JUDITH A. SCHICKEDANZ

*Syracuse University*

MARY E. YORK

*Portland State University*

IDA SANTOS STEWART

*University of Houston*

DORIS A. WHITE

Virginia Commonwealth University

# STRATEGIES FOR TEACHING YOUNG CHILDREN

## second edition

Prentice-Hall, Inc. Englewood Cliffs, New Jersey 07632

**Library of Congress Cataloging in Publication Data**

Main entry under title:

Strategies for teaching young children.

Includes bibliographies and index.
1. Education, Primary—Curricula.  2. Education,
Preschool—Curricula.  3. Kindergarten—Method and
manuals.  I. Schickedanz, Judith A., 1944–
ISBN 0-13-851139-X
LBI523.S77  1983        372.13        82-23190

Editorial/production supervision: Barbara Kelly Kittle
interior design: Richard Kilmartin
Cover design: Diane Saxe
Manufacturing buyer: Ron Chapman

Printed in the United States of America

10  9  8  7  6  5  4  3  2  1

ISBN 0-13-851139-X

Prentice-Hall International, Inc., *London*
Prentice-Hall of Australia Pty, Limited, *Sydney*
Editora Prentice-Hall do Brasil, Ltda., *Rio de Janeiro*
Prentice-Hall Canada Inc, *Toronto*
Prentice-Hall of India Private Limited, *New Delhi*
Prentice-Hall of Japan, Inc., *Tokyo*
Prentice-Hall of Southeast Asia Pte. Ltd., *Singapore*
Whitehall Books Limited, *Wellington, New Zealand*

# CONTENTS

# 6

# PERFORMING ARTS 140

# 7

# LANGUAGE ARTS 179

# PREFACE

Today, five years after the publication of the first edition of this book, concern about children's learning is perhaps more intense than ever. We remain dedicated to helping teachers help children learn, but we remain steadfast as well in our belief that concern for the whole child must be uppermost in every early childhood teacher's mind. This second edition, like the first, attempts to respond to these dual needs.

The first chapter presents an overview of three views of learning and their implications for education. Included also is a statement of the author's theoretical orientation. Chapter two, a new addition to this book, deals with classroom management. Chapter three covers the basics of planning and organizing instruction and evaluating children's learning. Chapter four, which is also a new addition, deals with issues and techniques relating to special-needs children who are mainstreamed into the regular classroom. The remaining six chapters are organized around the following content areas: (1) Visual Arts, (2) Performing Arts, (3) Language Arts, (4) Mathematics, (5) Science, and (6) Social Studies. Within each of these chapters, the reader will find a discussion of the nature of the subject matter itself, the nature of young children as it relates to the content area under discussion, skills and concepts in the content area that are appropriate for young children, and specific activities that serve as *examples* of ways a teacher can support children's learning in that particular content area. The introductory material to the activities in each content chapter has been updated and expanded.

This is especially true of the Language Arts chapter which incorporates the latest information about how young children learn about written language.

This book has been written primarily to meet the needs of undergraduate students studying early childhood education, although it would serve as a valuable resource for teachers already working in the field. The book helps the student who has had little background in child development or the content areas by including sections that discuss these considerations in each curriculum chapter. This makes the book appropriate for students in programs that integrate developmental and content area theory with methods or practicum courses, or those in which field work begins in the freshman or sophomore year before the student has completed theoretical work. Students in programs that require theory courses in development and the content areas before methods or practicum experiences will find the discussions useful in helping them see the implications of previous learning for their practical work with children. Teachers in the field will find the theoretical rationale for the practical ideas helpful in explaining and interpreting their program to parents, community, and colleagues.

Because the book deals with curriculum ideas appropriate for children between the ages of three and seven, it can be used by teachers and future teachers of preschool, kindergarten, and early primary school children. The activities are keyed to indicate their level of difficulty, but most activities are accompanied by "Suggestions and Variations" that illustrate how teachers can make them more simple or complex to meet the needs of individual children.

Activity suggestions rely heavily on materials that are inexpensive and teacher-made. Materials needed for each activity are listed and described, and often, several suggestions are made for materials that would work well for the same activity. Reference material at the end of each chapter includes resources for both teacher and children. The list of children's books indicated at the end of the Social Science chapter is annotated to help the teacher select those best suited for specific purposes.

## ACKNOWLEDGMENTS

The authors are indebted to many who have indirectly contributed to this book. Many of the photographs used in the first edition have remained in this edition. This speaks well for the quality of the work done by Jack Adams, who is affiliated with the University of New Hampshire; Jim Fety, who is also a teacher at Rogue River, Oregon; and Judi Jones, who was a teacher at the time the pictures used were taken. Many of the new photographs were taken by Mary York, while on visits to schools in the United States and England. We believe the pictures have captured the spirit of children and express ideas and feelings that are difficult to put into words.

There are also the children, and the teachers of children, who contributed to the development of the book by providing opportunities for obtaining photo—

graphs, testing out ideas, and observing. These schools and teachers include the University of New Hampshire, Judi Jones, head teacher; E-Kosh-Kosh Day Care Center, Urban Indian Coalition, Portland, Oregon; the Harold E. Moon Head Start Center, Alexandria, Virginia; the first grade class of Sharon Lewis; Beaverton School District, Beaverton, Oregon; Clinton Path Preschool, Brookline, Massachusetts; Radcliffe Child Care Center, Cambridge, Massachusetts; Technology Children's Center, Cambridge, Massachusetts; Crispus Attucks Children's Center, Dorchester, Massachusetts; and Ruggles Street Nursery School, Boston, Massachusetts.

The writers are also indebted to Mrs. Julia Bursch, instructor of parent education classes for Portland Community College and former director of a parent cooperative center, for many of the diagrams and drawings and for her comments and contributions to the Visual and Performing Arts chapters; and to Dorothy Morgan for much of the chapter on Mainstreaming.

Above all, we are deeply indebted to our teacher, Professor Bernard Spodek, who introduced us to the serious study of early childhood education; and to those we now teach, who are a constant source of inspiration.

J.A.S., M.E.Y., I.S.S., D.A.W.

# STRATEGIES
# FOR  TEACHING
# YOUNG  CHILDREN

# 1

# THEORETICAL
# FRAMEWORK

## INTRODUCTION

If you visited several early childhood classrooms, you might find that each provides different experiences intended to help children learn about written language. For example, one provides picture books, read-aloud stories, manipulative alphabet materials, and functional print, such as names on cubbies, labels on classroom objects, and experience charts posted on walls. Perhaps another provides few, if any, experiences relating to print. Yet a third provides children with daily lessons in alphabet recognition, letter formation, and letter-sound correspondences and gives children tangible rewards for paying attention and completing papers. You may wonder why approaches to teaching children vary so dramatically. You may also wonder which approach is the best and how a teacher chooses among them.

While there are as many ways to teach children as there are ways to do most other things, teachers do not employ the whole range of available approaches. Rather, they select some approaches and reject others. The basis for their decisions is a set of assumptions about *how* children learn and a set of values concerning what they think children *should* learn. When teachers say that a particular way of teaching children is good, they mean that it is consistent with their assumptions about how children learn and with their beliefs about what children should learn. Teachers select methods that are consistent with their philosophy of teaching.

The authors hold certain views about children and schooling. In this chapter, we make these views explicit; in later chapters, we discuss specific methods of teaching young children.

## HOW CHILDREN LEARN

Newborns cannot walk, talk, read, or compute numbers. In just a few years, however, children can do all these things. What accounts for these changes?

Three basic theories that can help explain children's learning are (1) the genetic-maturational theory, (2) the environmental-behavioral theory, and (3) the cognitive-developmental or interactional theory. Each offers a unique view of why children do what they do and why their behavior changes. Each theory also makes assumptions about the nature of knowledge and motivation. We will consider each in turn.

### Genetic-Maturational View

A genetic-maturationist thinks changes in behavior are due primarily to physical maturation of the nervous system, which is controlled by the genes. Thus, if one child walks at nine months of age while another does not walk until fifteen or sixteen months of age, a genetic-maturationist explains the difference by saying that the children differ genetically and therefore in their rates of maturation. In short, within broad limits, differences in behavior are not attributed to differences in experiences—such as having been placed prone on a blanket and surrounded by interesting toys—but to differences in heredity.

But how does this view account for intellectual development? While it seems reasonable that maturation of the nervous system would lead directly to the emergence of physical skills such as walking,[1] can such maturation also explain the emergence of talking or reading behavior? Does the theory suggest that with maturation these abilities simply blossom or unfold from within? While the theory does not say this explicitly, it appears to indicate that this is the case. Consider language development as an example. A genetic-maturationist does not say that knowledge of a *specific* language is innate; otherwise, the theory could not explain why children growing up in different societies learn different languages. However, a theorist of this persuasion would say that abstract aspects of language, the basic grammatical relations that are expressed by the syntax of a language, are built into the brain. (The *syntax* of a language refers to ways in which words are combined to express various relationships.) This aspect of the brain has been referred to as the *language acquisition device* (Chomsky, 1968; McNeill, 1970). This theory suggests that a part of the brain is literally programmed to be sensitive to language in a specific way, and that children learn to speak the language to which they are exposed when this part of the nervous system reaches a certain level of maturity.

In this view, learning to read is accounted for in much the same way as is learning to talk or walk. A degree of perceptual, motor, and intellectual maturity is assumed necessary before children are capable of learning, and certain experience is thought to have little effect, or even to be harmful, prior to the onset of this maturity.

The theory says little about how to promote learning when a child is ready to learn to talk or read. It assumes that when children are ready to learn something, they are well equipped to learn it. It also holds that learning will occur without any special means being employed, as long as the child is exposed, to a reasonable extent, to the knowledge we wish to impart. For example, once a child is ready to talk, the theory suggests that we need do little more than make sure the child is around others who talk. If a child learns to talk or read less well than another child, even when growing up in an environment that is not deficient in any significant way, the theory assumes that the child has inherited less ability to learn these things.

The genetic-maturational theory assumes that motivation goes hand in hand with maturational readiness: When a child is ready to learn something (so the thinking goes), the child will feel a great desire to learn it.

---

[1]There is not agreement on this point. Sylvia Fraiberg's (1975) work with blind babies, for example, indicates that vision mediates walking in sighted babies. This research suggests that the availability of toys or interesting sights (that is, experiences) influences onset of walking.

### Environmental-Behavioral View

An environmentalist-behaviorist sees things very differently from a genetic-maturationist. Experience, not heredity, is considered the key to readiness and ability. A child not ready to read is a child who lacks a history of appropriate experiences, rather than a child who is physically or mentally immature. (Getting ready involves providing appropriate experiences, not waiting for the child to mature.) In other words, environmentalist-behaviorists do not assume that children have special abilities within them that emerge with maturation, making it easy for them to comprehend or make sense of complex ideas. Instead, they assume that all knowledge exists in the external environment and must be transferred to the child little by little until complex ideas are built up.

This view holds that because children have no knowledge or internal structures available to them, it is important to simplify and carefully plan early experiences. Simplification is usually accomplished by dividing up knowledge or cutting it apart into subskills, which are then sequenced and taught one at a time. Instruction based on behavioral principles is more precise and structured than instruction based on views which assume that an active learner brings certain mental structures to the learning situation.

Motivation to learn, according to this theory, also comes from outside the organism. If children are to learn the desired behaviors, their behavior must be *reinforced,* that is, followed by a response that will increase the frequency of the behavior in the future. Behavior might also be *extinguished,* that is, ignored such that it will stop; or *punished*—followed by an unpleasant response which causes the frequency of the behavior to decline. An unmotivated child is considered to be a child whose behavior has not been appropriately reinforced, not a child who is lacking in physical readiness.

In short, this theory assumes that children are passive learners, contributing relatively little to their own development or knowledge, and that organization of stimuli from the environment is the key to learning. Children are molded, or shaped, by the environments created for them. The teacher's role, therefore, is more active and directive than that required by the genetic-maturational view.

### Cognitive-Developmental or Interactionist View

In the third major theory of development, both the child's contribution and the contribution of experience are recognized. However, the theory does not simply say that a little of each is required or that one must be present before the other can have an effect. Nor does it say that a combination of maturation and experience is necessary for development. If it did, it would not differ significantly from genetic-maturational theory. In this view, what is stressed as genetically given are *invariant functions,* to use Piaget's terminology. This means that children's mental processes enable them to construct knowledge as they act on their environment. Genetic endowment here does not consist of specific abilities controlled by maturational timetables, but rather of broader abilities, such as the ability to organize stimuli into categories to which behavior is then adapted.

Cognitive-developmental theory also differs from the other theories in its assumptions about where knowledge originates. Coming to know, according to this theory, is not a matter of maturation of certain structures that contain some aspects of knowledge, which then allow the child to comprehend other aspects of knowledge assumed to be "out there" (genetic-maturational view). Nor is it a matter of carefully organizing knowledge, all of which is assumed to be "out there," in order to transfer it efficiently to children (the environmental-behavioral view). Instead, knowledge is assumed to reside in *neither* place, but to be constructed through the interaction of the person and the person's environment.

The idea of knowledge construction is difficult to understand; once we know something, we literally "see" the world in terms of what we know. Consider, for example, a number such as 3 or 5 or a classification scheme relating a group of objects to each other. At first we might think that "threeness" or "fiveness" or a classification scheme based on color exist as part of the objects—obviously, we would need objects to count or to classify in terms of color in order to begin. But the notions of number and classification do not reside within the objects: If we take one object away from a group of three, "threeness" does not remain with the object. Number and classification are *relationships that we impose* on objects, or knowledge we create as we act on objects. While the objects are important to this creation, it is the coming together of the person with the environment that is essential. That is the very essence of *interaction*. The result of this coming together is *more* than the mere addition of each part; it is the creation of something unique to the interaction itself.

Motivation, according to cognitive-developmental theory, comes from the interaction between the individual and external experiences. From the moment of birth, the child is engaged in knowledge construction. Therefore, the child takes to each new experience all that he or she knows as a result of earlier interactions with experiences. But suppose that a particular experience provides no opportunity for creating new knowledge because it provides no new ideas or objects or allows no new manipulations of familiar objects or ideas. If there is no new knowledge to be gained from the experience, the situation will be boring and the child will not stay engaged. But then imagine the opposite situation. Suppose an experience is so novel that nothing in the child's current store of knowledge relates to it. In this situation, the child may be frightened or dumbfounded and is likely to withdraw from, or refuse in other ways to relate to, the experience.

Now imagine a situation somewhere between these two extremes. It contains a little that is familiar but a little that is novel. It is this situation that cognitive-developmentalists believe results in the greatest amount of learning (Kuhn, 1979). Motivation is shown by interest, or sustained engagement, in an experience. It does not result from some reservoir within the child, but from a situation in which the child and the experience confronting the child relate to each other in a certain way. The instructional problem of providing experiences that relate well to a child's current knowledge has been called the "problem of the match" (Hunt, 1969). When children react to an opportunity for learning with interest and delight, or when their involvement is sustained, it is assumed that a good cognitive match has been made.

### Summary and Comparison of the Three Theories of Development

The brief descriptions presented above illustrate how the three theories of development differ in terms of (1) assumptions about the source of knowledge and motivation, (2) emphasis on the roles of genetic endowment versus environment in setting the course of development, and (3) specificity of what they assume is given as part of the child's make-up.

The genetic-maturational and cognitive-developmental theories emphasize contributions of the individual more than does the environmental-behavioral theory, but they differ as to how they define this contribution. In the genetic-maturational view, the contribution is a genetic timetable which controls the emergence of specific mental and physical structures and sets limits on the amount of ability possessed by each individual. These structures, in turn, provide the foundation for specific content, or knowledge, gained through experience.

In the cognitive-developmental view, on the other hand, what is given are broader human abilities common to all children except those with gross physical or mental disabilities. These broad abilities permit the child to create knowledge as a result of interactions with the environment. While both the genetic-maturational and cognitive-developmental views assume an active child in the sense that characteristics of the child are considered to contribute to the course of development, the genetic-maturational view does not consider the child to be mentally active in the same sense as that intended by the cognitive-developmentalist—the child is not thought to create knowledge.

Similarly, the genetic-maturational and cognitive-developmental theories are alike because they both assume that motivation depends little on external measures. However, their assumptions about the actual source of motivation differ. In the genetic-motivational view, motivation to learn specific things is thought to come from within the individual, to be there as a reservoir of energy seeking the appropriate outlet, once a specific readiness is present. Disinterest in learning indicates a lack of readiness for engaging in an area of learning, and the recommendation of such theorists is to delay the introduction of such material. In the cognitive-developmental view, on the other hand, disinterest suggests that the learning experience needs to be altered, perhaps by adding something to make it more interesting, to provide a better "match." In other words, motivation for a specific area of learning is thought to originate from the *interaction* between individual and experience, although a general tendency to seek information is considered to be inherent in the organism.

An environmentalist-behaviorist explains disinterest as a problem with reinforcement and recommends specific social or physical rewards for on-task behavior. A behaviorist, like a cognitive-developmentalist, certainly is concerned about adapting instruction to "match" the child's level of understanding. However, the adaptation is usually of a very specific kind: backing up to previous steps or making the situation simpler and more likely to be successful in the way the teacher expects. In addition, specific rewards unrelated to the experience at hand may be introduced. Adaptation usually does not take the form of making the situation more meaningful, if that means putting learning in a broader context. Nor does it mean making the situation more interesting, if that means allowing for novel manipulations or experimentation, which may result in alternate ways of putting information together. The steps for arriving at knowledge are usually specified at the outset in behaviorally based programs, and the chief alteration is in pacing progress through the steps. If this does not result in greater motivation—more on-task behavior—then external incentives for increasing the child's attention to learning are often built in.

Similarly, a cognitive-developmentalist uses reinforcement to keep children engaged in learning experiences. For example, a teacher may spend time with children in the library corner reading or talking about books, but the teacher would not rely too heavily on attention, or anything else external to the experience, to keep children engaged.

The differences among the theories are basically a matter of the *extent* to which each advocates adapting the instructional situation to the child, as opposed to trying to get the child to adapt to the instructional situation. The environmentalist-behaviorist tries to get the child to adapt to the instruction by rearranging the environment and by applying reinforcement principles. While a cognitive-developmentalist is willing to go to similar lengths in adapting the instructional setting to the child, this theorist proceeds in a different way. The genetic-maturationist, on the other hand, tries to achieve better adaptation of the two by controlling when they are brought together. In one sense, this view favors adaptation of the child to instructional demands; however, the child is thought to adapt on his or her own with increased physical maturation. In another sense, this view favors adaptation of the environment to meet the needs of the child; however, here the adaptation takes the form of withholding experiences from the child until maturity, determined by age or other criteria, has been achieved.

While experience is considered crucial in both the cognitive-developmental and environmental-behavioral theories, its exact role is viewed differently in the two. In the environmental-behavioral view, experience is thought to become knowledge in a very literal way; What is "out there" is transferred to the learner without any alteration. But in the interactionist view, experience is merely an occasion for mental activity; what becomes knowledge in the child, in most cases, is something quite different from what is simply "out there." Rather, it is a product of the learner's actions on external material.

## THEORIES
## OF DEVELOPMENT
## AND THE ORGANIZATION
## OF INSTRUCTION

In this section, we are interested in the implications of each of the three theories for teaching young children. What will that teacher do who assumes children to be passive learners? What will that teacher do who assumes instead that knowledge is created? Certainly, teachers with such differing views will do things differently. The differences can be discussed in terms of (1) *what form* offered experiences take, (2) *when* the teacher offers learning experiences relating to a certain kind of knowledge, (3) what the teacher *accepts as initial evidence* of knowledge, and (4) how the teacher regards *errors*.

### Form and Timing

Let us consider first the question of timing. When, according to each theory, should a child be provided with various learning experiences? For the sake of discussion, we shall consider the question in relation to knowledge about written language. Posed simply, the question is: When should children begin to learn to read?

A genetic-maturationist would probably specify a minimum level of intellectual functioning, such as a mental age of 6.5 years, and perhaps a certain degree of fine motor control, such as the child's ability to draw a circle or square while looking at a model. If the child does not meet these or similar criteria, a theorist with this view would probably advocate delaying reading instruction and providing other supportive activities.

An environmentalist-behaviorist, on the other hand, would advocate beginning reading instruction when the child responds to instruction. This theorist would stress the importance of providing only the simplest information at first, allowing time and practice for mastery of one step before proceeding to the next. For example, a child might be taught to recognize letters of the alphabet as a first step in learning to read, with instruction focusing on one letter, or only a few letters, at a time.

A cognitive-developmentalist would probably not object to introducing written language early on, but would most assuredly object to the kind of experiences provided by an environmentalist-behaviorist. A cognitive-developmentalist would provide global or holistic experiences, such as story reading, play with sets of manipulative alphabet materials, and use of functional print in the environment, rather than sequenced instruction, practice, and drill. The differences between the two courses of action stem from basic differences in assumptions about the nature of knowledge and the learner, which we discussed above. When knowledge is assumed to be "out there" and the learner is not involved in constructing knowledge, it makes sense to subdivide adult knowledge, organize it into a logical sequence, and transfer it systematically to children. But when it is assumed that knowledge is a product of our interaction with what is "out there," it becomes impossible to think of instruction in terms of transferring pieces of information to children.

Let us consider a very specific example. Suppose we want children to learn after instruction or experience that each alphabet letter is unique.[2] Adults have differentiated each letter for so long that the uniqueness of each one seems self-evident. But a cognitive-developmentalist's view of perception suggests that arriving at this mature realization is the result of a long process of perceptual activity and concept development (Gibson and Levin, 1975). At first, we, like young children, probably did not see each letter as unique, no matter how carefully or how long we looked. Perhaps we first saw only two distinct groups of letters, those with straight lines, such as A, F, and H, and those with curved lines, such as C, O, and G. At that point, we did not consider an A and an F to be unique letters. Rather, they were considered to be the same because they were composed of straight lines. But then, with more exposure to alphabet letters, we noticed that not all straight-lined letters are the same. Some, such as H, I, F, and I, have only vertical and horizontal lines, while others, such as N, A, and Z, have diagonal lines. At that point we probably stopped confusing A and F because the A has diagonal lines and the F does not. However, we may have continued to confuse letters with diagonal lines, such as K and X.

The abstract features or characteristics of lines which are used to differentiate alphabet letters are known as *distinctive features* (Gibson and Levin, 1975). Gibson's perceptual theory holds that in learning to differentiate letters, children abstract distinctive features. As more and more distinctive features are discovered, more and more letters are seen as different from other letters. According to this theory, children do not learn individual letters first and then realize the distinctive features of print. Instead, they go about it the other way around. In short, Gibson says that children act on what is "out there" and develop categories or concepts for dealing with it. These concepts, in turn, change how children "see" things. In this view, the *same* materials, namely, a group of alphabet letters, result in *different* learnings over a period of time. The experience changes, not because the materials change, but because what the child does with them changes. In contrast, teaching children individual letters, one at a time, requires *different* materials at various points in time. The *teacher* changes the experience.

[2] Our use of learning the alphabet as an illustration here should not be interpreted to mean that we think this is the essential task in learning to read. Our views about this matter strongly contradict such a simplistic view as will be obvious in our discussion of reading in Chapter 7 on Language Arts.

The above example illustrates how a cognitive-developmentalist and an environmentalist-behaviorist view knowledge (constructed versus "out there") and the learner (active versus passive) and what they each consider to be appropriate instruction. A cognitive-developmentalist gives a child access to all, or at least a large number, of alphabet letters at once; knowledge of distinctive features is assumed to be what is needed for the child to "see" one letter as distinct from every other letter—to discover distinctive features, the child must see the same feature across a number of different letters. An environmentalist-behaviorist, on the other hand, insists on simplifying the situation by presenting only one letter at a time. Not surprisingly, each group of theorists sometimes accuses the other of making learning difficult for children. According to cognitive developmentalists, simplification of the kind employed by behaviorists makes it harder for children to learn, because it deprives them of the underlying structure or meaning that helps specific information make sense.

We can summarize each theory's assumptions about timing and form as follows:

| THEORETICAL VIEW | FORM OF THE EXPERIENCE | TIMING OF PRESENTATION |
|---|---|---|
| genetic-maturational | isolated pieces of adult knowledge | withhold until a specified level of maturity has been reached |
| environmental-behavioral | isolated pieces of adult knowledge | start early with simplest parts of knowledge—set pace depending on performance |
| cognitive-developmental | holistic activities in which complex forms of knowledge, rather than isolated pieces of knowledge out of context, are presented | early exposure to experiences from which knowledge can gradually be constructed |

## What Counts as Initial Knowledge, and What is Indicated by Errors?

We have already given some indication of how the different theories view errors, or some children's inability to do things in the same way as more knowledgeable children or adults. A genetic-maturationist views errors, such as matching A with an H, calling an L,I, or drawing a square almost like a circle, as evidence of immaturity. This theorist usually recommends withholding instructional opportunities involving this knowledge until the child is older and more mature. An environmentalist-behaviorist attempts to eliminate mistakes, and thus the formation of bad habits, by altering instruction. Teaching might be made simpler, practice on one thing might be provided before another is introduced, or the child's attention span might be increased through the use of external reinforcement. In both views, initial knowledge must look like a recognizable piece of mature knowledge to be counted as evidence of knowing.

A cognitive-developmentalist, on the other hand, tends to look for a pattern in the errors to determine the underlying concept or idea which governs them. It is always assumed that children know *something,* but their knowledge is thought to be qualitatively different from, and not as fully developed as, our own. (Children not only have *less* knowledge, they literally see things quite differently.) For example, cognitive-developmentalists would not focus on the surface confusion between an A or an H or a circle and a square, but rather they would look for what the child thinks or knows that is leading to confusion between the two. In the case of the letters A and H, the underlying idea or rule that makes up the child's knowledge could be stated: Some letters have straight lines and some letters have curved lines. Because the child does not know that some straight-lined letters have horizontal and vertical lines only while others have diagonal lines, certain unique letters are viewed as the same (A and H, for example), rather than different.

In the case of the circle and square, the problem is similar. The underlying idea or rule used by the child is: Some figures are closed (for example, 0,

□ , ◇  ) and some figures are open (for example,  ∪ C C    ). With only this limited idea of how figures vary, the child again considers figures we see as different (a circle and a square, for example) to be similar.

Gradually, knowledge becomes more differentiated and complex. For example, within the class of letters made with straight lines, the child develops subcategories of letters with horizontal and vertical lines and letters with diagonal lines, as well as of letters where lines intersect and letters where they do not. As the underlying knowledge changes, the errors also change and finally disappear. Children learn to understand, or know, the world in the same ways as adults. Cognitive-developmentalists are interested in describing the various stages children go through as they develop knowledge within a certain domain. In the earliest stages, what children know is often not a recognizable piece of mature knowledge—such as one letter of the alphabet—but an underlying concept or rule which leads them to deal with all or any of the pieces in a certain way; for example, grouping A, H, and L together or saying that two groups of eight objects each no longer contain the same number of objects when one is rearranged in space. Levels, or stages, of development are predictable signposts which emerge along the way to mature knowledge structures.

In summary, the three theories of development view errors as follows:

| THEORETICAL VIEW | WHAT ERRORS INDICATE | INSTRUCTIONAL DECISION |
|---|---|---|
| genetic-maturational | physical or mental immaturity | wait for readiness to emerge—withhold certain instructional experiences until some later time and provide generally rich environment in the meantime |
| environmental-behavioral | improper presentation of stimuli—"bad habits" | structure environment so that teachers control the reinforcers and then begin shaping behavior—when errors occur, return to earlier and simpler information until competence is achieved |
| cognitive-developmental | beginning stages of knowing in which the child's knowledge is qualitatively different from the adult's | provide experiences through which children can continue to construct knowledge—observe and study errors to try to understand the child's current understanding so that experiences enabling the child to go beyond this point can be provided |

## THE AUTHORS' VIEWS ABOUT CHILDREN AND LEARNING

Our orientation is eclectic and consists of elements from each of the basic theories, although we draw most heavily from cognitive-developmental theory. We consider children to be active learners. This means not only that young children employ physical activity in their learning but that learning is a matter of knowledge construction. In other words, mental activity is required.

Our assumption that children create knowledge leads us to design instruction in which broad experiences predominate over very specific lessons, although both are employed, especially in grades 1–3. Because knowledge construction requires that children act on experiences and relate one thing to another, a degree of complexity is required in the learning environment. We think many lessons, such as those appearing in workbooks and worksheets, are too narrowly defined and devoid of meaning to yield much learning based on understanding or to offer a basic framework of knowledge within which specific details make sense.

We do not emphasize process over product (that is, skills) merely for the sake of process. We would argue instead that the surest way to arrive at a product is to emphasize process. Often, children do not understand the information or specific skills they are taught because they have never been given opportunities to construct overall knowledge frameworks. Children who do develop basic understandings, on the other hand, appear to have little difficulty with skills. Developing one without the other seems unwise.

Children will learn most of the skills commonly specified, such as recognizing numerals and associating them with the correct numbers, recognizing letters of the alphabet, and learning to form alphabet letters, in the context of broad and meaningful experiences: for example, counting out napkins for snack, hanging up a coat in a cubby labeled with the child's name, attempting to write one's name on a painting, following a picture-word recipe chart to make applesauce, and so on. In addition, they will learn a great deal more; for example, (1) that the arrangement of objects in space does not alter their number (that is, conservation of number), (2) that the same letters can be rearranged to make different words, (3) that speech and print are related in very specific ways, (4) that context can be used as a clue to what words in print say, and so on. It is these broad understandings about a domain of knowledge that enable children to seek out, notice, remember, and skillfully manipulate specific bits of information, such as the fact that 3 is one less than 4, that $3 + 2$ and $4 + 1$ both equal 5, or that "was" and "saw" are *different* words, and "swa," "wsa," and "asw" are not words at all in English.

While we lean heavily on cognitive-developmental theory as a basis for creating learning experiences in content areas such as mathematics, language arts, and science, we rely somewhat on social learning theory (a branch of environmental-behavioral theory) in discussing social development and socialization. While we think that social development and socialization are influenced to a considerable extent by cognitive understandings, such as being able to see things from another's point of view or being able to think about what another person is thinking, we think that adult and peer modeling, standards and expectations, and social rewards and punishments (not physical) also play a large role.

## THE AUTHORS' VALUES
## RELATING TO SCHOOLING

Educators often disagree not only about *how* children learn, but about what children *should* learn. Our own values dictate that children's learning should be broad. It should include experiences in the visual arts, music and movement, the language arts, mathematics, and the social, physical, and biological sciences. In addition, we feel there should be opportunities for social interaction and decision making integrated throughout every aspect of a program.

## THE ROLE
## OF THE TEACHER

As we have indicated, what teachers do or how they teach depends on their philosophy of teaching. In this section, we will discuss the role of a teacher with the philosophy discussed above.

### The Teacher as Knowledge Imparter

When learning is in large part a matter of knowledge construction rather than of information transference, teaching must not consist mostly of "telling." This does not mean that the teacher is unimportant in the knowledge-construction process. For example, in the area of language, adults are the source of experiences that children act on in constructing knowledge about language. While language acquisition is not a passive process in which children parrot back what is said to them, they must still be talked to and with; if they are not, they have no language experiences out of which to build their own language. Similarly, the adult's action of reading print in the environment, such as the child's name on a cubby or a sign above a door, becomes an experience children act on to formulate ideas about print and reading. In short, a great deal of knowledge needs *social mediation*. While even in these cases teaching is not a matter of telling, part of the experience children act on consists of an adult's behavior. We may need to give particular care to this kind of experience in teaching because unlike concrete objects which are permanent and can be handled over and over by children, our actions are not permanent since they exist only while we make them. We may need to make them repetitious and redundant so that they can be effective. (Parents seem to do this when talking with their children and reading to them—they read the same story over and over, for example.)

### The Teacher as Planner, Organizer, and Evaluator

Planning, organizing, and evaluating are perhaps the most crucial aspects of teaching. Very little can occur in a classroom if extensive plans have not been made. Planning is of little use if an effort is not made to organize time and other resources necessary to implement the plans. Planning, to be most effective, must reflect evaluation of the experiences that resulted from previous planning.

Good planning and organizing free a teacher to teach and children to learn. For example, consider the difference in how the following two teachers spent their time one morning in a classroom when both had planned to provide children with tempera painting at a table.

#### Teacher 1

This teacher placed newspapers on the table on which the painting was to take place. The cups of paint were placed in facial tissue boxes in which holes had been cut. (The boxes offered support and kept the cups from tipping over.) Two sets of paints were provided, one to be shared by the two children who would stand on one side of the table. One brush was placed in each cup. Close by the table was a small rack for hanging paintings to dry. Plastic, pull-on smocks were placed at each of the four spaces at the table where painting was to occur.

While the children painted, the teacher occasionally stopped by the table to talk with them about their paintings, to help them write or spell their names, or to remind them to put on a smock. At other times, the teacher tended to children engaged in other activities in the room.

## Teacher 2

This teacher placed no newspapers on the table and placed the cups of paint on the table without providing support of any kind to keep them from tipping over. Four cups of different-colored paint were available. The teacher intended the four children who painted at one time to share the colors by passing the cups back and forth. Smocks (old shirts) were placed on a chair at one end of the table.

This teacher spent a considerable amount of time at the painting table. The first problem occurred when Jamie wouldn't permit Sandra to use the cup of red paint.

Sandra grabbed it, and in the process it was dropped to the floor, spattering Jamie's shoes. About fifteen minutes were required to clean up the spill. During this time, no one could use the paints on one side of the table, and the teacher could not attend to other children in the classroom who needed help with one thing or another.

The second problem arose when a child stepped on a wet painting that had been placed on the floor to dry. Its creator was distressed about the destroyed painting, and the teacher was distressed about the paint that was now being footprinted around the room. The teacher now had one child to console and another to clean.

By morning's end, the teacher was exhausted and children were on edge. The teacher vowed not to offer painting again soon because it was "too messy" and because the children were not "responsible" enough to use it. A little planning and organizing would have changed the situation considerably. The teacher's evaluation of the problems also left much to be desired. We are not convinced from her comments that the next painting experience (when and if one is offered) will be much better than the first.

## The Teacher as Disciplinarian

Learning is hampered in an atmosphere that is chaotic or personally destructive. It is the teacher's responsibility to help children behave in ways that promote self-respect and group cohesiveness. The first step in creating a classroom where relationships are harmonious involves planning and organizing. Poor planning and organizing (as described above) often lead to quarreling and other "misbehavior." On the other hand, attention to planning and organizing can prevent many problems from occurring and can make it possible for the teacher to give prompt and calm attention to problems that do arise.

The teacher also disciplines by being a good model of the behavior expected of the children. A teacher who yells loudly across the room to request that children quiet down is not likely to be successful. Similarly, a teacher who rarely pitches in to help children with cleanup or who rarely shares anything with children is likely to meet with difficulty in getting children to adopt the prosocial behaviors of helping and sharing. (See Chapter 2 on Classroom Management for further information.)

### The Teacher as Decision Maker

A teacher in a program oriented toward the cognitive-developmental theory makes decisions that are not made by teachers who hold other theories, because they do not base decisions on norms or on the internal logic of subject matter. For example, they may use curriculum guides in ways other than those intended by their designers. Nor does such a teacher eliminate from his or her program whole domains of knowledge considered by genetic-maturationists to be too complex for children of a given age. Instead, this teacher designs instructional programs, making sure to provide variety in order to give children numerous options. Once the basic program has been put in place, the teacher decides when and where to interact and what form each interaction will take. In addition, the teacher constantly observes children as they experience all aspects of the program so that modifications can be made.

## THE ROLE OF THE TEACHER: SUMMARY

In our view, the teacher is the key to the educational program. The teacher plans the environment, selects and arranges materials, guides children, poses questions, talks with children, answers questions, models desirable social behavior, observes children, keeps appropriate records, leads volunteer or other supplemental staff, meets with parents, and probably does a few dozen other things we have not yet mentioned. The teacher must do *many* things to make it possible for children to learn. In the chapters which follow, we will discuss in detail how a teacher might do all these things.

### REFERENCES

CHOMSKY, N.   *Language and Mind.* New York: Harcourt Brace Jovanovich, 1968.

GIBSON, E. J., and LEVIN, H.   *The Psychology of Reading.* Cambridge, Mass.: The MIT Press, 1975.

HUNT, J. McV.   *The Challenge of Incompetence and Poverty.* Urbana: University of Illinois Press, 1969.

KUHN, D.   The application of Piaget's theory of cognitive development to education. *Harvard Educational Review.* 49(1979): 340–360.

McNEILL, D.   The development of language. In P. H. Mussen, ed. *Carmichael's Manual of Child Psychology,* Vol. 1. 3rd ed. New York: John Wiley, 1970, 1061–1161.

# ADDITIONAL RESOURCES
# FOR TEACHERS

DUCKWORTH, E.    Either we're too early and they can't learn it or we're too late and they know it already: The dilemma of "applying Piaget." *Harvard Educational Review* 49(1979):297–312.

KAMII, C.    Piaget's theory, behaviorism, and other theories in education. In C. Kamii and R. DeVries, eds., *Group Games in Early Education: Implications of Piaget's Theory.* Washington, D.C.: The National Association for the Education of Young Children, 1980, 231–245.

MAIER, H. W.    *Three Theories of Child Development.* 3rd ed. New York: Harper and Row, Pub., 1978.

WEINER, I. B., and ELKIND, D.    *Child Development: A Core Approach.* New York: John Wiley, 1972.

# 2

# CLASSROOM MANAGEMENT: THE BASIS FOR INSTRUCTION

Since childhood was first conceptualized as a distinct stage of life, every society has been concerned with the behavior of its children and has offered wide-ranging recommendations for handling behavior problems. The topic raises many questions, both about teachers and schools and about education and society. First, what constitutes problem behavior? To one teacher, children who ask questions are intellectually alert and thinking for themselves; to another, such children are disrespectful. As regards what teachers ought to do about misbehavior, some teachers emphasize the importance of a personal relationship between teachers and children for socializing children to schooling and to adult society. Others of good intent advocate corporal punishment. Still others believe that children's behavior reflects the moral values of the society and that a change must occur in the greater community before an improvement can be realized in the classroom.

Perhaps no aspect of teaching receives as much attention and thought as discipline and classroom management. As every teacher knows, school is a place where whatever is done is usually done in the presence of others. It is no surprise then that how a classroom is managed determines the efficient use of both the children's and the teacher's time. When all or a large part of a teacher's time must be spent disciplining children, there is little time for instruction and learning. Whenever one child misbehaves, all the children as well as the teacher are affected. For all teachers, whether prospective, beginning, or experienced, it is important that children be well-behaved if learning is to occur in the classroom. In fact, discipline is cited as the main concern of teachers and administrators more often than any other aspect of teaching (Coates and Thoresen, 1976).

Classroom management includes practical duties, such as arranging materials and planning for the use of available time. It is also theoretical, in that the way teachers handle practical classroom details reflects their assumptions of how children learn and the role of teachers in this process. Although research on classroom management is replete with many suggestions for managing classrooms, the advice in the past has often been confusing and even contradictory. Nevertheless, there is a body of knowledge that can serve as a practical guide when teachers seek answers to questions such as: What is the most effective technique in handling misbehavior? Should teachers ignore, talk with, or redirect a child who misbehaves?

Classroom management is sometimes thought of as managing children's collective behavior so that they can spend their energies learning rather than pursuing nonproductive activities. In actual practice, the goal of classroom management is never merely the control of specific behaviors, but rather *the preparation and maintenance of a classroom that enlists the cooperation of children in learning activities.* There are specific techniques that have been identified and can be learned to help further this goal. Some are designed to prevent misbehavior, for example, having concrete materials available to the children. Others apply to handling discipline problems, for instance, redirecting children who are misbehaving to another activity. This chapter will discuss specific techniques for managing a classroom.

## THE EARLY CHILDHOOD
## CLASSROOM

Most children look forward to beginning nursery school or kindergarten. But school entry confronts them with a host of new stipulations as well as opportunities. Some children easily adapt to the social demands of classroom group life, whereas other children resist. We know that certain social behaviors are important for school success—children must learn to cooperate, be part of a group, take on responsibility, wait, work without disturbing their peers, and put away materials. Teachers need to find ways to help all children learn these social skills.

Despite differences in how teachers manage their classrooms, all classrooms have a management system (Tikunoff and Ward, 1978). Such systems are built upon values shared by both teachers and children. These values are expressed in classroom rules which include district policy (arriving on time), reflect teacher preferences (flicking off lights to get children's attention), or are related to specific activities (flushing the toilet only once). Although relationships in early education classes are less formal than in other classes, some rules are still necessary. No other level of schooling uses as many materials and groupings as do early education classes, and this complex approach cannot succeed without good management.

Management problems differ when teachers approach instruction in different ways. The more complex the mode of instruction, the more complex the management strategies needed. Regardless of the mode of instruction, management problems occur. For example, certain problems are created by total group instruction, where each child is at a desk or table and all children are working on the same page of a book. Keeping everyone's attention is but one problem. In addition, the lesson may be beyond the ability of some children and not challenging enough for other children. Problems are also created by differently structured classrooms in which instruction is individualized, for example. Such problems include keeping materials in good order and keeping track of the children's individual progress.

While teaching without flexibility is static, teaching without some agreed-upon ways to behave is not only chaotic but also nonproductive. *The notion that effective classroom management is necessary both for instruction to take place and for children to learn is illustrated by research suggesting that teachers who manage their classes effectively also tend to be more successful in helping children learn* (Rosenshine and Berliner, 1978).

## PERSPECTIVE ON CLASSROOM
## MANAGEMENT IN EARLY
## EDUCATION

Classroom management, as we see it, goes beyond concern with individual children *per se* and focuses on classroom conditions which affect the learning of all the children. On the other hand, it is the means by which classroom conditions are set up so that individual children can achieve personal goals. Within this conceptualization, *management is the physical, intellectual, and social-emotional preparation and management of a classroom so that children's learning is enhanced.* Instruction, which follows management, is the facilitation of children's learning. When we view teaching as being composed of two dimensions, classroom management and instruction, we have a useful way to talk about classroom management (Kounin, 1970).

Children welcome order in a classroom. By order we do not mean a quiet room with all children doing the same thing at the same time. Instead, we mean that there are clear expectations for teachers and children, that teachers and children feel it is right for them to conform to these expectations, and that there is some regularity in how teachers and children behave (Cohen, Intili, and Robbins, 1979). For example, in a recent study, Nash (1978) found that British children wanted and expected teachers to maintain order in their classrooms. When teachers did not do so, they lost the children's respect. Specifically, children expected their teachers to (1) keep order, (2) teach them, (3) explain, (4) be interesting, (5) be fair, and (6) be friendly. The children arrived personally at the same conclusions as educational researchers—*for the purposes of teaching, teachers must have a workable management system.*

A key problem in planning and maintaining a positive learning environment is that teachers are often unaware of the relationships between discipline and classroom management. Planning for a management system begins with a clear identification of the system and its purposes. We believe that the following principles are essential for a workable management system.

## BASIC PRINCIPLES OF CLASSROOM MANAGEMENT

- For the purposes of instruction, teachers must first have a workable management system.
- Classroom rules must be consistent with program goals.
- The goal of discipline is the cooperation of children in learning activities.
- Classroom management is the management of the collective behavior of children so that instruction and learning can take place.
- It is the responsibility of the teacher to develop and maintain an effective management system.

## VIEWS OF CLASSROOM MANAGEMENT

There are several views of classroom management which can serve as a framework from which teachers can make decisions about what to do in regard to management and discipline problems. Every model is not equally effective in every situation, nor does each one make an equal contribution to the efforts of teachers to improve their management skills. However, each approach has some merit and provides helpful suggestions for increasing a teacher's ability to manage a classroom of young children. We shall discuss three ways of looking at classroom management, including (1) a behaviorist model, (2) a psychological model, and (3) a group management model (Tanner, 1977; Weber, 1977).

### Behaviorist Perspective

The use of behavior modification as a management model is based on the belief that teachers can control everything that happens in a classroom by means of reinforcement. It focuses on the prescribed, systematic use of reinforcement in which primary attention is paid to what children do in the classroom in response to what actually happens in the classroom. Rather than relate what children do in school to home or community influences, teachers are asked to look only at what happens to the children within their classrooms. It is assumed in this model that children who behave well in classrooms are doing so because teachers use effective reinforcers selectively.

When using a behavior modification management system, teachers begin by identifying the behavior they want to change and then observing the extent to which the desired behavior is practiced. Once teachers know what needs to be done, they carefully plan a program to control the child's behavior. To begin this process, the desired behavior is made absolutely clear to the child. For example, consider the procedures for getting the teacher's attention. Are children to call the teacher by name, raise their hands, approach the teacher and wait for her to respond, or wait where they are for the teacher to be available and come to them? Whatever the expectation, children must know and understand it so that they will know how to behave.

Once the teacher and the children know the desired behavior, the teacher begins to ignore unacceptable behavior and reward acceptable behavior. According to behavioral principles, if unacceptable behavior is ignored, that is, unrewarded by the teacher, it will disappear. For example, when a child attempts to get the teacher's attention by calling the teacher by name, which is not acceptable, the teacher will not respond. On the other hand, when the child approaches the teacher and waits for a response, the child will be rewarded with a smile, which is a social reinforcer. It is expected that this child will continue to get the teacher's attention by waiting rather than by calling the teacher by name.

While problem behavior cannot always be ignored, Tanner suggests that it may be the best technique when the following four criteria are used (Tanner, 1979). First, if the problem is momentary and has stopped, it is best not to take teacher time to deal with it. (In a classroom with many children this makes sense.) Second, if the problem is not serious or dangerous, it is best to ignore it and use teacher time and energy for those misbehaviors that for safety's sake cannot be ignored. Third, if teacher reaction to the incident will attract the attention of the other children and interrupt the learning environment, it may not be worth paying attention to. Lastly, if the episode involves a usually well-behaved child who is unlikely to continue the behavior, it may best be overlooked.

Ignoring misbehavior, even when done for the correct reasons, is not usually sufficient to change behavior. It is also necessary to reinforce behaviors leading up to the desired behavior. The successful use of reinforcers depends on selecting reinforcers which the children value. Concrete reinforcers successfully used include candy, popcorn, and the traditional favorites, stars and smiling faces. Social reinforcers typically include attention, verbal praise, a smile, or just physical nearness.

Reinforcers are unlikely to be effective unless their use is

1.  Sincere (the teacher genuinely approves of the child's behavior).
2.  Valued by the child (for some children, candy may not be a reinforcer, but attention is).
3.  Matched with the desired behavior (the teacher pats the child on the back and says, "Thank you for waiting until I finished with Joey") (O'Leary and O'Leary, 1977).

CRITIQUE OF THE BEHAVIORIST PERSPECTIVE. There are practical problems in using a behavior modification management system in classrooms. Perhaps the major problem is that behavior modification is impractical. The most serious problem is the difficulty of using reinforcement strategies with entire classes. Behavior modification was developed to be used with individuals in a controlled environment, not in classrooms in which teachers are responsible for many children at one time and therefore cannot have complete control of the environment. It is no wonder that the greatest success with behavior modification has been in residential institutions in which greater control of the environment is possible.

Moreover, the cost of concrete reinforcers is not viewed kindly in schools with increasingly limited budgets. In addition, teachers have resisted the behaviorists' recommendations because of the time required in using concrete reinforcers. Also, some teachers consider behaviorist practices manipulative and impersonal and refuse to consider using such techniques with their children.

But of even more concern is the fact that little is known of the effect of ignoring children over a long period of time. What does such continued isolation do to young children? Also, teachers will surely have to use other, more direct techniques for many misbehaviors. Moreover, while behaviorism aims to change present misconduct, it makes no attempt to structure thought processes by giving children information that could lead to an understanding of their situation and thus to prevention of future violations.

Finally, in an era where the ideal of equality of educational opportunities is taken seriously, concern has been expressed that behavior modification, which encourages external and somewhat mechanical control, has gained widest acceptance in inner-city schools. Management systems used with more advantaged children, on the other hand, support internal and more reasonable control. Such differentiated classroom management systems may in fact be perpetuating inequality (Brookover et al., 1974).

Although these concerns limit the use of behavior modification with young children, some behaviorist practices can provide help in preventing or solving classroom management problems. The behaviorists' insistence that expectations for behavior be made clear and that praise be used is educationally sound. The necessity for sincerity in offering reinforcers and in linking them to the desired behavior has been successfully documented. Finally, the idea of looking at the behavior itself rather than at its antecedents has encouraged teachers to look in the classroom itself for the causes, prevention, and treatment of discipline problems rather than to outside influences, most of which are beyond the teacher's ability to change or even to influence.

## Psychological Perspective

Psychological classroom management systems are based on the idea that behavior change can occur only if teachers understand why children behave as they do. This approach developed as a result of interest in Freudian psycho-analytic theory with its emphasis on personality development and interpersonal relationships. However, Freud's therapeutic model of working with individuals to help free ideas and potential abilities was not applicable to teaching a roomful of young children. Therefore, over time this clinical model was reinterpreted as a psychologically based pedagogy which, instead of talking about the ego, spoke of children's personal adjustments to schooling and the creation of a social-emotional climate conducive to learning.

From this perspective, before teachers can provide a positive social-emotional environment, they must understand the children's behavior (Dreikurs, Grundwold, and Pepper, 1971). It is assumed that teachers cannot deal effectively with unruly children without first understanding what motivated the children to misbehave—why they did what they did and what they felt, believed, and intended to do. This requires that teachers understand how forces outside the classroom influence classroom behavior. It is also assumed that children cannot respond to instructional challenges until they have come to terms with themselves. This approach focuses on understanding the children rather than on controlling them, as in the behaviorist model. It also follows that teachers must first understand themselves in order to understand the children.

One of the most influential advocates of this approach is Carl Rogers, who believes that the attitudinal quality of the interpersonal relationship between teacher and children is the basis of teaching (Rogers, 1969). He urges teachers to be real persons in their relationships with children. Being genuine requires that teachers be aware of and accept their own feelings, and that they be free to communicate these feelings in the classroom. Further, the teacher's sensitive awareness to the children's own feelings is considered likely to increase the chances of understanding children.

Another psychological perspective toward classroom management is Robert Glasser's reality therapy (Bassin, Bratter, and Rachin, 1976). In this approach, the rules of classroom behavior and resolution of problems can be developed only through the cooperative efforts of teachers and children. According to reality therapy, there are two basic psychological needs—to love and to feel worthy. This means that teachers must first help unruly children fulfill their emotional needs. Only then can the children's behavior be expected to change so that they can be more responsible and educable.

Within this framework, children are taught to be responsible for their own behavior and, to a certain extent, for the behavior of other children. Class meetings are held to make children aware of class problems and to work out solutions through group discussion. For example, if during center time there is pushing at the science table to get to a new and interesting activity, a circle time would be called. With children seated in a circle, the teacher would guide the discussion by asking, "What can we do about the problem that only three children can use the science center at one time and that we have been interrupted several times today by children pushing to get to the science center's three chairs?" Such meetings would be held as often as needed.

A third subscriber to the psychological model is Thomas Gordon, who is also interested in the social-emotional climate of classrooms. Gordon views what goes on between teachers and children from a different psychological perspective, one in which relationships are determined by the quality of the teacher-child relationship (Gordon and Burch, 1974). Negotiation, rather than power, is the basis for the desired teacher-child relationship. Therefore, teachers and children are expected to talk together until they can come up with a solution that meets both the teachers' and children's needs. Children are encouraged to talk about what is troubling them. It is assumed that students have responsibilities along with rights and that if they fail to uphold their end of the negotiations, they suffer the consequences.

CRITIQUE OF THE PSYCHOLOGICAL PERSPECTIVE. Philip Jackson (1968) has pointed out that the psychological model presents problems for teachers who use it as a guide to classroom management. These problems derive from several important differences between the concerns of psychologists and those of teachers. Teachers, as a rule, do not look for explanations of behavior because their concern, unlike that of psychologists, is mainly in preventing disruption or in restoring order when necessary so that instruction can occur.

Further, teachers must relate to the class as a whole as well as to individual children, while psychologists typically work with one individual at a time. Group therapists are an exception, but even they seldom work with as many individuals as teachers do. Also, while psychologists take a nonevaluative stance in their interactions with patients, teachers are expected to judge children's performances, albeit with understanding and skill and without rejecting the children.

We must also note the influence of the classroom setting on children's behavior. Research on human behavior suggests that the context in which misbehavior occurs shapes the form that misbehavior takes.

Teachers do try to understand children who misbehave, but to succeed even partially involves a long and tedious process. Even so, understanding why a child has misbehaved does not automatically suggest a solution. A teacher can understand why Amy pushed Jim off his chair, but the teacher still has the problem of what to do about it.

Of the various perspectives, the psychological model has probably had the greatest impact on early childhood education thus far. Many teachers of young children feel very comfortable with the suggestions that the classroom's emotional climate is the starting point for curriculum development, that good teachers are concerned with the reasons for misbehavior, and that circle meetings to discuss behavior will lead children to become involved and to work out plausible solutions. The humanistic undertone of loving and accepting children as the basis of all teaching strategies has a familiar ring. The relatively informal, free-flowing climate of many preschools reflects the psychological model.

There are some educational benefits of the psychological perspective that cannot be denied. Regardless of the management model used, the success or failure of various techniques may depend to a great extent on the emotional climate of the classroom. It is also true that as teachers become more sensitive to the psychological underpinnings of their management system, they will understand that *if children like and trust teachers, they are more likely to behave well, no matter what approach is used.* Clearly, the insistence of this model that cooperative teacher-children efforts be used in seeking solutions to management problems has made both teachers and children more responsive to each other and classrooms more conducive to teaching and learning.

### Group Management Perspective

In the group management perspective, the classroom itself is seen as an example of a specific kind of group in which children engage in social interactions largely shaped by the conditions of classroom group life (Cartwright and Zander, 1962). In this approach, the dynamics of the group is the mechanism for children's socialization to schooling. Teachers and children are seen as part of a social network within the room, whether milk money is being collected or children are waiting to speak during a discussion.

Jacob Kounin's studies of classroom group management (1970) have provided a useful way to look at classroom social systems. Kounin analyzed classrooms and identified what successful teachers did that differentiated them from less successful teachers. Certain identifiable aspects of classroom management far outweighed disciplinary techniques in their ability to influence children's behavior. Perhaps even more relevant to teachers was the finding that those identified management dimensions were not only related to managing behavior, but also to producing the type of behavior leading to learning.

The four dimensions of teacher behavior found by Kounin to be correlated with effective classroom management were (1) "withitness," (2) overlappingness, (3) transition smoothness, and (4) learning-related variety. Teachers who have withitness are described as having eyes in the back of their heads. They see every-thing that goes on in the room at any given time—who is doing what, when, with whom, and where. They know at all times what is going on, and they clearly let the children know that nothing escapes them. For example, a teacher will re-mind a child to return the cubes to their prescribed place on the shelf with a wave of a hand while listening to another child read orally.

A related attribute is overlappingness, or the ability to attend to more than one thing simultaneously, such as acknowledging a child's bringing a note from a parent while guiding a language lesson. Overlappingness is significant because teachers who can handle two matters at one time are more likely than others to see when misbehavior is likely to occur and to do something to prevent it.

Overlappingness is especially important to teachers in early childhood classrooms because children are engaged in differentiated activities using concrete manipulative materials. A few children will be reading books, others will be mea-suring and weighing objects, and others writing a story. Still others will be paint-ing, making a collage, or working with clay. To orchestrate the children and all the ongoing activities, teachers need overlappingness.

The third important dimension correlated with effective classroom manage-ment is the smoothness of transitions between and during activities. Transition smoothness refers to effectiveness in both initiating and maintaining activities. For example, can the teacher have the children complete their independent ac-tivities and then come together as a group for a music period, without jarring in-terruptions? Can the teacher move things along at a reasonable pace but avoid hurrying the children?

Not all examples of smoothness or jerkiness occur between activities, however. Sometimes during activity times, teachers will attend to issues not related to the topic at hand to the extent that they interrupt the activity's continu-ity. For example, a teacher may interrupt the children's train of thought to give additional instructions, thus introducing jerkiness.

The final factor observed by Kounin is the ability of teachers to provide learning-related variety. Kounin's findings here are inconclusive. Nevertheless, observations of classrooms show that boredom and restlessness often precede misbehavior. Additionally, the data suggest that children involved in activities with little variation follow a predictable pattern of losing interest, becoming bored and restless, and finally, misbehaving. Or, they begin avoiding the repetitive ac-tivity by dawdling, daydreaming, or engaging in activities such as going to the bathroom.

Interestingly, several characteristics were identified which influence both the number of different learning activities and the management of the classroom. Since these are discussed specifically in other sections of this book, they will only be summarized here. The first factor is the appropriateness of the type and level of intellectual activity planned for the children. The second factor is the teaching style selected—are children allowed to learn for themselves in individual sensory-based action activities? Closely related to teaching style is the choice of teaching

This teacher has the ability to work with some children while knowing what the rest of the class is doing—overlappingness.

materials. Teachers of young children cannot be effective without making concrete, manipulative materials available to the children.

Still another factor in providing variety in learning activities and, in turn, motivating children to behave and to learn is the preparation of the physical environment—the location of activities (Is the block center out of the way of traffic?), the children's role in setting the pace of the activities (Were the children allowed to spend as long or as short a time to learn a skill or concept as they needed?), and the grouping practices, whether individuals, small groups, or total groups (Are children being prevented from learning because of grouping practices?)

CRITIQUE OF THE GROUP MANAGEMENT PERSPECTIVE. There are some striking differences between the group management perspective and the behaviorist and psychological perspectives. First, the group management view does not look at individual children *per se*, as the behaviorist and psychological approaches are wont to do, but rather looks at children and teachers as a group within the classroom social structure. It believes that the social character of the classroom is the predominant force in setting the stage for management, as well as for instruction. It discounts the children's individual emotional states and the reinforcement system used with individual children as key factors in the successful management of classrooms.

The group management perspective has several strengths. First, the suggestion that certain aspects of group management far outweigh disciplinary techniques in their ability to influence children's behavior has far-reaching implications. If this tenet is accepted, teachers will find themselves redirecting their energies from disciplining children to developing group management skills.

Equally relevant to the teaching process is the notion that management techniques are directly related to involvement in learning activities. Group management skills enable teachers to provide classrooms in which all children can learn and in which individual children are supported in their personal goals.

Perhaps the most important benefit is the separation of management and teaching, which has provided for a lucid analysis of the nature of the teaching process. The comparison of classroom management and instruction suggests that to be an effective teacher, group management skills, as well as instructional skills, must be mastered. In the best of all possible worlds, according to this view, management of the classroom would be done as efficiently and quickly as possible in order to get on with the primary concern of teachers—moving children toward greater development and knowledge.

## WHAT TEACHERS CAN DO

There are specific techniques for reducing misbehavior, limiting its influence, and increasing children's involvement in learning activities. It is the teacher's ability to prevent misbehavior from occurring and to prevent it from spreading when it does occur that is the crux of successful classroom management (Kounin, 1970).

### Preventing Misbehavior

Teachers are able to prevent most misbehavior by using specific strategies, such as assuming responsiblity for the management of the room, developing positive teacher-child relationships, making learning interesting, preparing the classroom, developing workable classroom rules, minimizing waiting, and limiting disruptions.

ASSUME RESPONSIBILITY. Even though outside influences affect what happens in the classroom, teachers are expected to manage a classroom in a way that will enable learning to occur in spite of conflicting pressures from without. Techniques available to teachers range from arranging the room before children arrive to stopping infractions and engaging the children's cooperation.

DEVELOP POSITIVE TEACHER-CHILD RELATIONSHIPS. It must be acknowledged that in the typical early education room, there is an interdepen-

A positive, caring teacher-child relationship is important in counseling a young child.

dence between teachers and children. In this close, personal relationship, teachers must not only know the children, but must also understand what impinges upon that relationship. In fact, the teacher-related factor most associated with children's misconduct in one study was insensitivity to the children's individuality (Kauffman, 1977). Getting to know children includes knowing something about what happens as children grow. All relevant information that makes each child unique and each teacher-child relationship individual is useful. It is also helpful for teachers to show an interest in what they do. Young children need teachers they can approach for comfort or help. *All management systems are based on a positive, caring teacher-child relationship;* without that as a basis, no technique will be effective.

MAKE LEARNING INTERESTING. Good classroom management is built on the teacher's ability to make learning exciting to young children. If experiences are too easy or too difficult because of the teacher's instructional limitations, misbehavior is likely to increase. In fact, making learning interesting has been found to be a powerful way to prevent problems—more powerful than talking with a child after misbehavior occurs or keeping the child isolated from the group (Morse, Cutler, and Fink, 1964).

SET THE SCENE. The importance of the physical setting in classroom management cannot be stated strongly enough. This first step, preparing the room for the children, shows that teachers know what they are doing by carefully arranging the physical environment to affect the children's behavior. A visitor should be able to identify a teacher's goals by looking around the room. Are children encouraged to develop language by the provision of opportunities to learn ideas and feelings? Are materials directly available to the children?

If teachers are to be able to supervise adequately to prevent problems from developing and, equally important, if they are to let the children know that *they* know what is going on in their rooms, then they must arrange the rooms so that every child can be seen. The setting of a room can make it easier or harder for children to behave. If there is a large open space, many children will use it for running or for rowdy play. On the other hand, if furniture is arranged so that only a pathway wide enough for walking is created, several discipline problems have been prevented. For basic information on preparing the room for learning, refer to Chapter 3.

HAVE WORKABLE CLASSROOM RULES. Classroom management begins with careful planning. The first step is to identify workable classroom rules that agree with the teacher's goals and are appropriate for children. All children will be expected both to learn and to follow these rules. There are times when routine behavior is appropriate and necessary. In a fire drill, children must file out of their classrooms in an orderly manner. Also, no teacher can supervise the beginning of each school day, toileting, or the movement of children from one activity to another without routine procedures.

One way a teacher can begin to identify classroom rules is to list all the daily occurrences that might require explicit rules. Established standards might include rules for arriving, beginning the day, toileting, getting the teacher's attention, snacktime, lunch, rest time, self-selection and self-pacing during center time, use and care of materials, storage of personal belongings, transition periods, and ending the day. For each of the above events, teachers need to spell out as simply and clearly as possible the rule(s) necessary for the accomplishment of the task.

Next, considering personal preferences, classroom conditions, and children's needs and interests, the teacher can eliminate as many rules as possible. It may well be that some rules are not really necessary and can safely be eliminated. Once the rules for each task have been reduced to the essentials, rank the rules beginning with the absolutely essential ones and ending with the lesser ones. It is wise to reduce rules to a minimum because young children are more likely to learn and follow a few rules than they are to absorb many.

Once the rules have been identified, the teacher can decide on the best wording so that in a few words, the intent of the rules is communicated in a concrete, positive way. Simple, declarative sentences stating the rules in positive terms are best. Also, it is far better to say, "We walk indoors," than to say, "Don't run indoors," when running occurs. The latter does not tell the children what they are supposed to do in place of running.

Some rules will be appropriate for the entire year; others will be needed for a limited time and can be discarded. For example, at the beginning of the year, when children are learning how to use materials independently in centers, one rule might be that the number of children at the manipulative center is limited to four. However, once children no longer push to get to the center, there may be no limit to the number of children permitted there at one time.

There will always be some children who cannot comfortably follow some of the routines. For example, some children, even young ones, do not need a day-time nap. If the children are young and at school for long periods of time, it is likely that a rest time is needed by the majority of the children. For the one or two who do not need the sleep, a compromise can be negotiated whereby the child can look at a book or hold a favorite toy; however, the child must take shoes off and lie down on the cot without getting up or disturbing the others. To allow the child to stay up, even if quiet, may have a ripple effect on others who will also insist on staying up even if they need the rest and *will* rest if undisturbed. Children who do not need a nap may be allowed to go into another room for quiet activities if they have been quiet for the prescribed time.

Workable rules should allow the children to do as much for themselves as possible. Young children can surely assume the major responsibility for the upkeep of their room if they are taught the required procedures. Young children can get the materials they need, use them appropriately, and return them to their assigned places. They can tuck in chairs when they get up to leave, dress and undress themselves, take care of toileting needs, and practice table etiquette. Such responsibilities will teach children to be independent, and will free teacher time and effort, which can be more judiciously spent in instructional practices than in managerial tasks.

One area of specific concern to early childhood teachers is the use of manipulative materials. Young children can become entirely responsible for the cleanup of the room, if a few basic rules are taught. The following rules are examples.

1.  Work within the designated area or center. For instance, if children want to paint, they may do so only in the art center. If rug samples or trays are used with the manipulatives, the children can learn to keep the materials on the rug samples or trays.
2.  Carry materials on trays for easier handling.
3.  Use both hands to hold materials, trays, and so on.
4.  Carry only one thing at a time.
5.  Return each material to its assigned place when finished and before getting anything else out.
6.  Carefully pull out chairs and push in chairs before leaving.

Once classroom rules have been identified, the rules must be taught to the children. Cohen, Intili, and Robbins (1979) have suggested that the most efficient way to teach class rules is to

1.  Clearly describe the rules, including examples of the desired behaviors.
2.  Precisely identify the situation(s) to which the rules apply.

3. Model the desired behavior, and have the children also model the behavior.
4. Provide many opportunities to practice the desired behavior.
5. Give consistent feedback on how the rules are being followed. (p. 138)

To introduce new rules to children beginning in school, teachers can (depending on the particular situation) teach the rules to individual children, to a small group of children, or to the entire group. Several considerations can assist teachers in deciding whether it is best to teach the rules to individual children or to the entire group:

1. *The age and developmental level of the children.* Surely, all two-year-olds, many three-year-olds, and children with unique needs will learn more effectively if the instruction is individualized.
2. *The complexity of the rules.* An example of rule complexity is toileting procedures, which are composed of many sequential steps. Children must get to the toilet, undress, put the seat down or up as necessary, use the toilet, flush the toilet, wet hands, use soap, replace soap, wash hands, get paper towel, dry hands, put paper towel in proper receptacle, shut the door, and return to the room or activity. Teaching these procedures to individual children as they use the toilet, or possibly to small groups of three or four children, has more effect than working with a larger group.
3. *The service of other adults.* If paraprofessionals or volunteer parents are available, they can be used to teach and reinforce the rules with individual children who need personalized instruction or with small groups that need more individual guidance and supervision.

Even when the above guidelines are followed, a fair amount of time will be needed before the children have practiced the rules enough to have internalized them. Once the basic class rules have been accepted and the class is operating smoothly, extend to the children the opportunity to participate more actively in the rule-making process. An assumption is that to the extent that young children can, discussions about the rules help them to begin functioning at a problem-solving level on issues relevant to them. What must be remembered is that problem solving requires a base of factual knowledge even at this initial level. Further, the teacher must play a stronger role with young children than with older children. Nevertheless, to the extent that they are able to do so, children should participate in identifying their classroom rules.

In the long run, good classroom management depends on children's sense of responsibility. To be responsible, children have to face and solve their own problems. To do this, children need to understand that sometimes they generate their own problems, while at other times classroom conditions create problems; but always, children can only solve the problems themselves with the cooperation and support of their teacher.

MINIMIZE WAITING. When young children have to wait too long, there is a high possibility that they will misbehave. Because of their need for physical mobility and their limited self-control, waiting is an anathema to them.

Sometimes children must do considerable waiting, and teachers are unaware of this. They may have to wait while the teacher gets materials or wait for a turn if there are not enough materials. Similarly, if children have to wait in line too long or if they have completed an assignment and must wait an unreasonable amount of time to begin a new activity, the seeds of misconduct have been sown by the unsuspecting teacher. Do children have to get personal permission from the teacher each time they want to begin a new activity? Are they dependent upon teachers to take care of routine needs the entire year? As one example, teachers can devise plans whereby children are responsible for their own toileting and thus save the children from having to wait in long lines to use the restrooms.

With the enormous number of manipulative materials used in early childhood education, putting away and cleaning up after use can be a troublesome time unless the operation is carefully planned and orchestrated by the teacher. It is very helpful to have all the needed materials within the centers in which they will be used. Equally important is a clearly identified place for each item so that even very young children can be responsible for keeping their room orderly. For example, placing objects in durable, see-through plastic boxes will enable materials to be obtained, used, and replaced without being mistreated or lost.

Many problems begin when primary children have to wait for teachers to check their work and provide feedback. Early childhood teachers have rightfully tried to keep track of individual children's progress systematically and to personalize feedback. We know, for example, that when teachers use regular means of providing feedback to children, children tend to continue working on their assignments (Robbins, 1977). The problem here is that such a system is often coupled with long waiting periods. One solution might be to have folders or boxes in which the children can place their assignments with the understanding that teachers will get to them as soon as possible.

For young children especially, it is difficult to wait patiently when the teacher is working with one child or with a small group and is unable to directly supervise the remaining children. In one way or another, these children must be persuaded to continue working on their tasks even though the teacher is not directly supervising them. One technique is to delegate more authority to individual children in regard to their own behavior and learning; another is to delegate more authority to small groups in which children can function as learning resources for one another. Of course, for those children who are not yet able to handle the independence and responsibility, more guidance and structure must be provided.

FACILITATING TRANSITIONS. Behavior problems may be most likely to occur during a transition period—that time between activities when all the children must move from one activity to another. Young children do not like to be interrupted when they are involved in an interesting task; unless the transition is carefully planned, confusion may result.

It is helpful if teachers prepare children for the change of activities by saying, for instance, "It's time for lunch. Please finish what you're doing and begin cleaning up." Or, the teacher can circumvent potential problems by offering an alternative, such as, "I'll help you pick up the blocks; it's a big job." If, however, a problem is serious, the teacher should remove the child, accompanying the removal with a brief explanation.

Without doubt, children will have to stand in line as part of their daily school life. Although too often misused, this is probably one of the most functional procedures and is usually among the first taught. For example, in some schools children must line up to get the school bus or the center van. Again, if children are socialized to schooling, a simple attention getter like flicking the lights and giving directions such as, "It's time to go home. Please line up," is all that is needed. This assumes, of course, that the children know where they are to line up; the order of lining up, whether it be one behind the other or the two-by-two rule; whether they are to use indoor voices or no talking; and whether they should follow the teacher or a leader.

However, if children are not able to line up as a group without arguments about who is first or without pushing one another, they need more help and direction for the time being. The following procedures may be used:

1. Assign a place in line and call the children individually to line up. Move along quickly; otherwise, the waiting can cause problems.
2. Randomly call a few children at a time. With young children, singing one of several ditties in which children's individual names can be used makes learning to line up fun.
3. As children are ready, they may line up on their own.
4. Allow the entire class to get in line on their own when it is time.

### Resolving Discipline Problems

All the available data on classroom management suggest that *it is mainly prevention of misbehavior, not just how teachers handle misbehavior, that is the key to effective classroom management.* But preventing all misbehavior is not always possible; inevitably, minor and even major discipline problems will occur. The severity of the misbehavior will determine to a great extent the options that teachers have in resolving the problem. Some techniques are more appropriate for minor infractions; others are more effective with major infractions. Some discipline strategies are intended to stop misbehavior once it occurs, while others are intended to get children involved in learning activities, which in turn stops the misbehavior.

This section will provide concise descriptions of numerous practical and effective techniques which can be used to solve the broad spectrum of behavior problems specific to young children. For each early childhood classroom discipline problem selected, appropriate management suggestions will be made. Teachers

It is better for this teacher to ignore the daydreamer rather than interrupt the class.

will have to choose those best suited for individual children and particular situations. For those management problems in which a multitude of effective techniques are available, we have arbitrarily selected from numerous options a few appropriate management strategies which, in our view, best enhance the growth and development of young children.

IGNORE MINOR MISBEHAVIORS AND MODEL DESIRABLE BEHAVIOR. Minor misbehaviors do not disturb other children and basically only interfere with the individual child's personal learning goals. When, for example, a child daydreams and does not pay close attention as the teacher tells a story, it is usually best to ignore it. It is a misuse of valuable teacher time to call attention to temporary infractions which are usually short-lived.

A simple, yet effective method to use along with ignoring minor behaviors is the modeling of desirable behavior by teachers. In fact, teacher modeling is an influential strategy to use with major, as well as minor, misbehaviors. When teachers do not pay attention to a child who is talking with them, and when teachers procrastinate, they are modeling the very behaviors they are trying to eradicate in the children. Young children tend to imitate the behavior of significant people around them—in this case, their teachers.

RECOGNIZE CONTINUED MINOR MISBEHAVIORS. If minor misbehaviors continue, however, the simpler techniques suggested above will not work. Extended minor misbehaviors, such as impulsiveness and excessive activity, require a more direct teacher approach. Warmly involved supervision is needed immediately to stop the misbehavior. The first step is always to secure the children's attention by moving near them and then to call the children by name before addressing the problem.

If the children are not applying themselves to their tasks, such as when they spend a large portion of the day daydreaming or when they attempt to avoid completing their assignments, teachers can initiate on-task behavior by making eye contact, motioning with their heads, or using a friendly touch. Sometimes, close physical contact such as joining the child or having her or him work near the teacher will be needed. At other times, referring to the desired behavior, "Just a little bit more, and you'll be finished," will be all that is needed to get the child back to the task at hand.

Still another serviceable technique is frequent, but appropriate, praise. Praise children for what they can do well on their level. However, to be effective, praise must be genuine and specific. As soon as you see children following the desired behavior, immediately reward them. "I like the way you turned off the water," may be effective.

Physical contact is one way of initiating on-task behavior.

Another technique is to call a restless child by name to gain attention and then in a clear, firm voice, redirect the child. Secure the child's attention first before continuing, for example, "Tom, use the crayons in the box in front of you." However, using redirection with young children is effective only when it is consistent with the children's interests. If other children are involved, the teacher might review the rule in question with just those children or with the whole class. In reviewing the rule, there is no need to overemphasize the misbehavior, but rather the stance should be to communicate the message that the teacher expects the children to follow the agreed-upon rule. It is also helpful for teachers to let children know that the classroom teacher, not the director or principal, will handle the problem.

If a child is restless, a simple and clear, "Paul, find a place that will help you to listen," will do, or you might involve the child in helping you if she or he can't settle down. "Brian, can you help me by holding this jar?" If restlessness pervades the entire classroom because of extended quiet activities, have the children sing an activity song with movements. If, on the other hand, the children are overstimulated, tell a story or play a quiet game.

A relatively simple management technique is to offer a choice only when there is a choice. Say, "Please come to our circle meeting now," rather than, "Would you like to come to our circle meeting now?" if you expect children to comply.

Knowing the logical consequences of their behavior enables young children to understand the link between behavior and consequences. For example, if upon completion of an activity, children refuse to pick up and put away the materials they have used, restricting those materials during the next activity period is the consequence. If children spill paint, they are expected to clean it up or they will not be able to paint the next time around. Logical consequences which young children can understand should always follow their behavior. Unless the culprits associate the punishment with their own misbehavior and not with the teacher, they are unlikely to change either their attitude or behavior.

Nothing disturbs most teachers more than the use of profanity in the classroom. There are many reasons why children use profanity. Reasons may include cultural models, excitement, and language limitations. Sometimes, teachers choose to ignore the cursing. At other times, they respond to the messages behind the curses by talking with the children, as in the following example. As Patrick knocked over the container of green paint, a loud "shit" echoed across the room. Patrick became tense as the others looked to see what the teacher would do, since profanity was not allowed in this room. The teacher walked over to him and said, "What a mess! I always get mad at myself when I have accidents like these. Here, I'll help you clean it up." This teacher interpreted Patrick's outburst as a response to frustration. The immediate need was to reduce the tension; later, the teacher spoke privately with Patrick and suggested ways in which he could handle his anger. She reviewed the procedures for removing paintings from the easel and helped Patrick to understand that the accidental spilling of paint can usually be prevented; however, if it does happen, it will not evoke punishment.

Temper tantrums occur when young children lose control and scream, bite, and kick. Such tantrums are usually seen in young children and seldom in children over the age of eight. Because temper tantrums are often maintained by the attention they receive, it is best to ignore the tantrums while at the same time using positive reinforcement for nontantrum behaviors.

Teachers of young children are often concerned about maintaining clean and healthful toilet facilities. Too often, the floor is littered with paper, toilets are unflushed, taps are left running, and water is left in basins to overflow. To promote cleanliness and proper use of toileting facilities, a few relatively simple techniques, such as more attentive supervision, teacher modeling, and praise when children put paper towels in the proper containers (for example) are needed.

There are, of course, countless other pedagogical techniques that teachers can use. Nevertheless, *the best technique is the one which is the fastest and least disruptive of the child's learning-related activity, of the other children, and of the teachers.* For the majority of children, minor misbehaviors will be the extent of their discipline problems. The consistent use of a positive teacher model, constructive preventive practices, and positive reinforcement and encouragement will be adequate to deal with these children.

RESPOND TO MAJOR MISBEHAVIORS. Although it is unusual for more than one or two children to engage in major misbehaviors in a classroom, these misbehaviors are usually such that they seriously impede the functioning of the children involved, their classmates, and their teachers. Such behaviors may include a fight among the children, the deliberate breaking of materials, or an act of defiance, as in the staunch refusal to get ready for lunch. None of these incidents can be ignored, and none can be handled indirectly.

Children count on teachers not to be impatient and not to lose their tempers. In tense situations, it is best for the teacher to remain calm and patient, using words and a tone of voice that will help the child feel reassured. The implication of a calm, confident voice and presence is that the teacher expects the child to cooperate; chances are, the child will. Screaming, wildly chasing children, or showing fear will not help. Instead, these actions communicate to the children that the situation is beyond the control of the teacher — a very frightening situation for young children.

When a major infraction occurs, such as a fight between two children, teachers should appraise the situation as quickly as possible to find out what happened and who is involved and to protect the rights of each child. Teachers will be able to act wisely only if they are alert to the activities of all the children, such as when a teacher says to a child, ''Those are Janie's blocks. Here are some more for you.'' It may be that given a few minutes longer, the children will be able to resolve the conflict on their own quite satisfactorily. However, if children involved in a fight are too upset to resolve the problem on their own, the teacher might begin by letting the children know that she or he understands their feelings and then giving them time to calm down and to gain some control. This may mean that the two children who are fighting need to sit down in ''time-out'' chairs until

A calm, understanding attitude on the part of the teacher is essential in responding to a major misbehavior between children.

tempers cool. For this technique to work, it is important that the cooling-down time be seen as nonpunitive.

Sometimes, it may be best to leave each child alone (but within supervision range, of course). When they are able to listen and to talk, speak with them in a private place away from the other children, allowing each child the opportunity to explain her or his perception of the situation. Discuss the problem in a quiet, but firm, manner and talk about possible solutions and accompanying implications. Avoid making comparisons between children. Tie the misbehavior to the violation of the children's personal goals and not to their relationship to you, the teacher. For example, if a child has misused the sorting cards, relate the misuse of the cards to the consequence of that behavior—if the cards are torn or lost, the child won't have the cards to help her or him learn to match things that are alike.

Do not finish the talk without helping children to understand what part their own behavior played in bringing about the problem. Try to reach a fair and just resolution with each child. For example, the consequence of misbehavior for children who misuse sorting cards might be that they cannot use the sorting cards for the balance of the activity period.

Whatever the problem, be sure that both the problem and its school-related antecedents and solutions are understood by the children. One way to assure this is to separate feelings about the misbehavior from feelings about the child as a person. Always return the child to the room as soon as possible, being careful not to isolate the misbehaving child from the other children for extended periods of time. Another helpful strategy is to model for all the children that, on your part, there are no lingering hard feelings or feelings of revenge and that the child has been fully accepted and reinstated. Finally, follow through on the agreed-upon discipline plans.

If the child misbehaves again, be consistent and remove the child. Repeat the process until the child behaves. Every child must continually be assured that the teacher is able to and will keep order so that no one and no situation will ever get out of hand.

Along with major misbehaviors, there often occurs a power struggle of some sort; sometimes the power struggle is between children, and sometimes it is between children and teachers. A cardinal rule of classroom management is never to allow oneself to be drawn into a confrontation with a child. Such a struggle presents a losing situation, not only for the child, but also for the teacher. Management confrontations tend to evoke winners and losers rather than solutions to problems.

AVOID USING PUNISHMENT WHENEVER POSSIBLE. For some teachers, the concept of punishment is limited to physically striking a child by spanking, pinching, slapping, shoving, and so forth. In that context, punishment is seen as synonymous with corporal punishment. That is not the definition we propose. We define punishment as those acts which are perceived by children as punishment. If a child does not perceive an act as punishment, then it is not punishment for that child because the effect of the punishment has been changed (MacMillan, Forness, and Trumbull, 1973). For one child, being corrected in front of peers is punishment; for another child, such singling out is rewarding, while having a favorite activity curtailed is punishment.

In most school settings, it is expected that punishment will include severe criticism, extended isolation from the group, time-out procedures, withholding of valued activities, and referral to the director or principal. All techniques which use words or actions that can cause children to lose respect for themselves, such as shaming, blaming, or humiliating, can never be successfully used to change behavior because they create undesirable side effects. They are therefore not recommended.

In the final analysis, however, what constitutes punishment is specific to individual children and classrooms. The only way teachers can be assured that an act constitutes punishment is by observing the child's response; if the misbehavior increases, it is reinforcement, not punishment.

We never recommend the use of physical punishment at any time or under any conditions in a school setting. When a teacher hits a child, the model of violence is clearly exemplified and advocated. There is always the risk that children will imitate the teacher's model and use violence in the future to get what they want. Therefore, physical punishment is unacceptable.

Most educators agree that punishment should be used only as a last resort. *Punishment should be used only after all other approaches have been tried and proven to be ineffective, and then only with major repeated misbehaviors.* Some teachers run quickly through other means and wind up using punishment regularly only to see that constant punishment diminishes its effect because children develop an immunity to it and stop being affected by it.

Because punishment engenders complex side effects, teachers need to understand the implications of using it. First, the teacher is communicating to the child that neither the teacher nor the child has been able to handle the problem adequately. This has far-reaching consequences in that it may not only damage the child's self-concept, but it also implies that the teacher is not equal to solving the problem. The damage done to the teacher-child relationship may be permanent, or at the very least give cause for concern. As Gnagey suggests, "If a control technique is selected that is too harsh or unfair, a deviant may become so angry or afraid that a constructive relationship with the teacher may be virtually impossible from that time on . . . it would be foolhardy to gain the control and lose the student" (Gnagey, 1968, pp. 32–33).

In reviewing the literature, Bandura (1977) carefully documented the position that the results of punishment are limited. Punishment will not teach the desired behavior; in fact, it can only control the behavior (Bandura, 1977). Furthermore, punishment does not reduce the need that made the misbehavior occur. *What it can do is stop the misbehavior at the time it is used—that is all.*

## SUMMARY

Children learn to misbehave, just as they learn to do everything else. Teachers sometimes make invalid assumptions about teaching young children and they erroneously assume that if they are skillful instructors, there will be no problems. Or they are certain that if they really care about the children, love and understanding will overcome whatever problems may arise. However, socializing children to schooling is best accomplished by a skilled teacher who knows how to prevent misbehavior in the first place and how to use techniques when it does occur.

## REFERENCES

BANDURA, A.  *Social Learning Theory.*  Englewood Cliffs, N. J.: Prentice-Hall, 1977.

BASSIN, A., BRATTER, I., AND RACHIN, R.  *The Reality Therapy Reader: A Survey of the Work of William Glasser.* New York: Harper and Row, Pub., 1976.

BROOKOVER, W., et. al.  Quality of educational attainment, standardized testing, assessment, and accountability. In *Uses of the Sociology of Education.* Seventy-third yearbook, Part II, National Society for the Study of Education. Chicago: University of Chicago Press, 1974, 162.

BROPHY, J. E., GOOD, T. L., AND NEDLER, S. E.    *Teaching in the Preschool.* New York: Harper and Row, Pub., 1975, 262–306.

CARTWRIGHT, D., AND ZANDER, A.    *Group Dynamics: Research and Theory.* New York: Harper and Row, Pub., 1962.

COATES, T. J., AND THORESEN, C. E.    Teacher anxiety: A review with recommendations. *Review of Educational Research* (Spring 1976): 159–184.

COHEN, D. H., and RUDOLPH, M.    *Kindergarten and Early Schooling.* Englewood Cliffs, N. J.: Prentice-Hall, 1977, 371–395.

COHEN, E. G., INTILI, J. K., and ROBBINS, S. H.    Task and authority: A sociological view of classroom management. In *Classroom Management.* Seventy-eighth yearbook, Vol. II, National Society for the Study of Education. Chicago: University of Chicago Press, 1979, 106–143.

DREIKURS, R., CRUNDWOLD, B. B., and PEPPER, F. C.    *Maintaining Sanity in the Classroom: Illustrated Teaching Techniques.* New York: Harper and Row, Pub., 1971.

GNAGEY, W. J.    *The Psychology of Discipline in the Classroom.* New York: Macmillan, 1968, 32–33.

GORDON, T., and BURCH, W.    *Teacher Effectiveness Training.* New York: Peter H. Hyden, 1974

HENDRICK, J.    *Total Learning for the Whole Child.* St. Louis, Mo.: C. V. Mosby, 1980, 91–109.

JACKSON, P.    *Life in the Classrooms.* New York: Holt, Rinehart and Winston, 1968, 170–174.

JOHNSON, L. V., and BANY, M. A.    *Classroom Management: Theory and Skill Training.* New York: Macmillan, 1970.

KAUFMAN, J. A.    *Characteristics of Children's Behavior Disorders.* Columbus, Ohio: Chas. E. Merrill, 1973, 136–138.

KOUNIN, J. A.    *Discipline and Group Management in Classrooms.* New York: Holt, Rinehart and Winston, 1970.

—— D., L., FORNESS, S. R , and TRUMBULL, B. M.    The role of punishment in the classroom. *Exceptional Children* 40(1973), 26–87

MORSE, C., CUTLER, R. L., and FINK, H. H.    *Public School Classes for the Emotionally Handicapped: A Research Analysis.* Washington, D.C.: National Education Association Council for Exceptional Children, 1964.

NATIONAL SOCIETY FOR THE STUDY OF EDUCATION. In D. L. Duke, ed., *Classroom Management.* Seventy-eighth yearbook, Vol. II. Chicago: University of Chicago Press, 1979.

NASH, R.    Pupil's expectations of their teachers. In Michael Stubbs and Sara Delamount, eds., *Explorations in Classroom Observations.* New York: John Wiley, 1976, 83–98.

O'LEARY, K. D., and O'LEARY, S. G.    *Classroom Management: The Successful Use of Behavior Modification.* New York: Pergamon Press, 1977.

ROBBINS, S. H.    An exploration of student choice in the elementary school classroom: Implications for implementation. Doctoral dissertation, Stanford University, 1977.

ROGERS, C. R.    *Freedom to Learn.* Columbus, Ohio: Chas. E. Merrill, 1969.

ROSENSHINE, B. V., and BERLINER, D. C.    Academic engaged time. *British Journal of Teacher Education* 4(1978): 3–16.

SLOANE, H. N.    *Classroom Management: Remediation and Prevention.* New York: John Wiley, 1976.

TANNER, L. N.    *Classroom Discipline for Effective Teaching and Learning.* New York: Holt, Rinehart and Winston, 1978, 161.

TIKUNOFF, W. T., and WARD, B. A.    *A naturalistic study of the initiation of students into three classroom social systems.* Report A-78-11. San Francisco, Calif.: Far West Laboratory for Educational Research and Development, 1978.

WEBER, W. A.    Classroom management. In J. A. Cooper, ed., *Classroom Teaching Skills: A Handbook.* Boston: Heath, 1977, 284–348.

# 3

# PLANNING, ORGANIZING, AND EVALUATING

Suppose we stepped into a classroom and watched a teacher interact with children. We might observe the following:

The teacher asks questions of a child who is experimenting with objects in water. Another child approaches and asks how "ambulance" is spelled. The word is needed for a picture that is one of the drawings the child has assembled into a book. The teacher moves to the box of scrap paper nearby and finds a suitable piece on which to write the word. The child takes the paper and returns to the table to continue making the book. The teacher starts to walk across the room, then pauses to watch a child who is jumping across the room. "Do you want to try hopping all the way back?" asks the teacher. "Hopping is a one-footed jump." The child turns around and begins hopping back.

The math table is the teacher's next stop. The child who is placing pegs in a peg-board there has been selecting numerals from the large upright calendar nearby and making the corresponding numbers with pegs. The teacher had observed this while with another child at the water table and had heard the child say each numeral aloud before making it: "14, 15, 21, 27, 31." Noting that the child was placing the appropriate number of pegs in the board with ease, the teacher sits down beside the child and asks what number is on the peg-board. "Thirty-one," the child answers. The teacher then asks the child what number there would be if all four rows were filled with pegs. The child hesitates for a moment and then answers, "forty." "That's right," says the teacher. The teacher then asks whether the child would like to make some very large numbers on the peg-board. The child says "yes," and the teacher writes 45, 50, 55, 65, and 70 on a piece of paper. Handing it to the child, the teacher promises to return later to see how things are going and then moves on to a group of children involved in dramatic play.

There are many questions the visitor to the classroom might ask. Why were water and objects provided? Why pegs and peg-boards? Why was the child asked to hop back rather than skip or walk? Why were different children doing different things at the same time? How was it possible for these children to work without constant teacher direction and yet progress in their learning? How did the teacher know what each child was learning?

These questions are answered by teachers as they perform teaching behaviors which often go unnoticed by the observer. These behaviors can be categorized into three types of activities: (1) planning, (2) organizing, and (3) evaluating. The visible aspects of teaching that were noticed by the observer are influenced considerably by these three less visible activities.

## PLANNING

Planning is thinking ahead. Planning includes thinking about *what* the teacher wants to happen, *why* it is to happen, *to whom* it is to happen, and *when* and *how* it will be made to happen. Why and to whom something should happen depends on the teacher's evaluation of what children have learned, of what is worthwhile for children to learn, and of what is appropriate for an individual child to learn. When and how the teacher will help learning to occur involves organization. It is in the planning process that planning, organizing, and evaluating merge.

### Setting Goals

The question of what the teacher wants to happen involves setting goals. Teachers determine goals for the children in their classrooms. They decide that children should learn to climb a cargo net and throw a ball, count objects and recognize shapes, handle a paint brush and work with clay, and share materials and listen while others talk. Teachers' goals are influenced by a number of factors. These include:

1. The teacher's assumptions about children, their learning, and the purpose of schools.
2. The age of the children in a teacher's class.
3. The community in which the school exists.

A teacher who views learning as a passive process will have different goals than a teacher who views learning as an active process. When learning is considered to occur passively, goals often include helping children learn to sit still, be quiet, and be attentive to the teacher. In contrast, when learning is viewed as an active process, goals often include helping children learn to interact and talk with one another and to decide to whom or to what their attention should be directed.

Similarly, goals will differ between two teachers when one thinks that the sole purpose of schools is to develop literacy skills, whereas the other thinks that the purposes include helping children develop a wide range of skills. Planning becomes more complex as the range of goals broadens.

The age of the children one teaches also affects goals, although age cannot be used as a precise predictor of appropriate goals for specific children. A teacher of three-year-olds who hopes to teach them to tell time, understand place value, jump rope, and tie their shoes will probably not be very successful. These goals need to be modified to take the children's developmental level into account, and age is a good first indicator of what children's developmental levels may be. Although children's development cannot tell us what we should teach them, it can tell us something about when and how to teach those things we consider to be valuable.

A teacher's goals are also influenced by the school community. Communities vary in their expectations of what children should learn and at what levels and in what ways they should learn it. Communities also vary in the skills required to live in them. Although one of the purposes of schooling is to enable children to cope with the larger community beyond the specific one in which they live, the teacher of young children in particular needs to be aware of the child's immediate community and to adjust teaching goals accordingly.

After considering the factors discussed above, teachers develop specific, tentative goals for the children in their classrooms. It may be helpful to generate goals in terms of categories. Such categories may include mathematics, language and speech, aesthetic appreciation and expression, small and large motor skills, peer relationships, adult relationships, self-help and work-study skills, social science, and science. Specific goals are then listed within each category. Not every child in the classroom will attain all goals. Teachers must always adjust and modify goals in relation to individual children.

Specificity of goals need not lead to highly prescribed learning situations. Teachers can and should think clearly about what they hope children will learn, but clarity of thought does not dictate that children must attain each goal in a specific and isolated fashion. Rather, children can spend much of their time engaged in experiences which contribute to several goals at the same time.

### Planning as a Process

Good planning starts with goals. The content of the activities and experiences provided in a teaching program should contribute something to the children's development and learning. The plans that are made for implementing activities and experiences should also be related to goals.

Suppose we were to observe what was going on in a classroom. We might notice an activity using food coloring, water, and eyedroppers. Three containers of water dyed with food coloring are available (red, yellow, blue) as are several small empty plastic test tubes. The tabletop is covered with a layer of newspapers.

If we were to ask the teacher to explain why he or she provided this activity, the answer might resemble the following:

Some children in the class are still learning to recognize and name basic colors. This activity provides an opportunity for them to work directly with substances of different colors. The activity also involves mixing colors. Children who may already be able to recognize and name basic colors may not know that some colors can be made from others. They can learn that. In addition to contributing to children's understanding about color, the activity helps children develop fine motor skills. It's really difficult to manipulate an eyedropper to obtain a small quantity of water and then squeeze out the amount you want. The activity is also a good one for helping children learn about vacuums and air. For example, the teacher can ask children what they think is in the eyedropper that keeps water from entering before the bulb is squeezed, or why the water squirts from the dropper when the bulb is squeezed.

I set up the activity to accommodate at least three children at one time. I want children to share ideas and information and have opportunities to explain things to each other. This activity is a particularly good one to encourage interaction among children. They become very interested in the changes that occur as the colored water is mixed, and they want to tell someone how they caused this to occur. Often, other children try to follow these directions to see if they get the same results. I make this activity available during activity time for as long as three or four weeks. This provides ample opportunity for children to have as many turns as they want. Some children spend a great deal of time there and take many turns. I want to encourage this kind of involvement and thoroughness in learning.

As we can see, this teacher had specific reasons for including the colored water activity in the teaching program. Some of these goals were met by the content of the activity. Others were met through the way the activity was implemented. Teachers must analyze activities in terms of all their possible effects and not just focus on the obvious effect of content. It is in the planning process that teachers develop learning experiences and activities that are congruent with teaching goals.

### Making Plans

General plans are usually made for the long term, and then details and modifications are made as needed from week to week, day to day, and moment to moment. For example, a teacher might decide before the school year begins that it would be nice to include several different types of dramatic play experiences for the children as the year progresses. The teacher then decides that the traditional house play area is the place to start and that other play themes will be added as the children seem to need a change. About two months into the year, house play seems to be waning. Deciding that it is time to introduce something new, the teacher refers to earlier notes and reconsiders ideas: A doctor's office? An airport? A grocery store? A fire station? Perhaps a grocery store would work best. The house area could stay and the grocery store could be placed nearby. Children could shop and then go home to cook and clean. In addition, the children have been making trips to a nearby grocery store to purchase items for their cooking projects. There might be great interest in a play store.

Having decided that a play grocery store would provide good learning experiences for the children in the classroom, the teacher decides when and how the activity will be introduced. It will be necessary to arrange for space and props and to determine what new knowledge children can gain, what seems to be of interest to them, and at what levels they can handle the concepts that are involved. The teacher also decides what limits are appropriate: the number of children who may be in an area at one time; times when the store is "open" or "closed"; and the kind of behavior that is to be expected of children using the store. These are broad plans that will have an effect on the activity for its duration.

More detailed plans for the store will be made, perhaps on a weekly basis. It might be decided that another trip to a local grocery store is necessary to help the children gain more information. For example, they can learn about the various departments of a grocery store or which things are refrigerated and which are not. Or, the roles of various people in a grocery store may need to be emphasized: Who places foods on the grocery store shelves? Who rings up the purchases? Who cuts the meats? Or, the teacher may decide to purchase produce because it must be weighed and this behavior will be encouraged in the children's store play.

The teacher would need to determine which children would go on the trip, which adults would accompany them, and what mode of travel they would use. In addition, it would be necessary to decide when to schedule the trip as well as when and how to explain to the children what is to occur.

No matter how carefully daily, weekly, or monthly plans are made, moment-to-moment decisions must be made as the reality of the specific situation emerges. It may begin pouring rain as the trip to the store is about to begin, and if the plan was to walk, the trip may have to be canceled or delayed. Maybe the high-school volunteer who was to take the children on the trip will become ill and call only half an hour ahead of time to say so. Perhaps one of the children who had been selected to go will be absent on the day of the trip or will unexpectedly become very upset about leaving the classroom. Or perhaps the day will start out bitter cold but then warm considerably, so that the teacher must decide whether snowpants go on the children or stay at school.

Experienced teachers can make these decisions on the spot. One of the ways to prepare for these moment-to-moment decisions is to make contingency plans. Wise teachers think to themselves, "If we cannot go to the store tomorrow, we can go the following day when we have another volunteer." "If we cannot use the fruit from the store for snack tomorrow, we'll have the graham crackers from the cupboard." "If John and Karen do not wish to make the trip, we will ask Carl and Greg if they would like to go." "If our thermometer reaches 32°, we won't dress the children in snowpants for short walks."

A teacher or the entire staff must devote time to making weekly plans. In addition, it is necessary for a teacher or staff to have at least a short time each day to discuss children and finalize plans. Sometimes teachers do this daily by talking "on the move" as they get materials ready for the day or put the room back in order at day's end. However it is arranged, time to talk and think about children and the program is important.

### Involving Children in the Planning Process

Children can contribute many ideas for classroom activities. If children are expected to become independent problem solvers and planners, they must be given opportunities to gain experience in these tasks.

Children could be included in planning for the store described above. By using discussions with the whole class and with individual children, the teacher can include children in decision making about where the store should be located in the room, what equipment can be used to build it, what items will make appropriate stock, and what limits will be necessary during store play. Children can also help decide what type of produce might be purchased at the store, how it will be prepared back at school, and when it should be eaten.

Just as teachers must learn to make decisions from moment to moment, so must children. Questions might arise regarding who will pay the cashier for the produce, who will carry the package back to school, or who will press the button to make the street light change from red to green. Perhaps each child can purchase two apples, and each child can take turns carrying the package of apples for one block. Children can express their ideas and alternatives can be discussed. Teachers can help children arrive at and implement satisfactory decisions.

### Recording Plans

Some teachers wonder whether plans should be written down. We think that plans are more useful if they are recorded. If several staff members are involved in implementing the plans, recording becomes essential. Sometimes it is impossible for part-time staff to attend all planning sessions and impossible for full-time staff to brief them personally on what they missed. In these cases, plans must be readily accessible and understandable in written form to ensure that staff know what they are to do when they arrive to work with the children.

There are dozens of ways to record plans. Teachers must develop a method suitable for their particular situations. We like the forms shown in Figures 3–1 and 3–2. The first is part of a monthly plan sheet for the entire year. On it are recorded such events as birthdays, holidays, and field trips that can be known or that must be planned well in advance. Teachers might also note seasonal activities such as planting flowers or vegetables outside in April or May. The purpose of the monthly plan sheet is to remind the teacher of major events that must be worked into weekly plans. For example, sites for field trips are often frequently visited by large numbers of school groups. A visit might need to be scheduled a month or two in advance. Parents must also be notified well before the trip if permission slips are to be obtained on time or if parent volunteers are needed to accompany the group. Sometimes a bus must be arranged for, and so on. Major events such as these simply cannot be arranged on a weekly basis.

The second figure shows a teacher's weekly plan. Any major events appearing on the monthly plan sheet that will occur during a specific week are recorded on the weekly plan sheet, as are plans for the more usual activities. It is also in-

**FIGURE 3-1**   Part of a teacher's monthly plan sheet.

Teachers' Monthly Planning Chart
October

|           | Week 1 | Week 2 | Week 3 | Week 4 | Week 5 |
|-----------|--------|--------|--------|--------|--------|
| Monday    | 3      | 10 Steve's Birthday | 17 | 23 Field Trip to Pumpkin Patch | 31 Halloween Party |
| Tuesday   | 4      | 11     | 18     | 24     |        |
| Wednesday | 5 Sara's Birthday | 12 | 19 | 25 |        |
| Thursday  | 6      | 13     | 20     | 26     |        |
| Friday    | 7      | 14     | 21     | 27     |        |

| Area \ Day | Monday | Tuesday | Wednesday | Thursday | Friday |
|---|---|---|---|---|---|
| Math | Chart Worms eaten by turtle. | | | | → |
| Science | (Steve) | | (Steve) Tubes, corks, water and food coloring. | | |
| Language Arts | | | (Sara) Write dictation. | | |
| House Area | (Ted) Add Materials for table. | (Ted) Applesauce- Sharon & Tom | (Ted) | (Ted) | (Ted) |
| Blocks | Add transporta- toys. | | | | |
| Art Table | Object painting | | Add new objects for printing. | | → |
| Music | Resonating bells. | | | (John) | |
| Story | (Jan) (Steve) | (Ted) | (Ted) | (Ted) (Susan) | (Ted) (Jan) |
| Group Time | (Jan) | (Jan) | (Jan) | (Jan) | (Jan) |
| Outdoor Play | Old tires for rolling down hill. | | Visiting goat. | | |
| Trips or Visitors | | | | | |
| Snack | Celery and peanut butter. | Applesauce | Juice and graham crack- ers. | Tapioca pudding. | Juice and raisins. |

**FIGURE 3-2**  Teacher's weekly plan sheet.

dicated on the plan sheet who is responsible for certain activities each day. Each person will need to make his or her own notes and plans as necessary to prepare for the assigned responsibility. For example, if applesauce is to be made on Tuesday, Ted will need to make sure the necessary supplies are available and that cooking utensils are on hand. If children are to shop for the apples, this will need to be planned. (See Monday under Trips or Visitors.) It must be decided who will make the trip and who will cook the applesauce. It must also be decided when it will be eaten. (See Tuesday under Snack.)

A weekly plan sheet for a preschool classroom organized in learning centers can be somewhat sketchy, as is the one in Figure 3-2, because a wide variety of basic materials is always available to the children. The weekly plan sheet needs only to note additions in materials and specially planned projects and events that are to be started and continued or that need specific supervision.

Part-time and volunteer staff assigned specific areas of responsibility are also noted on the plan sheet. The full-time teacher is not assigned to any particular area, but is to move from area to area as needed. The staff member who has this duty is often referred to as the *floater.*

Because the high-school students or other volunteers may not be available for planning sessions, additional information can be provided to them through notes posted on a bulletin board next to the plan sheet. When they arrive at the classroom to work with the children, they first refer to the plan sheet and then look for any notes posted for them. A note corresponding to the weekly plan sheet shown in Figure 3-2 might read as follows:

Sara:
Hi. Thought you'd like a turn at the table where children usually sit when making books. A few children can do the writing themselves. In order to find out who can do what, just ask them if they want to write the words or if they want you to write. They'll let you know what they can do.

Try to get the children to tell you what letter the words they want start with. If they're stumped, help them.

I gave you a manuscript letter guide earlier in the year so you could practice. There's another one on my desk if you need it for reference.

I've scheduled Ted for story so I can talk with you a minute before you must leave today.

Jan

Another plan sheet is also utilized in this classroom. It takes the form of a "helpers' chart." It is posted in the classroom at the children's eye level and the names on the jobs are changed at the end of each week. The name of each child is written on three cards, providing a small deck of name cards for each of the three jobs listed (water the plants, feed the animals, and help with snack). The name card of the child who has finished the week as helper for the job is removed from the chart and placed on the bottom of the deck, and the name on the top of the deck is put on the chart to indicate the new helper. If a child's name already appears on the chart for one job, that card, too, is put at the bottom of the deck and the next name is taken. Rubber bands are used to hold each of the three name-card decks securely.

In addition to the two planning charts discussed above, Jan, the full-time teacher in this classroom, keeps a notebook in which she writes ideas and tasks that are specifically for her reference. She typically writes plans in this book for one week at a time, although she is careful to leave adequate space under the daily headings to add further plans as needed. The entries are reminders to herself of materials to bring, activities to suggest to specific children, or of specific children who need special help or observation.

A teacher who works with kindergarten and primary age children can utilize methods which involve children in recording plans for their work. Kindergarten children can keep their own plan sheets, which may be similar to the one shown in Figure 3-3. By referring to these records, each child as well as the teacher can determine the work to be done.

In primary classrooms where learning goals for individual children may be much more extensive and specific, some of the teacher's plans are noted in children's individual folders. Perhaps one child decided with the teacher the previous week to complete certain math problems in a book during the following week. The child notes in his or her notebook which problems are to be completed. The teacher writes in the plan book, "Check with Paul on Wednesday about progress on math problems," but does not bother to note the specific problems Paul will be solving. Paul's notebook can be referred to for that information, if it is needed.

Even though more responsibility for keeping written plans is assumed by children at the kindergarten and primary-grade levels, teachers will usually find it necessary to keep a separate book of some sort for reminders and ideas for their own reference. For example, there will be plans made that affect the group as a whole and which may not be noted in any individual child's plans.

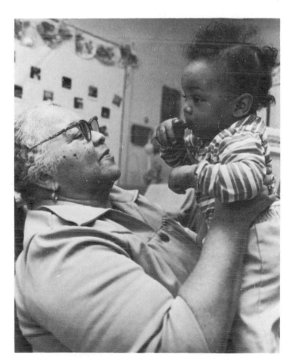

Senior citizens often enjoy working with children.

# Child's Weekly Plan Sheet

Name _____

| Areas | Planned | Finished |
|---|---|---|
| Puzzles and Alphabet Games ABC | | |
| Math | | |
| Listening Post | | |
| Books | | |
| Science | | |
| Writing | | |
| Blocks | | |
| Easels | | |
| Wood | | |

FIGURE 3-3  Child's weekly plan sheet.

## ORGANIZATION

Organization is a tool for achieving goals and implementing plans. It determines in large part whether plans are successful and thus whether goals are attained. Teachers must learn to organize space, time, materials, and staff if they wish to be effective.

### Organizing Indoor Space

Individualized classes may be organized into learning centers to allow different types of activities to occur simultaneously in the classroom. Learning centers are clearly defined physical areas with space for working. They offer children a wide range of learning options. They allow children to practice skills, pursue topics of special interest, use different learning styles, and proceed at their own pace. They also foster involvement required to integrate and consolidate learning.

Centers are attractive, inviting, and well stocked with materials. For example, a mathematics center might contain counters, string, felt numerals, numeral cards, 100's board, pegs and peg-boards, popsicle sticks and rubber bands, a pan balance, graph paper, geometric shapes, and geoboards. The center might also contain metronomes, clocks, hourglasses, and kitchen timers. All these materials would be present in the center so that different interests and levels of ability would be provided for. They would be arranged to enable children to obtain what they need with ease.

When the goals inherent in a center have been met, or when the materials in a center are no longer interesting to children, the center is dismantled or reorganized so that more current interests and needs are reflected. As new interests arise and children proceed with skill development, the teacher and children plan together for new equipment and materials and for the placement of new centers.

SELECTING CENTERS. There are four major factors to consider when selecting centers for a classroom. These are:

1. The teacher's goals for children's learning.
2. Individual characteristics of the children in the class.
3. The length of the school day.
4. The demands of group living.

What teachers want children to learn will determine the centers chosen for a classroom. If a teacher values art and music, then space for these activities will be provided.

Center selection is also influenced by characteristics of the children in the class. For example, younger children need larger amounts of space within a center than do older ones. This may require that fewer centers operate concurrently in a class of younger children. Differing amounts of space are also required for children with special needs, such as those confined to wheelchairs.

The selection of centers is also affected by the length of the school day. In all-day programs, provision must be made for storing cots and for cooking and eating facilities. Space needed for these activities may limit the number of centers which can be set up at one time.

Provisions for group living should also influence the selection of centers. Children need space to be by themselves, to work with other children, and to come together as a group.

ARRANGING CENTERS. After determining the different types of activities which will require classroom space, the teacher must arrange activity spaces within the classroom. Guidelines for planning the placement of areas include:

1.  Locate electrical outlets and place areas for activities requiring electricity near them. For example, a listening center would need to be near an outlet.
2.  Place the art area near a water source. If there is a sink in the room, the art center should be near it. If there is no sink in the room, the art center might be most conveniently placed by the door where access to hall sinks and bathrooms would be easiest.
3.  Separate noisy activities from quiet activities. The library and mathematics centers should be separated from the block and dramatic-play centers.
4.  Arrange the centers to divert traffic from areas where it would disturb work. It would be very distracting, for example, to have the main traffic patterns running through the block area.
5.  Determine sources of light and decide what activities require light. For example, light is important for growing plants or doing close work.
6.  Organize centers as distinct areas which are clearly defined.
7.  Arrange areas to make them readily visible to the teacher. This permits the teacher to see when children need help or guidance.
8.  Place interrelated areas adjacent to one another. For example, blocks may frequently be used to represent objects in dramatic play, or wheeled toys may represent the "work" that some member of the pretend family goes to in the course of dramatic play.

A sample floor plan which illustrates these guidelines is shown in Figure 3–4.

## Organizing Outdoor Space

Most teachers have less control over the organization of outdoor space than they do over indoor space. First, much of the equipment is large and stationary. In addition, the outside space may be shared with many other classes, making it difficult for an individual teacher to organize the space in terms of his or her specific needs and goals. However, in the event that a teacher can help plan the organiza-

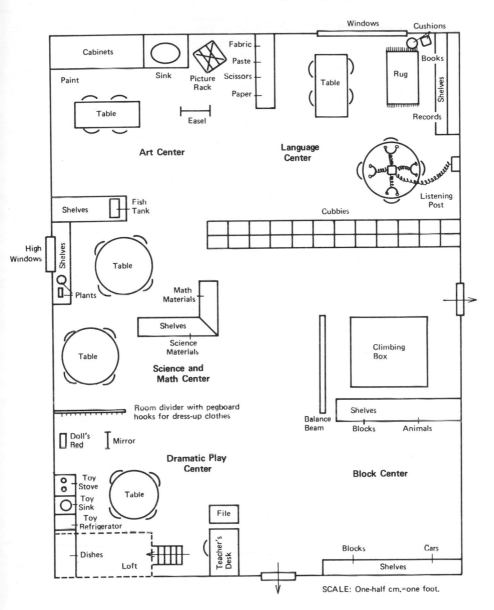

**FIGURE 3-4**  Room plan.

tion of an outdoor play area, it is helpful to know something about this topic. Furthermore, one can always add movable materials and equipment to what is permanently available. Finally, in urban areas in particular—where preschool children often walk to a community playground—knowledge of playground organization and design can guide teachers in deciding which of several available playgrounds may be best for the children to visit.

SELECTING PLAYGROUND ZONES. The areas of a playground are often referred to as *zones* (Frost and Klein, 1979). These are similar to the centers in a classroom. In choosing the zones to include in a playground, teachers must think about the experiences or kinds of play they want children to engage in. Large motor play is usually a high priority for outdoor activity, but there are many kinds of motor play: climbing, running, crawling, swinging, throwing, jumping, sliding, and twisting. Different kinds of equipment are needed to encourage the different forms of large motor behavior.

Other kinds of play are also important and need to be provided for. Small motor play; dramatic play; exploratory play with sand, water, and soil; creative arts; and construction play can occur outdoors if materials and equipment are provided. Both the weather and the season influence what is available at a time. For example, in areas where it snows during the winter, construction activities might include building a snowman or a snow fort. Containers for packing snow to make snow bricks can be provided to facilitate such play. In summer, on the other hand, large hollow blocks can be provided for building structures. Similarly, spoons, pans, pails, and other items can be used to play with snow in the winter, while in summer the same materials can be used with sand.

ORGANIZING OUTDOOR PLAY ZONES. Permanent equipment such as an inground sandbox, swings, or climbing platforms determine where other equipment and materials are placed. Wheel toys need a paved or other hard surface for proper use, and such toys must not be directed near moving objects such as swings or climbing apparatus. (Wheel toys parked near a climbing apparatus create a safety hazard.) Creative arts materials work best near a source of water if one is available outdoors, and perhaps near the classroom door, because tables, easels, and other supplies will typically need to be brought out and then taken in again. Areas for running need to be out of the way of swings, wheel toys, and play with objects such as balls. In general, when organizing an outdoor play area, one must consider (1) specific requirements for the use of equipment (a hard surface for wheel toys), (2) convenience and efficiency (placing the creative arts area near the door to the classroom), (3) traffic patterns (children should not have to cross through the wheel toy area or past the swings to get to other areas), and (4) safety (no other play zone should be placed near the swings).

## Organizing Time

Traditionally, time has been blocked into small subject-matter or activity segments during which all children in a class engage in the same activity at the same time. This organization is not functional in individualized programs because all children are not learning the same thing in the same way at the same time. Even so, time is still structured or organized, although differently than in traditional programs.

SCHEDULE COMPONENTS. A *schedule* provides the structure for the best use of student and teacher time. Components of a schedule are influenced by the same factors that influence the selection of activity areas (refer to page 00). For example, an extended nap might be needed in an all-day program for three-year-olds; whereas in a half-day program for five-year-olds, a nap would not be needed. In all-day programs, time will have to be scheduled for meals, but in half-day programs it will not. Components which are typical of individualized programs for young children are discussed below.

*Arrival.*   This is the period of time when children make the transition from home to school. During this time, each child should have an opportunity to talk with the teacher or with other children and to move at individual speed into the day's activities. In schools where children arrive at different times, this period will last longer than when they arrive at the same time.

*Planning meeting.*   This is a time for the teacher and children to clarify plans for the day. Sometimes they will review plans made earlier; sometimes they will need to make new plans. The meeting should be kept short.

The teacher should be well informed about the work children did the previous day. During the meeting, the teacher provides guidance by asking questions and making suggestions which help children plan their day.

*Activity and/or work time.*   The activity or work times constitute the major instructional time of the day. Rather than scheduling separate times for reading, mathematics, spelling, and so forth, the teacher sets aside a large block of time for these subjects. On any given day, some children might spend large amounts of time on a project which incorporates many areas of study, while other children work specifically on mathematics, reading, or science. Over a period of time, all children experience both kinds of days. This organization allows for attainment, practice, and consolidation of skills.

*Evaluation time.*   This provides an opportunity for the teacher and children to discuss the day's work experiences and plan for what is to follow the next day. The discussion may involve sharing the day's events, bringing each other up to date on projects, and making judgments about work that has been done. As the children summarize their day's experiences, the teacher asks questions and provides information which helps them to evaluate their progress. They then use this evaluation to plan for the following day.

For example, the teacher might ask what a child did with the fish tank during activity time. The child might report having added some more water to the tank. The teacher would then inquire why it was necessary to add the water. The child might or might not be aware that water evaporates from the tank. The teacher can supplement the child's explanation if necessary. The teacher might then point out that the gravel in the tank was disturbed when the new water was poured in and ask whether anyone has an idea how new water could be added without disturbing the gravel. Children will usually come up with suggestions. Some will be reasonably on target, while others will not. The teacher should accept all suggestions at this point by responding with a comment such as, "Yes, that might work." After a short time of brainstorming, the teacher should offer to provide materials at the water table so that the children can experiment to see how water can be poured from one container into another without disturbing the gravel the tank contains. Many children might clamor at this point to do this. The teacher might respond by assuring the children that the materials will be kept out as long as anyone wants to experiment with them. The discussion then passes on to another topic.

Perhaps some cooking is to be done the next day and it is the procedure in this class for the cooks to check the ingredient supply one day ahead to make sure they have what is needed. The teacher might ask one of them if the cooks did check and if everything is there. The child might report that milk and two eggs are needed. The teacher might say that milk will be available from the school kitchen, but that someone will need to bring the eggs. Two children volunteer to bring one each. It appears, then, that the cooking is all set for the next day, and the discussion moves on.

Evaluation sessions should be reasonably short; the length will vary with the age of the children and their ability to participate. Evaluation time is a crucial time in individualized programs. It provides a means for maintaining continuity in the children's lives. Children need to know what is going to happen next. In programs based primarily on textbooks and workbooks, the problem of continuity is solved. One simply goes on to the next page of the book or to the next book in the series. In individualized programs, continuity is established by means of evaluation and decision-making procedures through which children gain a sense of what has been done and what some of the next steps are to be. Evaluation time provides one of the ways in which this process can occur.

*Nap time.* This is a time when children are expected to rest. Most pre-primary children need to nap, and this requires that they lie down. The teacher may realize early in the year that a few children do not require naps but will still need to rest. Occasionally, there will be a child who does not require either a nap or a rest. Quiet activities should be provided for such children in a separate area where they will not disturb children who are sleeping.

Teachers often find it difficult to help children rest at naptime. Several techniques may be used to encourage children to rest. Sometimes, a soft animal or book will help relax children before they fall asleep. Quiet music is also helpful in relaxing some children. Others will quiet quickly if their backs are rubbed.

*Physical play.*    Young children are still learning basic motor skills such as climbing, skipping, throwing, and running. Specific provision should be made for such activity, particularly when limited classroom space reduces the range of activities which can be made available there.

Equipment facilitating the development of large motor skills should be provided. Teachers should encourage children to use this equipment independently. If some children do not play on equipment or participate in other rigorous activity, the teacher may engage them in activities such as jump rope, pitch and catch, frisbee, hula hoops, or games involving skipping, running, and jumping. When restricted facilities or inclement weather prevent outside activities, provisions for comparable indoor experiences should be made.

*Snack and lunch time.*    Because children burn up energy quickly, they need to eat frequently. Midmorning and midafternoon snacks should be provided. In full-day programs, lunch is also served.

Snacks should be nutritious and varied. Nutritious foods such as milk or natural fruit juices, raw vegetables, fresh fruits, whole-grain foods, nuts, raisins, and peanut butter should be used. Since the growth rate of preprimary and primary children has slowed considerably from what it was when they were infants and toddlers and their appetites have diminished accordingly, they should be served small portions. Those children who in fact can eat larger quantities can ask for more or take additional amounts when offered.

Snacks can be provided to the whole group at a specific time, or they can be made available early in the morning for a short period during which children may serve themselves. When snack is a group activity, it provides an opportunity for informal conversation between children and teachers. It should also be remembered that children like to help set the table, and to prepare and serve snacks.

Lunch in preprimary classes should be served much as has been described above. Care should be taken that meals are attractive, provide a variety of colors and textures, and follow nutritional guidelines.

*Music, movement, and story.*    These schedule components are self-explanatory. Experiences in music, movement, and story should be possible during activity/work time; however, because of constraints imposed by spatial requirements or noise, many teachers prefer that specific time be set aside for these activities. For example, although musical instruments may be available to children during some portions of activity/work time and a teacher may guide some individuals or small clusters of children in working with them, a time should still be set aside for musical activity involving all the children.

SCHEDULE SEQUENCE. Having determined the different types and lengths of activities which need a time slot during the school day, the teacher must determine their sequence. There are often external constraints on the sequence of a schedule. These include availability of shared resources such as gym facilities, eating facilities, special staff, and transportation accommodations. Fixed times should be noted first and other activities filled in later; it is here that teachers have some flexibility. In determining how to arrange the schedule, the teacher should try to alternate active and less active periods, quiet and noisy periods, and periods requiring different kinds of participation.

Schedules for various kinds of programs are shown below:

### HALF-DAY PREPRIMARY SCHEDULE

Arrival

Activity time (60–70 min.)

Cleanup (10 min.)

Group discussion and evaluation (10–15 min.)

Music and movement (15–20 min.)

Snack (10 min.)

Story in small groups (10–20 min.)

Second activity time or outdoor play (45 min.)

### ALL-DAY PREPRIMARY SCHEDULE

Arrival (can occur at different times for different children)

Activity time (60–80 min.)

Group discussion and evaluation (10 min.)

Snack (15 min.)

Story in small groups (15 min.)

Outside play (60 min.)

Lunch (30 min.)

Nap (90–120 min.)

Quiet time with quiet activities such as table games, puzzles, or art (30–120 min.; for those who do not sleep, this overlaps with nap time)

Music and movement (15–20 min.)

Snack (15 min.)

Physical play (outdoor or indoor 20–30 min.)

Story records, filmstrips, movies, story reading, puppet shows, flannel stories, quality TV programs such as *Mr. Rogers' Neighborhood* or *Sesame Street*

### PRIMARY PROGRAM SCHEDULE

Arrival

Group planning meeting (15–20 min.)

Work time (90 min.)

Group discussion and evaluation of work time (20 min.)

Lunch (30–40 min.)

Story read by teacher to small groups (15 min.)

Work time to continue work started in morning or begin new work (60–90 min.)

Gym or music (20 min.)

Group activity (student play or skit, puppet show, and so on) (20–30 min.)
Cleanup

In the above schedules, active and less active periods have been staggered throughout the day. Activity time allows for moderate activity, whereas the group discussion and evaluation which follow provide for relatively little activity. Story time is probably the least active period of the day, and it is followed by a more active period.

Quiet and noisy periods correspond closely to the less active and active periods, although there are some exceptions. Snack and lunch may be inactive, but not quiet. On the other hand, movement may be quite active, but quiet.

The kind of participation required of children in the activities listed also varies. During activity time, children participate individually or in small groups and make decisions about what they will do. This is followed by group discussions which require that children wait their turn to talk and remain quiet while others speak. Snack and meal times are group activities too, but they do not depend on the same type of participation or performance necessary in group discussion. Lunch is followed by story time, which requires a different group effort.

## Organizing Materials

SELECTING MATERIALS. The task of selecting materials is one of the teacher's major responsibilities. Materials should be selected on the basis of the following considerations: (1) safety, (2) durability, (3) cost, (4) instructional qualities, and (5) flexibility.

*Safety.* Materials used by children must be safe. Teachers should be alert to materials and equipment made with toxic materials such as lead paint. Materials should also be inspected to make certain that pieces do not come apart to expose nails and pins. The age of the children who will be using the equipment should also be remembered when teachers select materials for the classroom. Although pointed scissors may be used safely by an eight-year-old, they may be dangerous in the hands of a three-year-old.

*Durability.* Equipment used by a group of children will receive hard wear. The durability of learning equipment will be greater if suitable materials are used in its construction. For example, wooden blocks and puzzles last much longer than cardboard blocks and puzzles. Even durable materials deteriorate, however. It is essential, therefore, that materials are used and cared for properly. Paint brushes left in paint cups overnight soon become bent at the ends. Loose screws soon fall out and result in lost pieces.

Teachers can further the life of some materials and equipment. Paper materials can be laminated. Writing or drawing used to make teaching aids can be done with ink or a felt-tip marker, which leave marks that remain clear and dark, rather than with pencil or crayon, which do not. Paint and varnish can be used to prolong the life of materials made of wood or metal.

The containers in which materials are stored can also affect how long the items will last. Materials purchased in bulk or which arrive in flimsy containers will last longer if transferred to more suitable containers. If containers are too small for the amount of material stored in them, it is likely that some pieces will be spilled, damaged, or lost. The size of the container can also affect the care with which materials are put away and thus the amount of wear and tear they receive. Large Leggo pieces and one-inch cubes are often put away more carefully if they fit exactly into the storage containers. Similarly, materials with two distinct parts, such as lotto cards and pictures to match, will be put away more carefully if their storage containers are compartmentalized. Sometimes, fitting a smaller box inside a larger one works well. If the materials can be stored in this way, dumping and sorting by the next user are avoided and the materials receive less wear.

Teachers must also guard against the loss of a piece or two from a toy or game. For example, the loss of a puzzle piece ruins a puzzle. Putting a matching symbol, such as a number, on a puzzle frame and its pieces helps to keep them together. Carefully checking equipment each day at cleanup time can help rescue items before they are swept up or thrown out by mistake.

*Cost.*    The question of durability can present a dilemma for the teacher because it is often directly related to cost. Wooden unit blocks are expensive in terms of initial outlay, whereas cardboard building blocks are not. Many teachers purchase the cardboard blocks only to find that they do not withstand children's play. In the long run, the wood blocks might be a better buy.

When teachers face children every day and need materials and equipment immediately, they often trade durability for cost. This is unfortunate because teachers can often find or make things which work as well as the cheaper items they buy. Department stores, for example, are good sources for sturdy oblong boxes used as packing material. These make very adequate cardboard blocks. The only cost is that of the tape required to secure the box ends. In the short run, teachers have blocks; and in the long run, they will be able to put more money into equipment and materials which are of high quality. Over a period of years, the teacher will have a much better equipped classroom than if money had been spent at the start on many inexpensive materials.

*Instructional qualities of materials.*    Teachers should also consider the instructional qualities of materials. The consideration applies to equipment and materials designed for specific instructional goals. It is not uncommon for such materials to be designed so that children become confused. For example, arm balances designed to help children discover number relationships must be sensitive enough so that children receive accurate information.

Teachers also need to judge materials in terms of the range of opportunities they provide. This is not very problematic with flexible materials such as blocks or

Appropriate containers for materials encourage good care.

clay because children are able to adapt these to their own ideas. It is an important consideration, however, with items such as puzzles, books, and materials designed to teach specific skills. It is wise to purchase only one of anything that can be used for just one purpose or which is only appropriate for children at a particular level. If a certain initial-consonant teaching aid can only be used for its stated purpose, only one set needs to be purchased. Pegs and peg-boards, on the other hand, can be used to help children at various levels understand many math concepts. It may be wise to purchase several sets of these.

*Flexibility.*    Materials with specific attributes and purposes need to be included in a classroom. Puzzles, beads, books, records, a pan balance, magnets, and many other materials are quite specific in their design and use. In addition to these specific materials, classrooms should have abundant supplies of materials that lend themselves to many uses. Water, sand, blocks, cubes, clay, and paint are examples of materials which have flexible uses.

SOURCES FOR MATERIALS.    Teachers must know where to obtain materials at reasonable or no cost. Educational equipment companies supply catalogs of their products and often display them at conferences. Teachers can use these catalogs and displays to become familiar with and select materials.

The natural environment can provide materials and equipment at little or no cost.

Teachers also need to know where to obtain free materials. If teachers know where to look for what they want, this process can be simplified. Sources for free, natural, and waste materials are listed below:

1. Lumber yards
   Scrap lumber, sawdust, sturdy cardboard boxes, wood shavings
2. Department stores
   Ribbon and paper scraps, drapery and carpet swatches, packing materials, display racks, cardboard boxes
3. Hospitals or clinics
   Heavy paper from X-ray films
4. Pharmacies
   Bottles of all sizes and shapes, small boxes
5. Telephone company
   Colored wire, cable spools, telephone poles
6. Hardware stores
   Wallpaper books, paint chips, linoleum samples

MATERIALS AND CLASSROOM STRUCTURE. It is possible to create as well as to avoid problems by organizing materials in different ways. The arrangement of materials suggests something to children. It is important for the smooth running of individualized programs that classrooms not be in disarray. Cluttered shelves suggest that materials do not belong in a particular place. In such rooms children are apt to leave things out rather than put things away. This makes it difficult for the next person to find the materials needed. If quality work is expected, and it should be, then a quality environment is essential.

It is easy to keep materials organized. Designating specific and permanent storage places can help. For young children, pictures can be used to label storage areas. If woodworking tools are stored on peg-board hooks, their forms can be cut from colored contact paper and placed on the peg-board. These forms indicate specific places for the saw, hammer, drill, and screw-driver and remind children where the tools belong. A similar technique can be used to label block shelves or shelves where containers of crayons, paste, and magic markers are placed.

Organization of materials also affects the amount of traffic within a classroom. If items such as pencils, crayons, paper, and paste are placed in all centers which require them, rather than in just one center, traffic can be reduced considerably. In addition, multiple placement reduces the extent to which items are lost or misplaced; items are used near the place they are stored.

The organization of materials in a classroom can affect how children group themselves and therefore how they interact. For example, the quietness in the quiet area depends in part on the number of children who congregate there. A teacher who wants to ensure that small groupings form in the quiet area, but does not want to enforce this personally all the time, can present materials in ways

Equipment can help the teacher extend his or her time.

which suggest that only two or three children should work with them at the same time. For example, individual sets of crayons for illustrating stories might be placed in juice cans or plastic cups rather than together in large coffee cans or food jars. This arrangement suggests that a certain number of children are to use crayons at one time. If two sets are available, it suggests that only two children may work. If there are three sets, it suggests that three children may work. The number of chairs at a table, cushions in a library area, or smocks in the art area can have the same effect. In cases where small rugs are used as individual work spaces, the number of these placed in an area defines the number of people who may work there.

USING MATERIALS AND EQUIPMENT TO SAVE TIME. A teacher can extend instructional time by utilizing equipment and materials which can assume some instructional duties. A listening post can provide opportunities for children to hear more stories. Self-correcting materials can also be used. A game for matching initial consonants could be made. For example, the consonants could be written on cards and pictures of items which begin with phonemes represented by the consonants could be pasted on another set of cards. Each consonant and picture-card pair can be color coded to enable children to check their matches.

Assignment cards, or cards with questions or instructions pertaining to an activity, are also useful devices for making a teacher's time go further. While they are easier to use with primary school children who can read, picture assignment cards can also be used effectively with younger children. Several sample assignment cards are illustrated in Figures 3–5, 3–6, and 3–7.

By using materials similar to those described above, the teacher is using indirect instructional methods. Equipment and materials can help a child gain a skill or acquire information without constant and direct supervision from the teacher. Such items free the teacher during the school day to be able to spend time with children on tasks which they cannot do alone. However, even though such equipment and materials can be valuable as extenders of the teacher's instructional time, the teacher is still the key to instruction. Indirect instruction is only as good as the teacher's judgment about what kinds of experiences will be helpful to children and about what materials and equipment can provide good instruction.

MAKING MATERIALS GO FURTHER. The way in which materials are introduced into the classroom can affect their use. Children can explore an activity more completely if materials are presented carefully. By developing and extending activities over time, teachers can save preparation time; they can begin thinking in terms of small modifications of what they have, rather than in terms of major overhauls.

Clay, for example, may first be made available for several weeks without tools. The novelty of a new material will be sufficient to keep the children working the clay with their hands. Interest in this mode of exploration may last for several weeks. When it seems to be waning, one or two types of utensils such as cookie cut-

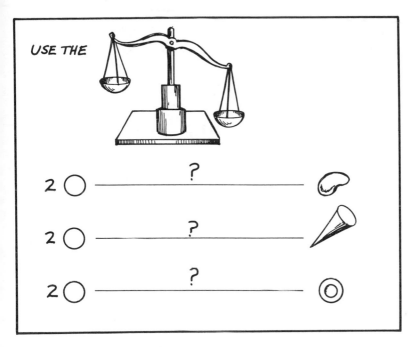

**FIGURE 3-5** Assignment cards.

ters, rolling pins, plastic knives, clay stamps, or wooden clay tools can be added. This addition changes the clay activity just enough to renew interest. After several more weeks, interest can again be revived by adding different utensils or tools. One reason why this procedure works so often to renew interest is that with the new tools, children find new ways in which to work with the materials.

The same principle can be applied to many other activities. New props for block play and dramatic play can be added from time to time. New utensils can also be added to the sand and water play areas.

**FIGURE 3-6** Assignment cards.

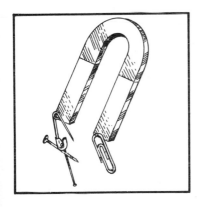

1. Place pudding mix in bowl.

2. Fill cup with milk.

3. Add milk to bowl.

4. Shake in jar.

5. Pour pudding into cups.

**FIGURE 3-7**  Assignment cards.

Another way teachers can make materials go further is to think of multiple uses for them. Dominoes can be used for several math skills, such as matching one to one, addition, subtraction, and multiplication. Cards from a rook deck can be used for a variety of mathematical skill games or as numeral cards with boxes containing different sets of materials. Not all the felt letters that come in a set are needed at the felt board. At least one letter from each set could be glued to a cardboard square to make a set of tactile cards.

### Organizing Activities

The organization of an activity has a great impact on how effective it is. Sometimes the content or the idea of an activity is excellent and the potential for learning is high, but because the teacher fails to organize the activity carefully, children are unable to profit from it. For example, recently this author observed in two different classrooms where an identical activity had been prepared for the children. The activity in both cases was a "fishing game." Fishing poles had been made from dowel rods, string, and magnets. "Fish" had been made from heavy paper, and paper clips had been inserted into each one in the mouth area. Children were to catch the fish by connecting the magnet and the paper clip. In both classes, the activity was provided as one of many choices during an activity period.

In one class, the student helper placed the fish in a small area on the floor and gave the poles to children who wished to fish. As the children fished, they sometimes stood very near the fish or even stepped on top of them. They also tangled their lines from time to time and bumped each other's arms. The teacher tried to help the children solve these problems by suggesting that they "stand back," "watch out," and "be careful." The children responded very little to these suggestions and in general continued to have difficulty. The teacher grew impatient as conflicts continued to arise and finally began telling children they could not fish if they did not do it "right." A fishing pole was taken away from one child who continued to step into the pile of fish on the floor.

In the second classroom, the teacher made a large "lake" on the floor with masking tape and placed the fish inside the boundaries. Sometimes, as children fished, they would step over the tape and the teacher would warn them in a playful tone that they would get wet if they didn't get out of the lake. Children quickly stepped back beyond the tape line when the teacher pointed this out, although the teacher did have to repeat the warning several times during the activity when children forgot to stay out of the lake. The circle made by the tape was big enough so that children had plenty of room to fish without bumping into each other. This spacing seemed to prevent tangled lines, too.

The simple addition of a lake made with tape seemed to make a difference in helping children be successful with this activity. It may have worked well because it appealed to children's sense of make-believe, or it may simply have provided more specific information about what to do than was the case with verbalizations such as "stand back," "watch out," and "be careful."

The different organization of the two fishing games seemed to have an impact on the children's learning. In the first classroom, the teacher spent so much time correcting children's behavior that both teacher and children had little time to talk about anything else. In the second classroom, the teacher asked individual children questions about the number of fish they were catching, about their color, and about the types of fish they might be. Children were also asked if they had ever been fishing and what must really be placed on the end of a fishing line if you want to catch a fish.

A teacher who plans an activity might first consider what type of behavior is to be expected in relation to the activity. The teacher can then analyze how to organize the activity to make it easier for children to meet the expectations. Many times, it is only after the activity has been tried that its difficulties are apparent. When difficulties do arise, we must be careful not simply to blame the children or chalk it up to a bad day. Sometimes children are to blame and sometimes it is the day; but often it reflects failure on the teacher's part to organize the activity in a way that helps children relate to it as the teacher expects. Good teachers analyze activities and make adjustments which improve them.

## Organizing Staff

Teachers who wish to provide individualized instruction are aware that a small amount of individual instruction is more effective than much longer periods of large-group instruction. Yet, faced with as many as thirty children in a kindergarten or primary classroom, a teacher may well despair of finding time to spend with each child. In most prekindergarten classrooms the teacher has a paid assistant, and in many kindergarten and primary classrooms paid aides are part of the staff. When this is not so, volunteers may provide the solution. Parents, high-school students, or retired persons may be called on to volunteer their services. Whether a teacher is working with paid staff or with volunteers, skill in using such help to best advantage is required.

UTILIZING STAFF EFFECTIVELY. Good communication among staff is a necessity. Only when assistants are aware of the teacher's purposes, plans, and methods can teacher and assistant work together as a smoothly functioning team. To achieve this, the teacher should be prepared to spend time with assistants when children are not present. Staff meetings for program planning, when the teacher can communicate plans and desires and elicit ideas, suggestions, and feedback about children from assistants, should be scheduled periodically. In addition, a relaxed chat over a cup of coffee after the children have left may do much to help the teacher gain insight into an assistant's strengths and allow the assistant a chance to ask questions.

Even though the ideal is to include all staff—part-time, full-time, and volunteer—in program planning, there are times when it is not possible. Then there should be some way to inform everyone of plans made or changed. A plan sheet such as the one on page 57 is one way to accomplish this; providing a "mail" box for each assistant where notes may be left is another (see page 52 for an example of a note left for a high-school volunteer).

To utilize volunteers effectively, it is particularly important to communicate a feeling of welcome, need, and appreciation. It is wise to suggest that a new assistant, whether volunteer or paid, take time to observe the class without participating and to follow the observation with a conference during which the new assistant can ask questions. Schedules for specific and regular times for the assistant to be in the classroom should then be arranged. Asking volunteers to notify the teacher when they cannot be in the classroom as scheduled serves the double purpose of emphasizing to them the importance of their help and allowing the teacher to make alternate plans. As has been suggested in the section on planning, it is important that assistants have a clear idea of what the teacher expects them to do.

*Using children as a source of help.*    Children themselves may also be utilized as teachers. If there is one child who is beginning to learn addition facts and another who needs additional practice, they could both benefit from working with flash cards. The beginner holds the cards with the facts and answers, which is what beginners need, while the other child is quizzed on recall, which provides a chance for practice and review. When children have developed a particular skill, teaching another child increases their feeling of self-worth and develops their ability to conceptualize what they have done.

In addition to helping with some of the instruction, children can be helpful

Children can teach each other.

in other ways. They can be responsible for many of the details of classroom life. The teacher can arrange the room to make it possible for children to get materials out, put them away, and clean up. For example, there is no reason for a preschool teacher to spend time tying or snapping children's paint smocks when simple, pull-on designs can be made. Similarly, a teacher does not need to spend time digging out blobs of paste onto pieces of paper each time a child needs some, when amounts that will last several weeks can be made available in small jars which can be stored on a shelf for children's use.

*Asking people to make things.* Though not all volunteers have the patience or desire to work directly with children, many would be happy to provide other kinds of help. Many of the preparation tasks teachers perform are not particularly difficult but require a substantial amount of time. It would be helpful if someone other than the teacher could do this work. There are many resources for such help. One frequently overlooked resource is older people. If older people live in group centers, they usually welcome requests for help to make things. Older people often have time on their hands and would like to contribute.

Parents, too, can help make things. Holding parent workshops is a good strategy for using parents' skills. Parents may visit with each other and the teacher while making materials. Workshops have the additional benefit of acquainting parents with materials their children will be using.

Teachers should not overlook the fact that it is difficult for some parents to attend meetings and workshops at school. This does not necessarily indicate a lack of interest on the parents' part. It is often possible for these parents to make things for the school while they are at home. This strategy for parent help can in fact be quite beneficial to the child. Sometimes the child can assist the parent in making items for school. When this is not possible, the child often is aware that the parent is making something for school and feels proud and special.

## EVALUATING

To evaluate a child's learning, the teacher first must have a clear idea of the goals set for each child. Progress or growth assumes movement from one level of skill or understanding to another. When a child's learning is evaluated, three steps are involved: (1) information is gathered to determine the child's skills and understandings, (2) current skills and understandings are compared to previous levels, and (3) current skills and understandings are compared to goals for the child's learning.

### Two Types of Information

There are basically two ways to secure information about what a child knows or can do: (1) the teacher can observe the child's behavior or look at work produced in the normal course of everyday classroom life or (2) the teacher can contrive situations in which certain kinds of information must be used or certain kinds of problems must be solved. Contrived situations take various forms, such as tests or specifically designed tasks. Each of the two basic techniques has advantages and limitations.

The contrived situation allows behaviors to be elicited relatively quickly in a standard way, that is, similarly for all children. If a teacher waits for all situations to occur naturally, information regarding some behaviors might take a very long time to collect. For example, a teacher wishing to know about the balancing skills of the children in a four-year-old group might set up a balance beam in the classroom and then watch children as they play on it. But some children might avoid it altogether, preferring instead to do other things during activity time. Or, the teacher may be busy with another classroom task when one or two children elect to walk the beam, thus missing the opportunity to observe their skill. Still other children may play on the balance beam, but their behavior may be influenced by the presence of other children. How steady can one be on the beam, for example, when a peer is screeching, "Don't fall off in the river. The snakes will bite you!"? It would be easier and quicker to obtain information by arranging a specific time to take a few children to the balance beam and asking each one to walk it from one end to the other.

On the other hand, contrived situations have some limitations. Perhaps a child who walks the balance beam for pleasure when it is made available for free use becomes tense when specifically asked to do it while someone watches. Apparent skill may decline under these conditions. Or perhaps motivation is not as high when something is done at the request of an adult rather than for one's own purposes: Trying not to "fall in the river and be eaten by the snakes" may, in fact, encourage a child to try his or her hardest to stay on the balance beam. Performing for the teacher may not elicit the same degree of determination.

Thorough teachers probably use both techniques to gather information, and they understand the pitfalls of each. Preschool teachers probably use tests and specific tasks to a much lesser extent than do kindergarten and primary teachers because they are not required to report at frequent intervals (grading periods) to school officials or to parents about progress in specific skill areas. In addition, preschool children usually must show in action, rather than with pencil and paper, what they can do.

## Collecting Information

ACTUAL WORK. Children's actual work may be used as information for evaluation. It is relatively easy to organize and store much of their work. A file folder can be made for each child and samples of drawings, paintings, and writing can be inserted. If the work is dated, the teacher can see the child's progress over a period of time.

Some products, of course, cannot be saved. Or, they may present a storage problem. Constructions made of unit blocks and Leggos must be dismantled if the materials are to remain in use. Sculpture does not fit into a file folder. A camera can be very useful for recording work of this kind, although photographic supplies are costly.

OBSERVATIONS. Much of the information a teacher collects comes from observing children's behavior. The difficulty here lies in noting in some way what has been observed. Some things are difficult to put into words, and all events take time to record. However, there are ways to make this type of recordkeeping less tedious.

Before one can decide on ways to record data collected through observation, one must have some understanding of the kinds of information that can be collected. The following is a sample of what a teacher might observe:

> Perhaps a discussion is conducted and the teacher notices the expression on several children's faces. John is gazing off into the distance, although he occasionally turns his face to a child who is talking. As Jim talks, he is smiling and maintains direct eye contact with the teacher. Maria yawns and rubs her eyes.
>
> As children work independently, the teacher notices that Susan has started her third activity without having finished either of the first two. John is in the blocks with Tim, and José is separating Cuisenaire rods into piles. The teacher hears Shawn tell

Tom he can not play with him any more if Tom does not give up the wooden truck and also sees Tom hand it over.

Stopping to work with one child and then another, the teacher notices that Ian loses the concept of one-to-one correspondence when there are more than four objects to count, that Shawn calls the numeral 3, "2," and that Tim can think of four words besides his name that start with a *t*. When asked how he learned to use a hammer so well, Ian responds by saying that his brother "teached" him.

The teacher needs some way to record and organize all the data collected through observation. Many types of information can be adequately recorded on a checklist. Information related to concepts and skills in subject matter are easily recorded in this manner. The teacher constructs the checklist on the basis of goals established for particular areas of study. A partial checklist for math skills is shown in Figure 3–8.

The teacher would have a checklist for each child, which can be kept in the child's folder. When data are collected through observation, it would be indicated on the checklist that on a particular date, the child showed evidence of having a particular skill or concept. When dates are noted several times in the boxes opposite a skill, the teacher can be rather certain the child does in fact have the skill.

It is important for such checklists to be detailed and specific. For example, it is not as helpful to have one item, "Can count," as it might be to have two items, "Counts to five," and "Counts to ten." It takes a long time for a child to learn to count to ten. Teachers need to know how far a child has progressed in order to give appropriate guidance. On the other hand, if checklists are too specific, their length will be burdensome.

**FIGURE 3-8**  Math skills checklist.

| Name: | | | | | |
|---|---|---|---|---|---|
| Classifies | | | | | |
| Matches one-to-one | | | | | |
| Names sets to three | | | | | |
| Counts to five | | | | | |
| Names sets to five | | | | | |
| Counts to ten | | | | | |
| Combines sets to four | | | | | |
| Names numerals to five | | | | | |

Checklists are also helpful in recording data about children's reactions to classroom routines, their physical abilities and health, their social-emotional behavior, and where they spend their time in the classroom.

Checklists are usually inadequate to record all the details a teacher might think important. Perhaps a child rarely cries except when required to attend gym class. Maybe another child accepts rules except when playing or working with a specific classmate. Yet another child may rarely lead in indoor play but often leads in outdoor play. These qualifications or details of behavior are important. They provide the necessary clues which a teacher would need in order to influence the children's behaviors in any way. In addition, they are idiosyncratic. They apply to individual children, not to everyone in the class. That is why it is difficult to construct an adequate checklist to handle this type of information. Children keep doing things for which there is no appropriate item to check. Clearly, another type of record is required.

*Anecdotal records* provide a structure for handling the type of data described above. Anecdotal records are detailed accounts of events. They include important details of the setting as well as of the event itself. Only the behavior itself should be noted. For example, rather than noting that "Johnny was happy outside today," the teacher should note, "Johnny jumped from the second bar of the climbing apparatus and laughed and smiled as he said, 'Hey, did you see that?'" Similarly, it will not be helpful to note that "Susan was awful today." Three weeks later, the teacher will not remember what Susan did that was awful. If teachers hope to support children's learning, they need detailed information which tells them specifically where an event occurred, under what conditions it occurred, and with whom it occurred.

The actual form of an anecdotal record does not matter. Complete sentences and neat handwriting are not necessary for such records when they are for the teacher's own use. When several teachers work together with the same group of children, legibility may be important; but when teachers read their own records, they may use shorthand, abbreviations, or any other system for making the writing less tedious. Entries may be kept on small pieces of paper which can be inserted into the child's file. Each entry must be dated to have value.

Sometimes, teachers have difficulty remembering what they have observed during the day. For this reason, some teachers carry pads of paper in their pockets so that they can jot down notes as they teach. Teachers do not have time to record events in their entirety, but sometimes these notes can serve as reminders for later. For example, a note which simply says, "Jill, blocks," might help a teacher remember a particular incident.[1]

STANDARDIZED TESTS. Sometimes, teachers wish not only to know if children are achieving the specific goals they have set for them, but if the children they teach know or can do what most children of their age and grade level know

---

[1]Teachers must be careful to keep records confidential.

and can do. Standardized tests are tests that have been administered to many children in order that age norms could be established for the various test items. It is possible to know how most five-year-olds perform, for example, or how most four-year-olds perform. Then, when any children in these age groups are given the test, their performance can be compared to the appropriate norms.

Standardized tests can be useful, but teachers must use them and their results with caution. The standardization sample, that is, the children used to develop the norms for the test, may not be completely representative of all children. For example, if all children in the sample are white, lower class, and rural; or black, middle class, and urban; the sample is not representative of all children. We would expect children from other racial, social, and geographic groups to have knowledge that differs in some ways from the knowledge of the children on whom the test was standardized; and we would expect their performance on the test to be different. While they might not know less, they might know *different* things. Therefore, the test would be an unfair measure of their skills and abilities.

The following story told by a kindergarten teacher illustrates how one's experiences can influence responses to test items. A series of questions on the particular test given to children in the class required that the children relate two objects. One picture was enclosed in a box to the left of the page, and to the right was a row of three pictures. The child was to select one picture from the row that represented an object that belonged with the key picture in the box. One of the key pictures was a shoe. The pictures from which the children were to choose a related picture included a sock, a chair, and a dog. The "correct" answer was the sock. Presumably, shoes and socks go together because they are both worn on the foot.

Most of the children in this class missed the item because they selected chair to go with shoe. The tester was somewhat alarmed at the apparent inability of these children to grasp such a simple relationship and expressed that concern to the children's teacher. Upon receiving the information, the teacher laughed and said their answers made perfectly good sense to her. She had been in the last months of a pregnancy during the first part of the school year and was unable to bend over to tie shoes. If someone requested help, she always asked the child to put the foot with the untied shoe on a chair so that she would not have to bend down to the floor. Thus, because of their experiences, children in this class learned that chair and shoe were related. The culture of this classroom influenced the views of the world developed by these children. This in turn influenced their responses to a test which had been standardized on a group of children whose experiences had not included this one.

There have been some attempts in recent years to develop "culture free" or "culture fair" tests (Cattell, 1971). Such tests would contain items not dependent on any particular cultural experience. However, it is doubtful that such a test can ever be devised (Anastasi, 1976). No matter what the test item, children with certain experiences are likely to do better on it than children with other experiences. Because experiences are systematically linked to one's culture, social class, and geographic location, test items will usually contain a bias against one group or another.

The issue of standardization samples is particularly controversial with IQ tests because many people assume that scores on these tests indicate basic or innate ability, rather than opportunities one has had to learn specific things. A low score, therefore, has often been interpreted as an indication of low learning potential, rather than as a lack of previous learning opportunities. As a result, children earning low scores may be placed in special classes, or teachers may expect less of them, thinking they can do little. Thus, their opportunities to learn may be further impeded. Teachers and schools must be careful in how they use IQ score information.

A second difficulty with standardized tests is that they sample behavior during restricted time frames, usually during one part of one day out of an entire year. If a child is upset or ill on that particular day, performance could be harmed. In such cases, typical classroom performance in school may provide a more accurate picture of the child's skills and abilities.

Other difficulties with standardized tests include misuse such as "teaching to the test." In this case, teachers plan instruction around test items to try to make certain that their children will score well on the test. The problem here is that tests include only a small sample of all that children should know, and teaching to the test narrows the range of what is taught.

Despite their limitations and frequent misuse, standardized tests can tell us something about how children compare with other children of the same age or grade level. When used wisely and in combination with other information, they are useful in the evaluation process.

JUDGING THE DATA. Evaluation requires making a judgment about the data one has collected. Judgments involve deciding whether or not a child is making adequate progress toward certain goals. For example, a judgment regarding the data discussed in the observation on page 75 might be that Shawn is not doing very well with names or numerals. He learns quickly and his interest in school is high. The teacher thinks he should be farther along. Another judgment might be that Ian's overgeneralization of verb endings is a typical pattern for a four-year-old and that he is progressing well in language development. A third judgment might be that Tim's ability to detect initial consonants is quite good and that he could profit from experiences to develop more ability in this area.

The above judgments are then used as a basis for planning. The teacher might plan to try to encourage Shawn to play numeral bingo with a friend who knows numeral names very well. The teacher might also plan to mention to Ian's parents that his language is typical for a child his age and might suggest that they do nothing more than repeat Ian's statements using the standard verb form. For example, if Ian says, "My brother teached me to saw," the parent might respond by saying, "Oh, your brother taught you to saw?"

The teacher might also plan to construct some initial consonant picture cards for Tim to extend his skills and plan to give these to him at the end of the next morning's planning meeting.

The above decisions indicate that the teacher has made some judgments about the data that were collected. Information is not very useful if teachers do not make judgments about what it means in terms of the child's progress in learning and in terms of appropriate learning experiences which should be planned for the child.

## REFERENCES

ANASTASI, A.    *Psychological testing.* Fourth Edition. New York: MacMillan, 1976.

CATTELL, R. B.    The structure of intelligence in relation to the nature-nurture controversy. In R. Canco ed., *Intelligence: Genetic and environmental influences.* New York: Grune and Stratton, 1971, pp. 3–30.

FROST, J. L., and KLEIN, B. L.    *Children's play and playgrounds.* Boston: Allyn and Bacon, Inc., 1979.

## ADDITIONAL RESOURCES

HOHMANN, M., BANET, B., and WEIKART, D. P.    Arranging and equipping the classroom. *Young Children in Action,* Chapter 1. Ypsilante, Michigan: High/Scope Educational Foundation, 1979, 35–57.

RAMBUSCH, N. M.    The organization of environment. In D. T. Streets, ed., *Administering Day Care and Preschool Programs.* Boston: Allyn and Bacon, 1982.

RHO, L., and DRURY, F.    *Space and Time in Early Learning.* Cheshire, Conn. Board of Education, 1979. (Adaptations of physical space for special needs children.)

TAYLOR, A. P., and VLASTOS, G.    *School Zone: Learning Environments for Children.* New York: Van Nostrand Reinhold, 1975.

# 4

# CHILDREN
# WITH SPECIAL
# NEEDS*

* Much of the material in this chapter was first published as "Mainstreaming in the Preschool"
by D. Morgan and M. E. York in *Young Children*, Vol. 36, No. 2, January 1981. Washington, D.C.:
NAEYC. We are indebted to Dorothy Morgan for this chapter. Ms. Morgan writes out of her long experience with young handicapped children and not only provided technical expertise for the original
article but expanded it to the present length.

A vivacious four-year-old thrusts her arms through the holes of an apron and backs up to a teaching assistant. The assistant ties the strings, pats the child affectionately on the shoulder and asks, ''Do you have all the colors you need?'' The child answers ''yes'' and scampers to the easels. It is only as she picks up a brush with two stumps that a visitor notes she has no hands.

The teacher calls out, ''Circle time! Finish what you are doing and come to the circle!'' Some children start directly toward the circle, while others put the finishing touches on their projects and put things away. Only one child does not respond to the teacher's call. The teacher catches the attention of a child next to the unresponsive one and motions toward him. The child walks over and touches him on the shoulder. When they are face-to-face, the child repeats what the teacher has said and points to the circle. Then they walk together to the circle and take places facing the teacher.

The children are eating midmorning snack at round tables in small groups. The teacher says to a small boy sitting nearby, ''Hold the cup with your one hand and pour from the pitcher with your other hand.'' After waiting several seconds with no response from the child, the teacher says, ''Let me help you,'' and asks the other children, ''What kind of juice do we have today?'' The teacher then puts one hand over each of the boy's hands while they pour the juice and describes what they are doing. When the juice is ready, the teacher continues, ''Pretty soon you'll be able to pour your juice by yourself.''

Three children with special needs have been described. The children's teachers and peers responded to each in ways that were both sensitive and natural. Not long ago, handicapped children such as these were routinely placed in special programs. In the past decade, it has become increasingly apparent that separating children with handicaps from those who are considered nonhandicapped deprives both groups of valuable educational experiences.

Pressure from concerned parents and teachers of handicapped children has resulted in legislation supporting the rights of handicapped children to a public (free) education. In 1972, PL 92–424 was passed by Congress specifying that all Head Start programs must enroll and serve handicapped children in order to retain funding. In 1975, PL 94–142 was passed mandating free education for all handicapped children between the ages of three and eighteen in ''least restrictive environments'' (Braun & Lasher 1978). Since the ''least restrictive environment'' may be a regular classroom serving nonhandicapped children, this legislation, known as the ''mainstreaming act,'' has caused concern among teachers in those classrooms.

The goal of this chapter is to provide teachers with information and suggestions for integrating handicapped children into their classes and to allay the fear of teachers who have not had special training for working with such children. The chapter will first consider the values of mainstreaming to handicapped children, nonhandicapped children, and adults. Information about handicapping conditions will then be presented and approaches to working with handicapped children will be suggested.

## VALUES OF MAINSTREAMING

### Values for the Handicapped Child

THE OPPORTUNITY TO CHOOSE FRIENDS. Receiving training only at home or in a special classroom restricts handicapped children to dealing only with persons in their immediate environment and usually with those who are like themselves. In an integrated classroom, they will come into contact with children with *and* without handicaps from whom they may choose their friends.

THE OPPORTUNITY TO REALIZE POTENTIAL SKILLS MORE FULLY. Typically, materials in special classrooms are geared to the children's handicaps. Because some materials are assumed to be beyond the children's ability, they are generally not obtained. But is such an assumption valid? Should a child not be allowed to try other materials? In most classrooms designed for nonhandicapped children, there is a greater variety of materials; the handicapped child may then have the opportunity to explore new avenues of interest and attempt to master different skills.

THE OPPORTUNITY TO LEARN FROM NONHANDICAPPED PEERS. Nonhandicapped peers serve as models and fill in the gaps in the experiences of handicapped children. When children with mental and physical problems are placed with children who are similar to them, the behavior patterns which set them apart are reinforced. On the other hand, they will adopt a wider range of behaviors when they observe and imitate nonhandicapped children.

Sensorially handicapped children, to whom life with sight or hearing is limited or unknown, are inclined to believe that all children are the same as they. As Piaget (1966) has suggested, young children are egocentric and tend to believe that all children think as they do. Exposure to those who are different widens their perspectives.

### Values for the Nonhandicapped Child

LEARNING TO ACCEPT DIFFERENCES IN PEOPLE. When children have positive early experiences with handicapped people, they learn to accept them as persons who, in spite of obvious differences, are very much like themselves. This happens most easily in the years before school. As Caldwell (1972) rather bluntly says, children before the age of seven are not usually "cripple kickers." They may show curiosity about the handicapping conditions they see and ask questions with typical candor, but seldom do they shun or denigrate the individual. Accepting differences in these early years may prevent the later hurtful name-calling that is so frequently heard from children between the ages of seven and twelve.

LEARNING TO BE HELPING, CARING PEOPLE. While the tendency to be altruistic appears very early (Rheingold, 1976), the tendency must be nurtured if children are to become helping, caring adults. Empathic distress (Hoffman, 1975) is often seen in very young children who see others who are hurt in some way. In the perception of young children, a handicapped child is a hurt child. If encouraged to do so, they will help that child. With such encouragement as well as with guidance and modeling from adults, children will exercise their altruistic tendencies when there are handicapped children in their classroom.

LEARNING HOW AND WHEN TO HELP. As pleasant as it may be to see one child help another, this helpfulness may be carried too far. A child's attempts to help a handicapped child are often inappropriate. As the relationship grows and with guidance from the teacher, the nonhandicapped child learns how to help and when helping is appropriate. For example, the teacher can say to a sighted child who wishes to help a blind child, "Let's help Sidney learn to climb to the top of the Jungle Gym by himself. Can you tell him how to do it? Tell him where to put his hand . . now his feet." Helping children learn to give directions to a child in need also helps them improve their communication skills.

## THE TEACHER OF CHILDREN WITH SPECIAL NEEDS

Mainstreaming is a frightening idea to many teachers. They feel inadequate to the task of meeting the special needs of both handicapped and nonhandicapped children. Many feel that they do not have the intellectual, emotional, or physical resources to work with children who have been labeled "handicapped." However, there are many ways in which classrooms using the approach to teaching recommended in this book are particularly suited to the needs of handicapped children. Some of the important factors they provide are:

1. A teacher knowledgeable in child development who accepts children on many levels of development. Such a teacher knows, for example, that four-year-olds tend to be boisterous and aggressive and can assure a parent of a developmentally delayed child that such behavior is seen in many nonhandicapped four-year-olds.
2. Consistency, a dependable schedule, and firm limits.
3. A curriculum with a multisensory approach.
4. A curriculum rich in a variety of hands-on experiences.
5. A curriculum which enhances growth in all areas of development.
6. An abundance of opportunities for play, for making choices, and for working at one's own pace.
7. A natural, appropriate setting in which learning may be directly applied with no need for delayed generalization from a highly structured and isolated lesson.

Teachers will find, however, that they have much to learn and will need to make adaptations in their teaching techniques.

## Learning about Children
## with Special Needs

Many adults have had little or no experience with persons who are handicapped in some way since, typically, handicapped people have been separated from the mainstream into programs especially designed for them. For teachers with little or no previous experience with handicapped persons, having handicapped children in their classrooms may provide them with the opportunity to learn to value such children for their unique strengths as well as to understand better their disabilities. Teachers and other adults may find that as they become acquainted with handicapped children, former beliefs about the handicaps are changed. For example, they may find that:

- Blind children do not use alternative sensory channels for information automatically; they must learn to use hearing, smell, and tactile senses as well as movement to replace sight. The adults must help them to develop these skills.
- Children with loss of hearing, even with severe or profound loss, are not necessarily quiet. They may be constantly babbling, chattering, or using jargon and other forms of unintelligible speech.
- Children with Down's syndrome typically appear to be cheerful, compliant, and loving, but they are not always so. They may surprise you with anger and stubborn resistance.
- Children with severe and multiple physical handicaps such as cerebral palsy may have normal or superior cognitive ability masked by their inability to express themselves readily.

## Adapting to Meet the Needs
## of Handicapped Children

The presence of handicapped children requires that teachers be creative and use different techniques for familiar activities. For example, when reading a story to hearing children, the teacher may read the words while the children look at the pictures and words at the same time. A child with a hearing loss, however, needs to be encouraged to observe all speech and facial movements closely. In order to allow the hearing-impaired child to watch the teacher's face, the pages being read will need to be shown to the children separately—before or after the reading, or both. All children may benefit, however, from having extra time to look at the pictures and words and perhaps from having some of the words pointed out or talking about the story as it progresses.

As teachers see handicapped children use unique ways to learn about their environment, they may become more aware and possibly more tolerant of the variety of ways in which all children learn. Shirley Cohen (1975) describes a blind

Hearing impaired children need to watch the teacher's face.

child entering kindergarten for the first time. As he began shouting, his mother explained to the teacher and children that since he could not use his eyes to get information as the other children did, he used his voice. From the way his voice sounded, from the echoes it made, he could tell whether the room was big or small.

Teachers will also need to make adaptations in the arrangement of furniture and to adjust their teaching in numerous ways. (Suggestions for ways of working with specific handicaps will be given later in the chapter.) They will also need to learn to call on volunteers, aides, and the children in the class to assist. Calling on the handicapped children's peers to assist provides a means of helping nonhandicapped children develop understanding and a sense of caring for people who are different.

## THE HANDICAPPED CHILD

Handicap may be defined as a physical, mental, sensory, linguistic, or emotional deficiency that prevents normal achievement (Fallen & McGovern, 1978). Some classroom teachers may recall a child who might be called "handicapped" and yet is not eligible for special services under P.L. 94–142. Whether or not a child is judged to be handicapped may depend on the screening test that is used or the attitudes of the teachers or parents (Safford 1978).

All handicapping conditions have a range of severity (Fallen & McGovern, 1978). If a child's handicap is judged so severe that coping with a regular classroom environment is clearly not feasible, the child will not be placed in a regular classroom. Knowledge of the handicapping condition does not predict a child's potential for success. A profoundly deaf child who has an engaging, outgoing personality will probably have a much more successful experience in a typical preschool than one with a mild hearing loss who also has emotional problems and few prior group experiences.

## Identification

Teachers need to be alert for signs which indicate that a child should be referred for professional diagnosis. It is not always easy to determine whether inappropriate behavior or apparent inability to learn is due to a specific handicap or to some other factor. Astute observation over time and in many different situations is needed to make that determination. Informal assessment which measures the child's behavior against that which is typical of others in the same age range also needs to be made. The following guidelines may be used:

1.  Is the problem chronic, that is, has it persisted over an extended period of time? Children demonstrate a wide range of normal behavior. When the behavior of a child is observed to be quite different from that of peers for an extended period of time, the teacher needs to analyze what those differences are. Using a developmental scale such as the Denver or Boyd scales (Frankenburg, et al 1970; Boyd, 1974) will help to pinpoint developmental lags. Keeping an anecdotal record is also useful (see Cartwright and Cartwright, 1974 and Rowen, 1973 for suggestions).

2.  Are there other factors which may account for a child's inappropriate behavior or failure to learn? For example, is English the language spoken in the home? (Children whose home language is other than English need time to learn a second language; typically, however, these children are not handicapped as defined above.) Has the family undergone a recent change or trauma such as divorce, a new baby, loss of job, or death? (Such crises may disrupt learning for some period of time.) (Hetherington, Cox & Cox, 1979) Is this the child's first experience in a group setting? (A child whose behavior is not typical or is out-of-bounds may not have had sufficient experience to know what behavior is acceptable in a group. Learning to be part of a group may supersede all other learning for a time.)

3.  How large are the differences between the behavior seen and behavior expected? When the problem is severe, specific intervention or different teaching approaches may be needed (Hare & Hare 1977). For example, if a four-year-old lacks certain speech sounds but is still intelligible, there is no cause for alarm. If, on the other hand, the speech is largely unintelligible, the child produces no sentences, and there are many omissions of *initial* consonants (Weiss and Liliwhite, 1976), a speech and hearing evaluation is indicated.

4.  Is the problem generalized to several areas of development? For example, a lag across all abilities of a year or more usually indicates developmental disability (mental retar-

dation). On the other hand, lacking a specific skill, such as being able to hop on one foot, while possessing abilities in other developmental areas similar to those of peers, simply indicates a lower level of maturity in motor skills. However, since there is a direct correlation between a specific handicap and lags in other areas of development, other possibilities need to be ruled out. For example, children with hearing problems will have difficulties with both receptive and expressive language; physically impaired children may have trouble with both large and small motor abilities and problems with speaking; while a visually impaired child may have difficulties with coordination.

If a teacher has observed over a prolonged period of time that a child behaves in a manner that is radically different from that of other children, and if usually successful efforts to change that behavior are unsuccessful, the child should be referred for professional diagnosis. When doing so, clear, objective, detailed descriptions of the observed behavior as well as possible causative factors (see 2 above) will be helpful to the professional making the diagnosis.

### Meeting the Needs of Children Who Have Been Identified as Handicapped

For a child who is assessed as handicapped, an Individualized Education Program (IEP) (Lerner, 1981) will be designed by a team consisting of a qualifed school official, the parent(s), the teacher, and, when feasible, the child (Fallen & McGovern, 1978; Souvaine, Crimmins, and Magel, 1981). Such an IEP is the child's right as mandated by P.L. 94–142. Having so many other people involved in determining goals and objectives for a child may at first seem threatening to classroom teachers accustomed to writing their own curricula. However, IEP's can be coordinated very well with classroom activities and the teacher will find that with practice, many of the activities recommended in other chapters of this book provide the source for achieving the goals of individual programs.

Teachers cannot be expected to provide for the special needs of handicapped children unaided. Most public school systems provide specialists such as speech therapists and others with special training in the education of handicapped children to work with the child and the teacher. In many communities, itinerant services are available. Some research into community resources may bring needed help to the teacher, the child, and the family.

Once a handicapped child is a member of the class, the challenge is to ensure maximum participation in as many activities as possible. Not all areas of the curriculum will present special problems for all handicapped children. In fact, for teachers using the approach recommended in this book, there are very few activities which are not appropriate for the handicapped child at some level. Obviously, there are exceptions. A cerebral-palsied child will not climb a jungle gym and a hearing-impaired child will have problems with playback equipment because of distortions.

## DESCRIPTIONS OF DIFFERENT
## HANDICAPPING CONDITIONS

Before discussing methods of teaching handicapped children, we will discuss some behaviors and common characteristics often seen among children with specific handicaps. Each child is unique and will not conveniently fit into a mold; we merely offer guidelines to assist in developing increased understanding.

### Hearing Impairment

Hearing impairment may range from mild hearing loss to severe deafness. Signs which suggest that a child may have a hearing impairment and should be referred to an audiologist are:

- Appearing not to respond to sounds.
- Needing to have instructions repeated many times.
- Not talking, speaking indistinctly, or speaking exceptionally loudly or softly.
- Unusually active, running around touching things.
- Unduly sensitive to visual clues such as movement, particularly facial movements. (Lerner, 1981)

The social and emotional maturity of hearing-impaired children varies as much as that of hearing children. If there have been low expectations in the family

Hearing-impaired children are sensitive to visual clues.

for behaving appropriately, children may exhibit an extreme amount of egocentrism. They may even appear not to notice other children in their way and may often relate more closely to adults than to their peers for a much longer time than is the case with other children. On the other hand, they may be delightfully caring as was Lisa, a four-year-old with a profound hearing loss. Lisa's greatest joy was watching her friends "win" when playing lotto.

Retardation in language development is directly related to hearing loss. Even here, however, there is not a consistent correlation between the severity of loss and the amount of language (Lerner, 1981). David's hearing loss was moderate, but it was not detected until age three. He lived with a series of foster parents, did not wear a hearing aid, and had little prior therapy. His vocabulary at age four was limited to three or four words, and he had limited understanding of concepts. Donna, on the other hand, had been profoundly deaf since birth but had received intensive therapy. Also, she had parents who were able emotionally and intellectually to work consistently and continuously to nurture language. Donna spoke in understandable phrases, watched others' talk very closely, and had good receptive language.

Hearing-impaired children, with or without prior therapy, tend to be even more concrete than other young children. They relate much more easily to events occurring here and now than to those of yesterday or tomorrow, and they have less difficulty with objects they can manipulate than with ideas.

Specific suggestions for working with the hearing-impaired child include the following:

1. Be sure the child can see the speaker's face easily.
2. Speak clearly in well-modulated tones, using short concise phrasing and inflection.
3. Position child to make maximal use of the hearing that she or he has. For example, when there is more hearing in one ear, place the child so that the better ear may be used to best advantage.
4. Remember that listening is hard work and that therefore the child's attention span may be shorter.
5. Speak more, not less, to the hearing impaired. Encourage the child to use expressive language by your active listening. (Safford, 1978)

### Visual Impairment

Children may suffer a wide range of visual impairment. For those whose vision can be corrected by glasses, behaviors may include squinting, bringing objects—particularly books—very close to their eyes, rubbing their eyes, or having difficulty judging distance (Lerner 1981). Once the vision is corrected, their behavior tends to differ little from those with no impairment.

Even for those whose impairment is such that they are termed legally blind, there is a range in the ability to see. Some may see shadow forms, colors, light, or even large pictures. If they see light, they may become so fascinated by it that their play is inappropriate. Closely watching the type of activity a child engages in while using such light-catching materials as crystal climbers will indicate whether these materials should be alternated with other materials frequently.

Some blind children may have developed mannerisms such as hand movements, rocking, and noises which may serve as self-stimulation or be a reaction to frustration (Safford, 1978). Rubbing their eyes is also typical of some and may stimulate their vision in some way. Others will have fewer facial expressions since they have been unable to observe others express their feelings in this fashion (Safford, 1978). Lack of facial expression should not be construed to mean that these children lack feelings; teachers and caregivers must be alert to vocal and postural clues and respond with touch and voice.

While sighted children can imitate others through watching, visually handicapped children need direct adult help. A child may hold the head down or walk on tiptoe or with short shuffling steps. For such a child, many experiences in moving about *without* physical help and *with* verbal guidance are needed. Verbal guidance using correct meaningful words will help develop long-range goals of independence. For instance, taking a walk around an area where there are a variety of levels and surfaces can be a challenge for both teacher and visually handicapped child. Specific clues such as "There are two steps up to the block area just in front of you" or "the blocks are on the shelves you can feel with your right hand" are more helpful than "Watch out for the steps!" or "The blocks are over there."

## Developmental Delay

Children in this group have been referred to as mentally retarded. However, since in some cases the apparent retardation may be the result of an impoverished early environment or a lack of experience due to a severe illness or other physical impairment, and not the result of a genetic anomaly, *developmentally delayed* is a preferred term. Even with a genetic cause for the developmental delay, it has been found that early discovery and treatment can greatly benefit such children (Heber, 1974).

There are tremendous differences in abilities, personality, and social skills among developmentally delayed children (Safford, 1978). As a group, their development in all areas will probably be at least a year behind that expected for their chronological age. A four-year-old Down's syndrome child will look awkward, walking with a wide-spread gait, for example. Fine coordination will develop more slowly, so that the child may need physical help in order to pour from a small pitcher at juice time. Self-help skills such as dressing, toileting, and using a tissue will be less well-developed than those of peers. Vocabulary will be smaller, sentences shorter, and understanding limited (Lerner, 1981). The teacher may quickly discover that a developmentally delayed child will try to avoid certain tasks or activities which the child may be capable of doing. It is necessary

Direct positive assistance will be required by developmentally delayed children.

to balance realistic expectations with an understanding of the child's limitations. As much as possible, expectations for behavior similar to that of other children should be the goal.

Many preschools require that children be completely toilet trained before admission. For most developmentally delayed children, this skill is not complete until much later and sometimes not until they are three or four years old. The benefit of a preprimary experience to a developmentally delayed child may well outweigh the inconvenience to the staff when this restriction is eliminated.

When independent behavior is expected, as in free choice of activities, two extremes of behavior may be seen. Some developmentally delayed children will be unable to choose an activity by themselves and will need direct adult help in order to become involved and to move on to a new activity. Others will become very excited by the large amount and variety of stimuli presented and flit from one activity to another without using any material constructively. Direct, positive assistance will be required for several months. Keeping a log of those activites the child enjoys will remind the teacher that a developmentally delayed child needs a variety of activities from which to learn. In one daycare center, a Down's syndrome child enjoyed playing the piano in the large-muscle room. It was difficult to get her to use other materials until one of the teachers began allowing use of the piano as a reward when the child completed some other activity. Behavior modification techniques are sometimes essential to get the child to move forward in learning (Safford, 1978).

A four-year-old developmentally delayed child may react to groups much like a $2\frac{1}{2}$-year-old.

Large groups of more than four or five children may be intolerable for a developmentally delayed child; teachers should anticipate that a four-year-old developmentally delayed child will react to a structured group situation much like a two-and-a-half-year-old. If expectations are too high, a power struggle may begin and what was intended as a pleasurable activity can become a torment for all. Flexibility and balance are extremely important.

## Speech Impairment

Teachers may be the first to recognize a communication problem. Because parents are accustomed to and understand the sounds and gestures a child uses, they may not see a communication problem (deVilliers 1980). Conversely, through inadequate knowledge of the range of normal speech and communication development, parents may be unduly concerned over some apparent defect in a child's speech.

Guidelines to determine whether or not a child needs referral to a specialist for diagnosis and help include the following:

- Is the child's speech noticeably deviant from what is typical of children of the same age, particularly of the same mental age?
- Is the child's speech unintelligible, that is, is communication difficult?
- Is the voice noticeably different, for example, louder, softer, nasal?
- Does the speech rhythm lack fluency to the extent that it causes the child distress? (Weiss & Liliwhite, 1976)

Speech development charts, which may be found in sources such as Weiss and Liliwhite (1976), will help in determining how much of a lag there is in a child's speech. Most children between the age of three and five hesitate, repeat, and revise as they talk; such stuttering is no cause for alarm unless accompanied by grimaces and other signs of discomfort. However, if inappropriate efforts to correct stuttering at this age are made, it may exacerbate and prolong the problem. Maintaining a nonstressful environment; listening to what the child has to say in a patient, interested manner; providing a calm, well-articulated language model; and refraining from interrupting the child or supplying words will do much to help a young child overcome a tendency to stutter (Weiss & Liliwhite, 1976).

For a child whose speech is impaired, the speech therapist and the teacher working together will reinforce the child's learning. Making it a point to engage the child in conversation daily is possibly the most important single step a teacher can take. Children who have had the interested attention of adults in conversation have been seen to develop speech more rapidly than those who do not (deVilliers & deVilliers, 1979). Specific suggestions for helping children develop language competence include:

1. Attend to *what* the child is saying rather than *how* it is said. (The *how* will come later and usually as a result of a favorable language environment.)
2. Comment on what the child has achieved: "How did you know this puzzle piece fits here?"
3. Ask questions as you share pictures.
4. Encourage spontaneous speech.
5. Avoid "yes" and "no" questions. Language is encouraged when you use "what," "when," "where," and "how," questions. ("What did you do at the park?" rather than "Did you go to the park?")
6. Describe what you are doing and what the child is doing.
7. Give the child time to think of an answer; encourage other children to give time also. Be aware of nonverbal signs of impatience.
8. Restate a child's comments rather than correcting them. (Child: "I *goed* to the park." Teacher: "What did you do when you *went* to the park?")
9. Use visual clues and props such as pictures or a wonder box. (Peaches, 1978)

### Physical Impairment

There are many different kinds of physical impairment in addition to vision and hearing impairments. Safford (1978) lists seven specific types: cerebral palsy, convulsive disorders (epilepsy), spina bifida, congenital or surgical amputation (missing limbs), osteogenesis imperfecta (brittle bone disease), arthrogryposis (stiffness of joints), and temporary (or correctible) orthopedic disabilities such as clubfoot. Birth defects such as club feet or malformed or nonexistent hands and impairments due to accidents generally are not accompanied by mental deficiencies unless there has been brain damage. If the parental attitude has been to help the child become as independent as possible, such children may fit into the classroom as easily as the child in the opening illustration.

However, when the physical impairment is related to brain injury as in cerebral palsy, children may be multihandicapped, that is, there is more than one problem that may interfere with their learning in school (Hare and Hare, 1977). Due to the lag in motor development and because a good deal of time and energy is needed to care for the child, the parents of such a child may have found it impossible to talk and play with the child as much as they might have with a nonhandicapped baby. Such a child may have visual and language impairments so severe as to prevent enrollment in a regular school or preschool class.

There is one characteristic multihandicapped children may have which will determine whether or not they may be successfully placed in a regular classroom. A child with a warm and engaging personality will make friends with other children and become an asset to the program despite severe handicaps. Mary, a child with limited hearing and vision in addition to the need to wear leg braces, would laugh infectiously and clap her hands when the teacher put on a musical activity record. She was determined to participate and loved to "spin like a top." Mary was able to participate in a morning preschool program with the assistance of a special education student. During the afternoon, she attended a specialized program for deaf-blind children—a full, intensive day for a four-year-old!

Teachers dealing with severely physically handicapped children will need support and assistance from both professionals and aides. A child on crutches and/or with leg braces will need extra time and space to move from one activity to another. A child who has little control over the back muscles may need to be tied securely to a chair for circle time. A child who cannot move about alone may need to be placed on a pillow on the floor near materials such as blocks and moved from time to time. Yet, when a teacher is willing to take on such a responsiblity, a very rewarding experience may result.

### Behavioral and Emotional Problems

Typically, psychotic children, that is, children who have been diagnosed by a psychiatrist or psychologist as having some form of mental illness such as autism, will not be enrolled in a regular class. Occasionally, however, a child in a group exhibits aggressive or withdrawn behavior that is beyond the normal range. While the aggressive child usually *gets* the most attention, it may be the withdrawn child who *needs* the most attention. If a child does not participate readily in activities, quiet loving encouragement may be all that is needed. However, if the child seems unresponsive and also has unusual mannerisms such as rocking back and forth or shaking the hands, the child should be referred to a psychologist.

Most teachers have had experience with children who are termed "hyperactive." Uncontrolled excessive movement is the principal characteristic of hyperactivity (Hare and Hare 1977). Whether, in fact, hyperactivity has its roots in a neurological anomaly, in diet, or is learned behavior is a matter of much controversy. For the teacher, the most productive consideration is the role of learning. Hare and Hare (1977) suggest that hyperactive children have not learned to control their own movement and may be described as impulsive, distractable, or inattentive. Such children may avoid participation for fear of failure. They may talk well but not listen to directions completely. When seeking help for such children from a professional—special educator or psychologist—it is wise to ask the professional to observe the children in the classroom, for their behavior may be quite different in the one-to-one clinic situation.

Aggressiveness may or may not be part of the behavior pattern of a hyperactive child. By aggressiveness we are referring to all the undesirable acts one occasionally sees in any child, such as knocking over another's block structure, painting on another's picture, or grabbing toys without asking. Such behavior does not necessarily indicate emotional disturbance. Instead, it may be caused by emotional problems, lack of knowledge of appropriate social behavior, or reinforcement by important adults in the child's life (Katz, 1972). Each cause suggests a different method of effective treatment. If the child is undergoing an emotional crisis, opportunity to express feelings in constructive ways, for example, with a doll house or sand play, may be needed. Modeling appropriate behavior as well as verbal instruction may be all that is needed by the child inexperienced in working in groups. For the child whose only means of getting adult attention has been misbehavior, a consistent program of attention for positive behavior may be the answer.

Suggestions for helping children with emotional problems include:

1. Establish a relationship of trust with the child.
2. Make extra effort to commend appropriate behavior of both the child and classmates.
3. Provide verbal notice a few minutes prior to the end of an activity as well as giving final notice.
4. Pair the child having a problem with a good model in two-children activities.
5. Provide a consistent reaction to inappropriate behavior which is nonreinforcing to the child (ignoring, removal, or loss of privilege). When possible, intervene before behavior has happened; if impossible, respond immediately following the behavior. This will determine the direction and strength of that behavior when it next occurs.
6. Maintain good communication with the parents as to any special effort you are making with a particular behavior in order to encourage consistent follow-up in the home. (Peaches, 1978)

## APPROACHES TO TEACHING CHILDREN WITH SPECIAL NEEDS

When teaching handicapped children together with nonhandicapped children, it is important to remember that there are more similarities than differences between them. If the teacher shows acceptance of each child, acceptance by the other children will usually follow. Napier, Kappen, and Tuttle (1974) stated: "All children can learn from their relationships with those who are handicapped. It is the able teacher who makes the presence of a blind child an advantage rather than a disadvantage as he works with his students throughout the year." Of course, this applies to *all* handicapping conditions.

Teachers should tell blind children which colors they are using.

A blind child uses the fingers of one hand to locate the paint can.

The recommendations that follow suggest ways in which children may be helped to become more accepting of each other as well as adaptations and activities which are appropriate to teaching children with specific disabilities.

EXPLAIN, ANSWER QUESTIONS, AND DEMONSTRATE REASONS FOR A HANDICAPPED CHILD'S BEHAVIOR. The teacher's role is crucial in this area. Anticipating some initial reactions from the class can help bring about a smooth adjustment. Children will have many different reactions to a handicapped child depending upon the amount of understanding and experience they possess. In one program in which a blind child was enrolled late in the school year, there were several responses from the children:

- The children tended not to talk directly to Todd. Because he did not see them and initiate conversation, they watched but did not interact.
- They were surprised that Todd's eyes were not covered. "Why can't Todd see if he's not wearing a mask?" asked a child giving a natural reaction directly related to a personal experience.
- They exhibited curiosity and shock that Todd still had some behaviors they knew were "naughty." For instance, they wondered why Todd continued to throw blocks across the room. It was as difficult to help the children understand that not being able to see the results of our actions makes it particularly hard to learn some things as it was to help Todd learn that although blocks may make a nice loud sound as they hit the floor, they were for building only!
- They showed a genuine interest in some of the different ways Todd did familiar things. For instance, in order to pour his own juice, Todd needed to put the index finger of his helping hand inside his glass to feel the level of the juice while he poured with his dominant hand.

Explanations of Todd's behavior were given quite naturally in answer to the children's questions. Sometimes, explanations of why a handicapped child cannot participate in some well-liked activity are needed. For example, the children wanted Karen, a child with a severe hearing loss, to use the earphones in the language center. It was necessary to explain that using the earphones on top of hearing aids would be loud and painful. Discussing common experiences of hurtful loud sounds helped the children to understand this point.

Sometimes, nonhandicapped children may be uncertain about or afraid of standing up for their rights with a handicapped child. To avoid accentuating a difference and reinforcing inappropriate behavior, children need to be helped to verbalize their feelings to an aggressive handicapped child. A teacher can say, "You need to tell Kenny that he can't grab the truck you were holding. He can't hear your words, but you can look right at him and tell him." Reminding the child to tell Kenny that he can have a turn when he's finished is important for developing the social skills of both children.

Demonstrating that a handicapped child has a special skill helps nonhandicapped children to appreciate the child and builds the handicapped child's self-esteem. In one preschool, the children sat on some steps at the bottom of a stairway to their class prior to the beginning of school. As they sat there, Lisa, a blind four-year-old, sat on a step, fingered the shoes of a playmate, and identified the person. At other times, she felt other parts of friends' clothing, such as belts, and told the group who it was. This intrigued the other children; they knew Lisa had developed a special skill.

Sometimes, the reason for a special adaptation may need to be given. At circle time, while saving a nearby chair for Todd, the blind child, the teacher said, "It's easier to find the chair next to me because it's closest to Todd's cubby."

Answering the questions asked by the other children about behaviors of handicapped children may provide important feedback for the handicapped child. When a child asked, "Why does Todd keep his head down?" the teacher answered, "Todd's eyes don't help him find the large blocks like yours do, so he doesn't need to look up like you do. I like it when he looks up, though, because I like to see his face."

All children need equal acceptance. A teacher will need to give sympathy when a classmate continues to bother or annoy as well as to direct the offending child to appropriate behavior. A teacher might say, "I know how upsetting it is when Rachel keeps knocking your building down. She really has a hard time remembering and we need to be patient and keep telling her. I'm here to help you both."

Throughout the day, there will be many situations which present opportunities for the teacher to model acceptance of all children, handicapped and nonhandicapped, by explaining why certain actions are taken, demonstrating appropriate verbal and nonverbal responses, and answering questions as simply and honestly as they are asked.

ENRICH THE CURRICULUM FOR THE WHOLE GROUP BY MEETING NEEDS OF HANDICAPPED CHILDREN. The presence of a handicapped child may provide the teacher with an incentive to be creative in conducting special activities. The following music experiences are examples of ways in which meeting the needs of a hearing-impaired child enriches the program for all children.

- Remove the front of the piano so that the children can see the action.
- Have children touch the sounding board of a piano when it is played.
- Have children observe vibrations of other instruments, for example, sand or seeds on a drum.
- Give visual cues for the beginning and end of music.
- Use standard signs for high and low.
- Share words of songs being learned with parents. (PEACHES, 1978)

ENCOURAGE CHILDREN TO TRY NEW EXPERIENCES. Often, a child with a handicap lacks a skill because of lack of experience, not because of inability to accomplish a specific task. For instance, a blind child may have an aversion to fingerpaint because the child has never encountered it before. Linda Croft, a blind adult recalling her experiences as a child says: "In kindergarten—it was a 'normal' one for sighted children—I was given no special treatment but encouraged to do everything just like the others. How do you play in a puppet theatre when you can't see the puppets? 'You can do it,' said my teacher, 'Here's how' . . . and I did it and had great fun. Afraid of the hammer? 'Not if you practice a little,' said the teacher and helped me feel it and hold it correctly. The day I brought home the two boards I had nailed together all by myself was a red letter day" (Croft, 1979).

GIVE REAL EXPERIENCES WITH REAL THINGS. Whenever possible, the real experience should precede any activities on a more abstract level. Field trips, cooking, water play, blocks, woodworking, and dramatic play are just a few real experiences. For Todd, the blind child mentioned earlier, walks on the trail in back of the school provided much more learning than a field trip to the zoo. At the zoo, there were sounds, smells, much walking, and many descriptions of the animals. But how can a blind child learn about the shape, girth, height, and movement of an elephant?

Think, then, about the increased understanding of outside space Todd learned on his walks with his class. The teacher made this a valuable experience by describing what was happening while walking beside or slightly in front of Todd. When he gets older, his sighted guide will walk a half-step in front of his arm, bent ready for a grip if needed; this method, therefore, has long-range applications. The teacher made comments such as, "After you take three or four more steps, the ground will get bumpy. Can you tell the ground is bumpy now? Now we're going to walk over a little bridge, right in the middle. It's made of wood and we sound like the Three Billy Goats Gruff. Now get ready to go downhill. Bend your knees to make it easier. It's slippery, isn't it? You're doing a good job. Now we're at the bottom; reach out and feel the tree with your right hand." Todd was encouraged to put his arms around the tree, to feel the bark, to find the roots, and to walk around the tree. This is the kind of hands-on approach that is needed. Consider how confusing and inappropriate it would be to give Todd a toy replica of a tree and hope that it would teach him the properties of a tree.

Whenever possible, present real objects first, then models, then pictures. Learning the difference between real apples, wax or plastic apples, and pictures of apples is important. Even nonhandicapped children may have problems with some materials. For example, children who were raised in the sunny South had learned about snow in their school readers but were surprised to find that it was cold and wet when they encountered the real thing.

STRUCTURE THE ENVIRONMENT TO MEET SPECIAL NEEDS. Being willing to alter a task somewhat so that the handicapped child can perform successfully is essential. For example:

- A sufficiently protruding coat hook at an appropriate level (perhaps wheelchair level) allows even a severely physically handicapped youngster to hang up his or her own coat.

Physically handicapped children may need special equipment and help.

- Providing a blind child with the same chair in the same location at snack time will provide a sense of security and help to orient the child to the classroom.
- At snacks and/or meals, it is wise to seat some handicapped children next to the teacher. Accidents can more easily be averted and physical guidance is more readily available. Sometimes, a developmentally delayed child needs to be reminded to keep hands away from other children's food.
- For art projects, the physically impaired will be helped by taping paper to the surface to avoid slipping. For a cutting project, a clothespin may help the child to hold the paper while cutting with the other hand.
- When trays or boxes are used for sorting the many small pieces of some games or sets of materials, such as puzzles, peg-boards, or tinker toys, such toys can be more easily handled by a poorly coordinated child.
- In planning field trips, decide on and practice using a common hand signal to indicate "wait" or "stop." Also, use a buddy system.
- Since story time is a visual as well as auditory activity, the blind child misses the added enjoyment which sight brings. Finding real objects that relate to the story and letting visually handicapped children handle them before hearing the story adds much to the experience.

PROVIDE ADULT AND PEER BEHAVIOR MODELS. Preschool may be the first unstructured group experience for a handicapped child. Providing only the setting may not be sufficient to elicit appropriate participation. Adults may need to take more active roles as models or interpreters for the child. When possible, try to pair a handicapped child with a good peer model, but if unsuccessful, physically guide the child to demonstrate what is expected.

- Walk the child through the action you wish to teach, directing the action both physically and verbally. For example, you might put your hand over the child's hand, leading it to pick up a small block. Then move the hand and block to the top shelf, saying, "We'll put the small blocks on the top shelf."
- Model, label, and direct the child to imitate. "I'm putting a small block on the top shelf; now you put one there."
- Verbalize the child's behavior and commend appropriate actions. "You're putting the small blocks on the top shelf. Good for you!"

PROVIDE ADULT AND PEER LANGUAGE MODELS. In an early childhood program where children have a balance of individual, small group, and total group activities and opportunities to work independently, there is rich potential for language development. The adult may need to serve as a model not only as conversations are held with each child but when guiding children's activities. Taking an active interest in children's play and describing events and materials may lead not only to increased language skill but also to sharpened observations and conceptualization for both handicapped and nonhandicapped children. For instance, when a group of children is playing with blocks, it is wise to describe or encourage the children to talk about what is being built. In this way, vocabulary may be expanded and concepts such as color, size, shape, location, and comparison may be introduced or reinforced. This much direct involvement may seem intrusive to some teachers, yet the teachers' presence may be the most important factor for the handicapped child's successful participation in play.

CHANGE THE LEVEL OF HELP GIVEN AS A CHILD LEARNS. Gauging the amount of help necessary for each child is an individual matter. The amount of help needed will usually lessen as the year progresses. For example, orientation to the room will be of prime importance for the severely visually handicapped child, but as the child becomes familiar with the surroundings, less and less direct assistance will be required. The mentally handicapped child, on the other hand, may need to be reminded many, many times throughout the year to use a tissue.

MAKE TIME AND SPACE ALLOWANCES TO MEET SPECIAL NEEDS. Helping may mean giving the child more time to accomplish the same tasks as the other children. The physically, mentally, or visually handicapped child will not be able to wash hands and prepare for snack as quickly as other children. Having the child begin a few minutes earlier for many self-help tasks will avoid the last-minute tendency to do the task yourself. It may take cerebral-palsied children five to ten minutes to hang up their coats, but this is an important task for them to do. Entrances, exits, pathways, and accessibility to materials for children on crutches or in wheelchairs will need to be examined and appropriate adjustments made.

FIND NEW WAYS TO ENABLE THE CHILD TO PARTICIPATE. When a child cannot participate in the same way as the other children, a new way should be found. Look for strengths, interests, and skills, and share observations with the other children, for example, "Toby will help you skip by playing the drum."

## WORKING WITH PARENTS

A good working relationship with parents benefits teacher, parents, and child. An important trust relationship may be established if there are get-acquainted visits prior to the beginning of school and ongoing communication prior to formal conferences. Remember that parents are an invaluable source of information about their children.

If a handicap is known prior to school enrollment, the classroom teacher will not be the first person to discuss possible problems. In all likelihood, the parents are already seeking ongoing specialized help. Teachers need to realize that parents of handicapped children go through stages of grief and need support and understanding at all stages.

Hare and Hare (1977) remind us: "Teachers cannot be expected to provide all the answers, to allay all the fears. However, they can be expected to point out the attributes of the child that make him like other children; to identify goals for the year and objectives for the present; to plan activities for the day; and to report what the child has been doing. Together the parents and teacher can determine how to manage the temper tantrums, how to encourage desired behavior, and how to respect each other's concerns and contributions."

The following suggestions for communicating with parents of handicapped children apply equally well to parents of nonhandicapped children.

1. Ongoing conversations about the child's work; keep examples for art, language, and positive social interactions in mind or on hand to share with the parents.
2. Telephone a parent to tell of an unusually positive event.
3. In conferences, listen as well as talk, seek parental advice, and, of course, exhibit the child's work.
4. Provide frequent news bulletins which discuss concepts being taught, songs and finger plays, and goals for specific parts of the program.
5. Organize social gatherings so that parents of handicapped children may become acquainted with those of nonhandicapped children and share common problems. This helps to break the feeling of isolation.
6. Start a discussion group to discuss problems common to all parents, such as behavior management, fears, nutrition, and so forth.
7. Invite all parents to actively participate in the program.

In addition to working with parents of children already identified as handicapped, a teacher may be faced with an even more difficult problem. During the year, a child may display behavior that indicates a specific disability, for example,

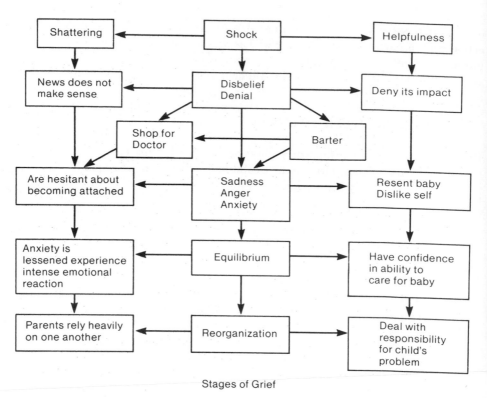

Stages of Grief

**FIGURE 4-1**   Children with special needs.

loss of hearing. Taking responsible action, the teacher recommends a conference with a pediatrician and a consequent hearing test. This may result in a diagnosis of a moderate hearing loss accompanied by the information given to the parents that their child will require specialized education and must now use a hearing aid. In addition, intensive therapy is prescribed, meaning many hours of additional time and work for the parents. If this happens, the parents will suffer tremendous shock, grief, anger, and guilt. Negative feelings may be directed toward the teacher as the bearer of bad tidings. It may not be easy for the teacher to keep a proper perspective, but it is at such a time that parents desperately need to know that there is someone who cares. Teachers can provide the sympathetic ear and the support the parents so badly need.

## SUMMARY

When teachers remember that handicapped children are more *like* nonhandicapped children than they are *different,* the idea of mainstreaming may be less frightening. Handicapped children have the same needs for affection, achievement, self-esteem, and companionship as do other children. They need rest and activity as well as a sense of self and of others; they need to have dependency needs fulfilled and to be independent; and they need to gain competence in as many areas as possible and to enjoy life. They also need to develop control over their own behavior. Yet, one must be realistic. Teaching most, if not all, handicapped children will require thought, imagination, and extra time and effort.

## BOX 4-1    SUGGESTIONS FOR WORKING WITH SPECIFIC IMPAIRMENTS

### Hearing Impairment

ARTS AND CRAFTS
1. Provide multisensory experiences.
2. Provide vocabulary appropriate to activity.
3. Avoid complex verbal directions.
4. Demonstrate, if necessary.

MUSIC AND MOVEMENT
1. Have other children demonstrate movement or action.
2. Use items and individual flannel boards to illustrate songs. As children sing, have them hold up appropriate items or flannel cut-outs.

GROUPS OR CIRCLE TIME
1. Translate to group what child says, when possible.
2. Seat for best vision of teacher and other children.
3. Talk in natural tone of voice; avoid exaggerated or loud voice.

GENERAL SUGGESTIONS
1. Provide names of objects with which child is working.
2. Draw picture of fire drill and children in line; practice drill.
3. Practice use of commonly understood sign for "wait" and "stop" before field trips.
4. Pair child with a hearing child for field trips.

DO
1. Let child choose another activity when telling a story with no visual interest.
2. Encourage total communication; that is lip-reading, signing, and pantomime.

AVOID
1. Playback equipment which requires removal of hearing aids.
2. Films with long dialogue not closely related to action.

## Visual Impairment

### ARTS AND CRAFTS

1. Mark paint cans and brushes with some tactile code, for example, circle = red, triangle = yellow, and so on.
2. Use variety of textures in paint; for example, Rice Krispies.
3. Praise efforts of child to overcome distaste for touching wet or sticky substances.
4. Have child help make play dough from dry ingredients. It will help child accept the final product.

### MUSIC AND MOVEMENT

1. Let child explore each instrument.
2. Use one-handed instruments first (maracas, clappers, bells, tambourine).
3. Use two-handed instruments later (sand blocks, sticks, drums, triangle).
4. Physically guide child in handling instruments.
5. Use peer as partner by having blind child place hand on partner's upper arm or shoulder.

### GROUP OR CIRCLE TIME

1. Have assigned places to help child learn classmates' voices and names.
2. At beginning of year, ask other children to identify themselves before speaking.

### GENERAL SUGGESTIONS

1. Keep furniture stationary until child is familiar with room.
2. Warn child when changes are made.
3. When child loses toy, allow child time to retrieve; assist with verbal guidance.
4. Identify coat hook with some other object, for example, "next to the door."
5. Water play is usually a favorite; provide it often.
6. Cut out tactile shapes and attach to shelves for block storage.

### DO

1. Provide many activities which use senses other than hearing.
2. Use short films in which story may be understood without seeing the action.

### AVOID

1. Long films.
2. Activities that are primarily visual in nature.

## Physical Impairment

### ARTS AND CRAFTS

1. Substitute large-handled brushes and large crayons or felt markers for small crayons.

2. Use training scissors if necessary.
3. Tilt surface for better visibility.
4. Outline fingerpaint paper with tape to help child with severe involuntary movements.

MUSIC AND MOVEMENT

1. Substitute "hands on knees" for walking; "hands up high" for running.
2. Stabilize instruments: tape or tie to hand or wrist or place between child's knees.
3. Substitute hand and arm circling for body turning.
4. When singing a "who's missing" song, move child instead of sending out of room.
5. Be creative! Think what you can substitute for actions a child cannot do.

GROUP OR CIRCLE TIME

1. Use "sitting box" to replace wheelchair. Cut a box to simulate a seat. Cut holes for knit ties at hip level and place a pillow between the knees.

GENERAL SUGGESTIONS

1. Use tray or shallow box to hold small objects; make back higher, front lower.
2. Use nonslip mat, for example, a towel under items to prevent slipping.
3. In listening center, pair with nonhandicapped child to turn pages of book while both use earphones.

DO

1. Put child's feet on a small stool when placing child at a table.
2. Move child to proximity of ongoing activities.
3. Place child with balancing difficulties behind others in a line.

AVOID

1. Allowing normal children to push wheelchair when in line. (Child may feel loss of control and become upset.)
2. Long periods of keeping child in same position (more than 20–30 minutes).

## Developmental Delay

ARTS AND CRAFTS

1. Use one-skill activities in the beginning.
2. Define edges of paper; use white glue or fold up edges.
3. Complete first two of a three-step activity others can do.
4. Send home written explanation of child's craft work.
5. Encourage independence; avoid doing for child.

MUSIC AND MOVEMENT

1. Use simple songs with strong rhythms.
2. Alternate quiet with active.
3. Use recordings which have a slower than normal tempo.

4. Pace speed of songs to children.
5. Provide many activities for walking, running, jumping, and so on.
6. Use wall or back of chair for support in activity.

GROUP OR CIRCLE TIME

1. Keep group small when possible.
2. Give praise for sitting and attending several times during session.
3. Make realistic expectations for attention span.
4. If sharing time is part of your program, ask parents to provide items from home (for example, kitchen utensils).

GENERAL SUGGESTIONS

1. If necessary, teach and use consistent verbal clues or signals for bathroom.
2. Have extra set of clothes available and plastic bag for soiled clothes.
3. Use velcro instead of buttons and snaps.
4. Model appropriate play.

DO

1. Pair child with a capable child who likes to help.
2. Be aware of length of time child has been present at an activity.

AVOID

1. Long films; 8–10 minutes are enough, especially at the beginning of the year.
2. Long periods of keeping the child in the same position (more than 20–30 minutes).

# REFERENCES

BOYD, R. D.   *Developmental Progress Scale.* San Bernardino, Calif: Inland Counties Regional Center, 1974.

BRAUN, S. J., and LASHER, M. G.   *Are You Ready to Mainstream?* Columbus, Ohio: Chas. E. Merrill, 1978.

CALDWELL, B.   The importance of beginning early. In J. B. Jordan, ed., *Not All Little Wagons are Red.* Arlington, Va. Council for Exceptional Children, 1972

CARTWRIGHT, C. A., and CARTWRIGHT, G. P.   *Developing Observation Skills.* New York: McGraw-Hill, 1974.

COHEN, S.   Integrating children with handicaps into early childhood education programs. *Children Today,* January/February 1975.

CROFT, L. A.   The daughter's story: Acceptance and perseverance are most important traits. *Visions Up News* 1(Spring, 1979).

DEVILLIERS, P., and DEVILLIERS, J. G.   *Early Language.* Cambridge, Mass.: Harvard University Press, 1979.

FALLEN, N. H., with McGOVERN, J. E.   *Young Children with Special Needs.* Columbus, Ohio: Chas. E. Merrill, 1978.

FRANKENBURG, W. J., and DODDS, J. B. and FANDAL, A.    *The Revised Denver Developmental Screening Test Manual.* Denver, Col: University of Colorado Press, 1970.

HARE, B. A., and HARE, J. M.    *Teaching Young Handicapped Children.* New York: Grune and Stratton, 1977.

HEBER R., et al.    *Rehabilitation of Families at Risk of Mental Retardation: A Progress Report.* Madison, Wisc: University of Wisconsin, 1974.

HETHERINGTON, E. M., COX, M., and COX, R.    Play and social interaction in the child following divorce. *Journal of Social Issues* 35 (1979): 26–49.

HOFFMAN, M. L.,    Altruistic behavior and the parent-child relationship. *Journal of Personality and Social Psychology* Vol. 31 (1975): 937–943.

LERNER, J., MARDELL-CZUNDOWSKI, C., and GOLDENBERG, D.    *Special Education for the Early Childhood Years.* Englewood Cliffs, N.J.: Prentice-Hall, 1981.

MORGAN, D., and YORK, M. E.    Mainstreaming in the preschool. *Young Children* 36 (January 1981).

MUSSEN, P., and EISENBERG-BERG, N.    *Roots of Caring, Sharing, and Helping.* San Francisco: W. H. Freeman and Company Publishers, 1977.

NAPIER, G., KAPPEN, D., TUTTLE, D. et al.,    *Handbook for Teachers of The Visually Handicapped.* American Printing House for the Blind, 1974.

PEACHES    (Pre-School Educational Adaptations for Children Who are Handicapped). Portland, Ore.: Portland State University, 1978. (A handbook designed for the use of a regular preschool teacher with handicapped children.)

PIAGET, J.    *Judgment and Reasoning in the Child.* Totowa, N.J.: Littlefield, Adams and Co., 1966.

RHEINGOLD, H. L., HAY, D. R., and WEST, M. J.    Sharing in the second year of life. *Child Development* 47 (December 1976).

ROWEN, B.    *The Children We See.* New York: Holt, Rinehart and Winston, 1972, 36–57.

SAFFORD, P. L.,    *Teaching Young Children with Special Needs.* St. Louis, Mo.: C. V. Mosby, 1978.

SOUWEINE, J., CRIMMINS, S., and MAZEL, C.    *Mainstreaming Ideas for Teaching Young Children.* Washington, D.C.: National Association for the Education of Young Children, 1981.

WEISS, C. E., and LILLIWHITE, H. S.    *Communicative Disorders.* St. Louis, Mo.: C. V. Mosby, 1976.

# 5
# VISUAL
# ARTS

Recently, the overriding concern that children learn the basic skills has caused many to relegate the arts to the category of an enjoyable pastime and not see the importance of the arts to the developing child. Yet, there is evidence to suggest that a program rich in the arts is one in which children will more readily learn the basic skills (Brittain, 1979; Williams, 1977) and benefit in many other ways as well.

In this chapter, we will consider the visual arts. The chapter is designed to help teachers understand (1) the values of experiences with visual arts, (2) the levels of development in using and expressing oneself in art media, (3) goals appropriate for young children, and (4) methods and activities which can be used to help children develop competency in and appreciation of the visual arts.

## VALUES OF VISUAL ARTS

### Enjoyment of Art Activity
### for Its Own Sake

As a teacher encourages young children's self-expression in art forms, the children develop confidence in their own ability, which may result in the enjoyment of art for its own sake. The long-term benefit of teaching art at an early age may be to provide a worthwhile, lifelong, leisure-time activity.

### An Acceptable Way to Reduce Tension

Children are often under far more pressure than we realize. The demands of the family, the strangeness and confusion of a new situation, and the imposed need to learn to control emotions all tend to make children tense. Painting, working with clay, or working with other media are potent means of expressing hurt and anger or other emotions in acceptable ways.

### Means of Self-Expression
### and Communication

Pictorial representations are the first means of putting thoughts into graphic symbols. Often, children have difficulty putting their thoughts and feelings into words but can express them in art forms. Happiness, joy, sadness, and hurt can be expressed in this way. Enjoyable or troubling and puzzling experiences may be recreated, prolonging the enjoyment or making the experience more understandable through working with paints, clay, sand, or blocks (Erickson, 1950; Brittain, 1979). While such self-expression may satisfy children's own needs without the conscious intent to communicate thoughts and feelings to others, the children's actions do in fact communicate these to the sensitive teacher. At other times, children may use art media purposefully to tell a story or communicate impressions of an experience to others.

### Increased Perception
### and Concept Development

In order to express a sight, sound, or complete experience in an art form, observations must be sharpened and reconstructed in the mind. While initial perceptions are formed through the avenue of the senses, it is accompanying mental activity often coupled with physical action that leads to conceptualization or better understanding. Such understanding is reflected in more accurate art forms.

### Eye-Hand Coordination

Coordination between the eyes and the hand and developing fine motor control have long been considered essential to effective learning and living. Working with implements such as brushes, scissors, crayons, and pencils provides the practice necessary to develop control. For example, before a child can write, he or she must be able to make a pencil or pen do what is desired.

### Aesthetic Appreciation

The foundation for appreciation of beauty may be laid when the child is young. The teacher who brings order and beauty into the classroom through the arrangement of furnishings or the addition of a bouquet of flowers or an art object expresses an appreciation for aesthetic values which may well be imitated and long remembered by children. Such a teacher's comments about children's work may also help in the development of aesthetic appreciation.

### Appreciation of Cultural Heritage

The values, lifestyles, and flavor of a people are reflected in their art. The immortality of countries and communities resides in their art. This art becomes the cultural heritage of the descendants of those people. Through knowledge and appreciation of their own cultural heritage, children develop a sense of pride as a representative of that culture.

## CHILDREN AND
## THE VISUAL ARTS

The competencies children are able to develop in the visual arts are influenced by their level of development. Skill in painting, drawing, or sculpting is related to the child's psychomotor and cognitive development.

As children are introduced to new experiences in any area of the fine arts, a period of *exploration* followed by a period of *integration* and then of *creation* will enable them to proceed at their own pace. In other words, if children are not asked immediately to make something in a specific way, they may make their own discoveries and conceptualizations. Actually, the cycles of exploring, integrating, and creating continue as long as people continue to study an area of the fine arts. However, each cycle occurs at a more complex level. Problems encountered while making something often lead to further exploration to learn more about what the medium can offer.

The stages discussed above are helpful as general guides for ways to approach fine arts with children. However, specific information is also available which has implications for judging what kinds of experiences will be most successful with children at a particular developmental stage. Information on the developmental stages in relation to the visual arts is given below.

## Stages of Development in the Visual Arts

In the visual arts, materials are used to make representations of objects, feelings, or experiences. In order to make a representation of something, or to appreciate a representation made by someone else, a clear concept of that which is represented is needed. Children develop such concepts and the skill to make representations of them very gradually. In using art media, children show a progression from purely sensory enjoyment to making recognizable representations. This progression is marked by stages which have been described by Lansing (1971), Brittain (1979), and others. The first three stages are often referred to as "scribbling."

STAGE 1: MANIPULATIVE. Young children's first involvement with visual arts materials is not for the purpose of making representations of anything at all; they become completely caught up with manipulating the materials. They make random scribbles with crayons or pencils. They may paint with tempera over an entire piece of paper until it is so thickly coated it will crack when dry. They pound, squeeze, or tear off small bits of clay. However, they make "nothing." This does not mean that what they have created is not highly valued by them, for it is. But if you were to ask what the child had made, you would receive a blank stare. Such a question is inappropriate to ask children at this level, for they are not making a representation of anything. It is what it is; nothing more, nothing less. This stage is appropriately called the *manipulative* stage.

STAGE 2: DESIGN OR PATTERNING. Somewhat later, usually by the age of four, children begin to organize their visual art creations. They may make lines, dots, or large separated areas of color with tempera paint. Collages may show areas where similar materials have been placed in close proximity on the paper. Even yet, however, the child is not using media to make representations of something. Children at this stage are still experimenting. But they are learning to control and organize their work and are gaining mastery over the implements they use. They are also discovering various kinds of lines—straight, curved, open, closed, vertical, horizontal—and spacing on the page. This stage is sometimes called the *design* or *patterning* stage.

STAGE 3: NAMING OR SYMBOLIC.    There comes a time, often during the fourth year, when children do begin to make a picture or model of something. At first, the representation does not resemble the thing represented well enough for another person to determine what it is. Children will voluntarily tell what it is, however, and often this telling will take the form of a story with the child pointing to each squiggle, dot, or line and naming it. This naming behavior is the first indication that children are truly using the medium for representation.

Many children in this stage do not seem to have a clear and sustained objective in mind as they *start* to work. Often, they will announce that they are going to draw one thing and when they are finished will say that it is something quite different. It may be that children are reminded of something by the form that appears in the still imperfectly controlled media, or an overheard comment or new thought may cause them to change direction. At any rate, names are given to their completed work causing this to be termed the *naming* or *symbolic* stage.

STAGE 4: REPRESENTATION.    During the fifth or sixth year, and very often somewhat earlier, children's art work begins to resemble the objects represented. Because children's mental representations of things are often incomplete, however, their graphic representations lack detail and often do not match many aspects of reality. For example, a picture of a cat may contain only a circle for a head, a line for the body, and two lines for legs. In addition, the drawing may have been made with red or blue crayons rather than black or brown despite the availability of both. As children's mental representations become more accurate and complete, their pictures become more accurate and complex.

In addition to making progress in terms of including details of objects represented, children make progress in their ability to plan and coordinate the parts of individual objects. For example, in early pictures a cat's legs may be drawn as if they extended from the cat's head rather than from the body, just as a child's picture of a person will often show appendages attached to the head. In addition, parts may be jumbled. For example, eyes, ears, nose, and mouth may all be drawn on a head, but not arranged accurately. It is as if the child thinks of one item at a time, draws it, and then goes on to another part. Perhaps because the child does not plan the whole before starting, he or she often does not leave room in the appropriate places and therefore just draws features where there is space.

Not only must children learn to coordinate parts within an object, but they must relate all objects within a picture as well. Mastery of spatial relationships comes gradually (Piaget, 1967). In addition to relating the objects to the space as a whole, the children must learn relationships between objects, such as *beside, inside of, outside of, above, below,* and, of course, relative sizes. A picture drawn by a young child may contain a flower, a house, and a child. In the picture, the child or flower may be bigger than the house. Gradually, the actual relationships are represented more accurately, but it will be a very long time before the relationships will be to scale or the relative positions of the objects consistent with reality.

The apparent lack of conventional inhibitions in the artwork of young children gives their work a special charm often admired by adult artists. The drawing of a house by a young child may show you the inside and the outside at the same time. A child's expectant mother may be portrayed with the baby drawn in the appropriate position. That you cannot see the interior of a house when looking at the outside or that an unborn baby is not visible seems not to concern the young child. Picasso's portrayal of a lady showing the full face and profile at the same time has the same quality. For Picasso, the effect was intentional; for the young child, it reflects both vivid imagination and lack of understanding.

Piaget's mountain experiment (Piaget, 1969) shows us that children do not understand that what can be seen at any one time depends on the view from which one is looking. At first, children include all views they may be familiar with in the same picture—the inside and the outside, the front and the back, or the top view and the side view. Later, as their understanding of space is developed, they will select one point of view and stick to it.

Children's art work is also influenced by their ability to distinguish between the coordinates within objects and coordinates in external space. Coordinates refer to horizontal and vertical axes. Young children have no appreciation for coordinates in space external to objects. For example, in Piaget's tilted bottle experiment (Hunt, 1961), young children drew water lines in drawings of bottles in terms of the coordinates of the bottles themselves, not of external space.

These miscalculations are revealed in young children's pictures. Chimneys on houses jut out peculiarly because children orient them to the roof line they have drawn rather than to the space around the house. Trees on mountain sides are given the same type of orientation. Only after children gain an appreciation for space as a total system and realize that objects are themselves in a coordinated space do these features disappear from their drawings.

Perhaps the most difficult understanding required for work in the visual arts is that involving the relationships of objects on a plane from foreground to background. The first pictures drawn by young children contain no technique for organizing objects on a plane. Objects simply float in space. Later, around age six, a baseline usually appears. Sometimes this is simply the base of the paper, or it may be grass or water on which other objects rest. Still later, children will use multiple baselines in order to indicate that all objects are not at the same point on the plane. Not until the age of eleven or twelve have most children gained the sophistication required to understand perspective, although occasionally a younger child may draw objects in the distance smaller than those in the foreground or show some other idea of perspective.

Teachers should keep this developmental information in mind when they teach visual arts. The making of representations is a highly cognitive activity, and what children are able to create will depend in large part on their knowledge about things and their ability to plan, organize, and create. In other words, the ability to make graphic representations depends on the ability to think. In turn, art experiences provide opportunities for planning, organizing, and creating. Contrary to what is often assumed, art experiences probably make a substantial contribution to cognitive development. It is this aspect that is slighted when children are given outline pictures to fill in or are given specific directions to follow. When the latter methods are used, the thinking has already been done by someone else.

## GOALS AND SKILLS
## FOR INSTRUCTION
## IN THE VISUAL ARTS

There are two major goals for teaching visual arts: (1) the development of skills for self-expression and creativity in art forms and (2) the development of aesthetic appreciation. To attain these general goals, the teacher needs to identify specific objectives or competencies which young children may be expected to gain.

For young children at any level of development, using art media with ease and enjoyment and producing work that is personally satisfying are appropriate objectives. Such objectives are gained through experiences and guidance, both of which are discussed later. The production of work which communicates thoughts and feelings to others is a competence which may begin to appear around the age of four or five, and the work can be expected to become increasingly more complex, recognizable, and reflective of the child's world.

Finally, in the production of art work, children will need to learn the technical aspects of working with various kinds of materials and tools. In addition, they must learn how to care for them properly. Even the youngest children can begin to understand how to control and care for materials and tools. For example, the teacher might make suggestions for preventing drips in a painting and for washing the paint out of a brush and storing it so as not to damage the bristles.

In developing children's aesthetic appreciation, the teacher should encourage responsiveness to what the child sees in the environment. The teaching aim is to help the child become sensitive and enjoy both natural and manmade beauty. Basic to such enjoyment is the ability to identify distinguishing features. To develop the ability to identify forms, shapes, colors, and sizes is a realistic goal for three- to five-year-olds, whereas older children may be expected to develop the ability to identify and appreciate the additional features of design and balance. Asking children to help set up an aesthetic display (see page 137) will help children attain this ability.

Children should also be helped to develop personal standards for judging the merits of their own work as well as the artistic efforts of others. This starts with simply being able to say, "I like this because_____," giving a reason in terms of specific features of the art object or of the affective response it evokes or both.

# METHODS AND ACTIVITIES
# FOR INSTRUCTION
# IN THE VISUAL ARTS

In this section, we will deal with methods and materials in general terms. This will be followed by specific activities which illustrate how the methods and materials can be used.

## Guiding Work in the Visual Arts

Teachers should have a concept of art which goes beyond craft projects or coloring outline pictures. There are many craft books to help the teacher who is looking for these kinds of ideas, and we will not deal with these here. Crafts do have a place in the classroom: They help the child develop eye-hand coordination, skill in using small muscles, and a sense of accomplishment and pride. They also provide experience in working with different kinds of materials. Only in a limited sense, however, can they be considered the expressive art which is consistent with the goals and values indicated earlier. Only insofar as children are free to use the materials given them can crafts be considered to provide opportunities for self-expression.

VISUAL ARTS CENTERS.    Well-planned and stocked art centers lead to self-reliant and responsible use of art materials. Portions of the room should be selected where children may work undisturbed by others and without interfering with the work of others. Often, there are two or more separate art areas: one for relatively clean and quiet table work such as drawing with crayons or cutting and pasting, and one or more for messier or noisier activities such as painting, working with clay, or different kinds of construction, including carpentry. A wide variety of materials including homemade and recyclable items as well as commercial products should be available. The materials should be stored in appropriately labeled boxes. (Lists of suggested materials may be found on pages 121–25.)

It is unwise to put out a vast selection of materials at the beginning of the year. Too large a selection is bewildering. A moderate selection of commonly used materials may be put out first and other materials introduced as children are ready for them. When new materials are introduced, children should be allowed a period of exploration as we have said, but limits may need to be set. Rules such as where the materials are to be used, under what conditions they may be used, and what needs to be done before a child leaves the area may be explained to the whole class, but follow-up will be needed. For younger children, new materials are best introduced in a small group with an adult present to encourage exploration and remind children of limits.

For a rich experience in the visual arts, centers should include easels for water-mixed paints; separate flat surfaces such as tables, desks, or wide low shelves for cutting and pasting work, clay modeling, or drawing, and areas for construction work such as carpentry and the making of three-dimensional things from household recyclables.

It is particularly valuable in early childhood education to have an area in which there are shelves with construction paper, 12-by-18-inch (or smaller) newsprint, scissors, crayons, chalk, felt-tip pens, and paste neatly arranged on them and an adjacent work table. Such an area provides the materials which may be used for any part of the curriculum. When a large project such as a mural or scenery for a play is to be made, a large area of floor covered with a sheet of heavy plastic or linoleum is ideal. If there is not enough space inside the room, larger pieces may be taken into the hall or outdoors.

A carpentry area will work best if it is located in an area where the noise of hammering will not disturb others and where it is easily seen and supervised. (Suggested materials for the carpentry area may be found on page 123.) Good quality tools kept in good condition will enable children to make constructions with some degree of ease. A peg-board with outlines of tools showing where tools are to be hung helps keep the area tidy and provides children with practice in matching an object to an outline picture. A low, sturdy workbench equipped with a vise for holding pieces of wood for sawing and other work provides a good base for the work.

Two other areas common to prekindergarten and kindergarten but which provide opportunities for self-expression throughout the childhood years are block and sand areas. Both are multipurpose areas providing activities related to other areas of the curriculum such as math (see p. 291), social sciences (see p. 340), and science (see p. 246). Children often make quite elaborate representations with blocks or sand and use these areas for dramatic play as well.

The block area needs to be located out of the line of traffic so that block buildings are not accidentally knocked down. If the area is reserved solely for block play, structures may be left up for some period of time to be admired and perhaps photographed. Children may wish to dictate or print signs to be placed near their structures.

Sand may be made available outdoors or indoors or both. A shallow metal-lined box on 1½-to-two-feet legs is generally used for indoor sand play. Wet sand provides a medium that can be molded; therefore, sand is preferable to cornmeal, which is often used as a substitute to prevent damage to floor coverings.

In addition to a wide variety of shapes and sizes of blocks in the block area and to implements for scooping and molding sand in the sandbox, numerous accessories such as toy animals, people, cars, and trees allow children's play to be elaborated. It is wise to arrange such accessories in sets; for example, there might be sets for building farms, zoos, cities, or garages. The teacher may wish to make only one set available at a time to fit a theme used in class or to match the interests of the children.

In the case of unfinished projects, materials may be left out ready for work on another day. Before stopping work for the day, children need to put caps on bottles, clean brushes, and put unneeded materials away. Being able to find materials in good condition on the following day helps to continue the work. When projects are finished, all materials need to be returned to assigned storage areas so that others may find them. Also, surfaces must be cleaned to be used for another purpose.

In order for children to clean up easily by themselves, materials for such cleanup must be accessible. A nearby source of water, sponges, rags, soap, paper towels, and buckets make cleanup manageable. Although children can be expected to do their own cleanup, if cleaning is made a tedious chore it will deter children from working in the art centers. Working side by side with an adult makes cleanup a special occasion for many young children.

SENSITIVITY TO CHILDREN'S FEELINGS.    In guiding the art of young children, the teacher must develop sensitivity to their readiness to accept suggestions. One primary rule to follow is to determine how children feel about their own work. Is a child satisfied or dissatisfied? This is often tricky: The child may verbally deprecate the work, but in actuality may be saying, "I hope you like it." Sometimes, young children are unable to verbalize their own feelings adequately. Gentle, sensitive questions and comments may help to draw them out. The teacher as teacher helps children improve their work by offering suggestions. A teacher might ask why a child thought an art product was "no good" and if the child is unable to verbalize the reasons, say, "I'm sorry you don't like it. I do like it. Would you like to know why?" and go on to point to the specific aspects of the work that are liked. "What shall we do with it?" the teacher might then ask the child. In other cases, such questioning may reveal a child's readiness to use ideas for improving the work and suggestions may then be given.

HELPING THE CHILD SEE THE WORLD.    As children move into the representational level, they need help to become more aware of the color, shape, form, and other characteristics of the environment. The sky isn't always blue or all blue; clouds have many different shapes and colors. The teacher through comments to children about features of the environment helps them look selectively at different features. Eliciting comments from the children also helps the teacher to see the world through the children's eyes and to appreciate those things to which individual children respond. Because the aim is to help children focus on selected features of the environment to include in their drawings, the teacher must avoid telling the children what to draw. Children's responses to features of the environment should be elicited through questions about what they see and like.

There is also a kinesthetic form of "seeing": the feel of things which translates into drawing. "How does it feel to bend over and touch your toes?" "Is your head above or below your knees?" As children perform these actions, they become more aware of the nature of things.

HELPING CHILDREN CONTROL MATERIALS.    Only by having ample opportunities with art materials do these items come under the child's control. The teacher may make suggestions to children about how to hold their brushes loosely so that the color flows from the tip rather than scrubbing it into the paper; about how to hold the brush against the edge of the jar before transferring paint to the paper; about how to wash the brush in clean water or use separate brushes to keep colors clean. Such tips help children learn to control materials. Teachers should realize, however, that such tips may be followed more by older children than by younger ones. It is not easy to hold the brush loosely if you have little skill in using your hands. Younger children tend to grasp the brush tightly with a fist grip and make wide strokes using the muscles of the upper arm.

HELPING CHILDREN COMPLETE PROJECTS.    Often, a child starts a project, works on it awhile, and brings it to the teacher before it appears complete. For example, an incomplete human figure is drawn near the edge of the paper. Children who bring their pictures to the teacher at such a point may be acting from a variety of motives. They may be tiring of art work and want to go on to something else; they may simply want approval and attention; or they may want suggestions for adding to their picture. The teacher must draw out the motives through conversation. Questions such as "Is it winter or summer?" "How could you show it is winter (summer)?" "What is the girl wearing?" "Does she have a friend with her?" might lead the child to think of other things to add to the picture. On the other hand, the child's responses may indicate the desire to turn to something else, which is to be accepted without further comment. For nonrepresentational pictures, a question such as "What colors would look nice with what you have?" might help a child continue the art work.

CONSIDERATION IN PRESENTING MODELS.    What models should be presented to children? Should a model be used at all? This is a matter of some controversy. In some cases, the act of studying the drawings of another helps children gain a skill which is transferable to drawing pictures they decide on. Much depends on the teacher's response to the child's efforts. If some children have met with appreciation of their efforts and have thereby developed self-confidence, they may learn from looking at the work of others or watching adult artists at work. But for others, the presentation of an adult model may be devastating. In general, the use of models is inappropriate with preschool and kindergarten children.

When there are enough adults in the room to provide the necessary supervision, participating in art work oneself is a rich experience for both teacher and child. There is a comraderie as teacher and children engage in an art activity which occupies hands and eyes. Teacher participation, however, does not mean that the teacher demonstrates to children how to draw a picture or create a model of an object. Brittain (1979) found that in the presence of a teacher, children were more involved in art work for a longer time and made more comments about the work.

ENCOURAGING EFFORTS AND HELPING CHILDREN EVALUATE.    Hoping to encourage a child's artistic efforts, some teachers praise children's work indiscriminately with phrases such as "That's lovely, Leslie; my, you always do such nice work!'' Such praise is seldom helpful. Children know that not all their products are equally good.

It is dishonest to say that a child who has used many different colors of paint which have all run together to produce a muddy brown has produced a lovely picture if you do not really feel that it is. The comment ''Sidney, you used a lot of different colors today'' provides honest feedback and encouragement. When praise is given a child's work, the child will appreciate knowing why you like it. Point to something specific and comment on it in an approving way. Conversations between teacher and child which elicit the child's own judgments will help the teacher suggest directions for future work.

DISPLAYING ART PRODUCTS.    When children have put their best efforts into an art product, they deserve to have their work displayed in a worthy manner. Flatwork may or may not be mounted, but should be attractively displayed. Three-dimensional work should also be displayed attractively and not left in a jumble on a shelf. Suggestions for displaying products can be found in the illustrations in Figure 5-1.

Although there should be an opportunity for each child's work to be displayed, not every work a child does need be displayed. If space permits, a wall space may be alloted for hanging a picture of each child's choice. It is important to foster discrimination in selecting a work to be displayed. The rare work of a child who seldom uses the art center, however, should be selected no matter what the quality. The child who uses the center daily should be asked to choose the best product for display.

### Materials for the Visual Arts Center

#### BASIC MATERIALS

Crayons—both large primary size and regular
Pencils
Library paste
White glue
Scissors—include some for left hand
Powdered paint—red, blue, and yellow; and other colors later
Plasticene (sometimes called plastolene)
Felt pens
Colored construction paper
Manila or white paper—larger sizes for younger children
Newsprint—24 by 36 inches
Brushes—long handles, half-inch; and other sizes later

#### OTHER COMMERCIAL MATERIALS

Ceramic clay
Pipe cleaners

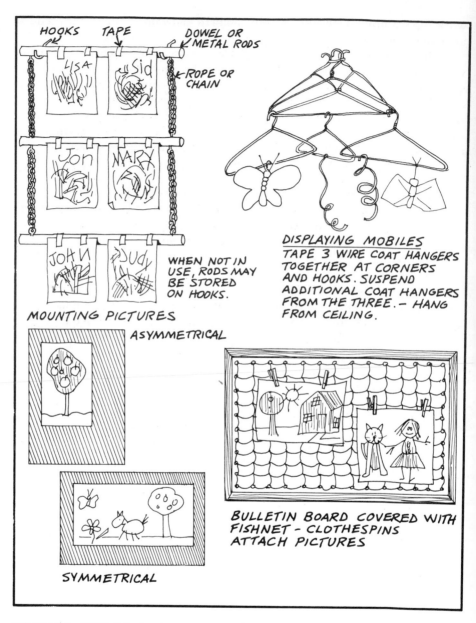

**FIGURE 5-1** Displaying artwork.

Colored tissue paper
Colored chalks or pastels
Paper plates
Balls of string

Craft materials—glitter, sequins, raffia, balsam, and so on
Wire—different thicknesses for different purposes: mobiles, papier mâché and so on
Wire snippers
Wallpaper paste
Yarn
Gummed tape—various types, sizes, colors: transparent, masking, plastic
Watercolors

## WOODWORKING MATERIALS

Carpenter bench and peg-board for tool storage
Vise or clamps
Hammer
Nails—variety of larger sizes
Saw
Screwdriver
Nails and screws
Pliers
Hand drill
Nuts and bolts
Wrench
Wood—soft wood scraps from lumber yard

## RECYCLABLES

Frozen juice cans
Coffee cans and plastic lids
Egg cartons
Styrofoam meat trays
Cottage cheese cartons
Oatmeal cartons
Scraps of contact paper
Scraps of gift-wrapping paper
Pill containers
Droppers from plant food or medicine bottles
Plastic squeeze bottles
Baby food jars
Tuna fish tins and other tins

## INGREDIENTS FOR HOMEMADE MATERIALS

Linit starch
Soap flakes
Flour
Sugar
Powdered alum
Salt—non-iodized

Food coloring
Salad oil
Cream of tartar
Oil of clove

RECIPES FOR HOMEMADE ART MATERIALS

*Finger paint base (1 gallon)*
3 cups Linit starch (dry)
Slightly more than 2 cups cold water
(Mix above together)
Add 9 cups boiling water and bring just to boiling point. Remove from heat and add 2 cups soap flakes (Ivory, Lux, or other).
Beat while hot, approximately 5 minutes.
Food coloring (1 large tablespoon per pint container) or tempera paint (dry) may be sprinkled on mixture as children use it.

*Tweedle Paste*
Stir in top of double boiler:
½ cup sifted flour
½ cup white sugar
½ tbsp. powdered alum
1½ cups cold water
Add to above stirring constantly:
1½ cups boiling water
Cook over hot water until clear. Add 15 drops of oil of cloves. Beat well. Store in wide-mouth jars with lids.
*Hints:* Powdered alum is available in the spice section of the grocery store. Oil of cloves may be purchased at a drugstore. A one-ounce bottle may cost $1.00 but will last through many batches of paste.

## PLAY DOUGH #1

½ cup salt (non-iodized)
2 cups cold water
Food coloring (optional)
Bring above ingredients to bubbling on medium heat.
Remove from heat. Add 2 tbsps. powdered alum.
Add 3 scant cups of flour slowly, stirring well.
Pour onto board and knead well. It will still be hot. If it seems sticky, add flour until desired texture is reached.
*Note:* It is best not to add the 3 cups of flour all at once. Start with about 2½ cups and add more if needed.

## PLAY DOUGH #2 (NEW TARTAR)

1 cup flour
½ cup salt
1 cup water

1 tbsp. salad oil

2 tbsp. cream of tartar

Mix above ingredients together with food coloring (optional) in a large sauce pan. Place over high heat, stirring constantly. As the mixture heats, it will thicken and form a ball leaving the sides of the pan. When this happens, remove from heat and allow to cool until it can be handled. Knead until smooth.

## CORNSTARCH CLAY

1 cup cornstarch

2 cups baking soda

1¼ cups cold water.

Mix together, cook over medium heat stirring constantly for about 4 minutes until mixture thickens to moist mashed-potato consistency. Cover with damp cloth to cool. Knead. Figures made with this clay will harden overnight.

## Activities for Instruction in the Visual Arts

## DEVELOPING SELF-EXPRESSION IN THE VISUAL ARTS

1. **Activity:**   Brush painting (PP–P)

*Materials:*   Easels, tables, or floor space; aprons, smocks, or old shirts to protect clothing; large (24-by-36-inch) sheets of newsprint, butcher paper, manila, or other paper; powdered tempera paints and water; a variety of brushes with long handles; sponges, rags, water, paper towels for cleanup.

*Procedure:*   Prepare an area near a source of water. Cover floor with oilcloth, heavy plastic, or linoleum rug. Set up easels and clip on paper (or have it nearby for children to obtain).

Mix paint in clear plastic or glass containers such as large baby-food jars. Cans may be used, but colors are not as easily seen. Choose containers which will not tip over when brushes are left in them. Paints may be set on a table next to the easels or in the trays of the easels.

For best results, place powdered paint in the containers first and add water in small amounts until desired consistency is obtained. For beginners, a brush may be placed in each color. Clean brushes may be stored in a can, brush-end up. Children can select brushes as needed. Teach children to wash out brushes between dippings and when finished painting.

When children want to paint, the teacher should print or have the children print their names in the left-hand corner of the paper. Names may be printed on the reverse side to avoid obscuring the name with paint.

When painting is finished, help the child place painting in a safe place for drying. A clothesline is useful for this purpose, and if it is hung low enough, children can hang their own pictures.

*Suggestions and Variations:*    A selection of colors in containers on a table adjacent to the easel area allows children to choose the colors they want. From time to time, teachers should comment on specific features of a child's work, such as colors used. For older children, provide brushes in a variety of shapes and sizes.

Start children with the primary colors: blue, red, and yellow. Add secondary colors: orange, green, and purple. Black, white, and brown may complete the collection. Use good quality, true colors. After children have had some experience with painting, they may like to mix their own colors. Provide the primary colors and black and white. Small palettes may be used for mixing, or muffin tins may be used. Children will need a cup of water to wash their brush each time they wish to use it in a different color.

A mural may be a group painting activity for primary children. Spread out a long sheet of butcher paper on the floor or on a long table. Plan with the children for a mural depicting an experience or interest which is held in common.

## 2. Activity:    Finger painting (PP–P)

*Materials:*    Flat washable surface (table or floor): shallow pan (larger than 12 by 18 inches) with water; glazed finger-painting paper, fingerpaint base (recipe on page 124), powdered tempera paint. Clothing protectors and cleanup and picture drying-materials as for brush painting.

*Procedure:*    Print child's name on a sheet of glazed paper. Draw the paper through the water in the shallow pan. Put dollops of fingerpaint on several areas of the paper.

Fingerpaint may be precolored or fingerpaint base may be put on the paper and powdered tempera sprinkled in it. For each dollop of fingerpaint base, a different color may be used.

*Suggestions and Variations:*    Encourage children to use whole sweep of palms and arms up to the elbows and to experiment with various ways of using hands and arms.

For beginners more interested in the feel of fingerpainting, painting may be done directly on a table which has a hard finish or on trays. Prints may be made by pressing paper on top of finger-painted table or tray if desired.

Finished finger paintings may be used as covers for five-gallon ice-cream-carton wastebaskets, scrapbook covers, gift-wrapping paper, or storage-box covers.

It is essential to have water for cleanup within easy reach.

## 3. Activity:    Rubbings (P)

*Materials:*    Paper; crayons, chalks, pastels, or charcoal; leaves, embossed flat metal, burlap, or other textured materials.

*Procedure:* Lay textured material on table and cover with paper. Using the side of the crayon (paper removed), piece of colored chalk, pastel, or charcoal, rub firmly over entire surface of the paper. Outlines of materials underneath the paper should appear. If chalk, charcoal, or pastels are used, spray with fixative (in well-ventilated area or outside).

*Suggestions and Variations:* Use a variety of textures as base for one rubbing. As it will take practice to use just the right touch—neither too hard nor too soft—this variation should be reserved for children who have developed a degree of motor skill.

4. Activity: Crayon–water-color etching (P)

*Materials:* Water-base paint, crayons, sharpened stick or nail file, paper, brush.

*Procedures:* Cover the paper completely with one or more colors of thin paint; water color is best. Allow to dry. Color over the paint thickly with a dark colored crayon (black is commonly used). Scratch designs with a pointed stick or nail file.

*Suggestions and Variations:* This is not recommended for beginners, for it requires patience for a series of processes. In addition to pointed tools, a flat-edged tool may be used to scrape off a width of crayon as may be desired for drawing a building.

5. Activity: Collage (PP–P)

*Materials:* Paper plates; medication cups, egg-carton cups, or jar lids; white glue; scissors; miscellaneous materials such as scraps of cloth, yarn, colored construction paper, colored tissue paper, colored glass, pebbles, beans, macaroni, seashells, old magazines, old greeting cards.

*Procedure:* On a table, spread out trays of selected scraps of material: paper plates, egg-carton tops, shoe-box lids, or paper for a base; and small containers of glue. Demonstrate ways of applying glue to objects to be used in the collage. Small objects may be dipped in glue, while popsicle sticks may be used to spread glue on paper. When finished, set aside to dry.

*Suggestions and Variations:* Have children select items wanted for their pictures and arrange them on the dry paper before starting to glue. (This sort of planning should not be expected from young preprimary children who are more interested in manipulating the materials than in making a picture.) Holes may be punched in the edges of paper plates, egg cartons, or heavy paper for lacing with yarn to give a framed effect.

For tissue-paper collage, paint the base with a thin coat of diluted glue or liquid starch. Then place the pieces of tissue on top and press.

Combine a neighborhood walk with this activity by having children pick up materials for collage. "Just what you can hold in your two hands" is a good rule.

6. **Activity:**   Styrofoam printing (P)

*Materials:*   Flat pieces of styrofoam of rectangular form (a trimmed meat tray cut into a piece about 4 by 6 inches would be fine); thick poster paint in shallow pans big enough for the pieces of prepared styrofoam; a roller (rolling pin or printer's roller); paper, pencils or pointed sticks.

*Procedure:*   Draw a design on a piece of styrofoam with a pencil or pointed stick. Press hard enough to make an indentation in the styrofoam. Lightly lay the styrofoam, picture side down, on the paint or cover the surface with paint using a printer's roller. Press the styrofoam, paint side down, on a piece of paper. Being careful not to move the styrofoam, roll over its top to make the print. Carefully lift the styrofoam from the paper.

*Suggestions and Variations:*   The raised surfaces will print; not the indentations. This idea may not be easy for a preoperational child to grasp. For younger children, carrots or potatoes carved into designs (by the adult), onion or orange halves, or objects such as frozen juice cans may be dipped into thick paint and pressed onto paper.

7. **Activity:**   Modeling (PP–P)

*Materials:*   Salt-and-flour dough, plasticene, or ceramic clay; popsicle sticks, orangewood manicure sticks, toy rolling pins, cookie cutters, and so on.

*Procedure:*   Have clay readily available for children to work with as they wish. If clay is stored in two- or three-inch diameter balls in a crock, children can easily get it on their own. Ceramic clay and salt-and-flour-dough clay will harden if exposed to air for more than a short period of time. Older children who have developed some skill may wish to make objects, let them harden, and then paint them. Plasticene and salt-and-flour dough made with oil will not harden readily if kept properly covered.

*Suggestions and Variations:*   Cut out shapes from rolled clay. Cover with textured material and press evenly with rolling pin for textured medallions. If made with ceramic clay and fired, these may be Christmas-tree ornaments, wind chimes, or pendants. Remember that for young children who have had little experience with modeling, the clay itself is enough for the first few weeks. Add tools gradually. Also remember that the younger children will not set out to make "something" with the clay. They are more interested in how it feels and what it does.

## 8. Activity:    Carpentry (PP–P)

*Materials:*    Workbench, hammer, saw, nails, vise, glue, hand drill, screwdriver, screws, nuts and bolts, wrench, pliers, plane. Soft wood in a variety of sizes.

*Procedure:*    Start a woodworking center with just a few tools, such as hammer, screwdriver, and hand drill. Add other tools later after children become accustomed to the center. Demonstrate safe use and care of tools in a planning period or to small groups as they use the area.

*Suggestions and Variations:*    Children's first woodworking will probably consist only of driving nails into wood. An example of this kind of work can be seen in the photo of two three-year-old girls below. Children are very proud of this accomplishment and value these creations very much. When first introduced to the saw, they will probably only cut wood into pieces and not attempt to put them together to make anything. It would be a very serious error in judgment to assume that these pieces mean nothing to the child and attempt to place them back in the stockpile of wood. These are precious pieces and the child will want to take them home. Again, it should be remembered that young children are far more interested in manipulating and

Early woodworking creations may consist only of a few nails in a piece of wood.

controlling the materials than in making "something." As children gain experience working with wood, they will want to begin making things. It is important that materials are available for their work. Nails should be provided in a variety of sizes. Wood of all shapes and sizes should also be available. Materials such as soda pop bottle caps or discs cut from dowel rods may be used for wheels. Popsicle sticks resemble airplane propellers. Paper and fabric scraps are often useful as boat sails, and upholstery can be used for a car seat or chair. Felt-tip pens can be used to add details to wood constructions.

Use only real tools and keep them in top working order.

## 9. Activity:   Mobiles (K–P)

*Materials:*   Quarter-inch dowel cut in varying lengths (less than twelve inches); strong black string or picture wire; miscellaneous materials such as scraps of cloth, yarn, pipe cleaners, construction paper, old magazines, old greeting cards.

*Procedure:*   Show a variety of mobiles and talk about how they are made. The teacher may initiate this "showing" and "talking" by hanging several mobiles around the classroom. Children are sure to notice them and ask questions.

To illustrate Activity 10: Blocks.

Demonstrate tying or other means for fastening strings or wire and testing for balance. Pictures from magazines or greeting cards may be mounted on tagboard before being attached to the mobile. Ceramic clay medallions may also be used.

*Suggestions and Variations:* A wire coat hanger may be used as the top bar and objects suspended from it. Show children how to cut spirals for a spring effect and how to fold paper for a snowflake effect. The wire frame of a small lampshade would make an interesting variation.

10. **Activity:** Blocks (PP-K-P)

*Materials:* A set of unit blocks in various shapes and sizes including cylinders and arches. (Catalogs of companies manufacturing unit blocks give suggestions for amounts and sizes. If economizing, use catalog as guide for making blocks from scrap lumber.) Sets of accessories such as zoo animals, farm animals, cars, people.

*Procedure:* Place like blocks together on open shelving. Diagrams drawn or pasted on shelves will indicate where each shape and size belongs, providing a guide for children to use in returning blocks to the shelves. Accessories may be placed in labeled trays or displayed on shelves. For three- to four-year-olds, putting one set out at a time may encourage cooperative play and help to focus the play on one theme. Select an area free from drafts and out of the line of traffic for building. A smooth, hard-surfaced rug or carpet is warmer for children to sit on than a bare floor; it is also quieter and may lessen wear on the blocks.

*Suggestions and Variations:* Children often use blocks in a linear arrangement laying out walls, fences, and roads. Such an arrangement may or may not be combined with vertical and roofed structures. Both cooperative and individual work is common in the block area. As children mature and gain experience in block building, their structures become more complex. Dated photographs of a child's block structures over time gives evidence of progress. A child in a wheelchair may enjoy having unit blocks placed on a table for building.

11. **Activity:** Sand (PP-K-P)

*Materials:* A box approximately 3 feet wide, 4 feet long, and ½ foot deep on 1½-to-2-feet legs for indoor or outdoor use; clean beach sand, water, shovels, spoons, cans or pails, flowerpots, sieves, plastic bleach bottles (bottles may be cut leaving neck and handle intact for a funnel or neck may be cut off leaving handle attached to the body of the bottle for a scoop); sets of accessories such as zoo animals, farm animals, cars, trucks and road construction equipment, people.

*Procedure:*   Place sand in box and moisten with water. (Older children may add water as they need it using sprinkling cans provided for them.) Provide shelves nearby or plastic stacking baskets for storing implements and accessories. As children work in the sand, they may need to be reminded of rules such as "Sand needs to be kept in the box"; "Sand may not be thrown"; and so on.

*Suggestions and Variations:*   Outdoor sandboxes may be made from 1-by-8-inch boards or from a large tractor tire. Provide mirrors or pieces of shiny metal to suggest bodies of water. Trees, houses, and other objects made by older children from construction paper and other materials add interest to scenes created in the sandbox. When children have completed an elaborate project at the sandbox, a photograph may be taken before returning materials to shelves and smoothing the sand.

12. Activity:   Papier mâché (PP–P)

*Materials:*   Newspapers, flour paste (commerical wallpaper or tweedle paste), a shallow basin or pan, water, string or picture wire, miscellaneous cartons and tubes (rollers from paper towels, wrapping paper, toilet paper, and so on). After figures are completed, you will need poster paints, brushes, scraps of construction paper, yarn, fabric, and other scraps for decorating; white glue.

*Procedure:*   Working with children, help them bunch and tie newspaper or used tubes for legs. To attach these, use strips of paper dipped in paste or use wide masking tape. Wrap tape or paper strip around the end of legs to be attached and also up over body.

Prepare flour paste in shallow pan to about consistency of thick pea soup. Tear newspapers into long one- or two-inch strips. Pull through paste and apply to base figure. Apply strips around joints first for extra strength. Continue until figure is completely covered and smooth. Paper toweling torn in strips forms a good final coat. Set aside to dry. Drying may take several days depending on size of figures, number of coats of papier mâché, and weather conditions. When figures are fully dry, provide materials for painting and other finishing touches. (See Figure 5–2.)

*Suggestions and Variations:*   Encourage children to work on their own, offering to help when requested or when frustration level appears beyond tolerance.

Younger children may not be ready for a project such as this, which requires an extended period of time. A papier mâché project should not be initiated unless additional adult help is available or children can work with minimal supervision.

Use a shared experience such as a well-liked story or a trip to a zoo or farm as a starter for using papier mâché as a medium. You can also make models in connection with social studies or science.

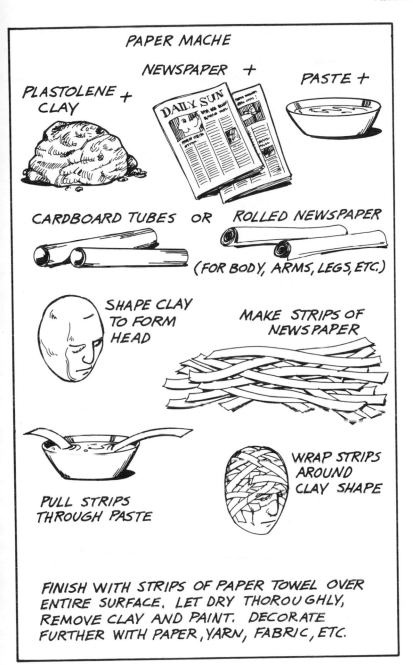

PAPER MACHE

PLASTOLENE + CLAY

NEWSPAPER +

PASTE +

CARDBOARD TUBES OR ROLLED NEWSPAPER

(FOR BODY, ARMS, LEGS, ETC.)

SHAPE CLAY TO FORM HEAD

MAKE STRIPS OF NEWSPAPER

PULL STRIPS THROUGH PASTE

WRAP STRIPS AROUND CLAY SHAPE

FINISH WITH STRIPS OF PAPER TOWEL OVER ENTIRE SURFACE. LET DRY THOROUGHLY, REMOVE CLAY AND PAINT. DECORATE FURTHER WITH PAPER, YARN, FABRIC, ETC.

**FIGURE 5-2** Papier mâché.

## 13. Activity:  Puppet (papier mâché) (P)

*Materials:*   Plasticene; materials for papier mâché.

*Procedure:*   Form a small head from plasticene. Be sure to make a good neck about the size of the middle finger. Cover with small strips of newspaper (about one-half inch wide) soaked in thinned paste as described above. Cover around neck but leave bottom uncovered. When dry, cut the papier-mâché head in half by incising with a sharp knife from bottom of side of neck in front of the ears and over the top. Remove plasticene and put two halves together, covering the joint with strips of paste-dipped paper. When dry, decorate as desired.

To make clothes, cut a piece of fabric twice the length of the hand from tip of middle finger to tip of thumb when hand is outstretched. Fold the length and cut a hole in the middle of the fold the size of the puppet's neck. Sew sides together forming sleeves which will fit over thumb and fourth finger. Trim. Turn right side out and attach to head. Add collar and trimming as desired.

*Suggestions and Variations:*   Copenhagen puppets: Use round balloons as base for molding head. Cover with papier mâché as for hand puppets and add features. Attach to broomsticks. A piece of fabric decorated as desired may be gathered and attached at joint of broomstick and head so that fabric drapes child who operates puppet with broomsticks. (See Figure 5–3.)

**FIGURE 5-3**   Copenhagen puppets.

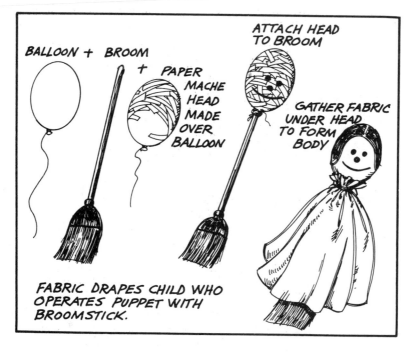

14. Activity:    Paper bag art (PP-P)

*Materials:*    Paper bags of various sizes; scissors; white glue or tweedle paste; construction paper scraps, yarn, and fabric scraps.

*Procedure:*    *For masks*—Choose large bags which will fit over head and shoulders of children. Show children how to help each other find proper places for cutting holes for eyes, nose, mouth, and arms. Demonstrate ways to decorate with construction paper cut in strips and rolled on pencils for curls, or with yarn and fabric for eyebrows, hair, and so on. Masks may be painted if preferred.

*For hand puppets*—Choose bags a little larger than the hand. The bag should be just large enough so that the bottom fold can easily be moved up and down with fingers inserted. Demonstrate placement of facial features on bottom of bag.

*Suggestions and Variations:*    Avoid leaving models; show child a variety of models to present ideas then put models out of sight after children have had opportunities to handle and examine them.

## APPRECIATING THE VISUAL ARTS

1. Activity:    Field trips (PP-P)

*Materials:*    Make advance arrangements (1) with personnel at site to be visited, (2) for adults—parents or others—to accompany children, and (3) for transportation. Obtain written parental permission for children to go.

*Procedure:*    Field trips may be taken to provide a core experience from which art and other learning activities will radiate. They may also be used to add needed knowledge to a project under way or to be a culminating experience. Field trips may be as simple as a walk in the vicinity of the school or as elaborate as a trip to a museum, the zoo, the state fair, a farm, a dairy, or other commercial establishment. En route and on arrival encourage comments on what children see and direct their attention to features which may be overlooked. Elicit reactions when returning to the classroom. Have children describe their experiences verbally or ask them to draw pictures of things they saw.

*Suggestions and Variations:*    Take a walk in the neighborhood specifically to see an animal, tree, or building. Ask children to tell and show with gestures how things look.

It is not necessary for the entire class to go on every field trip. An adult, volunteer, or aide may take a small group to visit something of special interest.

Do not require that all students engage in a follow-up activity; this should be optional.

Field trips extend children's experiences.

When making arrangements, ask for a guide who is skilled in talking with young children and in eliciting their questions, comments, and reactions. When visiting a museum, decide in advance which exhibits you wish to visit. Setting limits in advance may prevent very active youngsters from darting from room to room. It is more important for children to enjoy thoroughly one or two works of art than to have the buzzing confusion of sensory images resulting from trying to see everything in the same day.

For children who have shown a special interest in an exhibit arrange a return trip. A parent who has an interest in art may take them.

### 2. Activity:   Masterpiece of the week (PP–P)

*Materials:*   A file of prints of masterpieces. Cover the prints with clear plastic or laminate to preserve them for longer use. Prints that are prelaminated are available from the National Gallery. Talk with your local librarian or museum for appropriate suggestions.

*Procedure:*   Pictures displayed in classrooms should go beyond children's art and pictures designed to teach a concept. Trite, cute pictures of doubtful artistic value should be avoided. Art work selected from a wide range of periods and styles should be presented if children are to develop aesthetic appreciation.

Select prints for interest to children because of subject matter or for bright colors and vigorous design. Paintings of children, family groups, landscapes, and still-life and colorful abstracts (nonrepresentational art) may be included.

**FIGURE 5-4**    Aesthetic display.

Photographs or reproductions of statues should also be included. Photography is also a means of artistic expression and artistic photographs should be displayed.

Ask children to select "the masterpiece of the week" and hang it in a spot chosen for this purpose. Such a spot should be low enough so that children can examine the picture closely, yet be open to unobstructed long range view. (See Figure 5-4).

*Suggestions and Variations:*    Keep the file of masterpieces in the quiet corner for leisurely viewing.

On a trip to the art museum, select and purchase a print of some work seen there.

3. **Activity:**    Aesthetic display (PP–P)

*Materials:*    A small area in the classroom set aside for the purpose; shelf space, a small table, a chair; fabric, colored corrugated cardboard or other materials to provide background; any of the following: colored bottles,

musical instruments, flowers, leaves, fruit, interesting rocks, plants, seashells, statuettes, costumed dolls, bowls, vases, attractive dishes, model cars, and so on.

*Procedure:*   Setting up a display which has no other function than to be aesthetically pleasing helps a child develop a sense of design and balance and may be a stimulus for drawing or painting. There are many forms such a display may take. A chair draped with fabric falling in soft folds over the back and around objects of good design is one. Blocks may be used to form small shelves or pedestals and placed in front of standing rolls of colored corrugated cardboard. A piece of fabric may be tacked to a bulletin board and fall in folds which accent a display on a shelf below. Any of these three (as well as many other ideas) are possibilities for aesthetic displays. Teachers will usually make the first display. As the year progresses, encourage children to change the display and to make one of their own.

*Suggestions and Variations:*   Avoid sameness in composition. Some displays should be symmetrical and others asymmetrical. Curved lines may prevail one time and angular lines another.

# REFERENCES

BRITTAIN, W. L.    *Creativity Art and the Young Child.* New York: Macmillan, 1979.

CHERRY, C.    *Creative Art for the Developing Child.* Belmont, Calif: Fearon, 1972.

ERICKSON, E.    *Childhood and Society.* New York: W. W. Norton & Co., Inc., 1950.

FIRLICK, R. J.    Display as a teaching strategy. *Childhood Education* 57 (September–October 1980).

HILL, D. M.    *Mud, Sand and Water.* Washington, D.C.: National Association for the Education of Young Children, 1977.

HIRSCH, E. S., ed.    *The Block Book,* Washington, D.C.: National Association for the Education of Young Children, 1977.

LANSING, K.    *Art, Artists and Art Education.* New York: McGraw-Hill, 1971.

HUNT, J. M.    *Intelligence and Experience.* New York: Ronald Press, 1961.

PIAGET, J., and INHELDER, B.    *The Psychology of the Child.* New York: Basic Books, 1969.

PIAGET, J.    *A Child's Conception of Space.* New York: W. W. Norton & Co., Inc., 1967.

REED, J. P.    *Sand Magic,* Albuquerque, N.M.: JPR Publishers (privately printed), 1975.

WILLIAMS, R. M.    Why children should draw. *Saturday Review,* September 3, 1977, pp. 10–18.

# 6
# PERFORMING ARTS

Sound, movement, and imitative play are major interests and activities in a young child's life. When these activities are included in an educational program, they become music, dance (or movement), and drama, collectively known as the *performing arts*[1] A planned program in the performing arts promotes holistic development, that is, development that occurs simultaneously in the physical, affective, and cognitive domains. Also, activities in the performing arts, like those in the visual arts, support and contribute to children's academic skills.

The importance of physical activity to a person's well-being is increasingly recognized, and the performing arts provide such activity. Since many experts in physical education for the young child (Schurr, 1967; Flinchum, 1975) recommend movement activities as a major part of the physical education program, a separate chapter on health and physical education is not included here. In addition to the information on movement activities found in this chapter, activities in the chapters on science ("How Our Bodies Work," p. 263, "Healthy Bodies," p. 264, "Jumping Jiminy," p. 283); math ("Sand Timer Experiment," p. 328, "Outdoor Play," pp. 311 and 321, "Beanbag Toss," p. 314); and social science ("Wheels" p. 377, "School Safety Procedures," and "Traffic Signs," p. 371) are useful in planning health and physical education aspects of the total curriculum.

This chapter is designed to help teachers plan a strong program in the performing arts. It will (1) show why music, drama, and dance are essential parts of a well-rounded early childhood program, (2) give levels of development relative to each area and the implication for teaching, (3) suggest appropriate goals for each area, and (4) provide strategies for teaching in each area as well as descriptions of activities which may be used.

## THE VALUES
## OF THE PERFORMING ARTS

Mind, body, and spirit are involved when one participates fully in the performing arts of music, dance, and drama. There are many values that may be identified, of which the following are but a few.

### Enjoyment of the Performing Arts
### for Their Own Sake

The performing arts have the potential for involving one's mind, body, and feelings in total enjoyment. For a few, early introduction to the performing arts may lead to a lifelong vocation. Many, if not most, outstanding artists began developing their skill at a very young age. While only a few become professional musicians, dancers, or actors, many children develop an enjoyable hobby or appreciation for the performance of others.

---

[1] The term *Performing Arts* is used in the sense of action or process, not in the sense of entertainment. It is used to distinguish music, dance, and drama from the visual arts of painting, drawing, and sculpting.

### An Acceptable Way to Reduce Tension

When children seem "uptight," a change of pace which involves music or a movement activity helps them to relax and brings the group together. The power of music to soothe or raise the spirits has long been known. A movement activity may provide much needed physical exercise. Expressing feelings through dramatic play helps children deal with traumatic experiences.

### Means of Self-expression and Communication

Young children frequently express their feelings and their impressions of the world around them in music, movement, and dramatic play. A five-year-old imitating the sound of a storm with musical instruments, a three-year-old dancing joyfully on a beach, or a group of three-to five-year-olds playing out an experience in a doctor's office are all examples of such self-expression. While such play is not intended to communicate feelings and impressions to others, it does in fact tell the sensitive adult much about children's thinking.

### Increased Perception and Concept Development

As in the visual arts, recall of experiences must be sharpened to be reproduced in art forms. The sequence of events must be rehearsed in order to dramatize them. The sounds of falling rain or thunder must be held in mind while seeking the right instruments to represent them. Or the sight of a tree swaying in the wind must be remembered and imagined before its movement can be imitated.

### Physical Fitness and Acquisition of Motor Skills

Movement activities are particularly valuable for developing physical fitness and motor skills. Balancing, stretching, bending, running, and skipping are all involved in movement activity and increase physical fitness and coordination. Dramatic play, particularly outdoors, often involves lifting, pushing, pulling, climbing, and pedaling—all activities which stimulate circulation and build muscles. Singing increases respiration and hence circulation, while playing musical instruments involves coordination and fine motor skills.

### Aesthetic Appreciation

An important value of the performing arts is that they teach how to be an appreciative member of an audience as well as a performer. Providing a wide variety of styles of well-performed music for listening may lead children to develop a taste for good music.

## Appreciation of Cultural Heritage

All major ethnic groups have developed distinctive styles of music and dance. Listening to this music and singing the songs, and seeing and performing dances native to the country from which one's family comes helps a child retain a sense of identity. For those with different backgrounds, such learning engenders an appreciation and enjoyment of cultural diversity.

## CHILDREN AND MUSIC

In addition to the cognitive skills involved in perceiving the elements of music and synchronizing one's actions with them, one needs to remember the sequence of tones, the value given to each tone, and the rhythmic pattern. Perhaps what is said about children learning language can be applied here, for certainly children do learn songs quite easily from hearing them. Learning to read music comes much later, if at all. Notation is a complex and abstract symbol system which children may learn around the time they learn the symbol systems of reading and arithmetic.

Smith (1970) notes that young children match the three to five tones above and including middle C most easily and only gradually gain the ability to extend their range upward. Wendrich (1979) noted that three-to six-month-old babies could match D, F, and A when sung. It is not known how high a pitch can be matched by an infant, but the notes suggested are not inconsistent with Smith's comments. At any rate, it would seem important to give children opportunities to match tones within the appropriate range. It may be that there is a physical base as well as an experiential base for developing the ability to produce vocal sounds that match tones made by an instrument or by the human voice, resulting in tuneful singing.

There is an obvious physical base required for learning to play many musical instruments. Dexterity and strength in the hands and fingers are required to play instruments such as recorders, pianos, and violins. It is not surprising that instruments such as drums, bells, triangles, and cymbals are commonly found in classrooms for young children.

The learning of skills in music is influenced by the child's development in many areas. As in all areas of development, maturation and experience interact. It cannot be said that all children in any one age group will be able to perform music at a given level of ability. There will be as wide a variance in their musical abilities as there is in their experiences with music and their genetic structures. It takes both physical and cognitive development to master elements of music such as melody, harmony, volume, rhythm, tempo, and form. Children must develop not only the ability to perceive differences in these elements but also the ability to synchronize actions and voice with them. As in the learning of any language, in music the ability to perceive (reception) precedes the ability to perform (expression).

As recently as 1979 (McDonald, 1979), texts on teaching music stated that concepts of beat, tempo, and dynamics develop more quickly than concepts of pitch and melody, melodic rhythm, and harmony. Yet a study (Davidson, 1979) that same year indicated that infants match pitches at a very early age. Discrete pitches were noted at one-and-a-half years; characteristic bits (that is, sequences of pitches), rhythm, and pitch contour were noted in the first half of the third year; and there was continued progress until by five-and-a-half, a tune could be reliably reproduced. Moreover, both that and other studies indicated that before discrete pitches were isolated, babies noted and repeated continuous blends. It was hypothesized that every hearing baby is born with the tools of keen musical ability needed to match pitches but that these tools deteriorate because they are not environmentally reinforced.

## GOALS FOR INSTRUCTION IN MUSIC

From well-planned experiences in music, we expect children to develop some musical competence. The level of competence that can be expected will depend on the children's ages, experience, and special talents.

Basic to developing musical competence is the ability to distinguish variances in pitch, volume, tempo, and rhythm. Children from three to five can learn to distinguish high from low tones, soft from loud tones, those played in rapid succession from those played more slowly, and those played at equal intervals from those played at unequal intervals. When movement and music are combined, it is often bodily movement that tells you when the preschool child can make these discriminations. If appropriate descriptive labels are given, the child will later be able to describe such differences verbally (high–low; fast–slow; loud–soft; uneven–even).

Children should also develop the ability to distinguish between dissonance and harmony, noise and music. One measure of this ability is the way children play a xylophone or a piano. Does the child tend to select one note at a time? Which combinations of notes are repeated, and which rejected?

By the time children have reached seven or eight years of age, they may be expected to gain competence in reading musical notation and in producing music independently, if experiences and activities to teach these skills are provided.

Although young children may be able to respond to music with various expressions of pleasure—dancing, listening quietly with an expression of contentment, keeping time with a foot, hand, or head—there are some specific goals which the teacher should keep in mind in planning a program. For younger children as well as older children, the ability to distinguish among and recognize melodies is one such goal. Another goal is the ability to associate affective responses with characteristics of music.

A third goal is the ability to identify instruments by name and sound. This ability adds much to the enjoyment and appreciation of instrumental music. Even preschool children can learn to identify instruments as long as those presented differ substantially in timbre. For example, young children can easily distinguish a snare drum from a trumpet and a trumpet from a piano, although they would probably have difficulty telling the difference between a bass drum and tympani.

As children are given more experiences, they learn to distinguish between instruments very similar in timbre. For example, six- or seven-year-olds who have had two to three years experience in listening to and identifying instruments in music can easily tell the difference between a clarinet, a flute, and a piccolo. Around the age of eight, many children can begin to learn to play instruments that involve considerable finger movements. Instruction on a recorder or piano is appropriate at this time.

Young children begin to understand the elements of music as they sing songs, move their bodies to music, and create their own music on simple instruments. Some three- to five-year-olds develop a repertoire of songs they can sing recognizably, but more often they respond to and show preferences for songs without being able to sing them accurately. Children can also indicate the differences between music that is high and low, fast and slow, loud and soft, or even and uneven. Learning experiences which involve listening and responding to music, singing songs within their voice range which are simple and repetitious, and experimenting with rhythm instruments are most appropriate for preprimary children.

## METHODS AND ACTIVITIES
## FOR INSTRUCTION IN MUSIC

### Guiding Work in Music

Music is a large part of our lives. It soothes, inspires, entertains, and generally enriches us. Children should have many and varied musical experiences.

PROVIDING EXPERIENCES. Experience should be provided for the entire class as a group, for small groups, and for individuals. Having well-equipped centers allows children to have independent experiences with music. Although children need freedom to experiment with music on their own, they also need the guidance that can only come from the teacher-child face-to-face interaction. It is doubtful if children can learn to identify and discriminate among pitches, tones, rhythms, harmonies, melodies, and other musical concepts without the aid of the teacher.

In the early years, teachers will frequently include music as part of a class meeting. Sometimes, it may be singing as a pleasant way to start the meeting. This also serves as a transition from individual to group work. Other musical experiences such as listening to records or musicians can also be activities for the entire group.

Individuals and small groups of children who have a special interest in music also need opportunities to work independently. Much of the music competence a child acquires can only occur from exploring and practicing independently. Providing music centers is useful for this type of learning. Because the activities which take place in a center may be distracting, rules may be needed. Perhaps work in some of the centers will be permitted at certain times of the day and not at others. Perhaps appointments for teacher assistance with certain projects will be needed. When clearly understood by teacher and children, such limits provide more freedom for creativity than does the lack of such limits.

ENCOURAGING EFFORTS.    The fascination inherent in music is enough to get most children interested in exploring music. Participation by the teacher in musical activities at group time or other times of the day can also encourage children to become involved. In addition, knowing that a dance, an instrumental piece, or a song will be presented to an audience provides incentives for sustained involvement. When a small group of children becomes involved of their own choice in working on such a presentation, the teacher may suggest a time when they may perform for their classmates. A wider audience may be desired for a program the whole class has worked on. The audience may be another class or parents.

It is wise to remember that the important part of the musical production is not the final product, but the process. Performing for an audience should also be the children's decision. The teacher may reflect the wish, expressed by one or two children, or the teacher may suggest it if it seems the children need this kind of encouragement. Such performances, however, must be for the benefit of the children, not the teacher.

EVALUATING WORK.    Noting changes in quality of performance over time provides evaluation of progress in music. For younger children, the teacher may make an anecdotal record of observations. For example, having played a recording of "Raindrops Keep Falling on My Window," a child was heard singing the song softly at naptime. The teacher's recording of this incident provides evidence of the child's learning.

Older children might keep written records of their work in the center for exploring sound. For example, a child who experiments by filling glasses with water to different levels to duplicate the notes of a five-tone scale may write an account of procedure and findings.

Still another way to evaluate progress is to make tape recordings of children's performances at intervals throughout the year.

## Music Centers

A LISTENING CENTER.    Near a record player, in addition to story records, there should be a selection of musical recordings. A wide variety of music including nursery rhymes, jingles, folksongs, popular pieces, and classical music can be included there. Children are never too young to enjoy the finest music, and symphonic and operatic selections should be included. For a description of the enthusiastic response of four-year-olds to classical music, see *Discovering Music with Young Children* by Eunice Bailey (1958).

A FREE-MOVEMENT AREA. Some children may be content to listen to music with only small body movements such as rocking, gently tapping a foot, or waving a hand, but movement should not be limited to that. Another area is needed where children can move freely in response to music; where they can run and skip, gallop and glide, swing and sway, swoop and slither. Here they experience the mood of the music, the tempo, and the rhythm. They respond to these with their whole bodies.

In most public schools, the free-movement area would be a gym or auditorium which is available at periods of the day when unused by other classes. If the classroom is large enough, the teacher might consider designating an area there for movement activities. Such an area might also be used for dramatic play. In this area, small groups of children could independently explore music and movement. Larger, teacher-led groups could engage in music and movement activities in the gym when it is available.

AN AREA FOR EXPLORING SOUND. One center in the classroom can be an area where children are free to explore sound. It should be located at the farthest distance possible from the quiet corner and at sufficient distance from woodworking and other noisy activities so that the sounds of these activities will not interfere with children's listening to and discriminating among sounds.

In the area for exploring sound, there should be a variety of simple rhythm and musical instruments, both commercial and homemade. Materials for making musical instruments should also be available, but may be more appropriately housed in the art center.

Instruments which will be placed in the center may first be introduced to the class in a planning session. As each instrument is introduced, the children should be invited to compare it with other instruments. For example, children might be asked to compare bells with oriental temple blocks. The temple blocks have a nonreverberating, hollow sound, whereas the bells have a clear, ringing tone. If the children respond in terms of pitch instead of tone, the question of pitch might be explored.

## Music Materials

In the area of exploring sound, there should be a wide variety of musical instruments. Such equipment should include instruments which produce sound through being hit or shaken—percussion—through being blown—winds—and through being plucked or scraped—strings. Examples of instruments which may be purchased are:

## Music Materials

| PERCUSSION | WINDS | STRINGS |
|---|---|---|
| Drums | Recorders | Guitar |
| Cymbals | Flageolet | Autoharp |
| Rattles | Ocarinas | Ukulele |
| Triangle | Harmonicas | Violin |
| Bells | Flutophones | |
| Glockenspiel | Tonettes | |
| Xylophone | | |
| Oriental temple blocks | | |
| Blocks | | |
| Tone bars or resonator bells | | |
| Piano | | |
| Tambourine | | |

Instruments which have been made from inexpensive and scrap materials should also be available in the center for exploring sound. Some suggestions will be found among the activities in this chapter, but for further suggestions the reader is referred to Hawkinson and Faulhaber (1970).

Percussion instruments are the most commonly used instruments in the early years. They have relatively constant pitch and are not difficult to play. They can also be simulated readily with homemade instruments.

Though most percussion instruments must be considered rhythmic and not melodic, bells, xylophones, tone bars, the glockenspiel, and the piano are both. A variety of these instruments should be found in the center for exploring sound. There are many types and sizes of bells which should be included. Bells selected for this purpose should parallel the tones of the familiar C-major scale.

There are a variety of stringed instruments from various peoples and times, some of which are quite simple and may provide models for instruments that may be made in the classroom. In connection with studies of history and geography, instruments such as the sitar, psaltery, and viola da gamba may be introduced. Musicians often collect such ancient instruments, and the alert teacher looks for such resources.

Wind instruments are often omitted from classrooms for hygienic reasons. In a classroom which fosters self-reliance as well as good health habits, provision can be made for avoiding the transmittal of disease through the use of a common mouthpiece. A soap-and-water solution which includes a small amount of chlorine bleach may be used to clean the mouthpiece after each use. A small tray with cotton balls, the cleansing solution in one small bowl and clear water in another, and a supply of paper towels may be placed next to the wind instruments. The children may be taught to cleanse the mouthpiece effectively without damage to the instruments. Only kindergarten and primary children can be expected to follow such a procedure.

A piano is a valuable asset to a program for young children, but it is not essential. Should one be offered free for the taking, check it out first to be sure it can be tuned. The space a piano takes in the classroom is more valuable than a piano which cannot be properly tuned. An out-of-tune piano is damaging to the development of a sense of pitch.

Children should be allowed to experiment with playing the piano. Although there is a need for clearly understood, reasonable rules, learning may be inhibited by too-stringent, unexplained rules. When, within limits, children can freely explore sounds, they are building a firm background for musical expression.

**Activities for Instruction in Music**

## DEVELOPING SELF-EXPRESSION IN MUSIC

1. **Activity:**    Singing songs (PP–P)

   *Materials:*    Teacher's ability to sing a simple melody and repertoire of songs. Piano, autoharp, or guitar accompaniment is helpful but not essential. Recordings may be used when learning a song, if necessary.

   *Procedure:*    Select relatively short songs with simple, repetitious words and melody and strong rhythm. Four to six lines is a reasonable length. Single-word or phrase variations provide new verses in many well-loved songs.

   For example: "Where is Thumbkin?" names a new finger in each verse while the rest of the words remain the same. Once children are familiar with the base song, word changes are easily introduced. When teaching new songs, do not introduce too many verses at once. Teach one until children are reasonably familiar with it before going on to the next. One way to teach a verse is to go all the way through it several times and then ask the children to go through it with you.

   To emphasize the melody of a song, lead the children's singing by indicating with your hand when the melody goes up, down, or stays the same. More complicated rhythms can be emphasized by clapping your hands.

   *Suggestions and Variations:*    After children are familiar with a song and with the sounds of a variety of instruments, they may be asked what instruments they think would sound good in a particular place in a song. A child who suggests one should be allowed to try it. Other instruments may be added in the same way. Because children will probably play with any instruments in their hands, it is wise to keep the instruments next to yourself and hand them out only as needed. Have some children sing the melody while others sing rhythmic accompaniments, as in "The Little Drummer Boy," in which "vroom, vroom" is sung underneath the melody on a key-note in a low register on the accented beats. Older children may enjoy singing rounds. For example, "Brother John" has four parts. The class may be divided into halves or, for some advanced children, into four sections. Other adults may be needed to lead each section unless the children are able to sing the round independently.

2. **Activity:**   Mini-opera (PP—P)

*Materials:*   The teacher's good spirits, ingenuity, and pleasant voice. Scales, one or more familiar tunes, or improvised tunes.

*Procedure:*   Carry on a singing conversation with a child by asking a question on an ascending scale and having the child answer on a descending scale. A familiar tune such as "Frère Jacques" may be used, and the dialogue takes place like this:

Teacher and class: "Where is Susy? Where is Susy?"
Susy: "Here I am. Here I am."
Teacher and class: "How are you today, Miss?"
Susy: "Very fine, I thank you."
All: "Glad you're here. Glad you're here."

*Suggestions and Variations:*   Teacher and aide may demonstrate by singing questions and responses to each other. Call children together by singing your request or answer a child's question with singing.

3. **Activity:**   Exploring sound (PP–P)

*Materials:*   A variety of rhythm and melody instruments as they are available to you: drum, rattles, bells, blocks, tambourines, triangles, glockenspiels, oriental temple blocks, harmonicas, recorders, guitar, autoharp, ukulele, tone bars, xylophone, and so on.

Homemade equivalents of the above or other scrounged materials. Clay pots in graduated sizes hung from a horizontal bar by knotted ropes pulled through the holes; pop bottles filled with varying amounts of water; matched glass tumblers and a pitcher of water; pipe in varying lengths and thicknesses suspended from a bar.

Metal or plastic shakers containing materials such as rice, pebbles, beans, or seeds.

*Procedure:*   Arrange a selection of the above on a table in the center for exploring sound. Allow children to explore freely. Encourage them to guess what is inside the shakers. Play guessing games by having them shut their eyes and guess what instrument is being played. Talk about differences in sound.

For children who can read, provide activity cards with suggestions for further exploration. Examples:

Next to the xylophone or any instrument with a full major scale: "Can you find out how to play 'Mary Had a Little Lamb?' Hum the tune to yourself, then match the notes you play to your singing." Next to an assortment of per-

Pipes can be used to make chimes.

cussion instruments: "Can you make a sound like rain falling? a horse galloping? children skipping?" Next to five glasses and a pitcher of water: "Fill these glasses with water so they sound like C, D, E, F, and G on the piano or xylophone. When you find the right pitch, put a label on the glass."
*Suggestions and Variations:*    Have children shut their eyes and listen for sounds. It is ideal to do this when children are out of doors. Ask them to identify sounds they hear. Encourage them to imitate sounds and to use descriptive words. Talk about the effect and quality of sounds. Encourage children to have listening adventures independently. They may record what they hear by drawing pictures, writing a story, or telling about it on a tape recorder. Have more advanced children guess which bell was rung from a set of bells, which key of the piano was struck, which tone bar was hit. Tape record different everyday sounds and have children guess what they are.

4. Activity:    Rhythm instruments (PP-P)

*Materials:*    Drums, maracas, tambourines, triangles, gongs, sticks, blocks, cymbals, bells.
*Procedure:*    Using recordings or playing the piano, play music with well-defined rhythms. Lead the children in moving to the music, marching, skipping, hopping, or running as the rhythm suggests. Have children sit on the floor. Introduce a piece of music with a strong rhythm. Have children clap in

time to the music. As individuals show that they are responding well to the rhythm, hand out instruments to substitute for clapping. Introduce only a few instruments at a time. Have an instrument such as the tambourine struck only on the accented beats. Have children set instruments aside and listen to the music. Ask them to listen for points at which different instruments might be used: a triangle at the end of a phrase, sandblocks marking the rhythm of one section, and so on.

*Suggestions and Variations:*    March around the room in time to music and use rhythm instruments to accent beat. Use rhythm instruments as accompaniment for singing also.

5. Activity:    Music notation (P)

*Materials:*    Chart of musical staff and letter names of notes; stick-on labels, felt pen.

*Procedure:*    Place chart of the musical staff and letter names in back of keys on the piano. Put labels showing staff position and letter name on tone bars or xylophone. Write letter names with felt pen on piano keys. Refer by name to keys struck.

Introduce games suggested under exploring sound using letter names for different tones. Place beginners' piano pieces on the piano or next to other instruments for children to try.

*Suggestions and Variations:*    Transcribe tunes made up by children. Play them for their composers. Encourage them to pick out their tunes on the piano or xylophone. Utilize word recognition games substituting musical notes for words. Examples: Paint notes in staff positions on 8½-by-11-inch

To go with Music Activity #5 Music Notation.

pieces of cardboard covered with plastic. Scatter them on the floor. As one child or an adult calls the letter names, the other children scramble to put hands or feet on the correct note. Matching games of the lotto type may also be made.

6. **Activity:**   Composing original songs (P)

**Materials:**   Tape recorder, lined music paper, pencils, resonator bells, xylophone or piano.

**Procedure:**   With a group of children, introduce a short new song, leaving off the last line. Ask children to finish the song by making up their own tune. If children show ability to do this, they are ready to make up a tune for a favorite poem. Select a four-line poem. Have children say it with you, clapping the rhythm of the words. When you are sure they have the rhythm, ask if they think the song should start on a high note or a low note, and then whether it should go up or down. Having reached a decision like this, sing the first phrase together. Continue to elicit ideas for the remainder of the song. To record the tune, a tape recorder may be used as each line is composed or the tune may be written on the blackboard. To notate, short lines relative to position of pitches in a scale may be used. For an example of a familiar tune written this way, see Figure 6-1. The tune is "Twinkle, Twinkle, Little Star."

**FIGURE 6-1**   A simple notation for *Twinkle, Twinkle, Little Star*

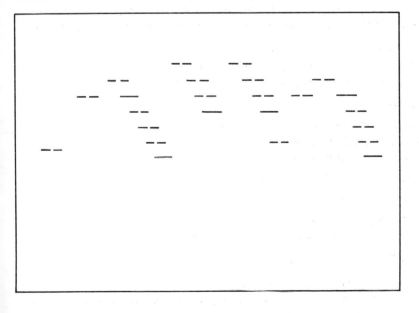

*Suggestions and Variations:*    After children have shown ability to do the above, encourage children to write their own verses and make up tunes for them. Although a few children may think of a tune first and then words, making up a tune for words which have been written is generally easier.

Individuals who make up their own songs may use the tape recorder during the process of creation. Later, the song may be transcribed. If you do not have the ability to do this, ask a musical friend to do it for you. After transcription, have the composer add words (if not written earlier) and illustrations. Then add the song to the class library.

Suggest that children try to compose their tunes on resonator bells or on the xylophone. This will be more successful if the F and B bars are omitted, leaving only the pentatonic scale—C,D,E,G,A. Persevering, talented children may be able to transcribe their own tunes with the help of charts and labels. Teach songs children have composed to other children in the class.


## DEVELOPING AESTHETIC APPRECIATION OF MUSIC

1. **Activity:**    Using recordings (PP-P)

    *Materials:*    Record player, earphones, selection of recordings.
    Recordings should be of good quality and include:

    > Children's songs
    > Folksongs
    > Jazz
    > Symphonies
    > Operatic selections such as "The Children's Prayer" from Humperdinck's *Hansel and Gretel,* "Barcarolle" from Offenbach's *Tales of Hoffman,* "The Toreador Song" from Bizet's *Carmen,* Menotti's *Amahl and the Night Visitors.*

    *Procedure:*    Play records at various times during the day. Show children how to select, play, and return records to storage. Encourage children to listen independently using earphones. Use recordings as accompaniment for movement and dance. Introduce a recording at a group meeting. Use records which introduce instruments. Recordings such as Britten's *Introduction to the Orchestra* or Prokofiev's *Peter and the Wolf* are especially good.

    The narration for the latter introduces the instruments used to portray the various characters. Have pictures of instruments available and show at appropriate times as indicated in the recording. Encourage children to identify instruments in other recordings by sound.

    *Suggestions and Variations:*    Have a comfortable, attractive listening area where children may curl up on soft cushions to listen to music.

2. **Activity:**  Visits from musicians (PP–P)

> **Materials:**  Invite musicians to visit the class. Brief them on what new kinds of experiences you want children to have, your expected outcomes, and the kinds of questions and curiosity they will encounter. Prepare the children by having them think of questions to ask and by discussing appropriate behavior. Listen to records which feature the instruments the visiting musician will bring.
>
> **Procedure:**  When the musicians arrive, children should greet them and show them the area where the class will meet. Gather all children together and enjoy the musicians.
>
> **Suggestions and Variations:**  Ask the musician to demonstrate the way the instrument is played and to play scales as well as pieces. Ask a group of musicians to demonstrate the way in which different melodies fit together into a harmonious whole.
>
> For older children, arrange with an organist for a field trip to hear and see an organ.

3. **Activity:**  Concerts for children (PP–P)

> **Procedure:**  In many urban areas, symphony orchestras play special concerts for children. As for any field trip, arrange for parental consent and assistance. Before going to the concert, obtain the program to be played and play recordings of some of the pieces. Discuss these with the children. When preparations are carefully made, the concert should be enjoyed by all who attend.
>
> **Suggestions and Variations:**  Follow-up activities might include drawing or painting pictures, writing stories, or learning songs based on melodies heard. If there have been many musical experiences in the classroom, even four-year-olds may enjoy a concert.

4. **Activity:**  Music in field trips (PP–P)

> **Procedure:**  Make usual arrangements for a field trip. Discuss with children sounds they might listen for. Obtain recordings of programmatic music in which the sounds of animals, of the city, or of the sea may be heard; for example, Saint-Saëns' *Carnival of the Animals,* Gershwin's *An American in Paris,* or Debussy's *La Mer.* Recordings of musical expression of visual impressions such as Moussorgsky's *Pictures at an Exhibition* and Holst's *The Planets* may be used when appropriate. On a field trip, suggest that children listen for sounds. Questions or suggestions which may be used are:

> > "Close your eyes; what do you hear?"
> >
> > "Tell me how it sounds; imitate it."
> >
> > "Is the bird call higher or lower than the dog's barking?"
> >
> > "How does a truck sound different from an automobile?"

"How does a truck going up hill sound different from one going down?"
"How does the rustling of leaves make you feel?"
"Can you hear the wind in the trees? What kind of sound is it?"

If appropriate, when returning to the classroom, listen to recordings of programmatic music.

**Suggestions and Variations:**    After a field trip, have children reproduce with homemade and commercial instruments the sounds they heard.


## CHILDREN AND MOVEMENT AND DANCE

Movement and dance involve skillful use of the body. The physical growth and development of the child is, therefore, crucial to skill development in these areas.

Physical growth and development occur in a very orderly fashion. The child must learn to control the movements of arms and hands. At first, movements are not specific or directed. The whole arm moves in a rather jerky fashion, and the hands move only as awkward extensions of upper arm movements. By the last half of the first year, hand and finger movements are no longer extensions of arm movements, but are independent. The child's wrist, however, is still a mere crease between a chubby arm and an even chubbier hand. The tendons that are noticeable on the back of an adolescent or adult hand are not apparent on the hand of a young child.

The lack of independence in the structure of the hand and arm in the young child can be seen in the imprecision of the movements made by the child's hands. As the wrist, hand, and fingers lengthen in the child from age four to six, skill in their use increases.

The child must also learn to move about in space. The sequence of skills which culminates in locomotor skill starts with children's ability to lift their heads off a surface on which they are placed prone and proceeds through abilities such as sitting up, pulling up, standing alone, walking, and running. All these require balance, and this is achieved quite differently by a young child than by an adult. As the child's trunk, arms, and legs lengthen in the years between two and five, the center of gravity shifts lower and balance becomes easier. The ability to move with speed, stop abruptly, and change directions while moving also improves as body proportions change.

Tissue growth also changes as children get older. During the first year, most weight gain is realized in fat tissue. After the first year, this fat production decreases rapidly, and bone and muscle tissue begin to grow at a faster rate than earlier. During the fifth year, about 75 percent of the child's weight gain is realized in muscle growth (Thompson, 1954). These changes have an effect on children's strength and ability to control their bodies. As children get older, strength and control gradually increase, and this pattern continues on through adolescence.

Physiological processes such as heart rate, blood pressure, and respiration also change with age (Thompson, 1954). These processes affect stamina. Generally, young children do not have as much stamina as older children, and this can be seen in the faster rate at which they become fatigued. As these basic physiological processes change through childhood and adolescence, stamina increases.

When teaching movement and dance, the teacher should carefully consider the physical growth and development of the child. Characteristics we often associate with movement and dance, such as grace and smoothness, come slowly in children for the reasons discussed above. Younger children need more space than older ones because they cannot control their movements as easily and often accidentally topple or run into someone. If fatigue is to be avoided, younger children also need more alternations than do older children between movements that require much exertion and those that require little.

The importance of developing motor skills should not be underestimated. Not only does such development contribute to the physical well-being of children, but there appears to be some evidence that mastery of gross motor skills may contribute to academic skills (Hallahan and Cruickshank, 1973). In addition, active, competent children have been found to be better able to cope with demands, challenges, and frustrations than are less active children (Murphy, 1962).

Experiences in movement and dance contribute to physical growth and development. As we stated earlier (see page 5), development results from the *interaction* of both maturation and experience. Therefore, the wise teacher does not wait until a child skips to introduce uneven rhythms in movement. However, if the teacher knows that a young three-year-old, who is just getting a good feel for even rhythms such as running and marching, is not maturationally ready, the teacher will not try to introduce skipping to that child.

## GOALS FOR INSTRUCTION
## IN MOVEMENT AND DANCE

A prime goal for a program of movement and dance is to impart the ability to use the body with grace and coordination. This includes the mastery of *locomotor movements:* crawling, sliding, walking, running, jumping, hopping, rolling, and climbing; *nonlocomotor movements:* pushing, pulling, stretching, curling, swinging, bending, and twisting; and *manipulative movements,* which involve prehension, dexterity, and coordination. Body awareness—knowing where one's body is in relation to the environment—balance, and eye-hand coordination are also involved in the ability to use one's body gracefully and with agility. Teachers need to determine appropriate levels of competence, reasonable for the children.

Participation in movement and dance activities may have the following results:

1. Increasing ability to respond with appropriate movement to words, music, and rhythms.
2. Increasing ability to participate with ease and enjoyment in singing games and folk dancing.
3. Increasing ability to express moods and concepts with movement.

From experience with dance, children should gain the ability to enjoy dancing either as watchers or participants. As a basis for participating in movement activities, the teacher may encourage children to become aware of and to develop an aesthetic appreciation for movement in nature: wind blowing trees, birds flying, animals moving, and plants growing. As a watcher, the child should develop the ability to interpret moods expressed by movement and to see the relationship between rhythms in music and certain steps, for example, skipping, hopping, running, and walking.

## METHODS AND ACTIVITIES FOR INSTRUCTION IN MOVEMENT AND DANCE

### Guiding Work in Movement and Dance

MOVEMENT.    Movement for young children includes gymnastics and games as well as dance. Gymnastics consists of the basic movement skills (locomotor, nonlocomotor, and manipulative, see p. 157), exercises, stunts, tumbling, and activities using equipment of different kinds and sizes (Schurr, 1967).

Typically, children are very active and will utilize all their basic movement skills when provided with the opportunity to do so. The major instructional strategy, therefore, is to provide a supportive environment as well as time for movement activities to take place. (See p. 161 for a list of recommended equipment.)

However, guidance is needed. Some children tend to be less physically active than others for one reason or another. Those without physical impairments may need simple encouragement to try new skills. A demonstration, guidance as the child tries an action for the first time, and a word of praise for the effort may suffice. Those who suffer physical impairment need more encouragement and specific guidance. Because an activity requires a great deal of effort, perhaps some pain, or because the child is clumsy, a child with a physical impairment may tend to avoid it. If a specialist such as a physical therapist has advised the teacher that the child needs to participate in a specific activity, the teacher may need to be quite firm in insisting that the child do the recommended exercise or activity; for example, it may be necessary to insist that a spastic child *walk* downstairs holding onto the railing rather than move down step by step in a sitting position.

When children are playing with equipment, guidance is generally minimal. Typically, children will run or walk, climb ropes, hang by hands or knees from bars, lift large blocks, pull or push wagons, throw balls, or pedal tricycles with little prodding from an adult.

However, ways to use equipment may need to be modeled or demonstrated. Safety rules will need to be established and enforced. Assistance may need to be given to a child wishing to try a new skill such as hanging from a bar a few inches beyond reach. Encouragement to try a new activity or a compliment for a good try or for the achievement of a new level of skill may be needed.

## Dance

TYPES OF DANCE. Dance for young children may be divided into two types: *creative movement*, which is related to ballet, and *folk dancing*. The two bear much the same relationship to each other that visual art does to crafts. In movement, the dancer is free to express feelings and thoughts, whereas in folk dancing the dancer performs the prescribed steps. Yet both may claim a legitimate place in the early years.

Although both kinds of dance should be experienced by young children, movement is particularly important. Movement requires intense involvement of body and mind. It increases awareness of self and of others and of the form and motion of things in the environment. At one and the same time, movement is an individual and a group activity; individuals respond to the words of the teacher or to music in their own ways, yet they are in the company of and may interact with others.

The receptive experiences which form the basis for expressive movement encompass virtually all the sensory experiences in life. The teacher's role is to raise these experiences to awareness by asking children to express their perceptions both verbally and motorically.

PROVIDING DANCE EXPERIENCES. Experiences with creative movement will usually be instigated by the teacher as a group activity, but opportunities may be provided for children to continue to explore movement as individuals or in small groups. If there is no room for a free movement area in the classroom, the record player might be taken outside for this purpose.

Folk dancing, which for younger children takes the form of singing games, is a social experience. In order to participate, children are expected to follow specified patterns of behavior—the rules. Some games are useful to promote skill in distinguishing between left and right and in using one side of the body and then the other. Folk dancing may aid in the development of gross motor coordination.

PROVIDING DANCE VOCABULARY.    Dimondstein (1974) states that the components of movement are space, time, and force. The teacher should direct children to explore the dimensions of each of these. The following outline indicates some concepts associated with each dimension:

### SPACE

Direction—backward, forward, diagonally, through
Level—high, low, middle
Range—size, shape

### TIME

Rhythm—pulse, beat, stress
Pace—mood, steady, changing
Tempo—fast, slow, moderate

### FORCE

Tension—resistance to pull of gravity or momentum
Balance—extending arms or legs, reaching, hopping
Dynamics—heavy, light, stronger, relaxed, fast, slow

While teachers direct movement through descriptive words and music, they should avoid modeling or giving precise how-to directions. For true artistic expression, the dancers must be encouraged to make their own interpretations and responses. Group expression may evolve from children's agreeing to use similar motions as part of their interpretation.

Folk dancing, on the other hand, requires direct teaching and modeling. The steps and motions of each dance have been handed down from generation to generation and can be transmitted only in this way.

ENCOURAGING EFFORTS.    As suggested earlier, generalized praise is seldom helpful, whereas commenting approvingly on specific actions gives useful feedback. As children participate in movement activities, the teacher should make specific comments such as ''John, you're taking slow heavy steps; you make me think of an elephant,'' when the suggestion was to think of something heavy and walk as heavily as it might move.

Older children may wish to present their interpretation of a poem or a piece of music in dance or mime, and arrangements for such a performance may be made. Such occasions provide an incentive for improvement but should not be an end in themselves.

## Evaluating Work in Movement and Dance

The teacher may evaluate progress by observing children and making anecdotal records over time or by using skill checklists on which initial ratings of competence and subsequent ratings over time are noted. The children's own feelings about increased competence—what they could do at the beginning of the year and what they can do now—may be elicited in conversation.

Progress in movement is measured both in terms of increased physical fitness and skill in basic movements. Strength, endurance, agility, flexibility, power, speed, balance, and coordination are components of physical fitness (Schurr, 1967). The basic movements, as we noted earlier, include: the locomotor skills—walking, jumping, leaping, sliding, running, hopping, skipping; the nonlocomotor skills—twisting, stretching, swinging, pushing, falling, turning, bending, lifting, and pulling; and manipulative skills, involving prehension, dexterity, and coordination (Schurr, 1967; Flinchum, 1975). In general, both the physical fitness components and the basic movement skills may be evaluated by watching children in active play. In some instances, however, teachers may need to ask a child to perform a task that requires the use of specific skills and attributes. For example, a child might be asked to throw a ball. By observing how the ball is thrown, the teacher could then rate the child's balance, prehension, flexibility, power, and coordination.

Progress in creative movement and dance is marked by factors such as greater expressiveness of movements, increased variety of movements, and additional ease in participation in movement as well as by the physical components mentioned above. In folk dancing, the ability to distinguish right from left and to synchronize movements with other dancers and with the music, in addition to basic locomotor skills, are marks of improved competence.

## Materials for Movement and Dance

Equipment and materials for children's play both indoors and outdoors should be selected with an eye toward the basic movements that will be involved when children play on the equipment or with the materials. Some of the following materials provide the opportunity to use several of the basic movements, while others are more limited. When choices are made, it is wise to choose those materials first which provide for the most varied opportunities.

Climbers—jungle gyms, climbing ropes, cargo nets, climbing stairs, rocking-boat stairs, ladders

Building materials—large hollow blocks, cardboard packing cartons, movable planks, sawhorses, milk cartons and carriers

Wheel toys—wagons, tricycles, ride-on trucks

Balls—large rubber balls, yarn balls, plastic whiffle balls of different sizes, balloons, beach balls, a small plastic bat

Walking beams—balance boards (2-by-4-inches by 10 feet), planks and trestles

Horizontal bars

Tunnels

Tires of various sizes

Sandbox—shovels, pails, plastic detergent or bleach bottles shaped into scoops, toy dump trucks, steam shovels

Ropes and hoops—hula hoops, jump ropes

Rhythm instruments—drums, tambourines, maracas

Phonograph and records

Parachute, scarves

Trampoline—large inner tube covered tightly with canvas, an innerspring mattress, tumbling mats

## Activities for Instruction in Movement and Dance

## PROMOTING PHYSICAL FITNESS

1. **Activity:**   Exercise session (PP–P)

*Materials:*   Sufficient space so that all may move without interfering with one another.

*Procedure:*   Have children stand in a semicircle facing you. Direct them to stretch out their arms full length to their sides making sure they do not touch their neighbors. Tell the children to reach up over their heads, out to the sides, down to the floor, out to the front, and out to the back, demonstrating as you speak. Having defined their own space, the children should now be ready to follow you in a series of exercises such as the following (see Block, 1977 for more exercises):

**tiptoe:**   Move slowly up on the toes with arms extended to the sides for balance and slowly lower the heels to the floor. Do this about ten times. Or have children alternate feet raising one foot at a time to the toe while the other remains flat.

**jumping jack:**   Move arms up to clap overhead while jumping from feet together to feet spread apart. Lowering hands, jump feet back together. Repeat ten times.

**climb the fireman's pole:**   Take a semisquatting position. Move arms upward as if climbing a pole and bring body up with them until standing on tiptoes. Then climb back down. Repeat five times.

**shoulder lift:**   Sit cross-legged on the floor with back straight. Lift shoulders up and forward and then up and back. Alternate lifting one shoulder at a time. May be done to rhythm—drum beat or recording.

**angry cat:**   Start on hands and knees. Look toward tummy. Pull in stomach and arch back to the count of five and relax to the count of five. Repeat seven times.

*Suggestions and Variations:*   Children may enjoy yoga exercises which imitate animals, for example: *The Cat* (on hands and knees, arch back, stretch legs); *The Bird* (on tiptoes, stretch arms in back, spread fingers); *The Rabbit* (kneel on floor, head touching floor in front of knees, arms reaching back through legs to grasp ankles); *The Stork* (stand on one leg with other leg bent behind, hold hands together as in prayer); or *The Fish* (lie prone on floor with hands flat on floor under shoulders, push head and shoulders up until arms are straight and head tipped back, open and close lips to imitate fish).

2. **Activity:**    Stunts—animals (PP-P)

*Materials:*    Space enough for children to move without interfering with one another.
*Procedure:*    Gather children in a circle at arms length from each other. Talk about different animals they might see, both domestic and zoo animals, or make up a story in which different animals appear. Then, taking each animal in turn, talk about how they move. Demonstrate, and have children imitate your actions. Both you and the children should use imagination with this activity. The following ideas may be helpful:
**puppy dog run:**    Bending so that hands are on the floor about two feet in front of feet, walk or run on all fours.
**elephant walk:**    With hands clasped together in front to simulate the elephant's trunk, bend forward and walk stiff-legged, swaying the "trunk" and head from side to side.
**duck walk:**    Put hands on hips and bend knees slightly. Waddle and quack, moving "wings" (elbows) back and forth.
**snake crawl:**    Lie prone with weight on elbows and lower arms. Crawl forward, dragging legs, and using the forearm to pull the weight. Hiss, curl up, and lunge to catch a frog.
**frog leap:**    Bend to an almost squatting position with hands on floor between the feet. Put hands forward on floor and jump feet to the outside of the hands. Add sound effects—"ribbit, ribbit".
*Suggestions and Variations:*    Saint Saëns' *Carnival of Animals* may provide inspiration and rhythm for imitating animals.

3. **Activity:**    Partner stunts (K-P)

*Materials:*    Space enough for free movement.
*Procedure:*    Match children in pairs by size, weight, and apparent strength. Teach children some stunts they can do cooperatively by demonstrating and by helping children move into the right positions.
**wheelbarrow:**    Have one child bend at the waist and put hands on the floor. Have a second child step between the feet of the first child and, grasping the ankles, lift the legs. Both walk forward, one on hands and the other on feet. They can then exchange places.
**Chinese get-up:**    Have children sit back to back with knees drawn up and feet flat on the floor. Have them hook elbows together. Children should push their feet on the floor and their backs against each other until they are standing without having unhooked their elbows.

**leap-frog:** This may be done with more than two children. All but one of the children kneel on the floor with their heads tucked between their knees and arms wrapped around to curl up small like round stones. The standing child places his or her hands on the back of each "stone" and, spreading legs, leaps over each. When finished, that child becomes a "stone" and the last child in line leaps over each stone. Continue until all have had a chance to leap over the "stones."

*Suggestions and Variations:*    These, and all stunts, need to be supervised carefully to prevent injury, particularly when first taught. For example, young children will need to be reminded to keep their heads down when playing leap frog.

## IMPROVING EYE-HAND COORDINATION

1. **Activity:**    Hula hoops (PP–P)

*Materials:*    One hula hoop for each child.
*Procedure:*    Have children form a circle, allowing plenty of space between children. Ask children to move around the circle trying to keep their hoops rolling. Then ask them to take partners and stand opposite each other, three to four feet apart. One child lays the hoop down in back of him or her. The remaining hoop is rolled back and forth between them. When the partners can do this without letting the hoop fall, have them try two hoops; each rolling the hoop at the same time and trying to catch the partner's hoop before it falls.
*Suggestions and Variations:*    The hoops may be laid flat and the children directed to walk around their hoops, to walk around the hoop with one foot inside and the other out, or to jump in and out of the hoop. Children may be asked to hold hoops vertically for other children to step through or jump through. In addition, hula hoops may be used in the traditional way, keeping them moving around by using the hips (not for younger children generally).

2. **Activity:**    Rolly-polly (K–P)

*Materials:*    A smooth, hard surface marked off in two rows of two-foot squares. Four, six, or eight squares may be used. Each square is marked with a number. A rubber ball such as a tennis ball with a good bounce.
*Procedure:*    Two or more children may play. Each child in turn bounces the ball in each square while stepping with one foot in that square. Having done that successfully, the child rolls the ball to the second square, bounces it twice, and then bounces it twice in each succeeding square. The ball is then rolled to the third square. The child steps quickly in square one, square two, and square three and stoops to catch the ball in that square. The child

bounces the ball three times in square three and in each successive square. The ball is then rolled to the fourth square and so on until the child misses. A miss is failing to catch the ball in the proper square, failing to catch a bounce, stepping on a line, or putting both feet at once in the same square. You can make the game more difficult by having children clap or stamp their foot before catching the ball or by having them hop on one foot.

*Suggestions and Variations:*   When introducing this game, use four squares. Practice in bouncing and catching balls will be needed before this game can be taught.

3. **Activity:**   Target practice (PP-P)

*Materials:*   Bean bags, yarn balls, plastic rings about three inches in diameter, boxes, coffee cans; plastic bottles weighted with sand and having long, narrow necks. A piece of plywood or strong cardboard with an easel back may be used as a target. The target may be about three feet tall and two to three feet wide with a hole cut near the center of the board. The board may be shaped and painted in some amusing form, such as that of a clown with an open mouth. The open mouth is the target.

*Procedure:*   Set up targets and provide children with objects to throw at or into the targets. As children succeed in hitting the targets, have them move further away from the targets. Each child may be given three projectiles or three tries.

**containers and projectiles:**   Provide boxes or coffee cans in three sizes and yarn balls or beanbags. Have children toss the balls or beanbags into the largest container, then the middle-sized one, and finally the smallest one.

**rings and bottles:**   Set plastic bottles in a row and have children toss rings over the necks of the bottles. A variation is to turn a chair upside down and throw rings over the legs of the chair.

*Suggestions and Variations:*   Children may enjoy these activities as individuals, in pairs, or in groups.

## IMPROVING LOCOMOTOR MOVEMENTS

1. **Activity:**   Running and chasing games (PP-K-P)

*Materials:*   Space for a circle of children which allows one or two children to run around the outside without bumping into anything.

*Procedure:*   Gather children into a circle and have them hold each other's hands. Check to see if children know the rules of the game. If necessary, review the rules and demonstrate how to play. Select a child to be "it."

**Tom, Tom run for your supper:**   "It" stands behind two children and taps both of them saying, "Tom, Tom run for your supper." The two children tapped run around the circle in opposite directions. The first child back to tap "it" on the arm becomes the new "it." The other children resume places in the circle and "it" selects two other children. Because this requires that children go in opposite directions, it may be difficult for younger children (Kamii, 1980).

**duck, duck, goose:**   "It" walks around the outside of the circle lightly tapping each child and saying, "Duck." "It" chooses a child to chase him or her by saying, "Goose."

*Suggestions and Variations:*   These are common folkgames usually known to one or more children in a group of five-year-olds. Children who know the game can help to teach it to others. Teachers playing the game with the children can help to ensure that each child has a chance to be "it."

2. **Activity:**   Obstacle relay (K–PP)

*Materials:*   A starting line and a goal line ten to thirty feet apart; tires, boxes, rubber cones (used to mark traffic hazards), or other objects which may be walked around, walked over, or jumped over.

*Procedure:*   Divide the children into two teams and put them in line behind the starting line. After arranging objects between the starting and goal lines, show children the way they are to go to reach the goal line. For example, three tires may be placed about two feet apart in a line between the starting line and the goal line. Instruct children to go to the right of the first tire, to the left of the second tire, and to the right of the third tire; they can then proceed to the goal line and return to the starting line in the same fashion. After returning, children touch the hand of the next child in line and go to the end of their team's line as the next child goes to the goal line and back in the same fashion. The winning team is the one whose last member first touches the hand of the first team-member.

*Suggestions and Variations:*   You might ask children to jump over a single tire, leapfrog over a cone, climb a set of movable steps, or climb over a sawhorse or any other obstacle requiring a different movement to get by it.


## DEVELOPING SELF-EXPRESSION
## IN CREATIVE MOVEMENT AND DANCE

1. **Activity:**   Body parts. (PP–P)

*Materials:*   A gymnasium or other large space; comfortable clothes which allow movement, for example, leotards or shorts, T-shirts, and bare feet or soft rubber-soled shoes. A large floor-level mirror and a drum or other percussion instrument are desirable.

*Procedure:*   Gather children in front of you and have them stand far enough apart so that they do not touch each other. Ask children to move their whole bodies in a variety of ways; for example, they can shake, stretch, bend, twist, swing, or sway. Selecting one part of the body at a time, ask children to move it in the various ways mentioned. For example: "Stretch one arm out from your body." "Shake your arm fast; slow." "Twist your arm into different shapes." Encourage children to watch themselves in the mirror if one is available. Children may be asked to move around the room while moving the specified body part—arm, leg, shoulders, or head—in some way.

*Suggestions and Variations:*   Have children pair off. Tell them to pretend they are looking in a mirror and to do a mirror imitation of each other's movements. After giving directions several times, ask children to choose just one body part to move in various ways. A drum may be used to indicate when to start and stop. Children should move as long as they hear the drum and stop when it stops. When they stop, they can either hold their position or sink to the floor completely relaxed.

2. **Activity:**   Space (PP–P)

*Materials:*   As in "Body Parts."

*Procedure:*   Start by asking children to find "their own space." This is a place where even with outstretched arms, they do not touch anyone else. Then ask children to explore their space without moving from where they are: "Down to the floor; up as high as you can reach; over to the side; to the front; to the back." While remaining in the same spot, children may be asked to "Make yourself as small as you can," "Make yourself as big as you can," or "Take up all your space."

You might ask children to move around the room remembering to keep their own space. Perhaps they might let one part of their bodies lead them around the room; or move very slowly or very rapidly; or change directions; or move close to the floor, at the middle level, or as high as they can. They might also make shapes with their bodies.

*Suggestions and Variations:*   Again, use the drum beat to indicate starting and stopping times as well as fast and slow movements. Your voice commenting on what you see and giving new directions keeps the children moving and concentrating on what they are doing. Call attention to what different children are doing, for example, "Look at the shape Sidney is making." "Marion is moving close to the floor."

3. **Activity:**   Force (K–P)

*Materials:*   As in the first two activities.

*Procedure:*   After children have defined their own space, have them run around the room as you beat the drum rapidly and stop quickly when you

stop. Ask them to drop to the floor and sit cross-legged. Elicit ideas from them
of things that are sharp and of things that are smooth.

Ask them to show you *sharp* movements and *smooth* movements. Having all
the children rise to their feet, direct them to move around the room making
sharp movements and then smooth movements. Follow the same sequence
with *strong* and *light* and with *tense* and *loose.*

*Suggestions and Variations:*    Props might be used to evoke a mental
image and feeling; for example, for *tense* and *loose,* a stiff doll and a limp rag
doll might be used and children asked to imitate the movements each would
make.

4. **Activity:**   Time (PP–P)

   *Materials:*   Records or a drum.

   *Procedure:*   Have children define their space and then have them move
   around the room at different speeds: fast, slow, or moderate. "Try to think of
   many different ways of moving"; "Listen to the drumbeat (or music) and let
   it tell you whether to move fast or slow"; "Move slowly and then faster and
   faster and faster and stop!" are some directions you might give.

   *Suggestions and Variations:*   Combine space, time, and force in the
   directions you give. Start with simple movements done for a rather short time
   and gradually increase the complexity and the amount of time as children
   move more freely and easily. A sharp rap on the drum can signal "stop!"

5. **Activity:**   Movement to music (PP–P)

   *Materials:*   Record player; selection of records including music that is fast
   and even (running), slow and even (walking), accented and even (marching),
   and uneven (galloping; skipping); lengths of nylon rope—seven feet for
   children, nine feet for adults; large chiffon scarves.

   *Procedure:*   Give children freedom to respond to music as they wish. At
   first, do not give children ropes or scarves; let them use just their bodies.
   Children may need some guidance to respond appropriately to rhythm,
   tempo, and mood of the music. Ask questions such as "Is the music fast or
   slow?" "Is the music high or low?" "Does the music sound like marching or
   skipping?" "Oh, it changed there. Did you hear that?"

   *Suggestions and Variations:*   Nylon ropes may be used to swing, twirl,
   skip with, or to draw a circle around each child. For the latter, have children
   hold ends of the rope in each hand and drop it in back of them. Stooping, the
   child may put the two ends in front and arrange a good circle. Scarves may be
   used by children to trail in the breeze as they run, to lift high to the sky and
   down to the ground, to wrap around themselves, or to become wings.

6. **Activity:**    Folk dance (PP-P)

*Materials:*    Recorded music, piano or guitar if desired. For the youngest children folk dancing usually consists of singing games such as "Ring-around-the Rosy," "Here We Go Looby Loo," "Doing the Hokey-Pokey," "A-Tisket A-Tasket," "Little Sally Walker," "London Bridge," "The Farmer in the Dell." Record albums and books which include these and others are easily found.

Older children may enjoy learning folk dances such as *Chiapanecas (The Mexican Hat Dance)*, the *hora, varsuvienne, polkas,* or the *Virginia Reel.*

*Procedure:*    Select the dance to be taught on the basis of your observations of children's ability to follow directions and respond to rhythm. Gather children in a line or semicircle so that you are all facing the same direction. Distribute older children or adults who know the dance among the children. Demonstrate steps for children to imitate.

When children have mastered the basic steps, put on the music. Step, evaluate, and reteach as necessary.

*Suggestions and Variations:*    The teacher should be aware of less popular and less coordinated children, making sure they are frequently chosen in games such as "Little Sally Walker" and "The Farmer in the Dell" and that they tactfully and discreetly are given help to master the steps. Some may prefer to play rhythm instruments for dancing. If you do not have a repertoire of dances, arrange for a physical education teacher or a dancer to teach some simple dances to you and others on the staff.

## DEVELOPING AESTHETIC
## APPRECIATION OF THE DANCE

1. **Activity:**    Visit from dancers (PP-P)

*Materials:*    Gym or other large space where the dancer and children may work.

*Procedure:*    Ask a dancer to visit the class and to demonstrate steps for the children. The dancer may be a ballet dancer, a mime artist, or one having a specialty such as Spanish dancing. The visit will be more meaningful if the dancer also works with the class, helping them to improve their dancing.

Assemble children to watch the dancer or to dance with him or her if this has been arranged.

*Suggestions and Variations:*    See suggestions in sections on art and music for similar activities.

Take the class or a group of children to see a ballet, mime show, or dance presentation.

2. **Activity:**    Awareness of movement (PP–P)

*Materials:*    Out of doors. Films.

*Procedure:*    Call attention to the way trees move or the way wind or different animals move. Time-lapse movies of plants growing may be used to illustrate slow movement in nature. Call attention to the way dancers move and the moods they express. For example: "Chrissy makes me think she's happy because she is whirling so lightly; Jon looks angry when he stomps his feet and shakes his fist."

*Suggestions and Variations:*    Have some children dance and ask other children to comment on the moods expressed.

After showing a time-lapse movie of plants, have children pretend they are seeds planted in the warm damp earth which are starting to grow.

## CHILDREN AND DRAMA

Skills in drama depend on children's abilities to organize and sequence, to take on roles, and to use language. Since language development is discussed in detail in the chapter on Language Arts (page 180), only role playing, sequencing, and organizing will be discussed here.

Children first begin to "pretend" at around age two. These first pretendings are often reruns of their own actions: they pretend to eat when they are not eating, they pretend to cry when they are not crying, or they pretend to be asleep when they are not sleeping. This is soon followed and combined with projection of these actions onto other objects: the doll eats, the doll cries, and the stuffed dog sleeps. Children also begin to use objects to stand for other objects which they do not resemble: a plain block is called a "car" or a "cup" (Hunt, 1961).

Finally, children begin to pretend that they are someone else. They are a mother or a father, the baby or the sister, a fireman or a garbage collector. Such role taking usually appears by age three-and-one-half or four.

The organization of this role-playing behavior into a coherent flow of events is a difficult task for young children. Typically, three- and four-year-olds playing together go about their role playing without much regard for the actions of the other children. They play in the same physical space, but not really together. Later, usually during the fourth year, children begin to coordinate roles. They are able to do this by talking over plans with each other. "You go to the store, and while you're gone I'll pack for the picnic." "You feed the baby while I fix dinner for us." "I'll mop the floor while you're out washing the windows so you won't walk all over it." This type of organization requires the ability to sequence and coordinate actions as well as to use and understand language.

In this type of role play, children perform the actions and say the words they have seen and heard, recombining these in their own unique ways. The roles are, then, their own creations, not reproductions of roles created by a story writer or a film maker. Indeed, children are not yet able to play out such unfamiliar roles. It is only in the primary grades that children should be asked to dramatize roles and events that are unfamiliar to them.

## GOAL FOR INSTRUCTION
## IN DRAMA

The verbalization of thoughts and feelings and the reliving of experiences are early goals for dramatic play. Later, goals for dramatic play include:

1. The ability to plan a sequence of actions.
2. The ability to assume a role in agreement with others.
3. The ability to use a variety of props and costumes with imagination.

Dramatic play builds on the children's own experiences and imagination. Dramatizing a story calls for children to recreate someone else's ideas. Such dramatization calls for other competencies, for example, assuming the role of a character in the story, recalling the sequence of actions in the story, and relating the actions of the character being played to those of other characters in the story. Guidance and activities which will lead to the development of these competencies are discussed later in this chapter.

As a result of guided experiences as watchers (as well as participants) of dramatic activities, children will hopefully gain a sense of story continuity and drama, learn to distinguish between fantasy and reality, and develop a growing sense of discrimination in choosing dramatic presentations to watch.

## METHODS AND ACTIVITIES
## FOR INSTRUCTIONS IN DRAMA

### Guiding Work in Drama

TYPES OF DRAMA.    There are three forms of drama for the early years: *dramatic play* or *role playing, creative dramatics,* and *formal drama* Dramatic play is a typical activity of young children which serves important functions in their social, emotional, and cognitive development (Bruner, 1981). At school, it will be found not only in the dramatic play area but wherever children play—the block area, the playground, and so on. Whenever one child says to another, ''You be the mother and I'll be the baby'' or ''You be the garage man and I'll be the lady who needs gas'' or ''You be Darth Vader and I'll be Luke Skywalker'' (or whoever the current heroes are), dramatic play starts.

Creative dramatics is a conscious and usually teacher-directed effort to retell a story in dramatic form. The story may be one which has been read and reread, or it may be one children have made up. In creative dramatics, the children may assume the roles or they may use puppets. Creative dramatics is particularly valuable in encouraging and extending oral language.

Dramatic play is common to all young children.

Formal drama is the presentation of a play using a script. The author's lines are to be spoken as directed in the script. As a form of dramatic expression for young children, it has little place in the classroom. Filmed or live drama, however, may be used for instruction and entertainment. The wise teacher will use films and television productions which dramatize stories from folk literature or present concepts in imaginative and dramatic ways, capitalizing on children's tendency to be captivated by such presentations.

THE DRAMATIC PLAY CENTER.    An area of the room should be designated for dramatic play. As children have such experiences as staying in a hospital, making a trip to the fire station, or visiting a parent's place of business, props in the dramatic play area could be changed to reflect the new experience. The basic equipment of this center may include child-size models of kitchen, dining-room, living-room, and bedroom furnishings. When such furnishings are chosen, models which are not realistically detailed offer more versatility and invite the children to use their imagination.

However, the addition of "real" things—a telephone, clock, foods—leads to the development of other concepts. For example, real fruit and vegetables have varying weights, a feature lacking in plastic or wax models, and they change over time. Children may learn to cut them up and serve them for the meals that are so often a part of dramatic play.

In the dramatic play center, the backs of shelf units may form the walls. On one of these walls, a picture of a landscape may be taped. Framed with strips of paper and draped with fabric, the picture simulates a window. When the center is used as a store or post office instead of a home, the units may be turned around to provide shelving.

With rearrangement of furniture and the addition of props, such a center may become, in turn, a home, a doctor's office, a store, a fire station, a bank, or an airport. If it is possible to retain an area as a home and add another area, the play is enriched and allows more children to become involved as some family member goes from home to work or whatever activity is suggested by children.

Racks, hooks, and shelves for various kinds of men's and women's clothes, including uniforms, shoes, hats, trousers, shirts, and party clothes, help to keep the clothing in order and well-displayed. Dolls and doll clothing are ever-popular.

The source material for dramatic expression is found in children's experiences. When children are involved in dramatic play, very little direct guidance may be needed. Occasionally, the teacher enters into the play with a comment or question which may add a new dimension. For example, seeing a group of children playing train, she may join the play. Buying a ticket, walking down the aisle, and taking a seat on the imaginary train, she may inquire about a dining car. If the children had not thought of this and are receptive, the play may be interrupted long enough to add the necessary equipment, a dining car steward, and waiters. As the play resumes with the additional children in the new roles, the teacher quietly leaves the scene to work with other children.

USING LITERATURE FOR CREATIVE DRAMATICS.   Stories, poems, and nursery rhymes provide material for creative dramatics. It is easier to guide the dramatization of a story if it is told rather than read. Children, too, should be encouraged to retell a story they have read or heard. The recall and relating of the events of a story in sequence must occur before it can be dramatized. The retelling of a story and the succeeding dramatization is valuable not only as artistic expression but as an aid to developing language competence. A flannel board and appropriate felt figures can aid practice.

ENCOURAGING EFFORTS.   The teacher's interest in dramatic play, shown by adding props or entering the play as suggested above, encourages participation and enriches the experience.

In creative dramatics, specific approving comments on children's performances will encourage efforts. If children show sustained involvement with dramatizing a story, they may wish to produce it for an audience. The addition of scenery, musical settings, and costumes will enrich the production and involve children with varying interests and talents.

EVALUATING THE WORK.   The younger child shows egocentricity in dramatic play. As children develop competence, they become aware of their own roles in relation to others and work together more cooperatively, building on each other's ideas. The scenes they play become more coherent; a logical sequence of events and a recognizable story line appear. They talk it out first and then play out what they have agreed on.

The same developmental trend appears in creative dramatics. Observation and anecdotal records provide material for assessing progress. An integral part of dramatizing stories is the children's evaluation of their own work. The teacher guides this evaluation by asking questions about the believability of the characterizations and the actions taken.

As in all expressive art for the early years, the process is of utmost importance. Yet it is the product which is the ultimate evaluation of the work. A sensitive teacher recognizes that a product which is the norm for one child may represent a great achievement for another. The speaking of a single line by a nonverbal child may give a teacher as much or more satisfaction as an acceptable performance in a major role by a verbal child.

### Activities for Instruction in Drama

## DEVELOPING SELF-EXPRESSION
## THROUGH DRAMA

1. **Activity:**   Doctor's office dramatic play (PP–K)

   *Materials:*   Chairs, tables, magazines, nurses' and doctors' uniforms and caps, flashlights, tongue depressors, soap, water, paper towels, thermometer, stethoscope, cot, sheets, band-aids, cotton, hypodermic syringes (minus the needle). A play doctor's kit will provide models of some of these things, but usually not enough for good dramatic play.
   *Procedure:*   Show children materials, which are introduced to dramatic play area. Talk about their experiences with doctors. Provide labels and demonstrate use of things such as a stethoscope and hypodermic syringe. Recall roles and activities of receptionist, nurse, doctor, and patients. Help children decide who will play each role. After children are involved, intervene, when ased, in order to enrich the play or to prevent injury.
   *Suggestions and Variations:*   The skill of knowing when to intervene and when not to is developed through sensitive observation and practice. The best single sign may be level of involvement. If it is deep and children are working well together, do not intervene. If involvement is light, children are beginning to quarrel, or an objectionable practice creeps in, intervene tactfully.

2. **Activity:**   Puppets (PP–P)

   *Materials:*   Puppets (see Visual Arts, page 134, for a variety of ways to make puppets); puppet stage (may be made from a packing case); material for making scenery.
   *Procedure:*   In dramatic play, gather children about you and introduce

the puppet by name as you would a guest. As the puppet speaks to the children and asks questions, the children will respond to the puppet as if it were a real person. The teacher also should converse with the puppet. When children show signs of readiness to use puppets, give puppets to them and help children think of things the puppet could do (wave bye, jump up and down, walk, shake its head "no," turn around, talk, and so on). Leave puppets on a shelf available to the children for their independent dramatic play. In creative dramatics using puppets, select a favorite story or poem. Decisions children will need to make include:

> Characters needed
> Sequence of events
> Scenery needed

Children may need assistance from time to time as they develop the puppet play. To the extent of their ability to do so, they should be encouraged to work independently.

**Suggestions and Variations:** Make a mock television set from a packing box. A hole the size and shape of a television screen may be cut and covered with clear plastic if desired. Paint on knobs and dials. A sequence of scenes may be drawn on long sheets of paper and rolled from side to side using dowels pasted on either end of the paper. As a story is read or told, the picture illustrating each event is shown on the screen. Puppets may be used instead of the drawings.

3. **Activity:** Creative dramatics (PP–P)

**Materials:** A story or poem which has a clear sequence of events, action, and simple dialogue. Props, scenery, and costumes enrich creative dramatics but are not essential.

**Procedure:** Guide the children's recall of the sequence of events or episodes. Name the characters which appear in each episode and the actions that occur. Review the content of the dialogue for each episode Exact words and the form the action takes are the prerogatives of the children as they set out the story. For example, the first two episodes of *The Three Bears* may be plotted as follows:

> Episode 1. Characters: The three bears.
> Actions: Sit down to breakfast, taste porridge, go for a walk.
> Dialogue: Mother tells when breakfast is ready; Baby says the porridge is too hot; Father suggests they go for a walk.
> Episode 2. Character: Goldilocks.
> Actions: Walks in woods, sings, sees house, enters, sees porridge, tastes porridge in each bowl, finishes porridge in one.
> Dialogue: Talks about what she sees, the temperature of each bowl.

This planning should be elicited from the children through skillful questioning. Once the story has been recalled and the action plotted, the cast of characters is selected. Following the selection, children should be called by the names of the character they will play. Before action is started, a few more decisions must be made. The locations of the scenes and the entrances of the characters are determined. When all plans are made, children enact the story with as little direct guidance as possible. After finishing, hold an evaluation session. Questions such as "Did Darryl really sound gruff like Father Bear?" "Do you think the way Baby Bear walks should be different from Father Bear?" "How can we make it better?" should be asked. Children should replay the story using the suggestions made.

*Suggestions and Variations:* Activity cards suggesting that children make a play or puppet show may be placed next to a display of a favorite book, appropriate props, and costumes. This technique for initiating creative dramatics would not be appropriate for children younger than primary age. A nursery rhyme which involves action may be used with the youngest children. For example, provide a candlestick and have each child jump over it as other children recite "Jack be nimble; Jack be quick. Jack jump over the candlestick." Allow children to make their own variations. For example, several small boys added several mice and a cat to their dramatization of *Hickory, Dickory, Dock.*

A story may be read and as a character, for example, a fox, is introduced, the teacher interrupts the story, looks at the children and asks if there are any "foxes" in the room. A child who volunteers is brought up front and assumes the role. As the story continues, the teacher turns to the player and repeats what the character is doing, if necessary, to encourage the child to perform the action. Characters are added as the story continues. This is a very effective method with a "new" class when the story is read dramatically and with enthusiasm.

# DEVELOPING AESTHETIC
# APPRECIATION OF DRAMA

1. **Activity:**   Television (PP–P)

   *Materials:*   Television set, cushion or rugs to sit on while watching.
   *Procedure:*   Select good quality programs which deal with human relationships. For example, *Mr. Rogers' Neighborhood* invites viewers to become part of the story and deals with feelings and human relationships. The puppets used in *Mr. Rogers' Neighborhood* help to distinguish between fantasy and reality. After viewing, elicit children's reactions to the programs, conversing with them about the events and characters.
   *Suggestions and Variations:*   Converse with children about home television watching. Solicit parents' cooperation in reducing the amount of

live and cartoon programs children watch which involve violence. When special programs for children are scheduled for early evening, send notes home with the children reminding parents of these programs.

## 2. Activity:   Attending a dramatic production (PP–P)

**Procedure:**   Arrange a field trip to see a dramatic production, or arrange for the children to watch a play or puppet show that older students in the school may be putting on. With young preprimary and kindergarten children, it is often helpful to familiarize them with the story line and characters before they attend the production. They delight in being able to recognize characters and predict what is going to happen next. Primary children can appreciate productions without having prior knowledge of the story line or characters.

**Suggestions and Variations:**   Many theater groups have special productions for children. Many puppet groups will come to the school to give a production.

Do not overlook the possibility of asking students from nearby colleges to come perform for the children. If they are enrolled in puppetry, creative dramatics, or children's theater classes, they are usually required to become involved in a certain number of performances as projects. If they know you are interested in having them come, they are often delighted to do so.

Remember that young children (under five) think that puppets are real. If the puppets pose questions, or find themselves in a problem-solving situation of which the audience has knowledge that would help solve it, young children often talk to the puppets to answer their questions or give them information. Children who respond in this way are not being "naughty" or "rude"; they are involved. This behavior does present some problems if all the children from a school are brought together in one room for the performance and there is a wide age range among the children attending. Older children can be quiet during the performance and should be asked to do so. But this is difficult to enforce if younger children who are talking are present. Perhaps the best solution is to try to arrange a separate performance for the younger children. Many children's theater groups are very sensitive to the way young children respond and have developed productions that actively seek to involve children both verbally and physically in the puppet plays.

*References for Teachers*

## Music

BAILEY, E.   *Discovering Music with Young Children.* New York: Philosophical Library, 1958.

BAYLESS, K., and RAMSEY, M. E.   *Music: A Way of Life for the Young Child.* St. Louis, Mo.: C. V. Mosby, 1978.

DAVIDSON, L.   The acquisition of song, *Project Zero.* Cambridge, Mass: Harvard University, 1979.

HAINES, B. J. E. and GERBER, L. L.    *Leading Young Children to Music.* Columbus, Ohio: Chas. E. Merrill, 1980.

HAWKINSON, J. and FAULHABER, M.    *Music and Instruments for Children to Make.* Chicago: Albert Whitman & Co., 1970.

McDONALD, D. J.    *Music in Our Lives: The Early Years.* Washington D. C.: National Association for the Education of Young Children, 1979.

SHEEY, E.    *Children Discover Music and Dance.* New York: Teachers College Press, 1968.

SMITH, R. B.    *Music in the Child's Education.* New York: Ronald Press, 1970.

WENDRICH, K.    The imitation of pitch in infants. *Infant Behavior and Development* 2 (1979): 93–99.

WISEMAN, A.    *Making Musical Things.* New York: Scribner's, 1979.

## Movement and Dance

BLOCK, S. E.    *Me and I'm Great: Physical Education for Children Three through Eight.* Minneapolis, Minn.: Burgess, 1977.

CARR, P.    *Be a Frog, a Bird, or a Tree.* Garden City, N.Y.: Doubleday, 1973.

CHERRY, C.    *Creative Movement for the Developing Child.* Belmont, Calif: Fearon, 1971.

DIAMONDSTEIN, G.    *Exploring the Arts with Children.* New York: Macmillan, 1974.

FLINCHUM, B. M.    *Motor Development in Early Childhood.* St. Louis, Mo.: C. V. Mosby, 1975.

FROST, J. L., and KLEIN, B. L.    *Children's Play and Playgrounds.* Boston: Allyn and Bacon, 1979.

HALLAHAN, D. P., and CRUICKSHANK, W. M.    *Psychoeducational Foundations of Learning Disabilities.* Englewood Cliffs, N.J.: Prentice-Hall, 1973.

JOYCE. M.    *First Steps in Teaching Creative Dance.* Palo Alto, Calif: Mayfield Publishing Company, 1973.

KAMII, C.    *Group Games in Early Education.* Washington, D.C.: National Associaton for the Education of Young Children, 1980.

MURPHY, L. B.    *The Widening World of Childhood: Paths Toward Mastery.* New York: Basic Books, 1962.

ROWEN, B.    *Learning Through Movement.* New York: Teachers College Press, 1963.

SCHURR, E. J.    *Movement Experiences for Young Children.* New York: Appleton-Century-Crofts, 1967.

SINCLAIR, C. B.    *Movement of the Young Child Ages Two to Six.* Columbus, Ohio: Chas. E. Merrill, 1973.

STEWART, G. L., and GALLINA, J.    *Playtime Parachute Fun.* Longbranch, N.J.: Kimbo Educational (undated).

STEICHER, M.    Concept learning through movement improvisation: The teacher's role as catalyst. In K. Read, ed., *Ideas that Work with Young Children.* Washington, D. C.: National Association for the Education of Young Children, 1972.

THOMPSON, H.    Physical Growth. In L. Carmichael, ed., *Manual of Child Psychology.* 2nd ed. New York: John Wiley, 1954, 292–334.

WILT, J., and WATSON, J.    *Rhythm and Movement.* Waco, Texas: Creative Resources, 1977.

## Drama

BENDER, J.    Have you ever thought of a prop box? In K. Read, ed., *Ideas that Work with Young Children.* Washington, D. C.: National Association for the Education of Young Children, 1972.

BRUNER, J.    Child's play. In R. D. Strom, ed., *Growing Through Play.* Monterey, Calif: Brooks/Cole, 1981.

# 7
# LANGUAGE
# ARTS

Perhaps nothing is more important to children and adults than the ability to communicate. We communicate in many ways, through music, visual arts, and gesture. However, language is the most direct and most important communication tool. But language, like all forms of communication, is not an end in itself. It derives its importance from social context and purpose. It is the need to give and receive information, to understand and to be understood, that motivates us to learn and to use all forms of language. In this chapter, we discuss (1) the nature of language, (2) how children learn and use language, (3) the language skills appropriate for young children, and (4) activities and materials for use in language instruction.

## THE NATURE OF LANGUAGE

### Language is Abstract

Tracks left by animals in mud or snow, the beep of a car horn, and a periscope above the surface of the water are all symbols. Art forms use symbols, too. In visual arts, materials are used to represent objects. In movement and dance, the body is used as a symbol. Symbols in these cases are not abstract; each bears a direct relationship to what is represented. In addition, in the case of visual arts and movement, the meaning of symbols is not determined by the social group. It can be interpreted differently by individual perceivers so that the meaning derived by one person is not necessarily the meaning derived by another.

Language, on the other hand, makes use of special symbols that bear no physical resemblance to what they represent. Their meanings are socially specified. The social nature of language makes it abstract in the sense that there is nothing in the language itself to indicate its meaning. Language is assigned meaning—it represents meaning. While we would probably be able to determine for ourselves that certain markings indicate the presence of animals, assuming we had some knowledge of animals, we could not determine an object's name merely by looking at it or touching it if someone had not identified its name earlier. Language learning depends on social interaction with mature language users.

An additional level of abstraction is involved in language. Much of what a person knows about language is never directly heard, but is inferred from what is heard. A child learns *more* than simply a collection of specific words and utterances. Abstract rules about language are also constructed as children act on and think about the language they hear. These rules guide a speaker in creating grammatical sentences, even though a sentence uttered may never have been heard before.

Children construct rules that apply to several levels of language structure. For example, they learn how words are combined to make sentences. These are *syntactic rules* and it is knowledge of these that enables children to recognize that "John hit the car" and "The car was hit by John" have the same meaning.

Children also learn *morphological rules*. These apply at the word level and govern how words can be changed to alter their meaning. For example, that verbs, in general, are changed to past tense by adding *ed* is one such rule. The fact that possession can be indicated by adding an apostrophe and an *s* to the end of nouns is another.

Learning the abstract rules of language, *which are never taught directly,* is the crux of the language learning process. Children formulate or construct rules as they experience language in meaningful social contexts. In short, children do a lot more with the language they hear than listen to it passively and parrot it back: They act on it mentally and formulate hypotheses about language in general.

## Language Takes Several Related Forms

Language may be written or spoken, produced or interpreted. Speaking, listening, writing, and reading are the four basic language skills. Although each requires unique skills, all four processes are closely related. For example, we use knowledge of oral language to predict words when we read. Imagine how difficult it would be to read "Colonel John Cavanagh rested his head on his knees to catch his breath after suffering a rough coughing spell" without having a good oral vocabulary. We probably would have difficulty pronouncing the words *colonel, knee, coughing,* and *rough* by sounding them out. Having them in our oral vocabulary is essential for pronouncing them correctly. In short, although being able to decode print—change words into their spoken counterparts—depends on knowing something about the unique characteristics of print, it also depends on having an adequate oral vocabulary.

# CHILDREN AND ORAL LANGUAGE

Adults who have tried to learn a second language might argue that the task is difficult. Indeed, a language is a complicated system. Surprisingly, though, children learn their native or first language with little or no formal instruction. In fact, they learn language merely by interacting with other language users.

## Stages of Language Development

By the time children are six or seven years old, their intuitive knowledge of the abstract rules of language is almost identical to that of adults. But what are the characteristics of children's language behavior between birth and the point at which they become skilled language users? In the following pages we shall trace the course of development in language behavior.

LANGUAGE BEHAVIOR IN EARLY INFANCY.    Infants are born with the ability to vocalize. They cry and make other sounds. By age three months, noncrying vocalizations begin to dominate, particularly during periods of social interaction with adults (Rheingold et al., 1959; Wolff, 1966). These vocalizations are called *cooing* and they consist at first of open, vowel-like sounds. Later, consonant-like sounds are added. By eight months of age, consonant and vowel sounds are combined to form syllables such as *mamamamama,* a type of speech called *babbling.* Around one year of age, babbling slows down such that the syllables become quite distinct. It is at this point that an infant is likely to utter its first word.

At this time, parents usually say the baby is talking. It is worth distinguishing, however, between *communicating* without using words and talking in words. Basic aspects of communication appear long before the first words. Six-month-old babies, for example, vary the pitch of vocalizations accompanying their interactions: They use one pitch when commenting on objects in hand and another when vocalizing to their mother (Bruner, 1975). In short, babies seem to use vocal cues to communicate before actual words are used, and parents respond to these.

Being around adults who are sensitive to such vocal behavior may be crucial for learning social aspects of communication such as turn-taking, and may teach the baby about the signals provided by *intonation* (the rise and fall of the voice when speaking). It may also provide information about how meaning is coded in language. For example, when baby vocalizes while reaching for an out-of-reach object, the adult may say, "Do you want that block? Here it is." The infant knows the general meaning of the adult's utterances because the child understands the context to which they apply. But the child's understanding is still at the action level. What the child has yet to learn is how to represent meaning in language. But learning this, it seems, depends on adult-child interaction in the midst of ongoing actions. ". . . infants learn their language first by determining independent of language, the meaning which a speaker intends to convey to them, and then by working out the relationship between the meaning and the language" (Macnamara, 1972, p. 1).

There is a lesson here for later learning in a first language as well as for second language learning: Language learning proceeds well in meaningful contexts when communication is the goal. The context provides clues to what is said and the desire to communicate motivates children to understand and to try to talk. Fillmore (1976) found that rapid second language acquisition in natural communication settings occurred when conditions matching those of first language acquisition in infants were present. McLaughlin (1978), commenting on Fillmore's work, summed it up this way:

> The important thing was to communicate, even if details of the utterances were incorrect. The native-speaking children cooperated by simplifying their speech, by including the non-native speakers in their play, and by directing their speech at objects and activities at hand. Furthermore, they believed that their friends would learn the language, encouraged them, and made an effort to figure out what they were trying to say. (p. 110)

Older children however can profit from organized instruction as well. When learning a second language in natural settings, children adopt some "prefabricated utterances" which are whole phrases or sentences repeated exactly as the child has heard them. For example, a child might say, "Oh, no!" "Stop that!" or "I want that." But the child does not learn the entire second language in this imitative way. Instead, the child adopts a few of these and then adapts these into other utterances. The constituents are freed from the original utterances and what the child learns are abstract rules which are then used to create other utterances (Fillmore, 1976). Teaching some prefabricated utterances to children may be helpful as long as teachers realize that it is what children do with these, not the learning of many specific utterances, that is important in the long run.

LANGUAGE BEHAVIOR IN LATER INFANCY.    Between the ages of one and two, children learn many new words which they utter one at a time. However, children often mean much more than they are able to say. When they say "milk," they may mean "That is milk" or "I want some milk." Adults must rely on context to determine the meaning.

At about eighteen months to two years of age, children begin to string words together. Children still do not linguistically code all aspects of the message they wish to convey. Therefore, adults must still make an effort to understand if "more cookie" means "I want more cookies" or "Do you want more cookies?"

LANGUAGE BEHAVIOR DURING THE PRESCHOOL YEARS.    After children begin combining two words to create utterances, they gradually add more words. But children have yet to master morphological rules. For example, they say "That daddy car," or "Two boy go." They leave out markers indicating plurals, possession, and past tense. By age three, some of these *inflections,* or additions to words that change their meanings, are used. Soon, however, the child learns the rules so well that the morphological rules are applied to words that are exceptions.

In English, not all verbs are changed to past tense by adding *ed.* Past tense is indicated by the use of a different word altogether. For example, the past tense of *teach* is *taught,* not *teached.* Similarly, the plural form of a word is not always formed by adding an *s* (*tooth-teeth; mouse-mice*). However, once children understand the general rule, they apply it to all words. Thus, they say "I *putted* it over there," and "The cat's *feets* are dirty." Sometimes, errors of this kind persist until the age of six or seven. When they do, children may translate a text they are reading orally into their own language patterns, such as reading "He felt much better" as "He *feeled* much better." Such errors do not indicate a reading problem. The child is comprehending the text well, and such errors will disappear when the child's language development progresses further.

Between the ages of two and four, children also learn to formulate fully grammatical sentences. Their earliest questions usually consist only of a *Wh* word (*who, what, where, why*) combined with one other word. They say "Where doggy!" or "Why go?" Then a few words are added to the sentence proper: "Where doggie is going?" However, the reversal of words that is required when formulating questions has not yet been mastered. Finally, the utterance is changed to the completely grammatical form of "Where is the doggie going?"

Negative sentences, too, begin simply with a *"no"* placed in front of one other word: "No go." The sentence then becomes more complete ("I no want to go") before becoming fully grammatical ("I don't want to go") (Menyuk, 1969). When older children and adults learn a second language, they often go through very similar stages in learning to formulate such sentences.

Children learn the correct use of morphological rules and the syntactic rules for formulating sentences the same way they learn other aspects of language—by interacting with mature language users who provide many utterances from which abstract rules can be inferred. A rich and stimulating language environment allows children to infer regularities that apply across many specific situations. In addition, communicating with the young child about things that are of immediate concern encourages talking and learning to talk. Specific instruction can also help, but it should stress communication. For example, in one guessing game, one child thinks about an object and other children must guess what is being thought about. Questions are posed by the guessers to gain clues. This exercise structures a situation so that children practice asking questions, but it is not meaningless drill on language patterns, such as a situation where children are simply asked to repeat questions formulated and spoken by the teacher.

Throughout the preschool years, children also add words to their vocabularies. But completely mature understandings may not develop until long after children begin to use these words. The child must learn *semantic categories,* or the characteristics of the things to which a word refers. Learning semantic categories is a complicted task. It is not enough for a child to be able to repeat the name of a specific object that has been named by an adult. Which variations in objects are significant? Which ones are not? When is something to sit on called a chair, a stool, or a bench? When is an object worn on the foot called a sock, a stocking, a shoe, a sandal, or a boot? Children cannot use and understand language effectively without experiencing language in the context of a large variety of objects and situations. General knowledge and experience, concept development, and adequate language models are critical for language learning.

LANGUAGE DEVELOPMENT DURING EARLY MIDDLE CHILDHOOD.    By the time children enter the first grade, they are skilled users of language, although they still confuse some complex syntactic structures. For example, they think that "John is easy to see" means "John can see easily" rather than "John *can be seen* easily." The first sentence confuses children because it has the same *surface* structure (word order) as "John is eager to see" (Chomsky, 1969). By and large, these misunderstandings are not very noticeable in children's language behavior, although they can be the source of communication problems or misinterpretations of written material.

What is noticeable in the language behavior of school age children is language play in the form of jokes, riddles, and puns. Jokes and riddles are funny because they involve a play on words, sounds, or sentences. For example, in the riddle "What is black and white and read all over?" the listener expects the word *red* in the question to be the color red, not its homonym, *read*. This riddle capitalizes on the ambiguous meaning of a word.

In knock-knock jokes, a play on sounds is sometimes utilized. For example, one knock-knock joke goes like this:

"Knock-knock"
"Who's there?"
"Duane."
"Duane who?"
"Duane the tub . . . I'm drowning."

Lexical (word-level) and phonological (sound-level) ambiguity are appreciated by primary age children, but syntactic ambiguity (sentences with double-meanings) is not appreciated until children are nine or ten (McGhee, 1979). Interest in jokes and riddles based on each type of ambiguity signals a new level of language ability. The child's knowledge of an aspect of language structure is no longer merely capable of being used, but can now be thought about and analyzed. Being able to think about and discuss language is known as *metalinguistic awareness*. Teachers can use children's interest in jokes and riddles to teach word meanings and attention to and analysis of sound. For example, reading riddles is a good way to involve primary level children in the study of homonyms.

## AN OVERVIEW OF DEVELOPMENT
## OF LANGUAGE COMPREHENSION
## AND PERCEPTION

In the discussion above, we have stressed language production—how children speak. We have commented little on how children understand what is said *to* them. It is this aspect of oral language we turn to now.

COMPREHENSION OF SENTENCES.    We have already discussed children's difficulty with syntactic structures such as "John is easy to see." Other syntactic forms, such as passive sentences, are misunderstood by children until they are about five. A four-year-old usually interprets the sentence "John was hit by Susan" as "John hit Susan," apparently because the child thinks the actor is always mentioned first in a sentence (Sinclair, 1969). Sometimes, however, passive sentences are interpreted correctly by a child younger than five if the probability of an incorrect interpretation is low in the real world. For example, when confronted with the sentence "The baby was fed by Mary," the child is likely to understand correctly that it was Mary who did the feeding because babies do not feed anyone else (Strohner and Nelson, 1974). Understanding language is not simply a matter of "listening carefully" or of making passive associations between language events and events in the real world. What the child knows about the real world seems to aid the child in thinking actively and making sense of what he or she hears.

COMPREHENSION OF WORDS.    Not only do children misunderstand the meaning of some sentences, but they misunderstand various words as well. For a period during the preschool years, children misunderstand the words *more* and *less*. When asked to indicate which of the two groups or sets of objects has more and which has less, children are likely to point to the group which has more objects when responding to *both* words. Apparently, they first understand that both words refer to quantity, not that they refer to *different* characteristics of quantity. Therefore, they point to a group of more objects even when the word said is *less*, because the larger quantity is the best indicator of quantity per se (Clark, 1978).

The words *on*, *in*, and *under* create similar problems. Young children at first realize only that these words are alike because they indicate location. As children gain more experience with language, they learn the specific meanings of each preposition (Clark, 1978).

These difficulties in language comprehension have important implications for teachers. First, statements or words that are clear to us may not convey our intended meaning to children. Therefore, we must be careful not to assume that children have failed to "listen" to us, but consider instead that they may not have understood what we meant. We must be willing to say things in a different way, or better yet, to demonstrate with actions what we mean.

Second, the discussion illustrates that children sometimes do not know what they *seem* to know. A child may respond correctly to the word *on* simply because the situation does not allow *in* as the interpretation. The child may, in fact, not understand the word *on*. Similarly, when a young child always responds correctly to the word *more* but responds incorrectly to the word *less* we would be wrong to think that one word is understood but that the other is not. The child probably understands neither word until both are used correctly.

Adults must be sure to use detailed verbalizations with children in a large variety of situations for a long time, even after children have appeared to understand words on one or two occasions. And, as in the case of misunderstood sentences, we need to take great care to be ready to consider that the problem is one of comprehension, not of poor listening.

Before leaving the discussion of comprehension of words, we will consider another type of misunderstanding. When children are taught songs or verses whose contents relate little to what they know or understand, they often "hear" the words said as different words entirely. For example, one child insisted on changing a refrain in the song "The Muffin Man" from "Who lives in Drury Lane" to "Who lives in the dirty lake."

Such examples illustrate how children search for meaning in language. What they "hear" is as much a matter of what makes sense as of what is said. If we want language to make sense to young children, we must be certain to provide it in the midst of concrete situations which can help children understand what we say, and to use songs and verses relating to children's experiences. Repetition of words or verses that are not understood does little to facilitate language learning.

COMPREHENSION OR PERCEPTION OF SOUNDS.    Finally, we must look at how language comprehension or perception relates to *sound*. To what extent do children hear speech sounds? How do they perceive what they hear?

Young infants are sensitive to speech sounds and perceive them in terms of the same categories as adults. They respond to differences *between* a *b* and *p* sound, for example. What is interesting about the distinctions that infants, as well as adults, make is that the actual acoustical differences among the various sounds represented by the letter *b* (behind, button, brake) are often as great as the difrence between any *b* and *p* sound. Yet, one kind of difference is perceived as a categorical difference, while the other (variations in *b*) is not (Eimas, 1974).

Research with infants is relevant to work with older children because it suggests that we need make little effort to help children "hear" the differences among various language sounds. However, if this is true, how are we to explain the difficulty older children have when asked to indicate words that begin with the same sound? For example, children may be unable to detect that the words *dog* and *dragon* have the same initial sounds, while *goat* has a different one. Or, they may say that *truck* and *top* begin with *different* sounds, but that *chicken* and *truck* begin with the *same* sound.

First, we must wonder if children understand the task. "What is a sound?"—a child may wonder. What do *beginning* and *start with* mean? What is a word? If children do not understand these words—and there is evidence that even first graders often do not—then they will have difficulty knowing what to do (Clay, 1975; Downing, 1970).

But there may be another difficulty, as well. In research with infants, sounds were presented in isolation by a machine which produces synthetic speech. When children listen to real language, they must segment a stream of speech into individual sounds. When listening to real language, the child's main focus may be on meaning, on what is said, and not on individual sounds within the words. Determining the meaning, after all, is the everyday task encountered in using language. In addition, in terms of the actual physical characteristics of speech, there is no such thing as an individual sound. We learn *to think about* speech in terms of individual sounds, but acoustically, segments that are syllable-like are necessary if we are to retain recognizable features of individual sounds. Individual sounds are abstract concepts—the way we come to think about the stream of speech—not a physical fact (Savin and Bever, 1970; McNeill and Lindig, 1973). We know from research (Gleitman and Rozin, 1977) that many preschool, and even some primary age, children (Savin, 1972) cannot segment real language into units smaller than the syllable. If they cannot do this, they cannot solve the problem of determining which of several words start with the same or with different sounds.

Children still have some problems when asked which words start with the same sound, even *after* the difficulty with segmentation is overcome. This problem is due to the tendency of preschool and early school age children to make distinctions among and create categories of sounds that adults do not. For example, the *t* in the word *truck* and the *t* in the word *toy* are different in one respect, and the *t* in the word *truck* and the *ch* in the word *chicken* are alike in one respect. If you pronounce the words *truck* and *toy,* you will notice that when saying the *t* in *truck,* you include the sound represented by the letters *ch* as well. That is because the *t* is followed by an *r.* But when you pronounce the *t* in the word *toy,* the *shh* sound is absent. Children are correct, then, in saying that *truck* and *chicken* begin with the same sound and that *toy* begins with a different sound, *if it is this* phonetic feature to which they attend (Read, 1980).

What children do not know is that this sound difference between the two *t*'s is disregarded in standard spelling, which is what the teacher has in mind when asking children to solve these same-different problems. What is attended to by the teacher and by standard spelling is *place of articulation* (where in the mouth the air is stopped to form a sound), not *affrication* (a certain way of stopping air which results in a *shhh* sound). Both the *t* in the word *truck* and the *t* in *toy* are articulated by pressing the tongue directly behind the teeth, while the sound represented by the letters *ch* in *chicken* is articulated in a different place. Attention to this phonetic feature makes the words *toy* and *truck* the same in terms of initial sound and the words *chicken* and *truck* different.

Apparently, young children are not less skilled in *discriminating* among sounds than are adults. They simply attend to different phonetic features and thereby categorize some sounds differently. What we know about this aspect of language indicates that we need not train children to "hear" sounds or to listen more carefully to exaggerated and strained pronunciations. What may be useful is exposure to meaningful print in the environment; children will see that words they have considered to be the same with regard to initial sounds are in fact spelled with different beginning letters, while words they have considered to be different are spelled with the same letter. Such conflicts in expectations may lead children to attend to certain similarities and disregard others, and to categorize sounds the way adults do.

It may also be useful to play oral language games with children, such as deciding which spoken words begin with the same sound. However, when children indicate that words we consider to be different in terms of initial sound are the same, we should refrain from saying that they are wrong or that they need to listen more carefully to the words as we say them. They probably *have* listened carefully but paid attention to phonetic features not represented in spelling. We might say instead that while the words they have grouped together are alike in some way, their choices do not sound as much alike to us as other words. This procedure would encourage children to trust their ability to hear the sounds in language and encourage them to continue to listen carefully. However, it would also encourage them to attend to the features that are significant to adults who are familiar with the distinctions made in standard spelling.

In summary, perception of speech at the sound level in terms of adult-defined categories is an extremely complicated task. It involves both the abstract concept of an individual sound and knowledge about which phonetic features should be attended to. It may be that speech perception at this level, which is crucial for learning to read and write (to spell, for example), depends on experience with the printed word. It may never occur to us to think about speech in terms of individual sounds if we never see how individual letters function—that they represent a segment of speech smaller than a syllable. Similarly, we may never learn to categorize sounds (such as the variations in the letter *t* when used in different words) in certain ways unless we see the words spelled. Experience with written language may be required for children to perceive oral language in these specific ways (Ehri and Wilce, 1979). If that is the case, then exposing even young children to functional print, such as their names, signs and labels in the classroom, experience charts, and simple picture books, may be as crucial as exposing them to rhyming verses and finger plays. In other words, exposure to oral language alone, even to experiences nicely structured to emphasize sounds within words, such as rhyming verses and songs that include alliteration (words beginning with the same initial consonants), may not be as effective as presenting these *along with* experiences with meaningful print.

### Summary of Oral Language Skills
### for Young Children

Young children must develop skill in *formulating fully grammatical sentences*. As we have seen above, skill in this area develops over a period of several years as children are talked with and have opportunities to talk. Young children also learn how to *articulate (pronounce) words correctly* as they hear words pronounced and have experience with talking. Here, also, there are normal deviations from the adult model throughout the developmental period.

When English is not a child's first language, or when a child's first language is a dialect of standard English, children must be given opportunities to learn standard English.

Children must also develop skill in *organizing and expressing thoughts*. This involves the ability to select and organize the information that is necessary to convey so that other people know what it is we are trying to tell them. This ability is supported by cognitive development in general, such as children's ability to think about things from another's point of view. Children can also develop skill in *communicating information to a group*. In addition to fostering the skills required to organize information around an idea and present it verbally in a coherent way, teachers can help children approach with ease and confidence situations involving verbal communication.

Children also need support in *learning to understand what is said to them.* While this involves *learning to attend or listen to the language directed to them,* it also involves learning about language. For example, it is important to know word meanings and how passive sentences work.

Finally, children must learn to *think about and perceive oral language in terms of individual sounds and to categorize these in terms of the phonetic features consistent with standard spelling.*

General methods for helping children gain these skills are discussed on pp. 209–17. Individual activities begin on p. 217.

## CHILDREN AND WRITTEN LANGUAGE

Three-year-old Monica is sprawled on the floor with paper and pencil, creating scribble marks. Monica's teacher comments that Monica is very busy today. Monica says, "I'm writing." The teacher takes a close look and notices that the marks have some characteristics of writing, although actual print has not been created.

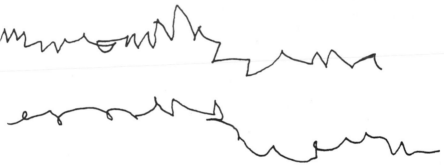

Monica is also interested in reading print in her classroom and in the world at large. She pauses as her teacher writes her name on a picture she has scribbled. She says, "That says me." When hearing familiar stories, she fills in many words when the adult reader pauses. Monica is exploring written language, although she has had no formal lessons in handwriting or reading. Monica, like most young children who find themselves in rich, literate environments, has noticed written language and has begun to make sense of it.

### Young Children and Writing

When we speak of writing, we refer not only to *handwriting,* the mechanics of creating specific print markings, but to many other skills relating to *composing* messages. Some of these relate to the function of writing—its purpose. Writing is permanent and can be used to communicate messages at a time removed from their creation. Unlike the receiver of an oral message, the receiver of a written message usually is not in direct contact with the message's creator. This characteristic of writing imposes unique demands on the writer for detail and clarity. Writing also differs in form depending on its purpose. Writing a story is one thing; writing a letter to a friend is another.

Children must also learn how print and speech are related. What level of sound in the speech stream is represented by each English alphabet letter? Adults know that letters are units used to represent speech at the sound level, but children at first do not know this. In addition, they do not know that words created in writing are marked by placing space between them. Learning these, as well as other, *conventions of print* is part of learning about writing.

DEVELOPING THE ABILITY TO CREATE PRINT MARKINGS.    The very first distinction children make about writing is between lines used to create print and pictures. Children notice that print is arranged in linear patterns organized horizontally. They also notice that it is composed of multiple units that are varied (Lavine, 1975). These understandings are seen in children's early "writing," which now differs from their attempts to draw:

Somewhat later, children notice the separations between the units of writing (Hildreth, 1936). Their scribble writing reflects this new insight:

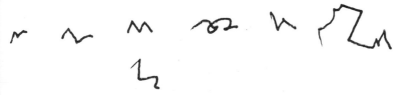

Next, children begin to discover what Gibson (Gibson and Levin, 1975) has called the *distinctive features of print,* or the various lines which, when combined in different ways, create the letters of the alphabet. One distinctive feature is curved lines versus straight lines. This feature makes letters such as *O, G, S,* and *C* different from letters such as *M, W, K, L,* and *E.* A second feature is open, curved lines versus closed, curved lines. This feature makes letters such as *C, G,* and *S* different from the letter *O.*

When children know some distinctive features of print, they create markings that look like actual alphabet letters, although they are not real letters:

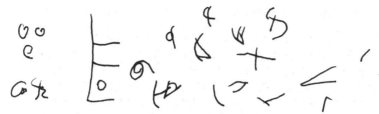

It would be a mistake to assume that the children who created these markings set out to make any of the individual alphabet letters. Children may not realize at this point that the alphabet letters are unique and stable and that they are a finite set (there are only twenty-six). Children may think instead that print is made by using various lines and that one literally creates a limitless number of print forms by combining these in all possible ways.

Finally, children learn enough distinctive features of print to create actual letters, and they realize that print consists only of these letters, each one of which is unique. However, errors are still made, even at this stage:

A 'B' with too many loops.

An 's' with two orientation errors.

A 't' with intersecting line placed too low.

An upper-case 'R' with a vertical line extending too far. (Shickedanz, 1980)

It is obvious that children still have some details to learn. Children appear to work actively on these details, to experiment to see what the limits of each letter are:

(Schickedanz, 1980)

Children also experiment to compare letters, apparently trying to see exactly what the differences are between one letter and another:

A child's experiment with
the letters *T, I, H, I,* and *E,*
all letters made only of straight, vertical, and
horizontal lines. (Clay, 1975)

Learning to create print involves increasing perceptual differentiation. Children do not learn to recognize the form of each alphabet letter one at a time, until each is learned. Instead, children differentiate groups of letters based on a discovered distinctive feature until finally they discover that each letter is unique.

Of course, to be able to make discoveries about print, children must have many opportunities both to see and to try to create it. Classrooms can provide manipulative alphabet materials, such as felt and magnetic letters and wooden alphabet puzzles. In addition, using children's names, classroom signs and labels, and simple picture books provides opportunities for children to see print used meaningfully. It is equally important to make available materials for drawing and writing—these will encourage the creation of all kinds of lines, which eventually become differentiated into specific symbol systems such as pictures and print.

When children have discovered most of the distinctive features of print and realize that alphabet letters are stable and unique, it may be useful to show them the customary way to form letters. In fact, children often ask for help: "I can't make the Z right. Show me how." "Show me how to make a little *e.*" Before this time, specific instruction in handwriting is not useful or efficient because children do not yet understand even what the distinctive features of print are or that these are combined in specific ways to form a finite set of unique letters. In addition, children have not yet had sufficient exploratory experience in creating lines to be able to benefit from demonstrations requiring that lines be combined in specific ways.

It is not possible to say at what age children are ready for specific instruction in handwriting. Some children who have been surrounded by print and have manipulated paper and pencil seem to seek such assistance between the ages of three and four. They may also continue to freely explore lines, but they do form real letters and often ask for help with some of them. Other children, particularly those who have not had a history of such experiences, may at age five only have begun to realize that print lines differ from picture lines. To give such a child formal lessons in forming each letter of the alphabet, without first providing an extensive period of exploration, is probably not very useful. Because such a child has little understanding of what to do, there is a further risk of creating disinterest and dislike for learning in general, and for writing in particular.

One of the questions teachers ask about instruction in handwriting is whether children should be shown how to form only upper-case letters at first, or both upper and lower case. We prefer showing children both upper- and lower-case letters from the beginning because both are in books and in other natural print settings. When only upper-case letters are shown first, handwriting is isolated from other aspects of writing and children are taught incorrect notions they must later unlearn. For example, in writing down a child's dictation, a teacher demonstrates more than correct handwriting if upper- and lower-case letters are used: The conventions for using each are also demonstrated. (An upper-case letter is used to begin a word following a period or other forms of punctuation marking the end of a sentence, and to begin proper nouns.) Young children do not at first understand these conventions, but they do begin to notice that sometimes one form of a letter is used, while at other times the other form is used.

When children request help in forming letters, a teacher might ask, "Where are you going to use it? Do you need a big *T* or a little one?" If the child is merely practicing writing letters, which is a task even preschool children often initiate themselves, the teacher can say, "I'll show you how to make both a capital *E* and a small *e* because sometimes you need one kind and other times you need the other."

In summary, it seems that there is no advantage in teaching upper-case letters first and lower-case letters later. What may be gained in more perfect initial handwriting (upper-case letters contain more straight lines and may be easier for children to form) is lost in terms of concepts about function and writing conventions. Children make errors in learning to make all letters. These bother them little when we do not fuss about them, and they generally disappear as children gain more experience. Expecting or aiming for perfection in handwriting, even to the point of sacrificing correct concepts about function, probably results in no real overall gain.

CREATING WORDS.    Not only must children discover how lines are used to create letters, but they must learn how letters are used to make words. We are not speaking here of knowing specific words, but rather of knowing, in general, what a word in print is. Children at first seem to think that single letters can function as words (Clay, 1975; Meltzer and Herse, 1969; Downing, 1970). For example, we observed one four-year-old make a "shopping list" by placing several letters on a piece of paper:

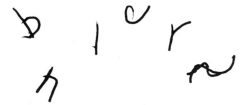

When asked what was on her list, she pointed to each letter and named a food.

Children's names can provide opportunities for learning about words.

In research studies in which children were asked to sort into "words" and "nonwords" cards with either single letters or strings of letters written on them, the youngest children often included cards with single letters[1] right along with the cards containing letter strings (Pick, 1978). It is possible that the children thought the cards with letter strings contained *several* words, not a *single* word, so that even with these the children considered single letters to be words.

With more print experience, particularly experience in seeing adults write and read words, children realize that a word usually consists of several letters. At this point, children may produce writing that looks like this:

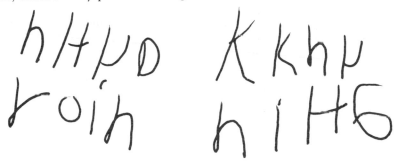

(Schickedanz, 1980)

[1] Some words such as *I* and *A* are formed using a single letter, but these are exceptions to the general rule that words are composed of several letters.

When children first create words using letter strings, they seem to think that all letter strings make words. They also assume we can make up the meaning of any string we create. For example, children place letters together and then show us their "word." "See my word. It says _____." A little later, children begin to realize that the meaning of a word is not designated by its creator. At this point, children string letters together and ask, "What does this say?" Often, of course, the string created does not make a real word. The child knows that a word's meaning cannot be made up, but he or she does not yet know that the order of letters in real words is systematic—letters must be put together in certain ways, and not all letter strings are permissible. When children develop this insight, they may spend long periods of time copying words available in the environment or in books and asking adults what they say. Some children ask adults for spellings or invent spellings of their own if they have some knowledge of how letters represent sounds. Word making from this point on consists of real words, although children's initial spellings differ from our own.

SPELLING.    Learning to spell is a complicated matter. First, children must realize that letters are not strung together at random to create words—their order is systematic. Second, children must realize that one good clue to letter order in printed words is the order of sounds uttered when the word is spoken—print and speech are related. Of course, children may spell some frequently seen words, such as their names, correctly before they realize that print and speech are related in any specific way. Learning to spell a small number of words in this way may even be crucial in helping children discover how spelling works—how it is related to words that are spoken. But it is the insight about the relationship between spoken and printed words that enables children to spell many words, rather than just a few familiar words.

Nevertheless, even after children know that speech and print are related systematically, they will not spell many words correctly. This, as we explained earlier (see p. 188), is because children do not categorize speech sounds exactly as adults do. For example, children place the sounds represented by a *t* followed by an *r* and the sound represented by the letters *ch* in the same category and represent both in writing with *ch* (*chray* for *tray* and *chrie* for *try*). Similarly, they represent the *d* before an *r* with a *g* (*giboll* for *dribble*) (Read, 1980). Young children also categorize some vowels differently, for example, they often use an *i* to represent a sound that adults represent with an *o* (*liv* for *love; diz* for *does*) (Read, 1980).

Thus, even though young children realize that spelling is related to how a word sounds, their spellings contain errors because they categorize sounds differently. The spellings they create as a result are known as *invented spellings.*

Children must also learn that the same sounds can, in some cases, be represented by different letters (c̲ity and s̲un) and that the same letter can represent different sounds (c̲omic and c̲ity). In addition, sometimes letters are used when spelling a word but not when speaking it (the *gh* is silent in *night;* the *e* is silent in *kite*). Further, spelling often violates phonetic transcription entirely: Sometimes the violations are made to allow lexical relationships to be retained. For example, in words such as *nation-nationality, muscle-muscular, anxious-anxiety,* and *medicine-medicate,* a nonphonetic spelling of one form of the word provides us with a clue about the word pair's similar meanings (Chomsky, 1980). Such a spelling system is useful to the mature reader and speller but confusing to the beginner.

In summary, children must master many complex understandings in order to spell skillfully. Mastering these skills takes many years, and nonconventional spellings persist throughout the primary grades, such as in the following sample written by a second grader:

> at the sercis
> I wood like to be a popsucl so someone cood lic me
> until they wer done and they wood throwe me a
> way so I cood see it all and I wood be with all the
> other popsucl stics and I wood be happy the e
>                                                n
>                                                d

(Donnelly and Stevens, 1980, p. 738)

It helps children learn to spell if (1) they are surrounded by print in the environment and in books from an early age, (2) they are encouraged to write meaningful messages, such as stories and letters to parents or friends, and (3) they are given simple picture dictionaries and their own word banks (a deck of cards on which are written words whose spellings they have requested).

Direct correction with colored pencil of invented spellings in children's creative writing is not recommended: It may discourage a child, and it mars the child's paper. However, it may be useful for a teacher to attach a note to the child's paper commenting on the content of the piece and listing words that the child spells differently. The child can then list his or her spellings beside these and compare the two. Or, the teacher might simply use some of the child's misspelled words in a note to the child, thus ensuring that the child sees the standard spelling. Seeing the letters that are actually used to spell a word leads children to revise their own spellings. If children select some of their writing samples for inclusion in an anthology for the class library, it is reasonable to expect them to copy the original draft over and make corrections. We are speaking here of primary level children; younger children should not be expected to achieve perfection in spelling. Simply trying to spell at all is enough for them, although children who are "experienced" writers at five often ask for spellings and revise their own hypotheses as the year progresses. This is particularly true if they see many samples of print in the environment, such as on labels and experience charts and in storybooks.

LEARNING THE CONVENTIONS OF PRINT.    Although the second grader who wrote the "sercis" piece (included above) had not mastered conventional spelling, she had mastered some of the basic conventions about arranging print on a page.

For example, she organized her writing from left to right and from top to bottom on the page. She also left space between each word to indicate where one ended and the next began. In addition, she consistently used lower-case and upper-case letters appropriately, except in the title, where upper-case beginnings would have been appropriate. Younger children who have not yet adopted these basic conventions may produce writing that looks like this:

This child arranged print from left to right and top to bottom, which is conventional, but did not leave space between words. She also did not yet know when to use upper and lower case letters, for even though she shows us that she *can* make both upper and lower case a's and e's, she often uses upper cases where lower case is the conventional pattern. (Klein & Schickedanz, 1980, p. 746).

Still younger children show less use of conventions regarding the arrangement of print and may place it on the page from left to right or right to left, or from top to bottom or bottom to top. They may even arrange print in vertical rather than horizontal linear patterns.

"Jessica" written down rather than across a page by a four-year-old.

The word *from* written from right to left with letters perfectly reversed, by a five-year-old

A message written by a four-year-old from left to right across a tiny piece of paper. Sharon then turned the paper around and wrote her name from left to right. Because the paper had been turned, the two rows of writing ended up not being oriented the same way.

As children write and encounter the writing of others, more conventions of print are mastered. Primary grade children begin to gain control over conventional usage of upper- and lower-case letters and punctuation. For example, they begin to confine the use of upper-case letters more and more to the first letter of words that begin a sentence and to the beginning letter of a noun, and they begin to insert punctuation marks. Alan, a third grader, says about punctuation: "If you want your story to make sense, you can't write without punctuation. . . . Punctuation tells people things—like if the sentence is asking, or if someone is talking, or if you should yell it out." A classmate of Alan's says, "It lets you know where the sentence ends, so otherwise one minute you'd be sledding down the hill and the next minute you're inside the house, without even stopping" (Graves, 1980a, p. 569).

Alan and his classmates learned about punctuation as the need arose, and as they wrote things they wanted others to understand. By third grade, these children knew the function of more than twice as many punctuation marks as did children in another third grade class in their school who had been given specific instruction and workbook drill on punctuation, without much opportunity to compose written messages (Graves, 1980). Alan and his classmates probably also learned a great deal more than the other classes about other important aspects of writing, such as how to start a piece so that it gets the reader's attention, how to write with detail to give exactly the effect you wish, and so on. While children do need to do a lot of writing to learn about conventions of writing, they need not be drilled on it.

COMPOSING MESSAGES.    Young children understand that oral language is not the only way to communicate. Thoughts, feelings, and stories can be pictured, for example, or written down. Children attempt to write down what they have to say long before they master conventional print. For example, the author observed a three-year-old boy in a bookstore writing notes to his mother. The store provided a play area with an old-style school desk. The mother gave the child a notebook and pencil to use while she browsed through books. The child drew lines of scribble print on a page, tore the sheet out, walked to his mother, placed the note (folded in half with the message inside) on the bookshelf near her, walked back to the desk, and then called to her "Mommy, there's a letter for you." Mother acted appropriately surprised and reached for the note. "What does it say?" she asked. "I love you," he answered.

Two more letters followed. Each was delivered to the bookshelf beside the mother. Each time, the child returned to his desk before notifying her of the letter's presence. This three-year-old seemed to understand the function of writing: He kept his distance from the receiver of the message when it was read, and he never gave the message directly to his mother. To have done so would have violated both the function of writing (creator and reader are separated in time and space) as well as the typical way that letters are received (obtained from a mailbox, not placed in our hand). In addition, the child folded the notes, perhaps in an attempt to make his mother open the letter as one might open an envelope. Because the child could create only scribble writing rather than conventional writing, he had to tell his mother what the letters said. However, he did his best to honor other social aspects of the writing situation.

Four-year-old Megan, who also uses scribble writing, shows us in the examples shown in Figure 7-1 that she knows the difference between the forms of writing used when writing a letter and those used when writing a story. Obviously, Megan has been exposed to both forms.

It is a long developmental process from these beginnings to being able to create writing that stands alone to convey exactly the message intended or to produce a desired effect. At the preschool level, children should be provided opportunities to "write" messages, *using whatever skills they have available.* Adult appreciation of and interest in the messages created is also crucial, as it provides support for development. In addition, adults can create messages to give to children. For example, in one preschool classroom, children wrote letters to a special classroom story reader requesting books of interest. "Writing" meant writing in whatever way the children could, from scribbles and pictures to conventional print. The

**FIGURE 7-1**   (Harste and Carey, 1979, p. 9)

Megan's letter: "Once upon a time—there was—wait—uh, huh. Dear Mary. I would like you to bring me . . . here everyday. The end. Megan."

Megan's story: "Once upon a time there was a ghost. Three ghosts family. One day they went out for a walk. They honked the horn cause they saw Mrs. Wood and said "I" then they went back to Mrs. Corners and they honked the horn and sa—said "Hi." The end."

story reader answered the children's letters with a letter, which was read to each child. Before long, many elements of the children's letters reflected those in the letters they had received. They included the closing *Love* before their names. They also included the word *Dear* before the name of the story reader to whom they were writing. Even children who used scribble writing read their letters by beginning with *Dear* _____ and ending with *Love* and their names (Klein and Schickedanz, 1980).

Simple questions such as "How will I remember who this letter is from?" can help children learn about the function and form of writing. A letter requires a response, making a signature necessary, while a story does not. Rereading a child's letter when that child complains that what was desired was a book about children, rather than animals, in the hospital can help the child understand that the message "I want a book about things in the hospital" can be interpreted in several ways. "I didn't know exactly what you meant," we could say, "next time try to tell me more." If letters are written in scribble writing and their contents told to us by their creators, we can ask "Do you want a book about the machines in a hospital, about people who work there, or about the sick people who go there to get well?"

Throughout the primary grades, the clarity and detail in children's writing will continue to improve if children are encouraged to write about topics of their choice. Having their writing read and responded to by others, including their peers, provides the necessary feedback which causes children to consider whether or not their writing is functioning well (Graves, 1979a). When children see that it is not, they often are willing, and even eager, to revise their first attempts. With experience and cognitive development, they learn to think about what readers will think of their writing and may revise several times before asking someone else to read it.

Eight-year-old Andrea wrote three leads for a piece of writing about learning to fly:

Lead One: Once when I was very little I got a hank to fly, so I tried jumping off things and tried to float up and across.

Lead Two: I always wanted to fly, but whenever I tried it, I always fell Kaboom on the ground.

Lead Three: Kaboom! That hurt! Why can't I fly? The birds do. Even with these wings, nothing happened.

Andrea stuck with the third lead: "It's happening now," she explained (Graves, 1979b, p. 317).

A nine-year-old child who has been in an environment that encourages writing tells us: "First you write down how you know it. Then you read it over and you think, 'Can other people understand this?' " (Graves, 1980b, p. 213). This kind of concern with audience is probably the effect both of experience with writing and of general cognitive abilities such as being able to think about what other people are thinking (DeVries, 1970). Such insights should be an important goal of writing programs in the primary grades.

### Summary of Writing Skills
### for Young Children

Skills in written language involve *distinguishing print from nonprint,* learning the *distinctive features of print,* learning to *form alphabet letters,* learning to form alphabet letters according to *conventional handwriting techniques,* and learning *conventions of print,* such as left-to-right and top-to-bottom arrangement, use of upper- and lower-case letters, and punctuation. In addition, skills include knowing that words consist of permissible strings of letters that are related to how words sound, and other conventions of spelling. Finally, with regard to creating messages, children must learn about the functions and forms of written language and how to communicate clearly in writing.

General methods for helping children learn these skills are discussed on pages 209–17. Specific activities begin on p. 217.

## YOUNG CHILDREN AND READING

Reading is interaction with printed language to obtain meaning. It is a complex behavior that involves the integration of several skills. When we read, we use what we know about language, the world, and specific relationships between print and speech (Goodman and Goodman, 1977). We discuss each of these strategies or skills below.

USING CONTEXT AS A READING STRATEGY.   Fluent readers do not depend solely on their ability to read individual words. They anticipate many words, reading them neither by sight nor by sounding them out. If all readers of this book filled in the blanks in the following passage, we would find striking similarities among the words chosen.

> The sky grew dark. It thundered and _____. Soon it began to _____ and _____ wind started to _____. My brothers started _____ cry. I told them not _____ worry. We were safe. Nothing could hurt _____ down here in Grandmother's fruit _____.

Certain words make sense because of their meanings. Lightning and thunder go together. We learn these associations through experience. Other words make sense because they fit our language patterns. What this illustration points out is that reading is influenced by general experience with the world and spoken language.

Concrete experiences, and many opportunities to talk about them, will do much to help children become good readers. In addition, experiences with storybooks and print in the environment can help children realize that thinking about what makes sense is useful in predicting what words say: Words are not arranged randomly, but in a way that is meaningful. But how does story reading, or other experiences with samples of print, lead to this conclusion?

When young children are read storybooks, they get a sense of the story—the context—long before they focus on the print used to tell the story. They also use the pictures—another context clue—to help them remember what each page of the story says. Gradually, as they learn the story and something about how print and speech are related (see discussion below on p. 206), they use their knowledge of what the story says to find the specific words which say it. Thus, context which includes knowledge of the story, pictures, and language, is used as a reading strategy from the start.

Use of context is not the only strategy needed in reading. Children also must know how speech and print are related and how print itself is arranged.

CONVENTIONS OF PRINT, SPEECH SEGMENTATION, AND MATCHING SPEECH AND PRINT.    Print has unique characteristics which children must come to understand. First, they must know that print is arranged from left to right and from top to bottom on a page. Children gain this understanding in many ways, including (1) seeing books read from front to back, (2) seeing a story reader refer, by pointing, to pictures, first on the left page and then on the right page, (3) seeing the story reader occasionally run a finger under a line of print as it is read, (4) seeing a story they dictate written down and then read back, with a finger pointing along the print, and (5) seeing the adult run a finger under print read in the environment, such as the words on a cereal box or a sign in a store window.[2]

Second, to be able to map speech onto print, children must learn how various speech units are marked or designated in print. Related to this is the ability to segment speech into units such as sounds and words. Although adults have difficulty appreciating the problem, young children are not at first aware of, nor do they consciously think about, the language they hear in terms of individual words or sounds. There are no clues in speech itself to indicate the difference between a syllable and a word. For example, many words have only one syllable, but there is little, if any, indication of the difference in physical speech between these and two- or three-syllable words. How is a child to know, for example, that to do is two words, with one syllable each, while today is one word, composed of two syllables?

A similar problem exists at the sound level—there is little physical difference between a syllable and the pronunciation of the "single" sounds in a word. For example, in pronouncing the sounds in the word bit, the teacher would say

[2]We feel that this characteristic of print should be taught using print, that requiring children to practice left-to-right movements in other settings is not necessary and may be detrimental to other learnings. For example, it is not necessary to insist that children count objects from left to right. In fact, insisting on this teaches them something wrong about counting—that it must be done in one direction! Objects can be counted in any order as long as each one is counted only once.

/bə I tə/, thus giving the word three syllables, while *bit* has only one. The children, of course, are supposed to solve the problem by blending /bə I tə/ into *bit*. However, without a concept of individual sounds and their relationship to syllables and words, children do not understand what to do (Savin, 1972). The problem is not with perceptual discrimination, but with knowing how speech maps onto print—how they are related (Menyuk, 1976)—and to what adults are referring when they use words such as *sound, word* and *letter*.

Maria Clay, an educator from New Zealand, gives the following example of how confused children can be about these things.

Suppose a teacher has placed an attractive picture on the wall and has asked her children for a story which she will record under it. They offer the text "Mother is cooking" which the teacher alters slightly to introduce some features she wishes to teach. She writes,

Mother said,
"I am baking."

If she says, "Now look at our *story*, " 30 percent of a new entrant group will attend to the *picture*.

If she says, "Look at the *words* and find some you know," between 50 and 90 percent will be searching for *letters*. If she says, "Can you see Mother?" most will agree that they can but some *see* her in the picture, some can locate "M" and others will locate the word "Mother."

Perhaps the children read in unison "Mother is . . . " and the teacher tries to sort this out. Pointing to *said* she asks, "Does this say *is*?" Half agree it does because it has "s" in it. "*What letter does it start with*?" Now the teacher is really in trouble. She assumes that children *know* that a word is built out of letters but 50 percent of children still confuse the verbal labels "word" and "letter" after six months of instruction. She also assumes that the children know that the left-hand letter following a space is the "start" of a word. Often they do not. She says, "Look at the *first* letter. It says s-s-s-s" and her pupils make s-noises. But Johnny who knows only "Mother" and "I" scans the text haphazardly for something relevant, sights the *comma* and makes s-noises!

Mother said,
"I am baking."

Teacher continues, "What do you think Mother said? *Look at the next word* and tell me what it says." That should be easy because most children learn "I" early, but for a child who does not know the difference between a letter and a word "the next word" will often be the second letter in "said." For other children who have not established left to right movement with return sweep the next word may be 'gnikab' because they are returning right to left along the second line. Still others may be conscientiously striving to decode the commas or the inverted commas, before they get to "I."

The lesson continues and the class makes a final unison statement "Mother said, 'I am cooking.'" Many have focussed on the quaint letter "k" in the middle. The teacher says, "Does it say cooking? Look carefully. Look at the beginning. Tell me what the first letter says." Many children may not locate the first letter. "Does it say c-c-c-c?" Children with an intuitive awareness of the phonic identity of "k" agree heartily. The teacher has now reached the new information for which her lesson was designed. "It says b-b-b-b–for baking." Some of the class are surprised to find that the "k" they are focussing says "b" and others gain the impression that "baking" says "b."

An earnest child may be found reading the story to himself later in the day. Matching the number of word impulses he says, to the number of word patterns he sees we might hear him *read* "Mother is cooking some cakes," and he could be very satisfied with his effort.

One could protest that if a good teacher was aware of such difficulties and was carefully pointing to letters and words as she spoke much of the confusion would be eliminated. But that assumes rather too much of group instruction where the young child's attention does fluctuate. If the teacher examines the things she says to her class, to small groups, and to individual children she may find that she takes for granted insights which some children do not have. (Clay, 1975, pp. 3-4)

What experiences help preschool children develop these understandings? Where might we begin? The truth of the matter is that we do not know for sure what experiences help; we have only recently begun to realize that learning to read involves solving such problems. However, we do know something about the experiences of children who have little difficulty with these understandings, and we have a few studies that suggest what might be involved.

First, it appears that experiences with speech alone may not be enough to teach these understandings. For example, learning verses that rhyme or contain alliteration may not accomplish what we assume they do—they may not transfer to insights about speech sounds at the level of analysis we wish or to insights about how these would be represented by print (Savin, 1972). What may be useful is for children to see print and try to map speech onto it. "Print helps readers learn to conceptualize words as sequences of discrete sounds and to become more keenly aware of which sound segments the words contain" (Ehri and Wilce, 1979).

But exactly how can we guide young children to do this? It is essential, first, for children to know what some samples of print say. These might include their own names, the names of friends, labels in the environment, and the story lines in favorite books. The last situation may be particularly important because it provides print that is sufficiently varied and complex to cause children to think about how print and speech are related. It takes time, and repeated reading of the print by adults, for children to know in a precise way what a variety of samples of print say. We all know, for example, that there comes a point when children who have been read favorite stories frequently, know these stories by heart. Until recently, however, we had little knowledge of what came before this step.

We now have data suggesting that developing this ability involves a long process of reconstructing the story and of realizing things such as (1) each book has its own specific story, not one made up by the reader to accompany the pictures, (2) the pictures and print are related—pictures provide clues about what the story says, (3) print, not the pictures, tells the story—it is what the reader reads, and (4) specific words are used to tell each story (Rossman, 1980; Doake, 1979; Schickedanz, 1979; Clay, 1975). These insights are gained gradually as children are read favorite stories over and over. For example, the experience of hearing several books read many times may be needed to help children realize that each book tells a specific story and that the story remains the same each time the book is read. Hearing each book even more frequently may then lead to the insight that not only does the story stay the same, but the specific words stay the same as well. Reading a book, children now realize, requires looking at the print.

After extensive experience with storybooks, children do begin to attend to the print in them and try to find the print that matches what they know the book says. Attempts to match speech and print are not successful at first, however, and children only gradually discover how the two are related. For example, children may at first point to letters when saying syllables. A child attempting to read the title on the cover of the book, *A Snowy Day,* might point to each letter when saying a syllable:

A    Snowy Day.   (text)

A    Snow   y   Day.   (speech with finger pointing to text)

The child runs out of words to say before running out of print to point to because the child does not know that each letter represents a sound, not a syllable or a word. Actually, as we explained earlier, the child does not even know what speech segments such as sounds, syllables, or words are. Speech is merely segmented into its most natural units, which are syllables (Rozin and Gleitman, 1977). What the child does discover, however, is that his or her initial hypothesis about the relationship between speech and print does not work as expected. The child knows what the print is *supposed* to say, but discovers that it doesn't work as he or she had guessed.

When adults see children make such errors in mapping, they explain that ''this says *A* (pointing to the *A*), this says *Snowy,* and this says *Day.*'' Children often repeat what was demonstrated, although they probably understand little about the basis for the procedure. Nevertheless, several such experiences seem to get children to revise their initial hypothesis that a single letter is pointed to, and they often start pointing to groups of letters marked by space—to words in print.

However, some problems remain. Consider the child who read a page from the book, *The Very Hungry Caterpillar:*

On Monday, he ate one apple, but he was still hungry. (text)

On   Mon   day   he ate one ap   ple, but he was still hungry. (speech with finger pointing)

This child knew that a word in print is a collection of letters set off from other collections by space, but not that some words have more than one syllable. (Of course, a child may still not know that a collection of letters in print is called a ''word'' or that speech is being segmented into syllables; the child is merely segmenting print and speech in certain ways.) Thus, the child at this point runs out of print before running out of the words the child knows the page says. This problem is the opposite of the earlier one where the child ran out of words to say with print left over. A child with this problem often reads the title of the book, *Where the Wild Things Are,* without difficulty because here each word has but one syllable.

However, children who have received instruction in sounding words out may begin to make a different kind of mistake; they may read *Where the Wild Things Are* like this:

Where the wild things are    (text)

Where    the    wil    d    things    are (speech with finger pointing)

What has happened is that sounding out has led to the creation of more syllables than the word *wild* has. One child whom the author observed read the title this way eleven times in a row. After several attempts, he exclaimed in exasperation, "This book's not working right!" (Schickedanz, 1981). The strategy of matching words in print to spoken syllables had worked for him so many times in the past that he insisted it should work now.

What the child failed to realize was that his exaggerated pronunciation of the word *wild* was creating an extra syllable. The author explained, "When you say the word *wild,* you say it altogether like this: *wild.* Here, see the *d* at the end of *wild?* When you say it, your finger should be no further than this word, which is the one that says *wild.* See the letter *d* at the end of it?"[3] The child then repeated what had been demonstrated and read the title correctly several times in succession. He also looked intently at the words, as if attempting to understand exactly why what he had done should work. This child may have been gaining real insight at this point about what blending sounds is all about. We can attempt to pronounce individual sounds in words, but we necessarily distort words when we do this. When children try to map speech to print, they discover the actual relationship between the two.

In summary, experiences in which children attempt to map speech to print may be critical in helping them discover that English alphabet letters represent speech at the sound level and that speech can be thought about at various levels including individual sounds, syllables, and words. The entire process of discovery probably takes several years. Children who are read to often beginning at an early age become proficient during the later preschool years. Children who are not provided with these experiences may have difficulty learning to read, particularly if phonics alone is used before children have any idea of what letters and sounds are.

---

[3]One of the reasons it is useful for children to learn letter names is because it makes talking with them about print possible. The purpose is not simply learning the smallest units of print in order to learn letter-sound associations, and so on.

Teachers help children learn letter
names.

USING KNOWLEDGE OF LETTER-SOUND ASSOCIATIONS AS A READING STRATEGY.
In the minds of many, reading is simply a matter of *decoding,* or of translating
printed symbols (letters) into the sounds they represent. We have seen in our
earlier discussions that the process is not quite so simple. First, children have great
difficulty in knowing what the segment of speech we call a *sound* is, and in isolating
these segments in the speech they hear. Second, children may not know exactly to
what we are referring in print when we use words such as *letter* or *word.* How do we
know a word in print when we see one? (We know, of course, that a word is surrounded by space.)

When matters such as these are understood, when children understand conceptually how print and speech relate, they are still confronted with difficulties
that arise because there is no one-to-one correspondence between letters and
sounds—the English alphabet is not completely phonetic. Therefore, in addition
to helping children learn the relationships between letters and sounds in general
through instruction which isolates this learning, it is crucial that children have
many opportunities to deal with whole print; because it is the context of a letter in
a word that determines what sound it will represent. Context clues, such as the
meaning of the text and knowledge of language, also help a reader determine what
a nonphonetic word says.

## Summary of Reading Skills for Young Children

Skills include learning *conventions of print* such as left-to-right arrangement of print and the use of space to mark words. Even more basic are insights such as knowing that it is the *print rather than the pictures that tell a story in a book,* that *print should make sense,* that *context can be used as a clue to what print says,* and that *print and speech are related in a very specific way*—individual letters represent individual speech sounds. Reading skills must also *include knowledge of the metalanguage used to talk about written language.*

General methods for helping children learn these skills are discussed on pp. 209–17. Specific activities begin on p. 217.

# GENERAL METHODS
# FOR TEACHING LANGUAGE
# ARTS TO YOUNG CHILDREN

### Encouraging Verbal Expression

From the moment children enter the classroom, language surrounds them. They exchange greetings with the teacher and with other children. They plan the day's activities by reviewing the previous day's work and agreeing on things to be done. At all times, they use language to solve problems, to share ideas, and to support ego development. Rich and stimulating experiences, encouragement in conversation with peers, and warm verbal adults who talk with them promote the development of language.

In an atmosphere of acceptance there will be talk, lots and lots of talk: child with child, child with small groups, child with large groups, child with teacher, child with other adults, and child with materials. The silent classroom where friends cannot sit next to each other because they talk is not a room that supports language development. Most of our talk is with friends.

When children are asked to share something verbally, it must be something the listener wants to hear. Sometimes, show-and-tell periods are one-way communications with aggressive, verbal children often making shallow comments about experiences that are largely irrelevant for listeners. Discussions for making decisions about what the class has done or will be doing that day would be more relevant to each child.

### Integrating Language Arts
### and Other Content Areas

Traditionally, schools have separated talking, writing, and reading even though their interrelationships have been repeatedly demonstrated. In the past, the emphasis in the lower grades was on skills development; the upper grades focused on learning content. Learning skills cannot be separated from learning meaning, however, even at the very beginning. In fact, skills learning within meaningful contexts may be even more important in the beginning when children do not yet understand the complex relationships between print and speech.

In all the content chapters in this book, activities incorporate the language arts. This integrated approach provides children with many opportunities to talk, write, and read in meaningful contexts; skill learning is made a tool, or a means to the end, of communication.

### Providing a Print-Rich Environment to Develop Readiness

Central to our approach to written language learning is a basic philosophy about "readiness." We have assumed that readiness for written language learning is not basically a matter of motor, perceptual (auditory and visual discrimination), or social-emotional development. Obviously, handwriting requires fine motor skill, and both reading and writing require detecting fine differences between one letter and another. Also, emotional well-being is essential to learning everything.[4] However, learning about written language is basically a conceptual matter—a matter of knowing about print, speech, and the relationship between the two.

Assumptions about motor and perceptual skills and other prerequisites have often resulted in our treating written language learning as something very different from any other kind of learning. For example, when children begin to walk, build with blocks, paint, or jump rope, they are not very skilled. Children stumble and fall down, the block structures fall over, the brush bristles are rubbed into the paper, or feet become tangled in the rope. But we rarely fuss and we do not remove the materials (and thus the opportunities for mastering them) until children are ready, that is, skilled enough motorically to perform more perfectly. In fact, we assume that access is necessary for mastery.

We suggest that motor skills should be viewed in the same way with regard to written language acquisition. Young children often wish to write long before they have perfect fine motor control. Its absence bothers children little, if at all, when adults refrain from making unreasonable demands such as insisting that children form letters perfectly, write on and within lines, arrange print on a page in conventional ways, and halt exploration of all the possible ways that lines and letters can be formed. If the beginning stages of writing are approached in ways similar to the beginning stages of picture making, alarm over scribbles and lack of fine motor control fade to the background. The emphasis shifts to providing tools for exploring and discovering the characteristics of print.

Similarly, assuming that learning to read is basically a perceptual prob-

---

[4] We would suggest that concern about emotional harm due to early introduction of written language is the result of inappropriate experiences and demands rather than of anything intrinsic to written language. For example, if we respond to a child's gift of a scribbled or imperfectly written "letter" as we would to a gift of a scribbled crayon drawing, the child's emotional delight will be the same. The problem has been that too often we have responded to the second with thanks and praise, and to the first with suggestions for corrections.

lem—a matter of learning ever more precise auditory and visual discriminations—has often prevented us from giving the youngest children access to print or
has led us to provide it in an isolated, fragmented fashion. For example, we may
have provided recorded environmental sounds for children to identify, but not experiences directly related to helping children segment and identify sounds within
actual speech. Or, we may have provided children with shapes to discriminate in
terms of overall form or orientation, but not provided alphabet materials. Our
assumption was that we must first train children to listen and to hear, to look and
to see, before they could hear speech sounds or see differences among letters.

In addition, we assumed that the errors we saw young children make were
essentially a matter of not listening or looking, rather than of not knowing about
print. Faced with a child who had reversed a letter in writing, we were inclined to
tell the child to *look* carefully at a model of the letter to see how it was different from
his or her own, assuming as we did that the child had failed to see how the letter
should be oriented. Armed with evidence that such problems abounded in young
children's writing, we tended to provide readiness practice such as asking children
to circle ducks or shapes in a workbook that faced the same direction.

However, the actual problem may be simply that children *see* these differences in orientation but ignore them because they don't at first *know* that orientation matters—after all, it does not matter with three-dimensional objects—a
duck is called a duck whether it faces right, left, up or down. But print is different—it follows different conventions—and we should not be surprised at such
errors. They can be overcome by exposing children to print so that its unique
characteristics can be discovered. Rather than telling children to "look carefully," we might simply explain "There's something very special about letters—
each letter faces a certain direction. You have put lines together the right way to
make an *E*, but an *E* faces this way, not the way you placed it. Would you like to
try to make an *E* that faces this direction rather than the other way?"

Similarly, we have assumed that children's problems in identifying similar
sounds is a matter of untrained listening or hearing. As we have seen in previous
discussions, much more is involved. Exercises in listening to environmental
sounds probably contribute little, if any, to children's understanding of speech
sounds. Speech has unique characteristics; the problem is essentially one of *knowing* how speech and print *relate*—how print represents speech. As worthwhile as
listening is, listening to environmental sounds does not provide adequate
"reading readiness" because it simply does not capture the essential problems.

We are suggesting that many traditional notions of "reading and writing
readiness" be discarded and that we consider instead that children read and write
from a very early age, but in ways that differ from conventional or adult ways. Errors in early attempts to use written language should not be any more alarming
than children's errors in early talking. David Doake, a researcher who has studied
how preschoolers learn to read storybooks, has talked about this issue:

> The concepts of reading readiness, pre-reading and even worse pre-literacy are
> misleading and harmful to young children and to continue to think of the child's pre-

grade one experience in these terms is a major hindrance to their progress in learning to read.

There is no such thing as readiness for reading. Children begin to learn to read from the time they begin to hear language and more particularly, from the time they hear their first nursery rhymes, jingles, or stories. They begin to learn that books have pages and that the pages can be turned . . . that books have a right and a wrong way up . . . At some stage they will make an important discovery about the stories they are hearing and often repeating for themselves. They will become aware, although not necessarily with a conscious realization, that the source of the story . . . is not in the pictures or in the reader's head, but is actually on the pages in the black squiggles that the reader has been pointing to from time to time. . . . Provided they are exposed and immersed in written language in functional ways, just as they are exposed to and immersed in oral language, children's reading behaviors will begin to emerge very early. . . . They are *reading behaviors* and as such are critically important to the child's continuing progress towards literacy. [Emphasis ours] (Doake, 1979, pp. 1–2)

In summary, experiences with written language are the experiences which enable children to learn about written language. (See Boxes 7–1 and 7–2 for suggestions about print-related materials to include in preschool and kindergarten classrooms.)

BOX 7–1   *WRITING MATERIALS SUGGESTED FOR CLASSROOMS*

## Materials to Include in a Writing Center

A variety of pencils, thick and thin, with erasers and without, black lead and colored*

Variety of magic markers, thick and thin tipped, various colors

Crayons

Typewriter

Alphabet letter print set and stamp pad

A variety of white and colored paper

Carbon paper

IBM cards

Magic slates

Pieces of cardboard of various weights and sizes

Index cards

Blank books**

Small chalkboards, chalk and damp sponge or cloth for erasing

Sand or salt trays (shirt boxes with lids will work)

Dittos with models of alphabet letters indicating the sequence for making strokes***

Picture dictionary

Deck of name cards for children in class and for teachers

Alphabet chart posted on the wall or on a room divider

Bulletin board to display samples of children's writing

## Writing Materials to Include in Other Areas of the Room

Pencils tied to easels to be used to write names on paintings

Cardboard and magic markers placed in block area to be used when children wish to make signs

Pencils, paper, small note pads, small chalkboard, and chalk placed in dramatic play area for use in making ''shopping lists,'' writing ''letters,'' leaving ''notes,'' making ''money'' or ''tickets,'' taking telephone ''messages,'' and so on.

Pencils and paper as needed in science and math areas for recording observations or keeping track of discoveries

\* Children who have not yet transferred from a fist grip to a mature pencil grasp exert a great deal of pressure on a pencil tip because their arm does not rest on the table. Thick pencils are needed by these children—thin pencils and crayons break.

\*\* These can be made simply by stapling a few sheets of paper together and using wallpaper from sample books for a cover. If a stapler is provided, children can make their own books.

\*\*\* Such dittos are for children who are ready for learning how to form the letters correctly. Sometimes, children who are not yet ready enjoy using the dittos, but typically, they do not attend to the instructions for sequence—they are merely playing with writing. There seems to be no harm when children self-select such materials, but they probably offer no help either. Teachers concerned about waste of such materials may wish to dispense these to selected children as appropriate.

BOX 7-2   *MATERIALS CONTAINING PRINT TO INCLUDE IN PRESCHOOL AND PRIMARY CLASSROOMS*

A library area with storybooks attractively displayed

Labels and signs

• storage containers can be labeled

| Pencils | Bristle Blocks | Play Dough |
|---|---|---|

• areas of the room can be labeled

| Block Area | Library Corner |
|---|---|

• reminders or rules can be written on signs

| Wear goggles | Talk quietly in the library |
|---|---|
| Wear a smock | Closed today | Open today |

Print props for dramatic play (see extensive list on p. 230)

Road and traffic signs for block play

Attendance chart

Helpers' chart

Poems or familiar songs and rhymes attractively posted on the wall

Manipulative materials in a learning center

- a deck of name cards for children in the class
- picture lotto games that have pictures labeled with words
- wooden puzzles with print on them (there are traffic sign puzzles, occupation puzzles, and puzzles of story characters which have print on them)
- concentration picture cards with pictures labeled
- wooden alphabet letters such as those from a Scrabble game
- picture-card sets to be used for grouping on the basis of same initial consonant or rhyming, preferably with pictures labeled
- see activity section for many more ideas for materials to include in this kind of learning center

## TEACHING THE METALANGUAGE OF WRITTEN LANGUAGE

As the example provided by Marie Clay on p. 204 illustrated, children often do not understand the language we use to talk about language. Knowing what we mean by terms such as *letter, word,* and *sound* is essential if we are to communicate effectively with children. Knowing the names of letters is important for the same reason.

Children can learn the language used in talking about written language in much the same way as they learn any other aspect of language—by hearing it used in meaningful contexts. For example, as a child manipulates felt letters on a felt board, a teacher might comment, "All the *letters* you have placed together up here are called *S*'s." Or the teacher might say, "This *letter* is in a *word* you know. What is the word you know that has a *B* in it? Does your name start with a *B?* Yes, that's the *word* you know that has the *letter B* in it."

When writing a child's name on artwork, the teacher might name the letters as they are written down: *M, a, r, i, a.* That *word* says *Maria.* The teacher might go on to say, "Your name and Marsha's name both start with the *letter M.* That's why your names *sound* alike at the beginning."

Before reading a familiar storybook, the teacher might point to the print on the book's cover and ask, "What do you think these *words* say? That's right, they do say *The Snowy Day.* This *word* says *The,* this word says *Snowy,* and this word says *Day.* Now, let's read all about what this little boy does on a snowy day."

In addition, children can be asked what various aspects of written language are called. Just as we might sit with a young child looking at a picture book and ask what the names of various pictures are, we might do the same with an alphabet book: "What's this letter's name? Uh-huh, that is an *A.* What's this letter called?

Children's names are often among the first sight words learned.

No, that one's not called *D;* it's called *G.* Here, let's look back and find the *D.* See how they are different? The big *D* is all closed. The big *G* has this open space. The little *d* has a circle and a straight line pointing up. The little *g* has a circle and a line going down with a curve at the end.''

After many experiences of this kind, children learn the language needed to talk about written language. They will make many errors along the way, but we need be no more alarmed by these than we are when a young child calls a cow a horsie. We respond to such errors with helpful information: ''We call that animal a cow, not a horsie. It doesn't have a mane or a bushy tail like a horse, and it says 'moooo,' not 'neigh.''' We can respond in the same way when talking about language, although we must understand in both situations that many encounters with print—or cows and horses—are needed for children really to understand the meaning of what we say.

## READING STORIES TO CHILDREN

Almost without exception, where children have learned to read at home before attending school, the children's parents read to them, typically on a daily basis (Durkin, 1966; Doake, 1979; Forrester, 1977). In addition, in studies of experiences that predict later success in reading achievement in school, early experience with stories appears again and again. Because the data are correlational, we do not know for sure whether it is the story reading experience or other experiences that such parents also provide that helps these children learn to read with ease. More recent studies on children's actual behavior with storybooks suggest that these experiences contribute something directly (Rossman, 1980; Doake, 1979). In any event, there seems to be sufficient evidence that story reading experience is useful and should be given emphasis in any program for young children.

Because classrooms differ from the home environment, especially in terms of the number of children present, story experiences in the classroom can differ markedly from story experiences at home. We would suggest that these differences may weaken the effect of such experiences in the classroom, and we suggest that teachers try to make story reading in the classroom as similar to story reading at home as possible. This would require, for example, that story reading not be limited to large groups in which children are sitting far from the book and cannot see the pictures or print. In addition, story reading in large groups prevents children from turning the pages, determining the pace of the reading, asking questions, relating the story content to personal experience, and so on. Reading to groups of three or four children provides a situation in which children can be more actively involved. In addition, we would strongly suggest that children be read to on an individual or very small group basis (two children) during activity time or at other times throughout the day. Of course, teachers cannot always devote undivided attention to children in the library corner. However, in preschool classrooms especially, staff can organize themselves so that at least one teacher spends some time each day reading to children in the library corner. Teachers in kindergarten and primary grade classrooms can arrange for volunteers to read to children. For example, high-school students often help out for several hours a week in the lower grades. Often, reading the stories is as helpful to the volunteers as hearing the stories is for the young children. (See Box 7–3 for suggested techniques to use in story reading.)

BOX 7–3   SUGGESTIONS FOR STORY READING

1. Read to *small* groups of children during organized story times.
2. Read to one or two children at a time during activity periods. Try to arrange for volunteers to help with this.
3. Read books children ask for. (Repetition of favorite storybooks is important if children are to master the story.)
4. Reread a book if you can when children request it.
5. Allow children to take favorite books home (one at a time) to have their parents read it. Better yet, set up a lending library for parents if this is possible.)
6. Run your finger under the line of print from time to time as you read.
7. Allow the child to hold the book and turn the pages.
8. Discuss pictures in the books with children. This helps children understand the story content and master the book.

9.  Store books attractively on low shelves where children can reach them easily.
10. Remove or repair torn books. Involve children in repairing books.
11. Add new books gradually and keep old, familiar books. It takes children many months to learn favorite stories. Children need access to books to be able to master them.
12. Ask children to read the story to you from time to time. Refrain from correcting children's "mistakes" unless it seems useful and appropriate. Allow children to read in their own way.
13. When using a listening post for storytelling, provide the book for children to follow along.
14. Include many books that contain rhyme, repetitions, verses, and story lines that match illustrations very closely. These characteristics of books make them easy for children to understand and learn.

## ACTIVITIES FOR LANGUAGE ARTS INSTRUCTION

The balance of this chapter consists of practical ideas for teaching language arts to young children. They are organized to follow closely the outline of goals presented earlier.

### Oral Language Development

### EXTENDING VOCABULARY

1. Activity:    Mystery box (PP–K)

*Materials:*    Attractively decorated box and assorted objects such as paper clips, yarn, cork, fabric, sandpaper, and so on.
*Procedure:*    Set up a box with an assortment of objects within it. Place box in an appropriate learning center. The children reach in, feel one object, and describe it to a peer or to the teacher. Teachers can supply descriptive words to help children. They may ask, "Is it soft or hard?" "Is it stiff or does it bend?" "Is it fuzzy or smooth?" In this way, children learn vocabulary.
*Suggestions and Variations:*    Rather than describe the objects hidden in the mystery box, children may be asked to identify the objects. A pincer clothespin, an acorn, a paper clip, a nut and bolt, a piece of velvet or corduroy, a piece of styrofoam, and so on, may be placed in the box. Children can try to identify the items by touch, but may not know what they are called. Teachers or other children can supply the new words. It must be remembered that encountering an object and its name once does not necessarily enable children to understand the semantic category referred to by the word. Providing many *different* objects that go by a particular name and naming objects in the natural environment must not be overlooked by the teacher.

2. **Activity:**   Picture file (PP-P)

*Materials:*   Pictures of all kinds of objects, plants, animals, and people, including those that indicate different feelings.
*Procedure:*   Place pictures where children can look at them. A picture album made from an old card album may be a good way to make them available to children. Children can look through the album and learn to identify the pictures by name. Teachers or other adults, or children who are familiar with some of the things depicted, will have to supply the words to children who do not know them.
*Suggestions and Variations:*   Pictures may also be used on bulletin boards or in other display areas. Pictures found in old magazines may be used by the children to make books. Teachers can then label the pictures or take other dictation children want to give. Several different pictures of objects, all of which go by a certain name, as well as related objects that go by different names, may help children learn the details and complexities of semantic categories.

3. **Activity:**   Field trips (PP-P)

*Materials:*   Various materials depending on the field trip taken.
*Procedure:*   Refer to field trip discussions on page 354. These experiences contribute much to vocabulary development. Teachers should familiarize themselves with special machinery, tools, and processes that might be used at the place the children visit so children can be provided with the names.
*Suggestions and Variations:*   Try to find pictures relating to the field trip so that discussions about the trip can be supported later in the classroom.
*Suggestions for handicapped children:*   Make certain that the place to be visited can accommodate children in wheelchairs, or whatever other special requirements will be necessary for a child. Arrange for children with sight problems to touch and feel items discussed, where possible, and to stand close to the items if sight is impaired but not absent.

4. **Activity:**   Color names (PP-K)

*Materials:*   A box of objects of various colors; a collection of paint chips from a hardware store; a set of commercial color plaques; a color wheel.
*Procedure:*   Place one of the materials listed above in a learning center. When children use the materials, help them use the appropriate names for the colors.
*Suggestions and Variations:*   Do not place all the materials in a center at the same time. Use one set for awhile, and then replace it with another set of materials. Remember, too, that colors surround children all the time. Use

natural opportunities to name colors: "That sure is a bright green shirt you have on today." "Your pants are red like my scarf."

5. Activity:   Singing (PP-K)

*Materials:*   Simple instruments to accompany songs, or tapes and records. The teacher's voice can also be used.
*Procedure:*   Sing all kinds of songs appropriate for young children. Songs in which children can substitute words are especially good for language development. "Wheels on the Bus" and "Where Oh Where is Dear Little Mary?" are two songs that are of this type.
*Suggestions and Variations:*   Songs that teach vocabulary best are those in which the experience the song talks about can be created by the children at the time the song is sung. For example, there are songs that call for patting one's tummy, head, or cheek, tapping one's foot, or clapping one's hands. Children can learn the meaning of these terms from these songs. Songs that talk about things children have not experienced and cannot experience do not teach new words to children, but merely teach them to repeat words (sometimes the wrong ones!) that they do not understand. (Refer back to the discussion on p. 186)

6. Activity:   Stories (PP-P)

*Materials:*   Storybooks.
*Procedure:*   Read books to children both during story time and, when you can, during activity time. Talk with children about words in the book. For example, if the book is about a ferocious lion, ask children if they know what "ferocious" means.
*Suggestions and Variations:*   When discussing words in stories, sometimes ask children to think of another word that could be used in place of the one appearing in the story. For example, if the story refers to a "ferocious" lion, the teacher might ask, "What other words could we use to describe that lion?" When children do not know the meaning of a word, try to explain it in terms of words they do know or experiences they have had. For example, if the word is *picnic* and a child does not know what this means, explain that when you have snack outside, this is really a picnic; eating outside is a picnic.

7. Activity:   Informal talk (PP-P)

*Materials:*   Nothing special.
*Procedure:*   Talk with children informally about anything and everything. For example, name the patterns (stripes, plaids, polka dots), weaves (cor-

A good story captures almost every child's attention.

duroy, gingham, flannel, seersucker) and fabric (wool, cotton, polyester) of their clothes. Help them learn the names for parts of school equipment (brush bristles, paint palette, fish-tank filter and pump, record-player arm and turntable, and so on) by using these terms yourself.


## DEVELOPING ACCURATE SPEECH

All the activities listed above in any of the other areas of oral language may also be used to help children develop accuracy in speech; when children talk, they are practicing speech sounds. The most important influence on the development of good speech is having good adult models to listen to. It should be remembered, too, that in normal development, children usually substitute some speech sounds for others or leave out some sounds in words they say. For example, they may say *gween* for *green* substituting a *w* for an *r,* or they may say *geen,* leaving out the *r* entirely. Attention need not be called to such errors in the speech of young preschool children. Good models and language activities such as those listed below will suffice.

1. **Activity:**   I said this, not that (K-P)

   *Materials:*   Tape recorder, tape, and words that are difficult for a child to pronounce. This list will vary from child to child and from class to class.

*Procedure:*   Children can practice pronunciation by recording words on which they have been working. Have children listen to their own tapes. Young children, for example, confuse "pin" and "pen." Spanish speakers find the word "yellow" difficult to produce.

*Suggestions and Variations:*   Ask a child to do this activity with a friend who will give help in hearing new or difficult sounds. If a child has a great deal of difficulty making some sounds, and it appears not to be typical immature speech, this child should be seen by a speech specialist. Ask the specialist for ideas to use in the classroom to help the child.

2. **Activity:**   Tongue-twisters (PP–K)

   *Materials:*   None.

   *Procedure:*   At group time, teach children tongue-twisters such as "Peter Piper Picked a Peck of Pickled Peppers." These give children practice in forming different sounds and sensitize them to correct pronunciation.

3. **Activity:**   Books (PP–K)

   *Materials:*   Books such as *One Bright Monday Morning* and *Over in the Meadow* that contain language with much alliteration or other characteristics that would focus attention on pronouncing words clearly.

   *Procedure:*   Read the books to children. Invite children to read along. Comment on the interesting ways the words start: "bees a buzzing"; "chirping cheery songs"; "worms a wiggling."

## SUPPORTING CHILDREN'S SYNTACTICAL DEVELOPMENT

1. **Activity:**   Dramatic play (PP–K)

   *Materials:*   Props for house or store play.

   *Procedure:*   Encourage several children to play together in the dramatic play area. Children usually talk to each other as they play. When appropriate, the teacher may join the children's play and interact verbally with them. It seems most helpful if this verbal interaction is directed toward the child's activities and interests. For example, if a child is "cooking" dinner when the adult enters and offers the adult a plate and says, "Eat," the adult might respond by saying, "Oh, you want me to eat lunch with you? Okay, I'll sit down over here." The adult might go on to inquire about what it is that everyone is eating. The child may answer, "Soup." The teacher might then say, "Good, it's cold outside. It's a good day to have soup for lunch."

2. **Activity:**   Reading books (PP–K)

   *Materials:*   Storybooks.
   *Procedure:*   Try to find time to read to individual children or small groups of children during activity time. Encourage children to talk about the story and the pictures. These conversations provide children with a chance to talk about things of interest and expose them to mature language from the teacher as well as from the book.

3. **Activity:**   Informal talk (PP–K)

   *Materials:*   Nothing special.
   *Procedure:*   Talk with individual children or small groups of children in all kinds of situations during the day. Such times might include arrival time in the morning, snack time, lunch time, and much of activity time. These conversations should be about children's ongoing activities or other topics that are of interest to them. This kind of meaningful talking between children and adults may be *the most important way* for children to learn about the structure and rules of language.

## USING STANDARD ENGLISH

1. **Activity:**   Stories and songs (PP–P)

   *Materials:*   Records and a listening post or record player.
   *Procedure:*   Provide records of stories and songs in Standard English for children to listen to during activity time. Children will enjoy the stories and songs and will at the same time gain familiarity with Standard English.
   *Suggestions and Variations:*   Provide an attractive assortment of books and encourage adult speakers of Standard English—volunteers, aides, parents—to read to the children. If there are children who speak a different language, for example, Navajo or Spanish, provide books in these languages also and encourage native speakers to read from them. Hearing books read in both Standard English and the native language will help children learn English as a second language while retaining their own. Care should be taken to see that there is a good balance between the two.

2. **Activity:**   Language master listening (K–P)

   *Materials:*   Language masters and blank language master cards.
   *Procedure:*   Language masters provide children with good language models and allow them to record their own words and sentences. In running through the cards, children can compare their language to the teacher's

model. Prepare cards to teach children their addresses. For example, on a card with John's picture clipped to it, tape "My name is John Taylor, and I live at 200 Main Street."

*Suggestions and Variations:*    Make up some language master cards which demonstrate Standard English forms of common phrases. Then ask a question which calls for a response using the same form. "My name is Mary. What is your name?" (Spanish speakers tend to say, "I am called Mary"—*"Me llamo Mary."*) "I am six years old. How old are you?" Spanish speakers tend to say, "I have six years"—*"Yo tengo seis años."* Black children may say, "I be six.") When the children record their answers to the question, they can hear their voices as well as the taped one.

3. **Activity:**   Conversations (PP-P)

*Materials:*   None.
*Procedure:*   Carry on conversations with children on the playground or inside about their block building, jungle-gym climbing, painting, sand building, or some experience they have in common. You should be able to carry on these conversations in the child's native language. Provide translations into Standard English for statements you know the child has mastered in the native language.

4. **Activity:**   Dramtic play (PP-K)

*Materials:*   Props for house or store play.
*Procedure:*   Encourage children to engage in dramatic play. If the class contains children who speak a language other than English as well as children who do speak English, the non-English-speaking children will pick up a great deal of language from the other children. (The English-speaking children will learn some of the other language, too, although the influence tends not to be very great when the non-English-speaking children are few in number.)

## ORGANIZING AND EXPRESSING THOUGHTS

1. **Activity:**   Block building (PP-P)

*Materials:*   Unit blocks; appropriate props, such as small people or transportation toys.
*Procedure:*   Make materials available to children during activity time. As children play together with these materials, they will inevitably talk with each other about what should be built and how they should go about building it.

These situations are excellent for giving children practice in organizing and expressing their ideas and feelings.

2. **Activity:**   Dramatic play (PP–P)

*Materials:*   Those described for dramatic play on pages 172 and 173.
*Procedure:*   Promote dramatic play by providing space and props. As children engage in dramatic play, they will talk with each other. They will often have differing ideas about how the play should proceed and these differences provide an excellent opportunity for children to organize and express their ideas and feelings.

3. **Activity:**   Discussion time (PP–P)

*Materials:*   None.
*Procedure:*   Often at group time at the end of an activity period, individual children offer to explain or are asked to explain how they did or made something or how something happened. These occasions provide excellent opportunities for children to organize and express ideas and feelings. Ask questions that help children express thoughts more clearly: "Did you build the house or the garage first?" "What are all the ingredients you used

Dramatic play provides an opportunity for children to organize and express complex ideas and feelings.

to make the apple muffins?'' ''Did you combine the ingredients before you stirred so hard?''

4. **Activity:**   Activities suggested in the chapter on Social Science that involve classroom visitors (pages 375 and 376).

*Materials:*   None.
*Procedure:*   Follow the procedure suggested for the activities. Experience listening to others who present complex ideas and feelings.

## RELATING INFORMATION TO A GROUP

1. **Activity:**   Discussion or evaluation time (PP–P)

*Materials:*   Materials will vary depending on the topic.
*Procedure:*   Children may describe to the whole group how they made something or what they found out about something during activity time earlier in the day.
*Suggestions and Variations:*   Avoid making these presentations routine and boring. Not every child needs to relay information to others in this way every day or even every week. When children have mastered a process or learned about something that is of interest to them and which they would like to share, then it is appropriate to encourage them to present the information to the group.
You may be able to arrange a visit by one of the students to a class next door to explain a process or give a talk on a special topic of interest. As children progress in the primary grades, it is perfectly appropriate for a teacher to help them organize such presentations, to encourage the child to practice the presentation before actually delivering it, and to help the child think of ways to make the presentation more interesting and clear to an audience.

### Listening

## DEVELOPING LISTENING ABILITIES

1. **Activity:**   Listening and discussing (PP–P)

*Materials:*   A designated place for group meetings.
*Procedure:*   Children and adults should be seated so that each one can easily and comfortably see everyone else. Encourage children to share ideas, achievements, and feelings. Individual children may tell about projects they have completed. Children can learn appreciative listening behavior by the teacher's model of looking at the speaker attentively, asking questions, re-

flecting about what the speaker has said, and communicating to the speaker an interest in what is being said. Encourage children to enter into the conversation by asking questions and suggesting possible uses for the project or possible solutions for a common concern.

*Suggestions and Variations:*   In order to come to any feasible conclusions and make a judgment, children must listen to each other. If children enjoy listening to a child describe a just-completed boat, this is appreciative listening. If children listen in order to make a boat of their own, this is attentive listening. Analytical listening is accomplished when the ideas presented are evaluated in terms of feasibility.

2. Activity:   Simon says (PP–P)

*Materials:*   None.

*Procedure:*   The leader, the teacher or a child, gives a command to each child by name to move in some fashion from a starting line toward a finish line. The called-on child is to perform the command if it begins with "Simon says." For example, if the leader says, "Mary, take a giant step," Mary should not move. But if the command is "Simon says: take a giant step," Mary takes the largest step she can.

*Suggestions and Variations:*   Children should be encouraged to give commands for a variety of unusual steps—scissor steps, skating steps, tip-toe steps—so that children learn to listen both for the words "Simon says" and the kinds of steps they are to take.

3. Activity:   Natural conversation (PP–P)

*Materials:*   None.

*Procedure:*   Talk to individual children in the normal course of the day about things that have happened at school or at home. Children learn to listen to our language in such situations and we can determine their understanding of what is said to them by noticing how they respond to our questions or how they proceed in a conversation after we have made a comment.

### Writing

## LEARNING THE DISTINCTIVE
## FEATURES OF PRINT AND
## THE NAME OF EACH LETTER

1. Activity:   Feely letters (PP–K)

*Materials:*   Letters of sandpaper, pipe cleaner, sand, felt, rice, and beans glued on cards; wooden and magnetic letters.

*Procedure:*   Young children need experiences with letters—to play with, match, or use in trying to make words. Make some of the above materials available where they may be used freely by children. Teachers or peers will need to provide letter names to those who do not know them.

2. **Activity:**   Letter bingo (PP–K)

*Materials:*   Bingo cards using letters; small cards with letters to be used by the caller; bottle caps for the players to use to cover cards as letters are called.
*Procedure:*   Follow the usual bingo procedures. Give one playing card and nine bottle caps to each player. Have a child be the caller. Encourage the child to say the name of the letter being called rather than just showing it to the players.
*Suggestions and Variations:*   Make the first bingo game using upper-case letters. Later, make another bingo game that contains upper- and lower-case pairs together in a square (*Aa, Bb, Cc,* and so on). In this way, children will begin to learn both forms and to recognize which letters go together.

3. **Activity:**   Typewriting (PP–K)

*Materials:*   Typewriter and paper.
*Procedures:*   Make the typewriter and paper available to the children. In working with the typewriter, children will learn some of the letter names. The teacher can provide these by telling the child what letters have been typed when a child proudly shows what he or she made at the typewriter: "Oh, I see. You typed an *A* over here, a *B* here, and lots of *T*s down here."
*Suggestions and Variations:*   A typewriter will be of great interest to many children and taking turns may become a source of conflict. Teachers can manage this situation by making a list of children who wish to have turns, by setting a time limit of five or ten minutes for each turn, and then calling the next child on the list (or having the child whose turn has just finished find the child). This provides experiences in finding one's name, and counting how many people are ahead of you, and so on.
After the typewriter has been in the classroom for a period of time, turn-taking may take care of itself.

4. **Activity:**   Letters in my name (PP–K)

*Materials:*   Magnetic letters and magnetic board or felt letters and felt board, or paper letters.
*Procedure:*   As children find letters for their own names, help them say the letter names. Often, children can pick out the letters in their names but do not know the names of the individual letters.
*Suggestions and Variations:*   When a child is near print in the environment, comment about any letters that are found in his or her name: "John,

there's a letter *o* in the word *stop* and there's an *o* in your name too.'' Point to the letter if you can.

5. **Activity:**   Writing (PP–K)

   *Materials:*   Paper and pencil or magic marker; magic slate; chalkboard.
   *Procedure:*   When children write, they may form letters even though they are uncertain about a letter's name. Name the letters a child creates, or ask the child which letter it is. When taking dictation, spell out at least some of the words the child is asking you to write: ''Mommy: m-o-m-m-y.''

## DEVELOPING SKILL IN CREATING PRINT

1. **Activity:**   Print in the environment (PP–K)

   *Materials:*   Labels in the classroom, manipulative alphabet materials, books.
   *Procedure:*   Provide print in the environment and call children's attention to it. Children will begin to notice print and how it differs from pictures,

**FIGURE 7-2**   Manuscript letter guide.

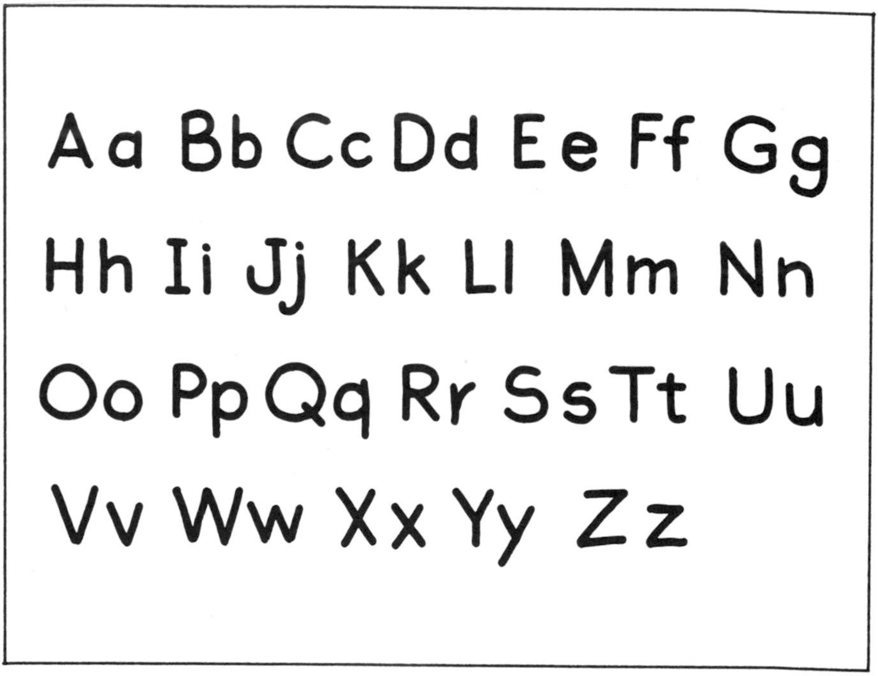

which is an essential understanding in learning how to create print. Children will also begin to notice the distinctive features of print. After some experience in trying to create print and words, children often copy words in the environment.

2. **Activity:**  Chalkboard writing (PP–K)

*Materials:*  Chalk, space at the chalkboard or a small portable board; eraser.

*Procedure:*  Encourage children to use the materials during activity time. They will at first probably just draw or scribble, but there will come a time when they want to "write." They may ask you to write their names or other words, and then try to copy them.

*Suggestions and Variations:*  Place some cards with manuscript letters written on them in the chalkboard chalk tray. Children will find these and be encouraged to try to make the letters. It is helpful to place a colored dot at the top of the letter card so children can hold the letters at the proper orientation. Provide pieces of colored chalk for variation, or give the children paint brushes and a can of water for writing on the chalkboard. Do not be concerned about errors in children's writing or about the creation of printlike forms that are not real letters. It is through experimentation that children learn how to form letters correctly.

3. **Activity:**  Names on work (PP–K)

*Materials:*  Individual work and pencil.

*Procedure:*  Encourage children to write their names on their paintings or drawings. Accept whatever kind of writing a child uses. You might also write the name of the child for a child who is still using scribble writing and merely say, "I'll write your name here the way I write it, which is different from how you do it."

*Suggestions and Variations:*  Children may at times refuse to write their names, saying they do not know how. This may indicate that they have achieved a more advanced understanding of how their name should look than they are currently able to create, or that they know it is to be spelled a certain way and they cannot remember exactly how. Ask the child if you can help, if the child wants you to write it or to spell it, or if the child would like you to write it on a piece of paper from which he or she can copy.

4. **Activity:**  Write and rub (PP–P)

*Materials:*  Manuscript letter guides enclosed in acetate sheet; wax crayon and towel.

*Procedure:*    Make materials available in writing center. Observe to see if the child is able to follow the arrows on the guide. For those who cannot, a simple demonstration can be offered. Sometimes, children attempt to do this activity before they are capable of doing it correctly. They should be allowed to use the materials in their own way if this is the case. Children may also need to be shown how to clean the acetate sheet with the towel.

*Suggestions and Variations:*    Copying letters is not as useful for young children as their own exploration of creating lines and combining them. A child who has not yet begun to create printlike forms and some actual print is probably not ready for copying letters, although he or she may wish to try.

5. **Activity:**    Meaningful writing (PP–P)

*Materials:*    Pencil and paper.

*Procedure:*    At all levels of skill, children should be involved in situations in which purposeful writing is going on. This may include writing a birthday card for a parent or friend, writing a grocery list to use while shopping in the dramatic play store, writing a thank-you note to a classroom visitor, or writing signs and building labels for structures made with unit blocks. Children need to be involved in situations that require writing so that they will realize that learning to write is a useful endeavor.

*Suggestions and Variations:*    Remember that the youngest children will at first scribble write and that it will be a very long time before children will be able to master all the skills involved in writing. Accept children's writing, whatever its level, and provide help and support when children seek it.

6. **Activity:**    Writing in a play (PP–K)

*Materials:*    Dramatic play area or areas; all kinds of props to support play *including* props that contain print and props for creating it (see chart in Box 7–4).

*Procedure:*    Provide print-related props along with other props. Children will incorporate these into their play to write ''letters,'' ''shopping lists,'' ''health charts,'' ''tickets,'' and so on.

BOX 7-4   DRAMATIC PLAY THEMES AND PROPS

**House Play**

1.  Kitchen furniture: a stove, sink, refrigerator, table and chairs, shelves.
2.  Tablecloth or place mats.
3.  Small chest of drawers and doll bed.
4.  Artificial flowers.

5. Several dolls and stuffed animals.
6. Dolls' clothes, blankets, and bottles.
7. Old adult clothes: hats, gloves, jackets, neckties, scarves, jewelry.
8. Plastic replicas of fruits and vegetables.
9. An assortment of dishes, silverware, pots and pans, and cooking utensils.
10. Empty containers from food, cleaning products, and toiletry items.
11. Dustpan and small broom.
12. Play telephones.
13. Brown paper bags or plastic net bags to use for "shopping" or "picnicking" trips.
14. Container of play-dough.
15. A "cookbook" consisting of a collection of recipe charts used in classroom cooking projects.
16. A "telephone book" consisting of children's names, street addresses, and telephone numbers.
17. Paper, pencils, envelopes, small note pads.
18. Wall plaques with appropriate sayings such as "Home Sweet Home."

### Fire Station Play

1. Climbing box or building blocks to use in creating a fire station.
2. Firefighter hats.
3. Old shirts to use as firefighters' jackets.
4. Small lengths of garden hose to use as water hoses.
5. A bell to use as a fire alarm.
6. Old flashlights.
7. Play telephones.
8. A sign that says FIRE STATION.
9. Very simple labeled maps of the classroom for use in locating "fires."
10. Picture posters with appropriate fire safety messages.
11. A large "log" book made with blank sheets of paper.
12. Pencils and note pads for "messages."

### Doctor's Office Play

1. Old, white skirts, shirts, and blouses for use as doctor and nurse dress-up clothes.
2. Medical props such as stethoscopes, popsicle sticks or straws (thermometer), strips of white cloth (bandages), plastic syringes, cotton balls, and old flashlights.
3. Play telephones.
4. Dolls and dolls' clothes.
5. DOCTOR IS IN and DOCTOR IS OUT signs.
6. An "appointment" book for the receptionist.
7. Pencils.
8. Model of clock face with hands that move.

9. An alphabet letter or picture "eye chart."
10. Exposed x-ray films obtained from a doctor.
11. Poster showing the human skeleton, or body parts.

### Grocery Store Play

1. A shelving unit.
2. Cardboard boxes that can serve as cases for "dairy products" or "produce." (Place smaller box inside larger one to make a raised surface.)
3. A large variety of empty containers from foods and other household products.
4. Plastic fruits and vegetables.
5. Play money.
6. A cash register (toy or old, real one).
7. Large food sale poster obtained from local grocers.
8. Brown paper bags of various sizes.
9. Newspaper pages containing food ads.
10. OPEN and CLOSED signs and paper and magic marker to create others.
11. Old shirts for store employee costumes.
12. A kitchen scale to weigh produce.
13. A large selection of food and household products coupons clipped from magazines and the newspaper.
14. A small pad or small pieces of paper, and pencils.
15. Magnetic board and letters to use in making signs for special sales.
16. Stamp pads and numeral stamps to put "prices" on foods.

## UNDERSTANDING HOW TO CREATE WORDS

1. **Activity:**   Manipulative alphabet materials (PP–K)

*Procedure:*   Make these materials available to children. Children will try to place letters together to make words.

*Suggestions and Variations:*   When children first begin to do this, their strings will not be real words, but they will tell you what "word" they have created. It is probably best to go along with their play at this point because they have, in fact, discovered that it takes several letters to make a word. Gradually, they will discover that each individual cannot decide what word has been made. At this point, they will probably string words together and then ask you what word it is. Here it seems helpful to try to pronounce the words they have made so that they can see that it is not a word. You might comment that only certain letter combinations make real words, and if they have letters that can be rearranged to make a word, you might help them do this. Still later, they might ask you how to spell certain words, or they may copy words posted in the classroom. At this point, some word cards may be useful to combine with the alphabet materials.

2. **Activity:**   Labels (PP–P)

   *Materials:*   Felt pen, cards, masking tape.
   *Procedure:*   Print the names of various objects in the room on cards and attach to appropriate objects (window, door, chair). Label storage areas for materials that are to be stored there. Label walls and corners to indicate directions—north, south, east, west.
   *Suggestions and Variations:*   On the playground, set up an area with road signs giving directions for tricycles and pedestrians. One child may act as officer holding up signs for tricycles to *stop* and children to *walk*. Seeing words in the environment helps children think about and discover what words are.

3. **Activity:**   Experience charts and story dictation (PP–K)

   *Materials:*   Paper and pencil or magic markers.
   *Procedure:*   Take story dictation from individual children or write an experience chart with a small group. As you write what children have dictated, say the words you are writing: "This is a little house with a tree." Children will observe that it takes several letters to write one word. Ask the children to help you spell words: "What letter would we use to begin the word *tree?*" This will help children come to realize that the sequence of letters used to write words is related to the sequence of sounds used in saying words. The exact behavior of the story or experience-chart writer needs to be based on the level of the child's understanding.

4. **Activity:**   Children's writing (PP–P)

   *Materials:*   All kinds of writing materials.
   *Procedure:*   As children attempt to write, they try to create words. The exact way in which they do this depends on their level of understanding. Repeated exposure to print, along with repeated opportunities to write, allow children gradually to discover exactly what words are and how they can be created.
   *Suggestions and Variations:*   When children begin to understand that a word's spelling is related (sometimes roughly) to how the word sounds, spelling dictionaries or word banks can be used. As children ask for help with the spelling of words for their stories, write the word, or have the child write the word, and place it in the ring holder to make a personal dictionary. New words should be placed on the ring in alphabetical order. As old words become unnecessary, they can be removed.

Children also invent spellings and then gradually modify them as they see the actual spelling of words they had previously created and as they gain a better understanding of phonology and of how spelling is related to it. It is probably not useful or necessary to correct children's invented spellings in a piece of writing. Children gradually change these spellings to conventional ones as they encounter more print and develop better understandings about phonology and our English spelling system.

## UNDERSTANDING THE CONVENTIONS OF PRINT

1. **Activity:**   Taking dictation (PP–K)

   *Materials:*   Paper and pencil or magic marker.
   *Procedure:*   Write the story or description dictated by the child. The child will observe that you write from left to right and from top to bottom and that you use upper-case letters in some places but not in others. Children will also observe the use of punctuation marks.
   *Suggestions and Variations:*   It takes children a long time (and much experience) to learn all the conventions of print. These should not be dwelled on at any great length when taking dictation. That a child observes your writing is often sufficient. After children have had many opportunities to watch you write, you might begin to ask them where you should begin to write, what kind of punctuation mark you need to place at the end of a sentence, or whether a word must start with a "small" or "big" letter. Be careful not to ask too many of these questions all at once.

2. **Activity:**   Reading print in the environment (PP–K)

   *Procedure:*   When children notice words in the environment, whether on store or traffic signs or in the classroom, run your finger or hand from left to right under the words or phrases when reading these to children: "It says *Cheerios,* right here."

3. **Activity:**   Reading storybooks (PP–K)

   *Procedure:*   When reading to children from a book, occasionally run your finger along under the print you are reading. When beginning a book, read the title on the cover and run your finger along under the words. You might also point out pictures as you go from page to page. This will help children get the idea that books are organized from left to right.

4. **Activity:**    Adult writing (PP–P)

*Procedure:*    Write letters or notes to children. Read these with individual children, running your finger along the words as you read.

5. **Activity:**    Reading what others write (P)

*Procedure:*    Encourage children to read each other's writing. The reading should be done out loud. A writer becomes more sensitive to using punctuation properly if someone else does not interpret the writing as the writer intended. In the process, writers discover where they need question marks or periods, and so on.

6. **Activity:**    Expressive reading (PP–P)

*Materials:*    Storybooks.
*Procedure:*    When reading a story to an individual child or a small group, point out the punctuation marks used in the story. Be sure to read the story with the proper expression indicated by the marks, so that children can observe their function.

7. **Activity:**    Class newspaper (P)

*Materials:*    Ditto master, paper, pencils, typewriter (optional).
*Procedure.*    It may be best to have a small group of children work on each newspaper, but change the composition of the group with each new issue of the paper. Help children decide what should be included in the newspaper and how it can be organized. Since the newspaper will be read by everyone, grammatical structure and punctuation will be of concern to the children. Have the children read each other's writing and suggest improvements and/or corrections. The teacher can provide suggestions for improvement, too.

## UNDERSTANDING THE DIFFERENT
## FORMS AND FUNCTIONS OF WRITING

1. **Activity:**    Shopping list (PP–K)

*Materials:*    Paper and pencil.
*Procedure:*    When you need to do some shopping for a classroom project (to buy ingredients for a cooking project, food for animals, and so on), make a list with the children. This introduces them to the function of writing (helps us to plan things, helps us to remember things) and to one of its forms (lists do not have the same form as stories or letters).

2. **Activity:**   Writing letters to children (PP–K)

**Materials:**   Paper and pencil, envelopes (envelopes can be old, and used).
**Procedure:**   Write letters to a child. They can be short notes in which you tell the child something you noticed about his or her work or in which you tell something about yourself. Read the letter with the child. Through exposure to letters, children come to understand the form of a letter.

3. **Activity:**   Children's letters (PP–K)

**Materials:**   Paper and pencil, envelopes, stamps.
**Procedure:**   Encourage children to write letters to you, to each other, to their parents, or to friends who live far away. Questions such as "How do we start a letter?" and "How will your mother know who it is from?" help children think about the form of a letter.

4. **Activity:**   Children's stories (PP–K)

**Materials:**   Paper and pencil, blank books, magic markers and crayons.
**Procedure:**   Encourage children to write stories. Writing stories enables children to think about the form stories take and to use this form.

5. **Activity:**   Writing invitations (PP–K)

**Materials:**   Paper and pencil, envelopes.
**Procedure:**   Help children write an invitation to the school secretary or some other important person to come to the classroom for snack or some other special event.
**Suggestions and Variations:**   If your school has an open house or a special event to which parents are invited, help children write invitations to their parents.

### Reading

## UNDERSTANDING THAT PRINT
## AND SPEECH ARE RELATED

1. **Activity:**   Taking dictation (PP–K)

**Materials:**   Paper and pencil or magic marker.
**Procedure:**   Write down what the child says about a drawing or an experience. The child sees that what he or she is saying can be turned into writing.

A listening post helps children focus their listening.

*Suggestions and Variations:* At first, because children do not understand the exact relationship between speech and print, they talk faster than you can write. Ask the child to slow down and point out where you are in writing what has been said: "I'm just writing the word *our* now. Let's see, we have 'This is our . . . .' What did you say after that?" It requires repeated experiences for children to learn to stay with you as you write what they say, because before they really understand that words are composed of letters, they think that one letter represents a whole word. Until they know that sound sequences within the words said are being represented by the letters you write, they have no way to correctly gauge the speed at which to dictate.

2. Activity:   Reading stories (PP–K)

*Materials:*   A good collection of picture books.
*Procedure:*   Read to children often, especially on an individual or very small group basis. Allow children to hold the book and turn the pages. Gradually, children realize that the words on the page tell the story and they

learn what the story says on each page. In time, children begin to try to find out how the story they know maps onto the print. They go from gross matching with errors (refer back to p. 206) to more precise matching. In the process of trying to match speech to print, they discover exactly how the two are related, that letters represent sounds, that some words have more than one syllable, and so on.

*Suggestions and Variations:*   Children must have access to familiar books over an extended period of time. Only when they have repeated exposure to the same books and have ample time to match their speech with the print in the books can they make significant discoveries about the relationships between print and speech.

3. **Activity:**   Print in the environment (PP–K)

*Materials:*   Signs and labels in the classroom; print on food cartons, traffic signs, and so on.

*Procedure:*   Point out print to children and tell them what it says. Children then become sensitive to print they see around them and try to read it.

*Suggestions and Variations:*   Often, children make rough guesses about contextual print, which is, of course, a positive first step. For example, a sign may say "Library Corner," but a child may read it as "books." Tell the child that his or her guess was a good one but that the sign has two words instead of one (point to the two groups of letters, separated by space) and that the sign says "Library Corner." Better yet, allow the child to think of what the two-worded sign might say. This feedback helps children learn what a word in print is (groups of letters surrounded by space). Knowing this helps children make more accurate predictions about what is said by print they encounter.

## USING CONTEXT CLUES
## AS A READING STRATEGY

1. **Activity:**   Print in the environment (PP–K)

*Materials:*   Signs and labels in the room; print on food cartons, traffic signs, and so on.

*Procedure:*   Point out print in the environment and ask children what physical surroundings provide clues to what the print says, for example, pictures on food cartons. From such experiences, children get the general idea that it is useful to think about what a word *might* say by considering many clues.

2. **Activity:**   Reading storybooks (PP–K)

> **Materials:**   A good collection of storybooks
>
> **Procedure:**   Read to children often, especially in groups of two or three. As children learn the content of their favorite stories and try to read them for themselves, they use the sense of the story, their knowledge of language, and picture clues to determine what the print on the page says. Children who have this kind of background are likely to try to predict new words when reading later on because they have learned that words must make sense in relation to the rest of the story.

3. **Activity:**   Reading books (K–P)

> **Materials:**   A good collection of trade books at various levels.
>
> **Procedure:**   Encourage children to read books of interest to them. You might read a book through the first time or provide a tape of it. Reading books with content that children already know something about allows and encourages children to predict new words from context.

## USING LETTER-SOUND ASSOCIATIONS IN READING NEW WORDS

As we discussed earlier, young children have difficulty conceptualizing spoken language as a series of distinct sounds. Therefore, it is not feasible to start the reading process with letter-sound associations when teaching preschool children, or even kindergarten and primary children, who have not had extensive experiences with print. For children who do have the essential insight that in our orthography one letter represents a sound, some activities dealing with the specific relationships between letters and sounds can be helpful. However, we would stress that such activities alone do not provide adequate experience for children; they make sense only when included in a much broader language arts program in which children are meaningfully engaged in real writing and reading.

1. **Activity:**   Picture card matching (PP–K)

> **Materials:**   Tagboard cards with pictures pasted on them. Pictures should be of items whose names start with consonants. Make sure you have at least three pictures for each consonant (house, hoe, hay; top, tie, timer; man, mouse, menu).
>
> **Procedure:**   Child sorts pictures into sets that all begin with the same letter.

**FIGURE 7-3** Consonant spinner board.

*Suggestions and Variations:* Depending on the context of the letter in the word (_truck vs. _toy; _dog vs. _dragon), children may sort the picture cards differently than we would because they pay attention to some similarities of sounds that we have learned to disregard. It may be useful in such instances to tell the child how you hear the beginning sounds in the names of the pictures ("I think *dog* and *dragon* sound the same at the beginning") and then write the names of these two pictures on a piece of paper so that the child can see that both begin with a *d*. It will take children awhile before they hear words the way we do because they must develop some concepts regarding how we categorize the different sounds we hear.

2. **Activity:**　Consonant-picture bingo (PP-K)

*Materials:*　Playing cards drawn so that there are nine spaces in which to paste on pictures (objects pictured should begin with single consonants); loose cards with one consonant written on each (to be used by the caller); blank pieces of paper or bottle caps for players to use as markers on playing cards.
*Procedure:*　Caller names letters drawn from the consonant deck. Players must cover pictures whose names begin with the consonants called.

*Suggestions and Variations:*    Children will make the same errors here that they make in Activity 1 above.

3. **Activity:**    Same first phonemes (PP–K)

*Materials:*    None.

*Procedure:*    In situations where you might want children to start doing something in small groups rather than all together (for example, getting coats on to go home; moving from the large group to a smaller story group), indicate which children are to go first by calling a phoneme and asking only those children whose names begin with that phoneme to go. For example, all children whose names begin with *B* might be asked to put their coats on first. This group might be followed by children whose names start with phonemes represented by *S* or *T*.

*Suggestions and Variations:*    Children who cannot segment speech into individual sounds will not know what you are talking about. When dealing with a group of children that includes some who have this ability and others who do not, merely tell children who seem not to respond when the appropriate clue for their name has been called that their name starts with this sound. It is not the least bit helpful to accuse such children of poor listening or inattention.

4. **Activity:**    Letter-sound books (K–P)

*Materials:*    Paper, pencils, paste, pictures.

*Procedure:*    Have children label pages with a consonant and collect the pages into a booklet. Children can cut out pictures of items whose names begin with the phoneme represented by the letter and paste them on the correct page. Children can also write the names of the items below the pictures or ask the teacher to write them.

*Suggestions and Variations:*    While this kind of "cut and dried" activity will not interest some children, it will be approached with great enthusiasm by others.

5. **Activity:**    Names that rhyme (PP–K)

*Materials:*    A collection of object pairs whose names rhyme (shell-bell; book-hook; can-pan) or pictures of objects whose names rhyme.

*Procedure:*    Help children pair the items or pictures whose names rhyme.

*Suggestions and Variations:*    Preparing word cards to accompany the objects (draw a picture of the object on the word card for easy matching) can help children see that words that sound alike have some similarity in spelling.

## 6. Activity:   Reading familiar print (PP–K)

*Materials:*   Print in the environment and in favorite storybooks.
*Procedure:*   Children must know what some samples of print say. This requires that you point out environmental print to children and read their favorite books to them often. When children know what some samples of print say and begin to match their saying of these samples with the print, they can make many discoveries about letter-sound associations. For example, they may notice that words spelled with an *m* at the beginning all sound alike at the beginning.

## 7. Activity:   Taking dictation (PP–K)

*Materials:*   Paper and pencil or magic marker
*Procedure:*   Take down exactly what a child says about a picture or an experience. When you think the child is ready, ask the child for help in spelling the words: "What letter do you think we need to begin the word *mommy?*"

## REFERENCES

BRUNER, J. S.   From communication to language: A psychological perspective. *Cognition* 3 (1975): 255–287.

CHOMSKY, C.   Reading, writing, and phonology. In M. Wolf, M. K. McQuillan, and E. Radwin, eds., *Thought and Language/Language and Reading.* Cambridge, Mass.: Harvard University Press, 1980, 51–71.

CHOMSKY, C.   *The Acquisition of Syntax in Children from 5 to 10.* Cambridge, Mass.: The M.I.T. Press, 1969.

CLARK, E. V.   Nonlinguistic strategies and the acquisition of word meanings. In L. Bloom, ed., *Readings in Language Development.* New York: John Wiley, 1978, 453–451.

CLAY, M.   *What Did I Write?* Auckland, New Zealand: Heinemann Educational Books, 1975.

DEVRIES, R.   The development of role-taking as reflected by behavior of bright, average, and retarded children in a social guessing game. *Child Development* 41 (1970): 759–770.

DOAKE, D.   Preschool book handling knowledge. Paper presented at the Annual Meeting of the International Reading Association, May 1979, Atlanta, Georgia.

DONNELLY, C., and STEVENS, G.   Streams and puddles: A comparison of two young writers. *Language Arts* 57 (1980): 735–741.

DOWNING, J.   Children's concepts of language in learning to read. *Educational Research* 12 (1970): 106–112.

DURKIN, D.   *Children Who Read Early.* New York: Teachers College Press, 1966.

EHRI, L. C., and WILCE, L. S.   Does orthography influence a reader's metalinguistic awareness of syllabic and phonetic segments in words? Paper presented at the International Reading Association/University of Victoria International Reading Research Seminar on Linguistic Awareness and Learning to Read, June 26–30, 1979, Victoria, British Columbia.

EIMAS, P. D.    Auditory and linguistic processing of cues for place of articulation by infants. *Perception and Psychophysics* 16 (1974): 513-521.

FILLMORE, L. W.    The second time around: Cognitive and social strategies in second-language acquisition. Unpublished Ph.D. dissertation, Stanford University, 1976.

FORESTER, A.    What teachers can learn from "natural readers." *The Reading Teacher,* 31 (1977): 160-166.

GLEITMAN, L. R., and ROZIN, P.    The structure and acquisition of reading I: Relations between orthographies and the structure of language. In A. S. Reber and D. L. Scarborough, eds., *Toward a Psychology of Reading.* Hillsdale, N.J.: Lawrence Erlbaum Associates, 1977, 1-54.

GOODMAN, K., and GOODMAN, Y.    Learning about psycholinguistic processes by analyzing oral reading. *Harvard Educational Review,* 47 (1977): 317-333.

GRAVES, D.    Andrea learns to make writing hard. *Language Arts* 56 (1979): 569-576. (a)

——.    What children show us about revision. *Language Arts* 56 (1979): 312-319. (b)

——.    Research update: When children want to punctuate: Basic skills belong in context. *Language Arts* 57 (1980): 567-573. (a)

——.    Research update: Children learn the writer's craft. *Language Arts* 57 (1980): 207-213. (b)

HARSTE, J., and CAREY, R. F.    Comprehension as setting. *Monograph in Language and Reading Studies,* Number 3 (October 1979): 4-22.

HILDRETH, G.    Developmental sequences in name writing. *Child Development,* 7 (1936): 291-303.

KLEIN, A., and SCHICKEDANZ, J.    Preschoolers write messages and receive their favorite books. *Language Arts* 57 (1980): 742-749.

LAVINE, L.    Differentiation of letterlike forms in prereading children. *Developmental Psychology* 13 (1977): 89-94.

MACNAMARA, J.    The cognitive basis of language learning in infants. *Psychology Review* 79 (1972): 1-13.

——.    First and second language learning: Same or different? *Journal of Education* 158 (1976): 39-54.

McGHEE, P. E.    *Humor: Its Origin and Development.* San Francisco, Calif.: W. H. Freeman and Company Publishers, 1979.

McLAUGHLIN, B.    *Second Language Acquisition in Childhood.* Hillsdale, N. J.: Lawrence Erlbaum Associates, 1978.

McNEILL, D., and LINDIG, K.    The perceptual reality of phonemes, syllables, words, and sentences. *Journal of Verbal Learning and Verbal Behavior* 12 (1973): 419-430.

MELTZER, N. S., and HERSE, R.    The boundaries of written words as seen by first graders. *Journal of Reading Behavior* 1 (1969): 3-14.

MENYUK, P.    Relations between acquisition of phonology and reading. In J. T. Guthrie, ed., *Aspects of Reading Acquisition.* Baltimore, Md.: John Hopkins University Press, 1976, 89-110.

——.    *Sentences Children Use.* Cambridge, Mass.: The M.I.T. Press, 1969.

NELSON, K. E., and NELSON, K.    Cognitive pendulums and their linguistic realization. In K. E. Nelson, ed., *Children's Language,* Vol. 1. New York: Gardner Press, 1978, 223-286.

PICK, A., UNZE, M. G., BROWNELL, C. A., DROZDAL, J. G., and HOPMANN, M. R.    Young children's knowledge of word structure. *Child Development,* 49 (1978): 669-680.

READ, C.    Pre-school children's knowledge of English phonology. In M. Wolf, M. K. McQuillan, and E. Radwin, eds., *Thought and Language/Language and Reading.* Cambridge, Mass.: Harvard University Press, 1980, 150-179.

RHEINGOLD, H. L., GEWIRTZ, J. L., and ROSS, H. W.    Social conditioning of vocalizations in the infant. *Journal of Comparative and Physiological Psychology* 52 (1959): 68-73.

Rossman, F. P.   Preschoolers' knowledge of the symbolic function of written language in storybooks. Unpublished doctoral dissertation, Boston University, 1980.

Rozin, P., and Gleitman, L. R.   The structure and acquisition of reading II: The reading process and the acquisition of the alphabetic principle. A. S. Reber and D. L. Scarborough, eds., *Toward a Psychology of Reading*. Hillsdale, N.J.: Lawrence Erlbaum Associates, 1977.

Savin, H. B.   What the child knows about speech when he starts to learn to read. In J. Kavanagh and I. Mattingly, eds., *Language by Ear and by Eye*. Cambridge, Mass.: The M.I.T. Press, 1972, 319–326.

————, and Bever, T. G.   The nonperceptual reality of the phoneme. *Journal of Verbal Learning and Verbal Behavior* 9 (1970): 295–302.

Schickedanz, J.   "You be the doctor and I'll be sick": Preschoolers learn the language arts through play. *Language Arts* 55 (1978): 713–718.

————.   What do preschoolers know about reading? Paper presented at the Annual Meeting of the International Reading Association, May 1979, Atlanta, Georgia.

————.   Data from Boston University Preelementary Reading Project, 1980.

————.   "Hey! This book's not working right." *Young Children* 37 (1981): 18–27.

Sinclair-de-Zwart, H.   Developmental psycholinguistics. In D. Elkind and J. Flavell, eds., *Studies in Cognitive Development*. New York: Oxford University Press, 1969.

Strohner, H., and Nelson, K.   The young child's development of sentence comprehension: Influence of event probability, nonverbal context, syntactic form, and strategies. *Child Development* 45 (1974): 567–576.

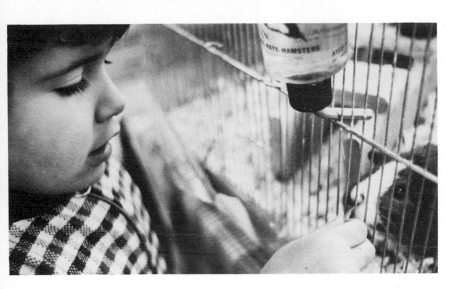

# 8

# YOUNG CHILDREN
# AND SCIENCE

Until about four decades ago, science instruction was almost nonexistent in early childhood programs. About all that was offered was incidental learning as part of nature study. This one-dimensional approach severely limited the opportunities children had to understand science. One reason for the limited consideration of science was that teachers thought that it was too difficult and complex for young children. That the basis for understanding science could be established in early childhood was not considered; that young children had a great deal of curiosity and interest in phenomena outside the realm of nature study was ignored.

Today, there is a much greater emphasis on science as part of the preschool curriculum. Part of the change has resulted from the unprecedented explosion of scientific knowledge and the accompanying technological and social consequences which have occurred in recent years. Science is more a part of everyone's world today than it was at any time in the past. Young children, like everyone else, live with this reality. In addition, numerous studies have explored what young children know about science and in particular whether they can learn the processes, as well as the content, of science. Partly as a result of Piaget's work on the development of notions of causality and logical thinking, we are now aware of ways in which children acquire and organize information. We now understand that not only do young children think about science in their own ways, but they also benefit from guided experiences which help them learn to observe, measure, classify, and infer.

This chapter will (1) introduce teachers to the nature of science, (2) help teachers recognize differences in children's thinking, needs, and experiences in relation to the developmental acquisition of knowledge about science, (3) organize selected science concepts appropriate for young children, and (4) provide teachers with up-to-date instructional strategies for helping children learn science skills and concepts.

## THE NATURE OF SCIENCE

What is science? What do we mean when we wish to teach "science"? *Webster's New World Dictionary* (1972) defines science as "systematized knowledge derived from observation, study, and experimentation carried on in order to determine the nature of principles of what is being studied." Science refers, then, not only to content—what is already known about plants, animals, minerals, and forces in the world—but to process, a method of inquiry into observed phenomena.

There are differences of opinion among scientists and science educators as to whether the major emphasis of beginning science should be on content or process. Nevertheless, all agree in varying degrees on a broader view of science as a dynamic process which helps us search for answers to questions about the world around us. For teachers and children, science has to do with finding out the what, why, when, and how of the children's world. Children can learn how information we call the content of science is acquired and, in the process, learn content too.

Learning about science is not limited to the classroom. Science can be seen everywhere in the children's world—when they watch the approach of a hurricane on television, see a meal cooked in minutes in a microwave oven, or observe parents using a home computer in working on the family budget. Because we cannot ignore our dependence on scientific and technological advancements, we might consider helping young children begin thinking not only about the content and processes of science but also about the social aspects of science and technology.

Scientific inquiry involves the use of several specific skills combined in certain ways. First, it requires observation and accurate description of phenomena observed. Next, it raises provocative questions from which inferences or hypotheses are developed. These inferences are then tested using instruments of science with appropriate precision. Experimentation follows, and then further observations are made. These lead to new inferences and further experimentation.

For example, if one wanted to determine why some objects sink while others float, one must first determine which items sink and which float. A variety of objects can be classified into two groups: "things that sink" and "things that float." Next, one needs to determine if there is a common characteristic which might account for the difference in the reactions of the objects tested. Are all things that float of one size whereas those that sink are of another? Are all things that float made of one material whereas those that sink are made of another?

The scientist, while testing out a large variety of objects in water, carefully records all observations. On the basis of the observations, hypotheses are formed about why objects react as they do: "If it is the weight which makes the difference, then the pin should float and the block should sink." But trying it out shows that it is not so in this case. A new question is then asked: "When does it make a difference and when does it not?" The scientist continues to observe, record, make inferences, and experiment until gaining an understanding of the relationship between objects and their tendency to sink or float in water.

The above example includes experimentation as part of scientific inquiry. Although it is often an important part, it need not and cannot always be included. For example, it is important for children to know that certain foods must be refrigerated or else illness will result, that electrical equipment can be deadly if not handled properly, and that life jackets can keep one afloat in water. It would be foolish and dangerous to have children acquire such knowledge through experimentation. Other information may be fascinating and safe for children to obtain but might be impractical in terms of cost or availability of materials. Knowledge of systems, interrelationships, and processes can be the result of scientific inquiry that may or may not require experimentation. Although it is important for some scientifically obtained material to be passed on for the sake of practicality and safety, it is important for teachers to understand that if children are really to understand science, they must be permitted to "abstract" knowledge on their own or at least be permitted to "verify" for themselves much of the information they are given.

## CHILDREN AND SCIENCE

The relationship between children and science depends on the nature of children as well as the nature of science. An infant sitting on a rug turns a baby bottle upside down. A few drops of milk spill. The infant pats the wet spot, looks at the bottle, deliberately turns it upside down, watches the milk drip, pats the wet spot again. In a similar manner, infants and toddlers explore the objects in their environments. The analogy to scientific experiments which explore cause and effect is evident.

Young children are natural investigators. They are always ready with questions. Why do some things float while others sink? Why do some objects cling to a magnet while others do not? Why do some substances change to a liquid when heated while others change to a vapor? Both scientists and children seek to make sense out of these phenomena. This longing for understanding is the focus of much of children's exploratory play, as well as of science.

By the time children begin school, they have lived science for at least a few years. They have been curious, identified problems, asked questions, and sought answers. School science, when it is offered, adds a new dimension, with children now being guided in their quest for answers through the provision of carefully selected learning activities and materials.

One of the dominant themes of Piaget's developmental theory is that children conceptually organize their environment in terms of sequential stages. The early childhood years, three to seven, straddle two of Piaget's developmental stages: ages one-and-a-half to about seven form the preoperational stage during which the child develops language and participates in symbolic activities, and ages seven to about eleven comprise the concrete operations stage where thinking remains concrete rather than abstract, but the child begins to perform elementary logical operations.

David Elkind (1972) has described the interesting and remarkable similarity between Piaget's paradigm of the growth of thought and the learning of science. Both are concerned with classification; relational skills; causality; and conservation of space, time, and number. Preoperational children believe that objects are alive in the same sense that the children are alive. It is a magical world to young, egocentric children. Events occur just for their benefit. What they say, do, and desire causes things to happen. The sun follows them around. The existence of lakes or snow has no cause or function other than to provide them pleasure in swimming, skating, or sledding. And when an older child chants "Step on a crack, break your mother's back; step on a line, break your mother's spine," the younger child is very careful about where she steps, fearful that it might really happen.

In science education, with its close alignment with the beginning of conceptual thinking, young children begin to show fewer instances of animistic beliefs and begin to give more explanations based on physical or mechanical considerations. At first, their physical explanations rely on the contiguity of two events in time or space as an indication of cause and effect (Piaget, 1969). When the sun shines and clouds move, the four-year-old might say, "The sun pushes them away." If a reel-to-reel tape recorder is shown to a child and the child is asked what makes the reels go around, the child might indicate by pointing that the moving tape causes the motion of the reels. In other words, though the child now seeks physical or mechanical, rather than magical, explanations, the child's explanations are still not always accurate.

Perhaps the most important application of Piaget's ideas lies in his insight that children learn by doing and thinking about what they are doing. Children need to experiment to see what happens under different conditions, and they must have the opportunity to discuss with their peers and teachers what they observed, did, and found.

Further, Piaget's research suggests some indicators that can be used in teaching science:

1. Science and thinking possibilities are present in every classroom.
2. In seeking to understand classification, causality, and relationships in firsthand experiences, children are developing meaningful abstract concepts.
3. All children cannot be expected to learn science concepts or develop science skills at the same time.
4. If a child cannot learn a particular concept, perhaps the objective is beyond the child's developmental level.

The way in which a child develops scientific ideas depends on both classroom experiences and information which will gradually help the child attain more complex modes of thinking. For example, if a teacher calls the child's attention to the fact that clouds move when the wind blows and do not move when the wind is still, the child may begin to consider the effects of the wind rather than the effects of the sun as the factor which controls the movement of clouds. Even more important, the child may begin to question any first hunches about the causes of phenomena and search for other possibilities.

One should not expect changes in children's thinking to occur quickly or in a straightforward linear fashion. The unique characteristics of young children's thinking limit their ability to understand things as adults do. What seems clear to an adult is not always clear to a child. For example, in the case of flotation, density (size in relation to weight), not absolute size or weight alone, helps determine whether an object sinks or floats. When asked to explain the floating or sinking of objects, for example, several five-year-olds gave the following explanation: "Because it's heavy," "Because it's little," "Because it has cracks in it," "Because I pushed it," "Because it has air inside," or simply, "I really don't know why" (Ducksworth, 1979). Because younger children are unable to make comparisons of two things simultaneously, it is not possible for them to think of the size and weight of one object in relation to the size and weight of another object. Given the opportunity to explore and experiment, four- and five-year-olds usually come to understand that flotation has something to do with size and weight, although typically they cannot integrate the two ideas into the concept of density. Their concept of flotation is, therefore, incomplete. It is important to note that this notion is on the right track, for their concept is not attached to irrelevant attributes such as the material of the objects or their color, which would be characteristic of the concepts of even younger children.

The teacher should be able to discriminate between different kinds of confusion resulting from (1) too much information, (2) information given in disorganized ways, (3) limited opportunities to obtain information, and (4) confusion which could be expected in terms of the child's level of thinking. Teachers should be prepared to provide continued exposure to experiences which will give children a chance gradually to refine and integrate into more accurate concepts the information they obtain.

In addition to limitations in understanding causality, young children have limited ability to reason logically. This has important implications, particularly for children's understanding of hierarchical classification, that is, subclasses within larger classes (Lavatelli and Stendler, 1972).

One of the ways in which knowledge obtained from scientific inquiry can be organized is through classification. For example, plants and animals are two major classes into which things in the world can be grouped. Within each there are subclasses, and within these there are more subclasses. This system provides a way to organize a vast amount of information. It also provides an efficient way to learn a great deal of information if one can comprehend the system. The categories can be used as cues to information applicable to all the specific things in the class. But young children cannot comprehend such involved systems. They may be able to learn that something is an animal, that it is a mammal, and further, that it is a goat, but the information remains specific and unintegrated in the child's mind. It is not used by the child to predict characteristics of other things similarly labeled "animal" or "mammal".

Despite these limitations, young children can make considerable progress in understanding science. They can observe events. They can acquire a great deal of descriptive knowledge about the world and begin to develop systems for organizing it. They can test out objects to see how they behave in relationship to a certain event, and they can organize objects according to their responses. If given some help, they can suggest several possible explanations for events they observe, and they can test these out. Although concepts formed by children may not become integrated into completely accurate concepts immediately, or even for a very long time, such incomplete concepts are the basis from which complete and accurate concepts eventually emerge.

## SCIENCE SKILLS AND CONCEPTS FOR YOUNG CHILDREN

Although young children are not yet able to perform all the formal operations for true scientific inquiry, teachers can help them attain basic science skills by planning a science program embracing both content and process. To begin, science should be a regular part of the total program and have a balance of content from all the sciences. Children need ample opportunities to explore in each of the three basic areas of science, (1) living things, (2) the earth and the universe, and (3) matter and energy (Blough, 1954). When helping children learn science, it is preferable to present a variety of science experiences to meet individual needs and interests. There must be enough materials with which to work and sufficient time in which to use the materials. Also, science learning needs to be integrated into the total curriculum. Finally, young children learn best when they are involved in action based, sensory, purposeful exploration.

This approach to science learning embodies the following basic science skills:

1. Observing
2. Classifying
3. Hypothesizing
4. Experimenting
5. Communicating
6. Interpreting and generalizing

**Observing**

Observing is the most basic skill upon which scientific inquiry is built; it precedes all the other skills. In fact, none of the other skills can exist without it. Observing involves describing with exactness what is observed. As acutely perceptive as young children usually are, at times they may look but not see. They often need direction in order to focus their perceptions on significant details.

Good observation requires perceiving subtle qualities as well as obvious ones. If children are to become more perceptive in their interpretations, increased attention must be given to meaningful details in observations. Have the children learned to use all their senses purposefully in gathering information? How do the children structure their information seeking and check their results? Do they know what questions to ask in order to gain an understanding of the observed phenomena?

The most important thing the teacher can do in guiding children to develop better observational abilities is to structure the classroom phenomena in such a way as to facilitate the children's sensitivity to the basic properties of the materials and equipment. For example, such a classroom would have a magnifying glass next to the terrarium to help children see more clearly and obtain more accurate information. Children would be encouraged to observe the sunlight as it comes into the classroom at different times of the day and asked to explain how shadows help us tell time. In such a classroom, children need to develop multisensory associations in order to observe accurately. Through hearing, seeing, smelling, tasting, and touching, they can sharpen basic sensory discriminations. Practice will allow them to observe and to distinguish relationships, likenesses, and differences.

### Classifying

Classification helps us make order out of what we have observed; it simplifies the world for us. Classification is so much a part of our lives that we are not conscious of its importance. Had you not learned both the concept and skill of classification, you would not be able to use the telephone directory or find items in a grocery store. Fortunately, it is unlikely that a child could completely avoid the development of some concepts and skills in classification. Many young children find great satisfaction in sorting objects into like collections based on physical properties. But skill development in classification goes far beyond simple grouping of objects on the basis of one characteristic, whether it be size, shape, or color.

As children continue to observe, they begin to gain insight into the classification process. The teacher may ask, "Can you think of another characteristic besides color as the basis to sort these objects?" Later, children can go beyond sorting objects into groups that share one physical property, to classify objects according to multiple physical characteristics. Still later, they will be able to classify objects in terms of function, rather than physical attributes.

Classification also involves subordinate categories within larger categories. For example, within the class of animals are subclasses of mammals and reptiles, and within each of these subclasses are further subclasses. Or, within the class of shapes we might have big and little shapes, and within each of these, triangles, circles, and squares. The logical skill involved in making subclasses and in realizing each part's relationship to the whole serves as a powerful tool for helping the scientist organize information. But children generally do not understand the logic of these relationships until they are about eight or nine years of age. It may be useful, however, for teachers to indicate that a particular creature is an animal, a mammal, and specifically a cow. But, teachers can not expect young children to grasp the relationship of one class to another.

### Hypothesizing

After making observations, children can generate possible reasons or hypotheses for the observed events. The children can then test these ideas. For example, when concrete experiences, such as real objects and water, are provided, children's natural curiosity will no doubt lead them to put the objects in the water. Children will discover through observation that some objects sink while others float. This observation might make children wonder, "Why do objects behave differently?" Some children will formulate their own explanations about why some things sink and some float. Perhaps they will say that it is because some will not float and others do not float; or because one object is red or green; or because some objects are big while others are little. A teacher can sometimes encourage further thinking and hypothesizing by asking questions such as, "If it is being red that makes something sink, why didn't the red piece of wood sink?" or "If it's bigness that makes something sink, why did this big piece of styrofoam float?"

Some children will shrug off the question and go about the business of making their own explanations. But other children will appreciate the conflict in their hypothesis and begin to explore again to try to see if they can figure out the problem. In this case the question has helped, but the child still needs to develop a new hypothesis.

As we discussed earlier, young children have not yet acquired the ability to search for all possible reasons for an event, nor are preoperational children able to deal with two characteristics at the same time. Instead, they tend to make explanations based on the fact that two events occur together in time or space or that two phenomena appear to have something in common, for example, hard carrots eaten by rabbits and ears that stand up straight.

Without guidance, children tend to be satisfied with such reasons and will not test them. The teacher's role is to help children verbalize what they have observed, to ask for a possible reason, to encourage predictions based on the reason given, and to invite the children to test to see if the reason is true. Hawkins advocates allowing children to explore materials freely on their own before guidance and information are provided. When materials appropriate to the demonstration of a new concept are placed on a table accessible to children for exploration, the exploration usually leads to observation and hypothesizing. The skillful guidance of a teacher can then maximize the learning with a few well-chosen questions such as "What would happen if. . . ." or other well-chosen comments about observations that had gone unnoticed by the child. It is impossible to know beforehand whether a question will be useful or will be ignored. All a teacher can do is pose the question and let the children either accept it or ignore it.

### Experimenting

In the past, the exploratory process was considered suitable only for the upper grades. Yet, young children are capable of investigating the effects of a single variable and of beginning to understand the need for exactness as an integral part of science experiments. This skill may involve the "let's-see-what-happens" exploration of materials or it may involve the systematic testing of a hypothesis. Children need to know which kind of investigation they are pursuing.

Experimentation is required to test hypotheses. It is the part of scientific inquiry which young children are most likely to enjoy. Children are always eager to get started and to test their ideas. However, experimentation to test a hypothesis is not random "messing about"; it is a thoughtful effort to collect solid information. For this reason, it is easier to do it with older children who are as interested in pinpointing principles as they are in exploring the properties of individual objects or just the "magic" of the objects' reactions. For example, a three-year-old may be delighted to discover that some things "like to be at the bottom" of the water table while others "like to be at the top." A five-year-old, on the other hand, can be terribly curious about exactly what makes some objects act one way and other objects act another. It is the onset of this kind of thinking that can signal a teacher to help children begin systematic experimentation.

In guiding children in their experimentation, the teacher needs to remember that the factor of control is very important. In order to find out what happens in the investigative process, certain variables or conditions must be controlled. As in the other processes, there are degrees of sophistication. With young children, for example, if the question asked in the investigation concerns the relationship of light to plant growth, the teacher should stress the importance of light. As many moderating influences as possible should be controlled, for example, the amount of watering must be the same for the sets of plants, the size and health of the plants must be similar, and so on. But the children will focus only on the amount of light needed by plants by keeping a few plants in the dark and a few similar plants in the light.

Preoperational children's (one-and-a-half to seven years) main interests are in doing experiments their own way. This is not to say that teachers cannot use this interest to extend science learning. It would be instructive at times to allow children to proceed without proper controls and then later question their conclusions with other conclusions that may be possible.

Care must be taken, however, to provide the necessary feedback and help: the term *experimentation* has too often been used loosely at the preprimary level. Young children in their enthusiasm and naiveté need teacher guidance in designing experiments in which variables are controlled to some extent so that their investigations will verify their ideas. Without taking away any of the fun of exploring, teachers should help children understand the need for exactness as an integral part of science investigations. Children who are ready for this find the very element of control stimulating and fun. They want to pin things down, to do things precisely, and to know for sure. As children grow older and enter the primary grades, they take more interest in thinking about what they have been doing and in planning what they might do next. They often get great enjoyment from being very precise and in keeping detailed accounts of everything that happened.

To direct children who set out to determine if things that float are lighter than things that sink, the teacher might ask, "How can we be sure that it is the weight of the objects and not something else that causes some objects to sink and some to float?" As in most investigating, the equipment needed is simple. In this case, a balance scale might be brought in to test the hypothesis.

Young children are more likely to conduct effective investigations if the following suggestions are considered:

1. Devise original investigations which test the children's hypothesis. Choose experiments which seek answers to the children's questions in preference to experiments in which the children have little or no interest.

2. Plan the experiment with the children so that they are not only actively engaged but also do more and more of the planning as the year goes on. (See Chapter 2, "Planning, Organizing, and Evaluating.")

3. Challenge children to move to higher levels of thinking. If incorrect generalizations and inferences are made, the teacher, guided by the maturity of the child and other relevant factors, can help the child correct the errors by asking the child for verifica-

tion, or the teacher should guide the child to see the necessity of further experimentation for clarification by asking, "Can we say that when. . . . ?" The important point is *how* the teacher goes about correcting a child's errors. It is useless to correct them verbally because the youngest children will not understand what is said.

4. Whenever possible, let each child actively conduct his or her own investigation at the science center. However, there may be times when a small group collectively working together is more effective than an individual child.

5. Keep the experiment as simple as possible. Young children cannot understand complex investigations. Complicated experiments can be broken down into simpler, more manageable investigations.

6. Control as many variables as possible. For example, in experimenting to see if mittens dry as quickly on the radiator as they do on a Formica® table, try to use mittens of similar size and equal wetness.

7. Provide feedback as the investigation proceeds. Young children need their teacher's perspective to be able to successfully complete the process. The teacher must give the children hints to guide them in finding solutions.

8. Plan different kinds of recordkeeping for different experiments. Some investigations will require more complete recording than others. Sometimes, children decline to participate in anticipation of the time-and-effort-consuming final report. Keep recording as simple as possible.

### Communicating

Communicating serves two purposes: (1) to ensure that knowledge of concepts and relationships is accurately recorded and (2) to share findings with others.

Communicating takes many forms. Drawings, experience charts, graphs, and booklets are all used in recording and communicating descriptions of science experiences and results of experimentation. "Products" themselves may also be records. A batch of fudge, scrambled eggs, a dead plant, and cornstarch putty are all results of chemical or biological processes. Another such product record may be collections of objects which have been sorted into labeled containers. For example, two containers are labeled with words and pictures "Things that sink" and "Things that float." Drawing on their experimentation, children fill the two containers with objects that fit the labels. Such records do have limitations, however. The products are difficult to preserve and they will show only the results, not the processes or conditions under which the results were obtained. They are best suited to the youngest children, who cannot make other kinds of records easily. For younger children, such product records may be sufficient, especially when accompanied with conversation which focuses observation and helps the children think about and interpret the experience. Teacher's questions during activity and evaluation times are particularly important to help children think about and report on what they have done. "John, how did you make the applesauce? What do you think made the apples fall apart?" "Franz, I noticed you didn't have any orange paint. Can you tell me what you did to get the orange color in your painting?" Such questions help children recall observations made, hypotheses tested, actions taken, and results obtained.

The children's responses can be recorded by the teacher on an experience chart. The chart, together with products from the experience, can form an attractive and informative display for the classroom and can initiate further discussion about the experience in the future.

Older children will be interested in making more complex types of records. For example, children may independently make records by drawing pictures to illustrate the process of experimentation, the objects used, and the products obtained. The degree of complexity of such illustration will, of course, depend on the child's stage of development. Beginners may draw only that which impressed them the most, while the more advanced may cartoon the entire process in sequence.

Graphs may also be made to illustrate changes which have occurred. Bar graph descriptions of simple phenomena can be used at first. For example, the growth of plants given different amounts of light over a three-week period might be illustrated in graphs as shown in Figure 8-1.

Later, children can use a graphic illustration of data that may be used to make an educated guess about the growth of the plants over a one-week period. With time and opportunities to use bar graphs, children might construct a record of this experiment as shown in Figure 8-2.

Children can also use a checklist to record the presence or absence of a particular property or action. An advantage of this kind of recording is that the child has only to put a mark next to his or her name; the disadvantage is that the child cannot describe quality or even the process. Using a checklist, the children could record measurement information such as in Figure 8-3 to see who has participated in an experiment.

Children who have developed some skill in writing may make booklets which record science experiences. In planning such a booklet, children can receive guidance which will help them include a description of materials used, procedures followed, results obtained, and interpretations and generalizations made. New words which children will need for their books may be written on a piece of paper for their later reference or may be added to their word collections. (See Chapter 7, Language Arts.)

Younger children, of course, can tell the teacher about their experiments. If a child draws pictures of the event, the teacher can then write the dictated sentence at the bottom of each picture. These can be bound into booklets with covers featuring the titles and the child's name as author. Again, the expectations for all these descriptions must be adapted to the child's stage of development.

Children can use the records they make. For example, they can trade records and repeat each other's work. Results can be compared. Preschoolers cannot be expected to do this with much sophistication. Though they may start out wanting very much to do what another child has done, they will typically do it in their own way. This should be accepted and encouraged.

As children grow older, they will become more interested in following precisely what someone else has done as well as in doing it their own way and comparing the two. By doing this, children will form clearer concepts of scientific inquiry and become aware of the variety of factors which may influence results.

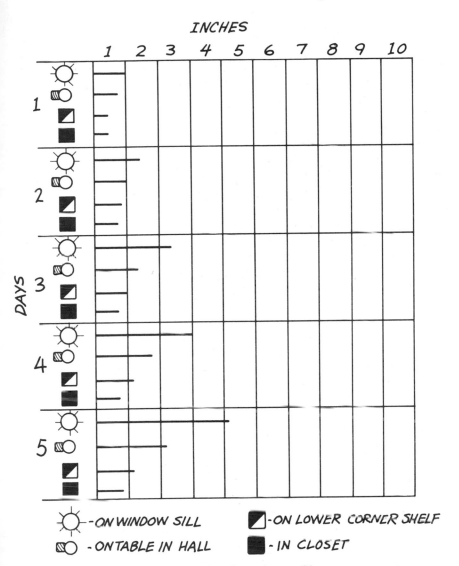

FIGURE 8-1   Graph showing plant growth under varying conditions.

## Interpreting and Generalizing

These may be considered the culminating steps of scientific inquiry. This sequence begins with describing the data collected; it progresses to relating the data to the hypothesis; and it leads finally to making a generalization. What has been learned through the processes described above is now translated into a concept on which more advanced learning may be built. The teacher must be careful to ensure that this step is made when the child is ready to render an opinion based on the investigation. Additionally, the child will need to support his or her position by

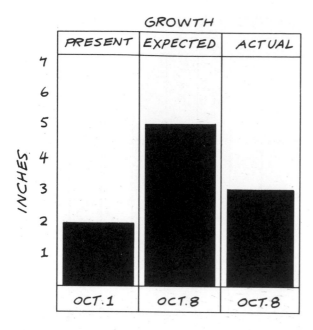

FIGURE 8-2

careful analysis of the data. It is not enough to describe the materials, procedures, and results of a science experience; one must also extract meaning from the experience. What do the results tell us about _____? If water travels downhill, then where would we put a bucket in relation to the aquarium we are emptying? If a box of nails spills, is there something we can use to pick them up?

With preschool children, it is important that interpreting and generalizing be done in context as things happen. Most preschoolers cannot sit down and think of the implications of an observed phenomenon, but they can relate an observed phenomenon to real situations that have occurred earlier or which might occur later. For example, if children are permitted to experiment with magnets and objects, a child might later think of using a magnet to collect nails spilled at the workbench. If a child did not think of it, the teacher might ask, "What could we

**FIGURE 8-3**

| WEIGHING EXPERIMENT | | | | |
|---|---|---|---|---|
| | ROCKS | SAND | WOOD | NAILS |
| GARY KIM BRAD | ✓ ✓ | ✓ | ✓ ✓ | ✓ ✓ |

use to pick up the nails?'' Better yet, a magnet might be included among the woodworking tools for just such occasions.

Primary age children are better able to think of implications of information they have obtained than are preschool children. This is partly due to their greater experience in the world. They bring many more experiences to school than do younger children. But some of the increase in skill is also due to progress in the ability to think, to understand, and to use language. This does not mean that primary age children need fewer concrete situations in which to apply what they have learned. What it does mean is that more interpreting and generalizing can be done through talking, reading, and writing.

## Key Science Concepts
## and Understandings

Just as science processes are subdivided into six basic procedures, science content, too, is organized into key concepts, which are the foremost ideas around which science is organized. Children can learn these key concepts as a consequence of their experiential inquiry. Although we believe that science programs should be weighted in favor of process over content, children must have something to inquire about. Victor (1975) suggests that we use those conceptual schemes that have been accepted for some time and are likely to continue being accepted. In the preschool, science concepts are specific enough to help children to understand and to generalize at their own level of functioning.

When teachers have a clear idea of the concepts they wish children to ascertain from an experience, the children will be more apt to learn those concepts. It is important, therefore, that teachers be as well versed in the subject matter of science as possible. Without understanding primary science concepts, teachers cannot arrange an environment from which children can abstract meaning; nor can they give suitable guidance.

The concepts selected as learning objectives for children should be based on the teacher's knowledge of the children and of the community in which they live, the nature of the larger society, and the main conceptual schemes found in science. What experiences have the children had? In what things do they show an interest? What kinds of knowledge and skills do they need to function safely and effectively in the community in which they live? What will they need to know and be able to do to participate and succeed in the larger society? Which of the basic science concepts are relevant to them at this stage of their lives? Questions such as the above should be asked and answered whether the teacher selects activities from this book or from specific commercial materials.

All the activities which follow later in this chapter are designed to involve children in the process of scientific inquiry in order that they learn key science concepts and develop the skills which have been described. The activities are grouped into three content areas which include (1) living things, (2) the earth and the universe, and (3) matter and energy (Blough and Schwartz, 1979). The content of each in terms of early childhood education is discussed below. Teachers who are not familiar with the concepts outlined in each area will find much good information in the references listed at the end of the chapter. Many of these are also appropriate for use by young children.

LIVING THINGS.    Concepts about plant and animal life and their relationship to each other and their environment are included in the study of living things. Subjects such as the variety of life are marvelous for observational walks and field trips. What plants live in our neighborhood? How are our class pets alike? Which seedlings shall we plant?

Many plants and animals can be brought into the classroom. The teacher may also capitalize on home experiences or take children on walks to observe plants and animals. Observation and experimentation are the best means of teaching these concepts, but informational sources can also be used.

Young children are naturally curious about their bodies. Although the study of the structure and function of the body does not lend itself to experimentation, other means of teaching about the human body, such as observations, talks, discussions, books, audio-visual aids, and other informational sources, can be used.

THE EARTH AND THE UNIVERSE.    The first area deals with features of the earth's surface and includes geology, meteorology, ecology, and geography. All belong in the realm of social science since they deal with the interrelationships between people and their physical environment. Observations of weather, of the surrounding countryside, and of interesting land and water features are most appropriate in teaching earth science to young children.

While some might feel that the study of the solar system, stars, and planets might not be interesting to young children, these children are already well acquainted with astronauts and trips to the moon. Observation of the night sky, sunrise, and sunset as well as visits to planetariums and the use of models of the solar system can all help children understand some basic concepts.

MATTER AND ENERGY.    In their firsthand, concrete experiences with various materials, preprimary children use all the senses to explore the characteristics of the materials as a first step toward discovering their properties. Children are intrigued with the changes that occur as materials are combined or exposed to air, water, and variations in temperature.

Further, even young children want to know how machines work. They want to understand how force, energy, and mechanics interact to distribute force. Children are enthralled and challenged by interactions which mystify them— gears, wheels, reflected sounds, and colors. The teacher's job is to help children identify what occurs as children work and play and to design activities and experiences which can help illustrate concepts related to matter and energy.

## ACTIVITIES FOR SCIENCE INSTRUCTION

### Living Things

## UNDERSTANDING ANIMAL LIFE

1. Activity:    Caring for animals (PP–P)

*Materials:*    Cages, food, water, and other equipment to care for animals in a safe and sanitary manner; animal books; writing and drawing equipment.

*Procedure:*    Before bringing an animal into the classroom, prepare yourself and the children by reading and talking about the animal, its habits, and the natural conditions in which it thrives. Plan with the children for the care of the animal to protect it from harm and to keep it healthy and happy. When the animal is brought into the classroom, the children should be asked to observe things such as what the animal likes to eat, when and how it sleeps, how it moves, what it likes to do. Children may record their observations by writing stories, drawing pictures, making tape recordings, or, as a group, making an experience chart.

*Suggestions and Variations:*    Gerbils and hamsters are playful and particularly popular for school classrooms. One drawback is that they tend to be nocturnal and sleep much of the time that children are present. Animals other than mammals might be considered. Lizards, poultry, rabbits, turtles, and snakes are interesting to children and make excellent classroom companions.

Place a simple bird feeding station on a nearby tree or post. Use commercially prepared birdseed, bread crumbs, nuts, or green vegetables as feed.

Wet a duck's feet in colored water and let it walk across a white sheet of paper. Be sure to rinse his feet off when finished.

Have children bring their pets to school and ask children to compare their various pets. Note similarities and differences. Group the pets according to whether or not they are nocturnal, the sounds they make, what they eat and so on.

*Adaptation for handicapped:*    For a blind child, be sure to have animals which can be handled without harm to the child or animal. The blind child may wish long periods for tactile exploration because vision cannot be used to gain information.

*Suggestions for parent involvement:*    Try to arrange for home pets to visit school and for the parent to participate in telling about the animal. Some parents may interact with animals in their work (for example, pet store worker, horse trainer, dairy farmer). These parents might be asked to come talk with the children.

2. **Activity:**   Animal sounds (PP)

   *Materials:*   Tape, tape recorder.
   *Procedure:*   Tape various animal sounds: a dog yelping or panting, a cat meowing, a gerbil chewing a carrot, a cow mooing, a horse whinnying, and so on. Ask, "What is this animal? What do you think it's doing?"
   *Adaptation for handicapped:*   An excellent activity for a blind child, especially if the child has had experience with animals. However, those with hearing loss may be left out when only a tape is used. A pantomiming activity will include these children.

3. **Activity:**   Aquarium (PP–P)

   *Materials:*   Kit of materials to establish an aquarium, including the following: five- or ten-gallon glass tank; sand; assortment of shells, stones, and other decorative materials; filter and pump; charcoal; glass wool; aquarium plants. (Although artificial plants are preferred by many because they are less trouble, real plants should be purchased in order to lay the groundwork for understanding the interdependence of plants and animals.)
   *Procedure:*   A small group of children may assist an adult in setting up the aquarium. Follow these steps: (1) Put clean sand in the bottom of the tank. If beach sand is used, wash it thoroughly by putting it in a shallow pan and letting water run in and over the sides. Swish the sand around with the hand until the water runs clear. (2) Add water until it is about an inch above the level of the sand. (3) Arrange plants and decorative materials. Anchor the plants in the sand, covering the roots. (4) Put about a quarter to a half inch of charcoal in the filter, then fill with glass wool packed lightly. Immerse in the water and attach plastic tube. (5) Fill tank with water until it is about an inch from the top. To avoid disturbing the sand and plants, pour water slowly over a piece of paper against the side of the tank. As the above is being done, discuss with the children why each item is needed: plants because they look pretty and provide oxygen; decorative materials for attractiveness; filter to keep the water clean and provide air. You should also explore how the pump works. When the tank is set up, let the water age overnight. Plan a buying trip to the pet store for fish. The pet store owner can advise on which fish are compatible in the same tank. Angel fish, which are showy, will eat guppies, for example. Guppies are a good choice because they are generally hardy, males are easily distinguished from females, they breed readily, and they are live-bearers (the birth process may be witnessed). Buy a catfish and a few snails to keep the tank clean. After the tank is installed, children should be encouraged to notice

things such as how fish eat and move about and which part of the tank different kinds of fish seem to like best. A magnifying glass helps children explore details in an aquarium.

*Suggestions and Variations:*    Add books on fish to the table where the aquarium is placed. If the tank has a good balance between fish and plants and fish are not overfed, the water should stay clean for as long as six months. A temperature of between 68° and 80° should be maintained. The tank should be away from direct sunlight to prevent rapid algae growth.

Have children assume responsibility for feeding. To avoid overfeeding, it is wise to use a feeding ring—a small plastic ring which floats on the surface. If feeding the fish is not exclusively the responsibility of one person, a tag with different colors on each side with the word "fed" on one side and "feed" on the other side may be hung near the tank. The teacher must remember to turn the tag "feed" side out before going home or when arriving in the morning. Water will evaporate from the fish tank, and children can be responsible for refilling it. Tap water kills fish because of the chlorine. Letting water stand for a few days will permit the chlorine to escape. Children can store water to refill the tank in open gallon jars. Ask children where they think the water goes (young children often think the fish drink it). The full water-level of the tank can be marked with masking tape so that children can see clearly how much water is being lost through evaporation.

*Suggestion for parent involvement:*    Try to find out if any parents have fish at home. Some adults' hobbies include this kind of activity and the set-up can be elaborate. This can make a nice field trip.

4. Activity:    How our bodies work (P)

*Materials:*    Models, charts, filmstrips, books which illustrate and explain in simple terms the systems of the human body.

*Procedure:*    Invite a pediatrician, pediatric nurse, or the school nurse to visit the class to explain body functions. Such arrangements should be made when a need or interest has been shown by the children. For example, a child is cut and bleeds. As you apply first aid, other children show concern and talk about what has happened. Their conversation reveals curiosity and misunderstanding about why and how a person bleeds. You provide simple explanations but note that questions are being asked which you are not prepared to answer. This interest may indicate readiness for a more extensive explanation by a professional.

*Suggestions and Variations:*    Follow-up conversations should be held to ensure that children understand clearly what was said by the visitor. When a child in the class is scheduled to go to the hospital for corrective surgery or has returned to class after a stay in the hospital, such explanations may help to reduce fear and increase understanding of the experience.

Make a class mural using the children's hands by having them dip their open hands in a pan of tempera and then leave their imprint on the paper. Have the children spatter paint over their feet. How can you tell what part of the body is shown? In what ways are hands suited for grasping and holding while feet are suited for walking?

Have children press their hands and feet firmly on a slab of clay.

5. Activity:    Healthy bodies (K–P)

**Materials:**    Audio-visual aids, pictures from magazines, paper, paste, scissors.

**Procedure:**    Present information on good health practices. This may be done by inviting a pediatrician, pediatric nurse, or school nurse to talk with the children; or by utilizing audio-visual aids. (Good sources for audio-visual aids are the state and local departments of health, which may maintain an audio-visual library; and the Dairy Council.)

**Suggestions and Variations:**    Make "do–don't" "cause–effect," or "good–bad" posters. To start this activity, ask children questions such as "What happens when you stay up to see the late show night after night?" "How do you feel when you've had a good night's sleep?" "Can you make a poster to show us what happens?" For readers, these questions may be on an activity card placed next to a selection of art and writing materials. As a class project, a large sheet of paper divided into two sections may be attached to the wall. The word "sick" and a picture of a pale, listless child may be pasted to the top of one side, while the word "healthy" and a picture of a robust, active child appears at the top of the other section. Encourage children to paste cutout pictures on the sheet depicting what they think the children do that makes them "sick" or "healthy."

6. Activity:    Snack (PP–K)

**Materials:**    Food for snack which can be prepared by the children; utensils for preparing food.

**Procedure:**    Select only foods of high nutritional value, such as fresh fruit juices, raw fruits and vegetables, whole grains and nuts, and milk products. Informally, as children are preparing and eating snacks, talk about the special value of types of food.

**Suggestions and Variations:**    Young children usually like to eat foods they have seen adults eat, foods they have had frequent exposure to, and foods that are prepared and served in an attractive way. "Preaching" and "lecturing" to children about what they should eat is usually only effective in strengthening their resolve not to eat certain foods.

**Suggestions for parent involvement:**    Send snack "recipes" home and encourage parents to allow children to help cook. Provide suggestions for how children can be involved and what they learn from it.

## UNDERSTANDING PLANT LIFE

1. **Activity:**   Inside a seed (PP–P)

   *Materials:*   Large seeds such as beans; pan or dish of water.
   *Procedure:*   Have children soak beans in water overnight. Have them open the seeds the following day. Children should predict what they will find inside the seed.
   *Suggestions and Variations:*   This is such a simple experiment that children can do it off and on throughout the year. The use of magnifying glasses can increase the children's ability to see details of the seed.

2. **Activity:**   Sprouting seeds to eat (PP–P)

   *Materials:*   Select seeds of fast-growing plants or seedlings of plants already started; alfalfa seeds, mung bean seeds; two large glass jars (institutional size); wire or fabric mesh to cover the jar mouths.
   *Procedure:*   Help interested children sprout the bean and alfalfa seeds in the jars. Follow the directions on the seed packages. This usually involves placing a layer of seeds in the bottom of a jar, covering the jars with wire or fabric mesh, rinsing daily, and keeping them in a dark place. The volume of the sprouted seeds will be many times that of the original seeds. Talk about eating seeds. How many seeds are there? What color are they? Are they all alike? How do seeds feel?
   *Suggestions and Variations:*   Guinea pigs and rabbits love alfalfa and bean sprouts.
   Sprouted seeds may be used in food prepared by the children, such as chop suey or fried rice.
   Tell the story of "Jack and the Beanstalk."
   Try rapid-growing, vinelike plants such as peas.

3. **Activity:**   What makes a plant grow? (P)

   *Materials:*   Eight or nine slips of coleus, a small pot for each slip, potting soil and several pebbles; graph paper (one-inch run on ditto); string.
   *Procedure:*   Help a few children pot the coleus slips, one to a pot. Place all the plants in the sun and water them for the first few days. Then select one plant to place in each of the following places:

   > A sunny place
   > A light, but not sunny, place
   > A place that is sometimes light and sometimes dark (a closet that is opened and closed often)
   > A place that is always dark (under a can; inside a heavy box)

Guide children to take appropriate care of each plant by controlling for the one condition (variable) being tested, in this case, the amount of light. Encourage children to check and care for their plants every day and to observe what is happening to their growth and color. Help children draw conclusions about what plants need if they are to grow properly.

*Suggestions and Variations:*    Select another variable (condition) to test. Ask, "What else does a plant need to grow besides light?" Then select one plant to treat each of the following ways, using the same amount when watering:

> Watered often (every day)
> Watered once a week
> Watered never

Ask what else besides light and water a plant needs to grow. Prepare various soil mixtures for testing (see sprouting seeds).

Plant growth can be measured with string or ribbon every other day and marked on a piece of graph paper (each plant should have its own piece of graph paper). The experiment can be continued for several weeks.

There may be appropriate times during the year to suggest that plants that are not doing well be placed in conditions which seem to be more conducive to growth. This helps children see the dramatic effect that such conditions can have.

"How long does it take for them to grow leaves (flowers)?" Keep a daily chart to check the length of time.

Set up the dramatic play center so that children can play at being farmers, and encourage them to draw aesthetic pictures of their gardening products (but also educational ones in which they label the parts—roots, stems, leaves, flowers).

## 4. Activity:    Terrariums (PP–P)

*Materials:*    Glass jars such as gallon pickle jars, candy jars, or goldfish bowls; potting soil; a variety of small plants such as ferns, moss, philodendrons, ivy, begonias, African violets.

*Procedure:*    Plants may be removed from their pots by striking them sharply against a table and turning the plant with root-structure and soil intact into the palm of your hand; or, if the container is large, the plants may be left in the pots. Arrange plants in the container and surround with moist potting soil. Cover. If container has no lid of its own, use clear plastic. Plants should not be watered until soil looks and feels dry. Water condensation on the glass will indicate the moisture level. Ask children to observe changes seen, for example, water condensation on glass. They can also guess where the water comes from and can be provided with books which explain the water cycle.

*Suggestions and Variations:*    A lizard may be added to the terrarium. In that case, however, insects will need to be provided as food. A desert terrarium can be constructed using sand as ground and cacti for plants.

5. **Activity:**    Starting plants (PP–P)

*Materials:*    Variety of seeds, some saved from food children have eaten (for example, avocado, apple, orange), others purchased at the store; variety of vegetables such as sweet potatoes, white potatoes, beets, carrots and turnips; slips of ivy, coleus, and wandering Jew; potting soil, dishes, glasses, pebbles, pots, and water. Parents might be able to help here. Send home a note and request such slips of plants as they may be willing to send to school.

*Procedure:*    Encourage a few interested children to do this project. Seeds may be planted in potting soil in dishes or pans. Vegetables should be suspended with toothpicks in water in dishes or glasses. The leafy tops of turnips, beets, and carrots should be trimmed. Avocado seeds require special procedures to start. Sprouting an avocado in water first (by inserting toothpicks to hold the pit suspended in a jar of water) allows children to watch the root emerging. However, planting a pit directly in moist planting soil with the top showing above the surface of the soil gives a better chance of success When the plant reaches ten inches in height, pinch off the top new leaves, and it will spread out.

6. **Activity:**    Good plants to eat (PP–P)

*Materials:*    Whole plants; portions of the same plants—roots, stems, flowers, seeds, leaves. (Real plants are preferable, but pictures or plastic models, or some combination of these may be used.) Display boxes or bulletin boards divided into two sections: one for whole plants and one for parts of plants; string or ribbon.

*Procedures:*    Arrange whole plants or their pictures on one side of a bulletin board or in a shallow box with one section for each plant. Arrange plant parts in random order on the other side. If a bulletin board is used, children can connect plant parts with the whole plant, using string or pens. If boxes are used, children can put plant parts in the same compartment as the appropriate whole plant.

*Suggestions and Variations:*    Nuts (walnuts, pecans), fruit (apples, oranges), flowers (broccoli, cauliflower), leaves (spinach, lettuce, celery, rhubarb), and various roots (carrots, beets, potatoes, onions) may be separated into things that grow above ground and those that grow below ground. Or, the classification may be by leaves, stems, roots, flowers, or seeds.

### The Earth and the Universe

## GAINING CONCEPTS
## RELATED TO THE MOVEMENT
## OF THE EARTH AND SUN

1. **Activity:**   Day and night (PP–P)

   *Materials:*   Mounted globe map of the earth; a flashlight or small light bulb.
   *Procedure:*   Begin a discussion with children about what they do during the day and at night. Lead into questions about what causes the change from day to night and from night to day. In a closet, a large packing box, or another place that can be darkened, set up the globe and station the flashlight or light bulb in such a way that it will shine most directly on the equator. Show children the approximate area where they live. Have them mark it with a piece of colored tape or with a pin. Have the children spin the globe and note where the marked area is in relation to the light.
   *Suggestions and Variations:*   The globe and light activity would not be appropriate for young preprimary children, although older preprimary children can understand the idea that at night they are "not where the sun shines." For older primary children, the globe may be moved around the sun (light bulb) in an ellipse to demonstrate where the sun's rays hit at different times of the year (the seasons); or, a model of the solar system may be used.

2. **Activity:**   Sunrise, sunset (PP–P)

   *Materials:*   None.
   *Procedure:*   Ask children to note where they see the sun in the morning and where they see it in the evening. Children could even change the position of plants in the classroom in order to keep them in the sunlight. Help children relate their observations to the activity of the earth and sun (primary age children).

3. **Activity:**   The seasons (PP–P)

   *Materials:*   Outdoor environment; pictures of outdoor environment.
   *Procedure:*   Help children notice changes in the seasons by commenting about new plant growth, cessation of growth, need for outdoor clothing, frequency and form of precipitation (rain, sleet, snow), and so on. For preprimary children, the focus should be observation of the indicators of

seasonal changes as well as the names for each. Help older children relate these observations to the changes in the movement of the earth around the sun.

*Suggestions and Variations:*    Spring flowers and autumn leaves are excellent materials to use for aesthetic displays in the classroom and can serve to initiate children's interest in other signs of a season. A large outdoor thermometer mounted where children can see it provides a good ongoing experience which ties in with the study of seasons. Preprimary children should not be expected to master reading the thermometer, but they can understand that "when the red line goes up it's hot outside, and when it goes down it's cold outside." Older primary children can read a thermometer and may keep a graph illustrating the variation in temperature over a period of several months. If a few annual plants of some type are placed outside, children can relate seasonal changes to growing seasons, because they will be able to see the adverse effects of low temperatures on plants.

## UNDERSTANDING THE EARTH'S SURFACE AND HOW IT CHANGES

1. **Activity:**  Trips (PP-P)

*Materials:*    Materials will vary, depending on the type of trip taken. They may include permission slips from parents, packed lunches, vehicles for transportation, equipment and supplies (camera and film) to record aspects of the trip, and maps (topographical if possible).

*Procedure:*    Plan a trip for the specific purpose of observing certain land features. Perhaps you can visit a river, some mountains, a large lake, or the ocean. Help kindergarten and primary children relate what they are seeing to the features on the map. (This task is too abstract for preprimary children.)

*Suggestions and Variations:*    Children can use sand or clay to make their own topological maps. Older children can be encouraged to build maps of places they have visited on family trips.

2. **Activity:**  Erosion observation (K-P)

*Materials:*    Walk in immediate surroundings.

*Procedure:*    Children can take walking trips around the school and neighborhood to see if they can locate signs of erosion. Look for street cuts, eroded gulleys, or construction excavations. Some of the things that might be observed are the color of the soil where plants are growing versus the color of the soil where there are no plants, the presence or absence of gravel or larger rocks, and the thickness of the soil. Call children's attention to any signs of soil being removed by the wind (swirl dust outside in order to help children understand that wind also contributes to erosion). If children locate areas that are eroding, help them plan what might be done to stop erosion (placing rocks along a vertical gulley in a hill; planting something in bare spots where the wind carries soil away).

*Suggestions and Variations:*    Using earth, sand, and a bucket of water or a hose, call attention to what happens when a bucket of water is dumped on, or a hose is aimed at, soft earth. Relate this to the force of running water after a hard rain in which quantities of soil and debris are washed away. Pour water from a teakettle on gravel. Notice how the gravel is moved around. The greater the flow, the more the gravel moves.

3. **Activity:**    Rock collection (PP–P)

*Materials:*    Rocks, books about rocks.

*Procedure:*    Encourage children to collect rocks and to bring them into the classroom. Help them match their rocks to pictures of rocks and label them using the names given in the books. Record where each rock was found. Group rocks into "soft rocks" and "hard rocks." Rocks which leave particles when rubbed are "soft"; those from which particles do not rub off are "hard."

*Suggestions and Variations:*    Older children are often fascinated by fossils and prehistoric times. Museum trips, as well as books, may help them discover what a fossil is as well as the great variation in size and structure of fossils.

4. **Activity:**    Testing for limestone (P)

*Materials:*    Small pieces of rock; vinegar; small pot; electric hot plate.

*Procedures:*    Put one-fourth to one-half cup of vinegar in a pot and heat until hot. Do not let it boil. Heat speeds the chemical reaction. Dip a small corner of a rock into the hot vinegar. If small bubbles appear, the rock is either limestone or marble. The bubbles are carbon dioxide.

5. **Activity:**    Picture study (P)

*Materials:*    Photographs, pictures.

*Procedure:*    Bring in photos of the community as it was at an earlier time. Compare and contrast with photos of the community as it is today. Call attention to changes in trees, streets, buildings, and so on. Sources of such pictures include the children's families, local newspapers, private collections, and local government agencies.

*Suggestions and Variations:*    Capitalize on current happenings which impinge on the life of the children; for example, the eclipse of the sun, the explosion of a volcano, a hurricane, flood, or draught. Such events are of interest to children and can help them understand the implications of various events.

6. **Activity:**    Digging to find out (K-P)

*Materials:*    An area about twelve inches square and six inches deep in which children can dig up all the soil; box; newspapers; magnifying glass.
*Procedure:*    Have children dig up all the soil in the area and put it in the box. Carefully examine the soil by spreading it out on newspapers. Use magnifying glass to see what is contained in the soil: parts of decomposing leaves, stems, roots, larva, insects, earthworms, spiders, and so on.

## UNDERSTANDING WEATHER

1. **Activity:**    Weather station (PP-P)

*Materials:*    Outdoor thermometer; large mounted calendar; drawings and paper to indicate different weather (yellow circle for sunny day, white irregular shaped paper to indicate cloudy day, white irregular shaped paper with black dots to indicate rain, white paper cut to look like a snowflake to indicate snowy days); large cardboard doll, mounted, with paper clothes suitable for all types of weather.
*Procedure:*    For younger children, provide the large cardboard doll and paper clothes. Have children observe the daily weather and dress the doll appropriately. Sometimes the weather will change during the day, so the doll's clothes may need to be changed more than once a day. (Be sure to include all types of clothes for the doll; do not design them to indicate that the doll is necessarily a boy or a girl.) Older preprimary children and kindergarten children will be able to place weather pictures on a daily calendar. It has been one author's experience that this activity works best as one of many during activity or work time, rather than as a routine function to be performed at group time. Some children will not become involved in it at all, but others will spend a great deal of time taking care of the weather calendar. Primary children may keep a record of the weather for each week in a weather book. They may record items such as the daily temperature, whether the sun is shining, whether it is raining or snowing and how much accumulates, and whether it is windy or calm.
*Suggestions and Variations:*    Kindergarten and young primary children can make a permanent weather calendar book from the daily records they keep on the large mounted calendar. At the end of each month, before the new month is put up by rotating the numerals on the calendar and changing the name, children can paste smaller replicas of each weather symbol onto a calendar drawn on construction paper. Because of the visual differences

among the various weather symbols, it is easy to see quickly whether a month was rainy or snowy, cloudy or sunny. Children can compare the months. The children might also retain such records for the next year. New records can then be made for the current year, and these can be compared with those from the previous year. Children could predict the next month's weather on the basis of the last year's record. Primary children may be interested in listening to local weather forecasts and comparing them with actual weather. Books about weather should be provided for children to teach them about some factors that determine weather.

The children might incorporate their weather study and predicting activities into plans made for class projects. For example, if a walking trip is being considered for some aspect of study, they may want to consider weather conditions in planning when it should be done.

2. **Activity:**   Humidity (amount of moisture) identification (PP–P)

*Materials:*   Cobalt chloride, salt, and white paper towels for blotting.
*Procedures:*   Mix one teaspoon of cobalt chloride, one-half teaspoon of salt, and one cup of water. Dip towel and let dry. Paper will turn blue on days with high humidity (wet) and pink on low humidity (dry) days.
*Suggestions and Variations:*   Extend experiment by holding paper near spout of boiling teakettle.

3. **Activity:**   Irrigation system (P)

*Materials:*   A section of the playground, preferably with a small mound where children can dig holes and trenches and run water. Pieces of plywood, sheet metal, or masonite approximately 6 by 8 by 1/4 inches may be provided for watergates. Other useful materials are tin cans with both ends removed (be sure there are no jagged edges), small pieces of garden hose, and aluminum foil or plastic for lining the reservoir. Towels or shovels are needed.
*Procedure:*   Digging trenches, watching water run, and building dams are such interesting activities for young children that providing the materials may be enough to start an irrigation project. For further learning, visit an irrigated farm or show pictures of one. Older children may build quite elaborate systems with reservoirs, canals, irrigation ditches, and small trenches between planted rows of "farmland." By using a can or piece of hose, a road may be built over a canal or ditch. Help older primary children relate irrigation to weather.
*Suggestions and Variations:*   Vocabulary: Reservoir—a lake formed by damming a stream. The amount of water allowed to remain in the stream is controlled by gates in the dam.

Canal—a manmade stream to carry water to farmlands. Canals are generally quite long and keep a constant flow of water.

Irrigation ditches—smaller ditches leading directly to the farms. Water from the canals is led into the ditches as needed by lifting gates.

Trenches—smaller spaces between rows of plants through which water from the ditches is fed.

Zanjero (zan-he-rō)—the person who lifts the gates to let water into the ditches. Usually, this is siphoned in.

This project is an excellent activity for integrating science, social science, language arts, and dramatic play.

4. **Activity:**   Wind blowing (PP)

   *Materials:*   Pinwheels (see page 282).
   *Procedure:*   Hold pinwheels upright so that they face the wind.
   *Suggestions and Variations:*   On a windy day, let the children feel the wind on their faces or have them look at flags flying or leaves and smoke blowing across the yard.
   Cut a strip of paper for children to use as streamers. Encourage them to run and to see what happens.

   **Matter and Energy**

## UNDERSTANDING SIMPLE MACHINES

1. **Activity:**   Wheels #1 (PP)

   *Materials:*   Tricycles, wagons, wheeled toys of all sizes. (Include some toys from which wheels may be removed and put on again.)
   *Procedure:*   Include a large variety of wheeled toys in the block area, on the playground, and in areas where there is space to run wheeled toys without disturbing other activities. Encourage free exploration and help children verbalize what they observe. For example, a child has a tricycle upside down and is turning the front wheel by moving the pedals by hand. You might comment with mock surprise: "The rear wheels aren't turning!" or you might ask questions such as "What's happening to the front wheel when you do that?" "Why does a wheel have an axle?" (Pointing to the axle as you speak).

2. **Activity:**   Wheels #2 (P)

   *Materials:*   Sturdy cardboard cartons or plywood cartons (cigar boxes, cheese boxes, and so on); drill and bit; lengths of dowel to extend beyond sides of cartons; plywood circles, jar lids, extra-strength cardboard circles; glue or hammer and thin nails.

*Procedure:*   Discuss with children ways in which wheeled carts might be made from the materials. Holes may be drilled in the cartons close to the base and exactly opposite each other. Holes need to be large enough to allow the dowel to turn easily. Wheels must be fastened on the dowel after it is inserted into holes in the cart. The dowel, when attached to the wheels in this fashion, is called an axle.

*Suggestions and Variations:*   The trickiest part will be fastening the wheels to the axle. Find the center of the cardboard or plywood circle and, using a bit the same size as the dowel, drill a hole. It would be wise to do this in advance. When wheels are fastened to the axle, coat the joint with glue. If jar lids are used as wheels, they should be nailed to the ends of the dowel-axle. Children may work in pairs on this project. Assignment cards may be useful and might take the following form:

> Can you make a wheeled cart with the materials on this table?
> Before you start, load the box with blocks and push or pull it across the table.
> Notice how it feels and how hard you have to pull or push. After cart is made, put the same number of blocks in it and again pull or push it across the table.

A display of all kinds of wheels might be set up and books about wheels might be provided. Children may be interested in speculating as to how people managed to move things before there were wheels.

3. **Activity:**   Gears and springs (PP–P)

*Materials:*   Old worn-out alarm clocks, gear-driven toys, music boxes, watches, and so on.

*Procedure:*   Place these on the table. Tell children that these are items that people have discarded because they no longer work well. Children may find out what made them work by taking them apart. Encourage children to describe what they see inside. Children may be able to move one gear with their fingers to see what happens to the one attached to it, or they may wind up springs.

*Suggestions and Variations:*   Children may draw pictures or write stories about what they see.

4. **Activity:**   Downhill racer (inclined plane) (P)

*Materials:*   Blocks, flat boards; matched pair of toy cars or balls; ruler, stopwatch.

*Procedure:*   While children are playing in the block corner, suggest the following, or set up a table with the above materials and an assignment card:

> Put two blocks under one end of one of these boards.
> Put three blocks under one end of another board.

Allow one car to run down each of the boards.

Measure how far the car goes on the table before it stops.

With a friend, race cars down the inclined boards.

Ask someone to time the cars using a stopwatch. (You will need to mark a finish line on the table with a strip of masking tape.)

*Suggestions and Variations:*    Provide extra blocks so that children may experiment with steeper slopes. Commercial toys such as trains and racing cars with tracks may be introduced. Set up a display of various inclined planes: doorstops (wedge shaped), axes, wedges of various types, pictures of ramps, dump trucks, and so on. Discuss how they help people do work.

Place two boards (about four feet and eight feet) as ramps leading to a table. Incline them enough for cars and trucks to travel on. Have children push or pull equal loads up the ramps. On which ramp must children exert greater force to move the car up?

5. **Activity:**    Circular inclined planes (P)

*Materials:*    Drill, variety of screws, screwdriver, screw-on lids and jars; pieces of soft wood 1 to 2 inches thick.

*Procedure:*    Make materials available for children. Help children to notice that the lines on a drill bit, a screw, and a jar lid slant as they go around, which makes them easier to use.

*Suggestions and Variations:*    Try to find screws that differ in terms of number and slant of lines. Have children compare the ease with which each can be screwed into a piece of wood.

6. **Activity:**    Clothesline pulley (PP–P)

*Materials:*    Clothesline; two pulleys attached to opposite walls of a room, one end high on the wall and the other end low enough to be easily reached by children; pincer clothespins.

*Procedure:*    Encourage children to hang up their own paintings on the clothesline to dry. Children can attach their paintings to the low end and then move the rope to send their painting to the high end. The rope goes around the pulleys at each end.

7. **Activity:**    Weight-lifting pulleys (P)

*Materials:*    Three simple and two double clothesline pulleys; clothesline; hook.

*Procedure:*    Make three different pulleys of successive strength as shown in Figure 8–4. Knot the end of each clothesline and place a hook at the bottom of the lower pulleys for attaching objects for lifting. Begin by having children

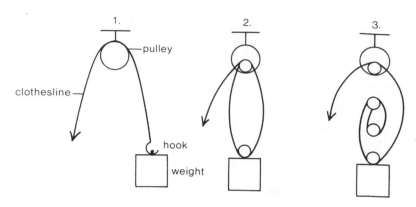

**FIGURE 8-4**

lift objects without using the pulleys. Then have them use the first pulley to lift the same object. Compare and note how much easier the pulley makes the lifting. Continue with pulley 2 and pulley 3. Compare the efficacy of the three pulleys. Watch the school flag being raised. Note pulleys in window shades and clotheslines.

8. **Activity:**　Seesaw level (PP–K)

**Materials:**　Playground seesaw or one made by placing a long board on a saw horse; two objects.
**Procedure:**　The teacher can ask where the objects must be placed in order to balance. Allow children to experiment.
**Suggestions and Variations:**　Use two objects of different weights. (Heavier one nearer the fulcrum; lighter one further out on the board.) Try putting the fulcrum at various locations. Construct a miniature seesaw for the doll playhouse.

## UNDERSTANDING LIGHT, HEAT, AND SOUND

1. **Activity:**　Making rainbows (PP–P)

**Materials:**　Jar and water, prisms, white paper; soap solution and bubble pipes.
**Procedure:**　Fill jar with water and place it on a window sill where there is sunlight, or hang prisms in a window. Hold white paper in front of the jar or prism so that the sun shines through onto the paper. Bands of color (a rainbow) will appear on the paper. Ask children to identify the colors and the order in which they appear. Ask them to recall rainbows they have seen.

What kind of weather was there when they saw the rainbow? Was it raining? Was the sun shining? Or both?

Give children soap solution and pipes outside on a sunny day. Encourage them to notice and talk about the colors they see in the bubbles.

*Suggestions and Variations:*   The light refraction, which appears as a rainbow, may occur when the sun shines through an aquarium and children may comment spontaneously. Follow up on such spontaneous remarks with the above activity.

2. **Activity:**   Light spots (PP-P)

*Materials:*   Bowl of water, small hand mirrors.

*Procedure:*   Place bowl of water on floor, table, or shelf where it catches the sunlight. The water will reflect the light onto the ceiling or wall depending on the angle at which it strikes the water. This may be done before the children enter the room. If children do not spontaneously notice and remark on the spots of light, call attention to them and start a search for the source. Use hand mirrors in similar fashion.

3. **Activity:**   Making things safe (PP-P)

*Materials:*   Collection of reflectors such as the ones found on bicycles; fluorescent materials such as those used to mark guard rails or mailboxes; stick-on fluorescent materials such as those provided by fire departments to mark clothing, bicycles, and bedroom windows.

*Procedure:*   Make a display of these items. Discuss with children how the items are used to prevent accidents. Enough stick-on dots can be obtained from the local fire department to mark the children's clothing.

4. **Activity:**   Shadows in sunlight (PP-K)

*Materials:*   Sunlight; children's bodies.

*Procedure:*   As children play outside, point out their shadows. If children go out at different times during the day, help them note how their shadows change.

5. **Activity:**   Heat transmission through air

*Materials:*   Thread, slick paper, candle or other heat source.

*Procedure:*   Cut a spiral shape from slick paper. In the center, tie an 8-by-10-inch knotted thread. Attach thread to a stick for easy handling. Hold paper above the heat source and watch it spin. Ask, "What makes it turn? What happens if we hold the paper way up here (too far above heat for reaction)?"

6. **Activity:**   Heat transmission through water and solids

   *Materials:*   Test tube and test-tube holder, candle or other source of heat, water.
   *Procedure:*   Put water into test tube and mark level with a rubber band. Hold over the candle flame and watch what happens. Call attention to little bubbles moving through the water as it nears boiling point. Note level of water.
   In science kits there is a metal ball and ring mounted on sticks. When heated, the ball will not go through the ring; but when cold, it will. As does any activity which involves fire or high heat, this project needs to be carefully supervised.

7. **Activity:**   Sound travels (PP–P)

   *Materials:*   Two tin cans, nails, ten or more feet of wire.
   *Procedure:*   Hammer nails into ends of cans. Wrap wire around nails. Have one child hold one can against an ear while another child talks into the can.
   *Suggestions and Variations:*   Two funnels stuck into the ends of a long piece of hose may be used as a variation. For other explorations of sound, see activities in the chapter on Expressive Arts. Call attention to vibrations.
   Place a clock on a table and have children place their ears on the table surface to discover that the wood, as well as air, conducts sound.

8. **Activity:**   Different sounds (PP)

   *Materials:*   Musical instruments—piano, triangle, drum.
   *Procedure:*   Have children identify the differences between high and low and loud and soft sounds by comparing each for a specific criteria, for example, higher than a given note or louder than a given sound, and so on.
   *Suggestions and Variations:*   Vary the sound made by having children blow, pick, or strike various instruments.

## UNDERSTANDING THE PROPERTIES
## OF DIFFERENT TYPES OF SUBSTANCES

1. **Activity:**   Water and oil (PP–P)

   *Materials:*   Clear plastic bottles with caps (such as the bottles cooking oil is sold in); water; oil.
   *Procedure:*   Fill bottle about three quarters full with water. Add two tablespoons oil to the water. Cap the bottle. Place bottle out where children

can use it. Encourage children to try to mix the two layers they see in the bottle. Ask children what they think the two materials are.

*Suggestions and Variations:*    Food coloring can be added to the contents of the bottle. It is soluble in water and so mixes with it, thus making the oil droplets stand out better. Encourage children to think of other substances (liquid) which could be added to water. As they come up with ideas, more bottles should be supplied so they can test out their ideas.

2. **Activity:**    Soap bubbles (PP–K)

*Materials:*    Water pans or plastic tubs; newspapers or terry towels, rotary beaters, wire whips, straws; liquid soap, *not* detergent; plastic or oilcloth aprons.

*Procedure:*    Children should wear plastic aprons. Water containers should be placed on newspaper or terry towels so any spills will be absorbed. Children (two or three at a time, depending on space) make bubbles using any pieces of equipment. Ask children what's inside the outer film of the bubble. Teachers can also ask children why they think some of the utensils make big bubbles while others make small ones.

*Suggestions and Variations:*    Cut straws in half to reduce cost of materials. Children do not need a whole straw. Half of one works well.

3. **Activity:**    Air-filled bottle (PP–K)

*Materials:*    Bowl of water, small bottle with lid or cap.

*Procedure:*    Encourage children to cover the bottle with its lid or cap and then submerge it in the water, where the lid or cap should be removed. Children will see bubbles of air emerge from the bottle as it fills with water.

4. **Activity:**    Cool snack (PP–K)

*Materials:*    Ice trays, refrigerator with freezing compartment; juice.

*Procedure:*    Help children fill ice trays and place them in the refrigerator to freeze. Help children remove ice from trays when it is ready and use it to chill their juice. Talk about how water changes from liquid to solid when it freezes and how ice floats on top of the juice in the cup.

*Suggestions and Variations:*    Children may enjoy a few ice cubes in the water-play tubs from time to time.

5. **Activity:**    Fun with magnets (PP–K–P)

*Materials:*    One bar magent, paper clips, rubber bands, large nails, scraps of paper, hair pins, and so on.

*Procedure:*   Have children try to pick up or move each object with the magnets. Separate objects into those which are attracted and those which are not.

*Suggestions and Variations:*   Let children experiment with picking up paper clips and nails using the magnet under water, through a glass, a paper, and so on.

6. **Activity:**   Making static electricity (PP-P)

*Materials:*   Balloons, small pieces of wool cloth.

*Procedure:*   Inflate balloons and tie the openings. Let children rub one side of balloons with the wool cloth and place the rubbed side against the wall. Have them see if the rubbed balloons adhere to other surfaces as well and if once-rubbed balloons also adhere. (The static electricity makes the rubbed balloons act like magnets.)

*Suggestions and Variations:*   Rub several balloons and drop one at a time into a large cardboard box. Because objects with the same static charge repel each other, the balloons will jump around away from each other for a few minutes.

7. **Activity:**   Many things have water (PP-P)

*Materials:*   Fruits, vegetables, hot plate, pan with lid.

*Procedure:*   Cut the fruit or vegetables and note the juice (water) accumulate. Heat the fruit or vegetable in a small pan with a lid and notice the moisture collecting on the lid. As food is heated, it loses some of its moisture. Spinach is particularly good for this. Wash, drain, then place fresh spinach in a tightly covered pan with no water. Note amount of water in pan after cooking.

8. **Activity:**   Smelling (PP-K)

*Materials:*   Small metal or plastic photographic film containers with screw-on lids, or other small containers; a variety of common substances which may be distinguishable by smell (onions, cinnamon, perfume, coffee, soap, pine needles, and so on).

*Procedure:*   Puncture lids of containers so fragrance can emerge, or use gauze attached by rubber bands as a lid. Be sure substance cannot be seen from outside the container. (Cover clear bottles with aluminum foil or opaque paper.) Mark each with a number or letter and prepare a key (a chart showing the number and a picture of the contents) so children can determine if their guesses are accurate. Children can sniff the containers and guess what each contains.

9. **Activity:** Touching (PP–K)

**Materials:** A variety of materials that vary in texture (sandpaper, velvet, fake fur, pine cone, satin, corduroy, flocked wallpaper, vinyl floor tile, mosaic floor tile, smooth wood, and so on).

**Procedure:** Place materials in a closed box that has on one side a hole large enough for a child's hand. Children reach in through the hole, feel the objects, and talk about the materials. Stop by as children are engaged in the activity and talk about how the materials feel, and provide vocabulary (hard, soft, rough, stiff, slick, and so on). Also, encourage children to guess what the materials are and for what they might be used.

**Suggestions and Variations:** A texture board can be made by gluing materials to a large piece of cardboard, with the interesting texture side facing out. Children can then feel the materials and also see how their appearance varies with their texture.

10. **Activity:** Tasting (PP–K)

**Materials:** Pudding, apples, celery, carrots, peanut butter, nuts, and other nutritious snack items.

**Procedure:** Proceed with snack as usual, but talk with children about the different smells and textures of the foods they are served. Two foods with contrasting textures might be served on the same day so children can compare them.

**Suggestions and Variations:** Teach children to classify food in various ways such as by texture, shape, color, size, or weight.

How many cherry tomatoes balance with an apple?

**Suggestions for parent involvement:** In newsletter or note, tell parents about this classroom experience. Suggest they continue at home.

11. **Activity:** Woodworking (PP–K)

**Materials:** Wood, nails, sandpaper, hammer, saw, plane, and other woodworking tools being used in the woodworking center.

**Procedure:** Encourage children to use the woodworking center. They will find that materials have different characteristics, such as hardness and roughness. They can determine uses of the material (nails are hard and can be driven into other materials; sandpaper is rough and can make wood smooth, and so on).

12. **Activity:** Cooking (PP–P)

**Materials:** Recipes and ingredients for jello, popcorn, cookies, hard-boiled eggs, salads, and so on.

*Procedure:*    Provide a rebus recipe (using pictures or drawings with few words) for the children to use in their food preparation. Guide them to count aloud, to measure carefully, and to follow directions. Discuss how the mixture of substances forms new substances, how some dry substances dissolve in liquids, and how cold solidifies some things and heat melts them. Ask them to close their eyes and identify ingredients by taste. They will learn that even though foods look alike, they may not taste the same.

## UNDERSTANDING FORCE AND PRESSURE

### 1. Activity:   Pinwheels (PP–K)

*Materials:*   Pinwheels, either commercially made or made from paper, pins, and pencils. (See Figure 8–5.)

*Procedure:*   Take pinwheels outside and hold them in the wind. Talk with children about what makes the pinwheel move. When the wind stops and the pinwheel is still, help children think of other ways to make the pinwheel move. Some possible solutions are blowing on them, using a small electric fan (with a good screen guard), or using the reverse end of a vacuum cleaner.

*Suggestions and Variations:*   On field trips and other outings, call attention to windmills, sailboats moving on bodies of water, and clouds moving across the sky. Relate these movements to experiences with pinwheels.

### 2. Activity:   Snack preparation (PP–K)

*Materials:*   Cans of juice, can opener.

*Procedure:*   Permit a few children to help prepare juice. Start by punching only one hole in the top of the juice can. It will pour with difficulty. Then punch another hole. The juice will now pour easily as air moves in to replace the juice.

**FIGURE 8-5**   Pinwheels.

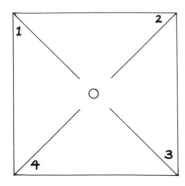
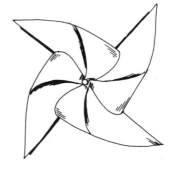

3. **Activity:**  Vacuums (K–P)

*Materials:*  Straws and milk or juice; medicine dropper and bowl of water; vacuum cleaner.
*Procedure:*  Permit children to use the above items in appropriate situations (straws at juice time, dropper and water during activity time, vacuum at cleanup time). Through discussion and questions, help children understand that when air is removed from something, an empty space or vacuum is created, and some other substance rushes in to fill the empty space.

4. **Activity:**  Pumps (PP–P)

*Materials:*  Hypodermic and bulb syringes, pump-type hand lotion or spray bottles, straws, water; old, hand-operated water pump mounted over a tank of water if possible.
*Procedure:*  Encourage children to explore freely these various kinds of pumps. As they work, ask questions which will further children's thinking. For example, as a child pushes the plunger down on a hypodermic syringe with the tip held under water, ask, "Do you see what's happening? (Bubbles.) What are those bubbles?" A child who does not know can be asked to hold an empty syringe with the tip about an inch above one arm and to push the plunger down. What does the child feel?
*Suggestions and Variations:*  These items are good for outdoor water play. When they are used inside, children will need to be reminded to point the water toward the tub!

5. **Activity:**  Jumping Jiminy (PP–K)

*Materials:*  Commercial canvas cover to fit over large inner tube. (Makes a small trampoline-like piece of equipment that children can jump up and down on.)
*Procedure:*  Permit children to play on the equipment outside on the ground or, if there is space, inside on a mat. When children jump on the piece of equipment, the air in the inner tube is compressed, but then it "bounces back" and propels the child upward. This illustrates how air exerts force on other objects.

6. **Activity:**  Inflatable things (PP–P)

*Materials:*  Balloons, plastic bags, inner tubes, inflatable balls; bicycle pump.
*Procedure:*  Allow children to inflate items and then to use them. These items illustrate that air has weight and exerts pressure.

7. **Activity:**   Water pressure (PP–P)

*Materials:*   Garden hose with nozzle attachment; pipes in a variety of diameters and types which fit together (one piece of the pipe should connect with a faucet or garden hose); tin can with a vertical line of holes punched about one inch apart from the bottom nearly to the top.
*Procedure:*   Pipes and garden hose and nozzle can be made available to children outside in warm weather. Children can discover that the narrower the pipe, the stronger the force of water as it emerges. Children should look at the nozzle to see how it is constructed and notice how it changes the force with which water comes out of the hose. The can with holes can be used for inside water play. A faucet works best to fill it. Children will notice that the water stream from the bottom hole is the longest, while the water stream from the top hole is the shortest. If no faucet and sink are available in the classroom, the tin can can be filled by being dipped into a bucket or pan of water.

8. **Activity:**   Water and tubes (K–P)

*Materials:*   Tubs of water; bowls and funnels; pincer clothespins; metal racks (perhaps from felt board or experience charts); wooden building blocks or other materials to use as platforms to raise the height of some water bowls; newspapers to soak up spills; pieces of clear plastic tubing varying in thickness from three-fourths to one-fourth inch. (Each piece should be at least three feet long. Some longer pieces of the smaller-diameter tubing would also be useful.)
*Procedure:*   Materials can be placed out together and arranged so that children can explore them. Children will discover many ways to combine the equipment to transport water from one bowl to another. Ask questions such as "Can you find out through which size tubing water travels the fastest from a given height?" or "Can you find something to stop the flow of water in the tube?" Clothespins can be used to stop the flow of water in tubes as well as to hang them on the metal racks.

9. **Activity:**   Sink and float (PP–P)

*Materials:*   Large variety of objects such as washers, ping-pong balls, golf tees, poker chips, paper clips, pins, colored wooden cubes, blocks of wood, plastic fishing bobs, bolts, buttons, spools, corks, rubber jar rings, erasers, pieces of styrofoam, pebbles, mothballs, and so on; container for water and soda water such as plastic dishpan or water-play table; two smaller containers labeled with pictures showing something floating and something sinking or with the words "sink" and "float."
*Procedure:*   Place water tub on terry towel or newspaper laid on a table or on the floor. Make objects available in appropriate container near water tub.

Encourage children to place objects in water to see if they sink or float and then to place them into the properly labeled containers.

*Suggestions and Variations:*   Do not provide too many objects at any one time. New objects can be added and old objects removed every three or four days. Encourage children to try to find ways to make sinking objects float.

Younger children will be content to sort objects into sink or float containers rather than seeking reasons for floating or sinking. This should be permitted. Older children will become interested in solving the problem of what determines flotation. At this point, help children generate possible hypotheses through questioning—"How are these objects different from these?" "Do you suppose all these are heavier than these?" A pan balance can be provided to find out. "Do you think size has anything to do with it?" "Are these alike in any way and different from the others in any way?" Older children might also be interested in altering the condition of the water to see if this affects the flotation of objects in any way. Ice, food coloring, sugar, soap, and salt should be provided so that children can experiment. Smaller bowls are helpful at this point so that a great deal of the materials is not consumed. Older children might notice that there are many gradations of sinking and floating. Some objects float, although almost totally submerged. Others float midway, while others are on top of the water. They may want to test objects for these fine distinctions. You might ask children to see if they can make a ball of plasticene float. Children who live near a port may find it interesting to take a trip to see large ships and find out about ballast. Fill a jar with three parts water to one part soda water. Place a few moth balls in the jar and watch them bob up and down. (Dissolved carbon dioxide in the soda water settles on the moth balls, lifting them to the surface like a raft. When the gas escapes, the moth balls sink.)

Place several ice cubes in a pan of water. What happens? Why do they float?

10. **Activity:**   Dissolving things (PP)

*Materials:*   Glass containers, such as baby food jars; salt, sugar, sand, bread, sponge, dye, water, shortening, cooking oil.

*Procedure:*   Add each of the above to a glass with water, stir thoroughly, and let settle. Which dissolve and which do not? Which disintegrate? Which absorb? Which color?

## UNDERSTANDING CHEMICAL CHANGES

1. **Activity:**   The shape of things (PP-K)

*Materials:*   Colored construction paper; flat objects such as a pair of scissors, a small book, a sponge, a key, and so on.

*Procedure:*    Encourage interested children to place the objects on the paper, which is then placed in the sunlight. Leave the objects on the paper for several days. The sun will bleach the color where the paper is exposed, but not where the objects have covered it.

2. **Activity:**   Rust (PP–P)

*Materials:*   Iron nails and other iron objects as well as metals that do not rust; shallow aluminum pie tin with water.
*Procedure:*   Put objects out for children to see. Encourage interested children to place the objects in water and then to observe for a few days to see if any of the objects change.
*Suggestion for parent involvement:*   Explain what is being studied at school and ask parents to show their children where rust forms on things at home, for example, the car, the gutters, a wagon, swings, and so on.

3. **Activity:**   Painting equipment (PP–P)

*Materials:*   Tricycles, swings, wagons, and any other metal equipment; paint to touch up equipment; brushes and cleaner to clean them after painting.
*Procedure:*   Point out to children any rust spots that appear on outdoor equipment. Involve children in preparing the spots for touch-up and also permit them to help paint the spots. Talk about what causes the rust, and mention that paint helps keep things from rusting.

4. **Activity:**   Cooking (PP–P)

*Materials:*   Ingredients and utensils to make cakes, cookies, bread, biscuits, and so on.
*Procedure:*   Select a small group of children to do the cooking. Discuss the changes that occur in the process of preparing the food and why they occur.
*Suggestions and Variations:*   With young preprimary children, the discussion should focus on changes in appearance (the bread dough was small and then it got big; the bread dough was soft, and the baked bread is hard; the cake batter was wet, and the baked cake is dry, and so on.). As children are able to comprehend the information, the discussion can include more and more reasons for the change (yeast ferments the sugar and a gas is formed, making the bread rise).

5. **Activity:**   Fizz (PP–P)

*Materials:*   Baking soda, vinegar; small dishes, spoons.
*Procedure:*   Have children predict what will happen if vinegar and soda are combined. Then permit them to combine the two and see what happens.

*Suggestions and Variations:*    For older children, this activity may be related to what happens when you put baking powder or yeast in baked goods. Buttermilk pancakes may be made. Children can notice what happens when soda is added to the buttermilk and can discuss soda's function in the pancakes.

## UNDERSTANDING LENSES

1. **Activity:**    Real lenses (PP–P)

    *Materials:*    Hand magnifying glasses, old box-style cameras, binoculars, small telescope, old eyeglasses.
    *Procedure:*    Make these materials available for children. They will notice that some of the lenses make objects appear smaller and farther away, whereas other lenses make objects appear bigger and closer. Help the children explore the curvatures of the lenses to see if they can discern the difference.
    *Suggestions and Variations:*    It is helpful to tape comic pages from the newspaper (Sunday, colored ones) to a tabletop or to the bottom of a water table and to place different kinds of lenses on them. Children tend to look at the comics through the lenses. This arrangement prevents children from wandering around the room with the lenses and misplacing them.

2. **Activity:**    Magnifying jar (P)

    *Materials:*    Glass jar or bottle with rounded sides (mayonnaise jars work well); water; objects to hold behind the jar (word cards, pencil, and so on).
    *Procedure:*    Have children fill the jar with water and put a finger in to notice that the submerged portion is enlarged when viewed from the outside. Then hold objects behind the jar and have children look through the jar to view them. Objects and writing will appear larger behind the jar because the jar's outwardly sloping sides make the water act like a lens. The teacher should explain to children that glass and water bend the light rays as they pass through and thus make objects look different.

3. **Activity:**    Mirrors (light reflection) (PP–P)

    *Materials:*    Two flat mirrors, flashlight.
    *Procedure:*    Arrange mirrors so that they reflect the flashlight beam onto the wall, ceiling, and so on. Try to trace the beam's light.

4. **Activity:**    Shadow profiles (PP–P)

    *Materials:*    Slide projector, large drawing paper, marker.

*Procedure:*   Tape paper onto the walls and sit children in front of the slide projector in order to cast a shadow on the wall. Trace the outlines of their profiles. See if children can identify each other by their silhouettes.

*Suggestions and Variations:*   Move slide projectors farther away from the wall. What happens to the size of the picture on the wall as the light source moves farther away?

Early one sunny morning, have children play shadow tag outdoors. Designate one child as the shadow chaser, who is to step on the shadow of another child. This child then becomes the shadow chaser. Another time play shadow tag at noon, when shadows are shorter.

## TEACHER REFERENCES

ABRUSCATO, J.   *Teaching Children Science.* Englewood Cliffs, N. J., Prentice-Hall, 1982.

ASIMOV, I.   *Asimov's Guide to Science.* New York: Basic Books, 1972.

BLOUGH, G.O., and CAMPBELL, M.H.   *Making and Using Classroom Science Materials in the Elementary School.* New York: Holt, Rinehart and Winston, 1954.

BLOUGH, G.O., and SCHWARTZ, J.   *Elementary School Science and How to Teach It.* New York: Holt, Rinehart and Winston, 1979.

BROWN, S. E.   *Bubbles, Rainbows and Worms: Science Experiments for Pre-School Children.* Mt. Rainier, Maryland: Gryphon House, 1982.

CANTU, L., and HERRON, J.   Concrete and formal Piagetian stages and science concept attainment. *Journal of Research in Science Teaching* 15(1978): 135–143.

CHITTENDON, E.A.   Piaget and elementary science. *Science and Children* 8(1970): 9–14.

CLARK, C.   Teaching concepts in the classroom—A set of prescriptions derived from experimental research. *Journal of Educational Psychology* 62(1971): 253–278.

COBB, V.   *Science Experiments You Can Eat.* New York: Lippincott, 1972.

COOPER, E.K.   *Science in Your Own Backyard.* New York: Harcourt Brace Jovanovich, 1960.

DUCKWORTH, E.   Either we're too early and they can't learn it or we're too late and they know it already: The dilemma of "Applying Piaget." *Harvard Educational Review* 49(1979): 297–311.

DURGIN, H.J.   From curiosity to concepts: From concepts to curiosity—Science experiences in the preschool. *Young Children* 30(1975): 249–256.

ELKIND, D.   Piaget and science education. *Science and Children* 10(1972): 9–12

GEGA, P.C.   *Science in Elementary Education.* New York: John Wiley, 1982.

GOODWIN, M., and POLEN, G.   *Creative Food Experiences for Children.* Washington, D.C.: Center for Science in the Public Interest, 1977.

GURALINIK, D.B., (ed.),   *Webster's New World Dictionary.* New York: World Publishing, 1972, 1275.

HARLAN, J.   *Science Experiences for the Early Childhood Years.* Columbus, Ohio: Charles E. Merrill, 1980.

HAWKINS, D.   Messing about in science. *Science and Children* 2(1965): 5–9.

KESSEN, W.   Statement of purpose and objectives of science education in school. *Journal of Research in Science Teaching* (1964): 3–6.

LAVATELLI, C.S., and STENDLER, F.   *Readings in Child Behavior and Development.* New York: Harcourt Brace Jovanovich, 1972, 9–14.

PIAGET, J.   *The Child's Concept of the World.* Totowa, N. J. Littlefield, Adams and Co., 1969.

SCHMIDT, V.E., and ROCKCASTLE, V.N.    *Teaching Science with Everyday Things.* New York: McGraw-Hill, 1982.

SHAW, J.M., and CLIATT, M.J.    Science is what scientists do. *Science and Children,* 18 (1981): 16-17.

SKELSEY, A., and HUCKABY, G.    *Growing up Green.* New York: Workman Publishing, 1973.

THURBER, W.A., and RILBURN, R.E.    *Exploring Life Science.* Rockleigh, N. J.: Allyn and Bacon, 1975.

VICTOR, E.    *Science for the Elementary School.* New York: Macmillan, 1975.

———. The pendulum never stops swinging. *Science and Children,* 16(1978): 25-35.

WATSON, F.    Learning science from planned experiences. In Rowe, (ed.), *What Research Says To The Science Teacher*—Volume I. Washington, D.C.: National Science Teachers Association, 1978, 83-94.

WEISS, I.R.    *Report of the 1977 National Survey of Science, Mathematics and Social Studies Education.* Research Triangle Park, N.C., 1978.

WYLER, R.    *First Book of Science Experiments.* New York: Franklin Watts, 1971.

———. *Exploring with Science.* Racine, Wisc.: Western Publishing Co. 1973.

## CHILDREN'S REFERENCES

ADLER, I.    *Energy.* New York: John Day, 1970.

ALIKI,    *Fossils Tell of Long Ago.* New York: Macmillan, 1972.

ASIMOV, I.    *What Makes the Sun Shine?* Boston, Mass.: Little, Brown, 1971.

BENDICK, J.    *The First Book of Airplanes.* New York: Franklin Watts, 1958.

———. *The Human Senses.* New York: Franklin Watts, 1968.

. *Living Things.* New York: Franklin Watts, 1969.

BLOUGH, G.O.    *Useful Plants and Animals.* New York: Harper and Row, Pub., 1959.

———. *Doing Work.* New York: Harper and Row, Pub., 1959.

———. *Water Appears and Disappears.* New York: Harper and Row, Pub., 1959.

BROWN, M.W.    *The Country Noisy Book.* New York: Harper and Row, Pub., 1940.

CAMPBELL, A.    *Let's Find Out about Color.* New York: Franklin Watts, 1966.

CRAIG, M.J.    *Dinosaurs and More Dinosaurs.* New York: Four Winds Press, 1968.

FREEMAN, I., and FREEMAN, M.D.    *The Story of Chemistry.* New York: Random House, 1962.

GIONNONI F., and REIT, S.    *Golden Book of Gardening: How to Plan, Plant, and Care for the Home Garden.* New York. Golden Press, 1962.

GUTHRIE, E.L.    *Home Book of Animal Care.* New York: Harper and Row, Pub., 1966.

HOONER, H.    *Animals at My Doorstep.* New York: Parent's Magazine Press, 1966.

HUNGERFORD, H.R.    *Ecology: The Circle of Life.* Chicago: Children's Press, 1971.

IRVING, R.    *Sound and Vetrasonics.* New York: Knopf, 1959.

KEENE, M.    *The Beginner's Story of Minerals and Rocks.* New York: Harper and Row, Pub., 1966.

SIMON, S.    *Let's Try It Out—Light and Dark.* New York: McGraw-Hill, 1970.

———. *The Paper Airplane.* New York: Viking, 1971.

STERLING, D.    *Fall is Here.* Garden City, New York: Doubleday, 1966.

ZAFFO, G.    *The Giant Book of Things in Space.* Garden City, New York: Doubleday, 1969.

———. *The Giant Nursery Book of Things That Go.* Garden City, New York: Doubleday, 1959.

ZIM, H.S.    *What's Inside of Me?* New York: Morrow, 1952.

———. *What's Inside of Plants?* New York: Morrow, 1952.

———. *What's Inside of the Earth?* New York: Morrow, 1953.

# 9

# MATHEMATICS

One of the major ways we organize the world is by quantifying the objects and substances we encounter. For example, we count objects or distribute them among places and people, and we determine the size of one thing in relation to the size of something else. As adults, we are so accustomed to performing these simple processes that we may assume erroneously that they are self-evident to young children as well. However, they are not. This chapter is designed to help teachers understand (1) the nature of mathematics, (2) how young children learn mathematics, (3) the mathematical concepts that are appropriate for young children, and (4) materials and activities that are useful in mathematics instruction.

## THE NATURE OF MATHEMATICS

To understand how young children learn mathematics, it is necessary to understand what kind of knowledge mathematics involves. To discuss this topic, we must consider four types of knowledge: (1) physical, (2) social, (3) logico-mathematical, and (4) symbolic (Kamii and DeVries, 1977).

Attributes such as color and texture are *physical knowledge*. We obtain this knowledge through direct observation of objects by means of our senses. We look at objects, pick them up, feel them.

*Social knowledge* is knowledge obtained from other people. It is arbitrary in that it is socially determined: we could place a fork on the right side of a plate rather than on the left, but we do not. We could celebrate Thanksgiving on a Tuesday, rather than on a Thursday, in November, but we do not. Social knowledge does not reside in objects, but in people, and it is from interaction with people that we learn it.

*Logico-mathematical knowledge* is very different from both physical and social knowledge. It differs from physical knowledge because it involves relationships between and among objects, rather than characteristics of individual objects. For example, if we gather together several objects and determine that we have four, fourness is not a characteristic of one of the objects by itself, it is a relationship we have imposed on the group of objects. However, the color of the objects, perhaps blue, red, yellow, and green, can be said to be a characteristic of each object and not dependent on any object's relationship to other objects. It is in this sense that physical knowledge is in the external world to be observed, while logico-mathematical knowledge is created by the learner. To create logico-mathematical knowledge, we act on objects, relate them to each other, and then observe these actions and relationships.

Logico-mathematical knowledge differs from social knowledge in that it is obtained from actions on objects rather than from people. In addition, logico-mathematical knowledge is not arbitrary, but logical or lawful. Fourness has a specific and unalterable relationship to fiveness and sixness. We could decide to give a relationship a different name (social knowledge), but we could not alter the relationship itself.

The fourth kind of knowledge, *symbolic knowledge,* tells us how to represent what we know. It includes the insight that one thing can be represented by another, the basic understanding or ability that Piaget called the *symbolic function* (Furth, 1969). The symbolic function underlies our use of all symbols, such as in dramatic play, drawing, language, and mapping. While symbolic knowledge involves systems for representing other types of knowledge, it is not a substitute for them. We can represent with symbols what we already know, but we cannot come to know if we are only given other people's symbols or representations of knowledge. We must have direct access to objects to obtain physical knowledge, and we must be able to act on objects to obtain logico-mathematical knowledge.

In many classrooms, there has been a tendency to teach mathematics as if it were social and symbolic knowledge; that is, as if its source were other people and as if the symbols used to represent mathematical relationships were the same as the relationships themselves. For example, teaching math by asking children to say the number words in order from one to ten, or by asking children to recognize math symbols without recourse to objects, assumes that math knowledge is social and symbolic.

Although it is necessary and appropriate to tell children about the symbols customarily used to represent the mathematical relationships created with objects (that certain collections of objects are represented by the numeral 5, while other collections are represented by the numeral 6, for example), the relationships themselves must be created by the learner through direct actions on objects. Unless young children are given this opportunity, they may learn to recognize, repeat, and write symbols, but they may also learn little about mathematics, which is basically understanding relationships among objects. As Kamii and DeVries (1976, p. 9) have stated, "Piaget's view is in contrast with the belief that there is a 'world of number' into which each child must be socialized." Admittedly, there are social and symbolic aspects to learning what we consider mathematics, such as which name is given to groupings of objects, but much more basic to mathematics is the creation of the logico-mathematical relationships themselves. This is not a matter of socialization, but of mental creation. Action on objects, performed by the child, are required if this kind of knowledge is to be obtained.

## CHILDREN AND MATHEMATICS

Children's ability to think influences their understanding of mathematical relationships. Children's thinking undergoes changes as they get older. For example, the child between two and six or seven years of age is in Piaget's (1965) *preoperational stage* of cognitive development, while the child between six or seven and nine or ten is in Piaget's *concrete operational stage.* We shall now discuss the characteristics of thinking in both these stages and the implications of these characteristics for learning mathematics.

### Preoperational Thinking

Thinking during the preoperational stage has several characteristics. First, the child's thinking is *dominated by perception,* or how things look, rather than by logic as adults know it. For example, if we show a child two rows of ten pennies each, lined up side by side, and ask if the two rows each contain the same number of pennies, the child will agree that they do. But if we then change the position of the pennies in one row such that they are no longer directly opposite the pennies in the other row, the child is likely to say that the rows now contain different numbers of pennies. The child could see that we did not add or take away any pennies, that we merely changed the position of the pennies in one row. The preoperational child, however, responds as if the number of pennies has been changed because it looks as if there has been a change. Even when we ask the child to count the pennies in each row, and the child determines that each has ten, the quality of the quantities is denied because the rows do not look equal (Piaget, 1965).

Second, the preoperational child's thinking is characterized by *centering,* which is the tendency to focus on one aspect of a relationship at a time. For example, with the pennies, adults would conclude that one row still contains the same number of pennies as the other even after the position of objects in one row has been changed; they reason that one row of pennies is shorter but more dense, while the other row is longer but less dense. Preoperational children, however, center on either the density of objects in the rows or on the lengths of the rows. They do not coordinate these two attributes into a coherent relationship. If they center on the density of the pennies, they say that the shorter row has more pennies. If they center on the length of the rows, they say that the longer, less dense row has more.

Third, the preoperational child's thinking is characterized by *irreversibility.* The child cannot reverse an action on objects mentally in order to reconstruct their original state. For example, after the position of one row of pennies has been changed, the child might simply imagine the action being performed in reverse order, such that the pennies in one row would again be directly opposite the pennies in the other row. But the preoperational child cannot do this.

These limitations of the preoperational child's thinking result in an absence of number constancy, or the ability to conserve number; the child cannot recognize that the quantity of objects remains the same despite variations in their spatial arrangement. Without this basic notion, children's understanding of number is very different from our own. When we count eight objects, eight has a constancy. It refers to the quantity of eight objects, and we know that this quantity does not alter when we arrange objects in a line, a circle, or a clump. But a preoperational child typically counts eight objects and then denies that there are still eight if the arrangement of the objects changes. (See Box 9-1 for a description

BOX 9-1    *CONSERVATION OF NUMBER TASK AND STAGES*
          *IN THE ATTAINMENT OF THE NUMBER CONCEPT*

## The Task

MATERIALS:    Discrete, identical objects such as poker chips, pennies, or cubes. At least twenty-five objects are required.

PROCEDURE:    *Step I.*
The adult introduces the task by explaining to the child that he or she is going to participate in a game. The adult starts the game by building a row with the objects. This row should contain at least eight to ten objects:

Adult's Row    ○ ○ ○ ○ ○ ○ ○ ○ ○

*Step II.*    When the adult finishes constructing a row, the child is then invited to build a second row which contains exactly the same number of pennies, cubes, or whatever object is being used, as are contained in the row the adult made. ("Make a row with just as many pennies as I put in my row.") The child should be given about fifteen objects from which to select the number of objects to build the row.

*Step III.*    If the child does not build a row containing exactly the same number of objects as the adult's row, the task ends with step II. But if the child succeeds in building a row with exactly the same number of objects as are contained in the adult's row, then the adult proceeds by altering the position of the objects in one of the two rows. The result of the alteration is that the members of one row are no longer directly opposite the members of the other row.

The Two Rows After Successful Completion of Step II

Adult's Row    ○ ○ ○ ○ ○ ○ ○ ○ ○ ○

Child's Row    ○ ○ ○ ○ ○ ○ ○ ○ ○ ○

Transformation of One Row Made in Step III.

Adult's Row    ○○○○○○○ ○ ○

Child's Row    ○ ○ ○ ○ ○ ○ ○ ○ ○ ○

When the transformation has been made, the adult then asks the child if the rows still contain the same number of objects or if one row now contains more or less objects than the other. If the child says that the rows no longer contain the same number of objects, the adult asks why not. If the child says the rows still contain the same number of objects, the child is asked to explain how he or she knows, or to prove it.

## Stages in the Attainment of the Number Concept

STAGE I.    Absence of One-to-One Correspondence
The child fails to make a row containing the same number of objects as the adult's model. The child judges equality of the rows solely on the basis of the spatial alignment of the ends of the rows. As long as the two rows begin and end together in space, the child assumes that they also contain the same number of objects.

Adult's Model  ◯ ◯ ◯ ◯ ◯ ◯ ◯ ◯ ◯ ◯

Child's Rows  ◯    ◯    ◯    ◯    ◯    ◯    or

◯◯◯◯◯◯◯◯◯◯◯

STAGE II.    Equality Depends on Spatial Correspondence between the Rows
The child is able to create a row with the same number of objects as the adult's model by matching the objects one to one.

Adult's Model  ◯ ◯ ◯ ◯ ◯ ◯ ◯ ◯ ◯ ◯

Child's Row  ◯ ◯ ◯ ◯ ◯ ◯ ◯ ◯ ◯ ◯

When the objects in one row are displaced in space, however, the child denies that the rows still contain the same number of objects.

Adult's Model  ◯ ◯ ◯ ◯ ◯ ◯ ◯ ◯ ◯ ◯

Child's Row Displaced

◯ ◯ ◯ ◯ ◯ ◯ ◯ ◯ ◯ ◯

The child says that the rows no longer contain the same number of pennies.

STAGE III.    Equality is Recognized Despite Alterations in the Spatial Arrangement of Objects—The Child Conserves Number

The child now recognizes that all the following groupings contain the same number of objects and can explain why.

Adult's Model  ◯ ◯ ◯ ◯ ◯ ◯ ◯ ◯ ◯ ◯

Child's Row Displaced

◯ ◯ ◯ ◯ ◯ ◯ ◯ ◯ ◯ ◯

or

◯◯◯◯◯◯◯◯◯◯

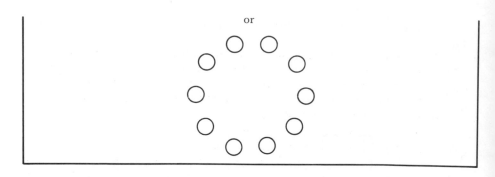

of the conservation of number task and the stages associated with attainment of conservation of number.)

PREOPERATIONAL THINKING AND MATHEMATICAL SKILLS.   The confusion between quantity and spatial arrangement has important implications for the mathematical skills young children can learn. For example, addition facts make little sense to preoperational children because the facts assume an understanding of number constancy across various spatial arrangements. The addition facts for the number 8, for example, are 8 + 0, 7 + 1, 6 + 2, 5 + 3, and 4 + 4. These are nothing more than different arrangements of eight objects among two subgroups. Preoperational children, however, will not understand that these facts all equal the same number; to them, different arrangements of a group of objects change number.

Preoperational children also do not appreciate the relationship between addition and subtraction, for example, that 3 + 1 = 4 and 4 − 3 = 1 are related by a specific mental operation. We explained earlier that one characteristic of preoperational thinking is irreversibility, or the inability to reverse an operation mentally and to appreciate how this transformation relates the end states to each other.

Preoperational children, then, are unable to understand operations on number (addition and subtraction, for example), although they often do appear to understand them to a limited extent. For example, a child might say "2 + 2 = 4" or "3 + 1 = 4." Or, the child might say "3 − 1 = 2" or "4 − 2 = 2," thus appearing to understand addition and subtraction. When working with objects such as cubes, preoperational children often can determine that six cubes and four cubes are ten cubes altogether. But what does a child who exhibits these behaviors actually know?

The child knows how to combine objects from two groups, counting to see how many objects there are altogether. What the child does not understand, however, is that 2 + 2 and 3 + 1 are related, that they are different arrangements of the same number. Without this basic understanding, it is impossible for children to go very far in learning addition or subtraction facts; each individual fact must be remembered specifically *instead of being placed in a coherent system of facts*. Although they may learn through independent manipulation of objects that two sets of two objects make four altogether and that two objects remain when a set of two objects is removed from a set of four, the child does not see the logical connection between the two actions. Each discovery remains isolated. Children cannot remember many bits and pieces of this sort. They can only learn the many addition and subtraction facts when they understand how the facts are derived and related. It is for this reason that teaching addition and subtraction facts to preoperational children is inappropriate. Unless a child can conserve number, specific instruction in addition facts is probably of little use. But what about teaching preoperational children to count? Is this skill of any value?

PREOPERATIONAL THINKING AND COUNTING.    Recall that when preoperational children count the pennies in each of two rows in the number conservation task, they remain unconvinced that the rows contain the same number of pennies when the pennies in the two rows are not lined up side by side. Despite counting, they deny that the rows contain the same number of pennies, because the lengths or densities of the rows look different. Counting obviously has a different meaning for the preoperational child than it does for us.

It is important to understand that counting does not provide the background for developing the concept of number as Piaget has described it. In short, teaching children how to count does not teach them to conserve number. It may, in fact, impede development of this basic idea about number if it is taught through rote verbal drill (saying the number words, one, two, three, and so on, in order without reference to objects) or only in connection with pictures on a workbook page. In the first case, children have no recourse to objects at all, and thus no way to create relationships among them; in the second, the objects (pictures) are not movable, which makes it impossible for children to discover through action that different arrangements of objects can contain the same number of objects.

Preoperational children, of course, can learn to count, and they often enjoy counting. It is not unusual for three- or four-year-olds to request that an adult watch them while they count something. When finished, they are extremely proud of their accomplishment. It *is* an accomplishment, and we can help children develop this skill. However, we must realize that *what the child is learning is a social and symbolic aspect of mathematics and that this alone does not lead to an understanding of the most important and basic idea of all—conservation of number*. Furthermore, if taught without the use of objects, children do not even learn the basics of counting.

Often, a young child will say to an adult, "I can count; listen!" The child then says the number words in order, usually from 1 to 10. But when confronted with a group of objects, the same child becomes confused. For example, given six objects to count, the child might say several number words when pointing to one object in order to use up all the number words he or she has learned; that is, the child would count to 10, even though presented with only six objects. Such a child has learned to *count by rote*—to say numerals verbally in order—but cannot *count rationally*—attach one and only one numeral to one and only one object to determine how many objects there are. If adults wish to help children learn to count, it should be taught with objects, and even better, with objects that are of interest to the child, such as the number of marbles brought to school in a pocket or the number of napkins needed when setting a table for snack.

PREOPERATIONAL THINKING AND LEARNING TO READ AND WRITE NUMERALS. The same problems can occur in learning to read and write numerals as occur in learning to count. These skills do not lead to an understanding of conservation of number, and they lack meaning if not learned in relation to the objects they represent. For example, it is common to encounter a young child who can recognize several numerals, perhaps the numerals 7 and 8, but who does not know what they mean—what seven objects or eight objects are. Children can even learn to write numerals, perhaps all the numerals from 1 to 10, and yet not know the meaning of any of them. Such isolated skills have limited use.

Preoperational children can learn to read and write numerals and enjoy such learning when it begins with curiosity about the symbols they see in their world, and when they are permitted to learn to read and write symbols in their own way and at their own pace. In addition, children enjoy learning to read and write symbols when they know what they represent and understand how they can function in meaningful situations. For example, a child who is playing in the block area is motivated to read the numeral 4 written on the sign that says "4 children may play here" when a fifth child tries to enter the space to play. The numeral 4 represents the number of children who may play in the space. Being able to point to the sign and read the numeral 4 when a fifth child tries to enter helps a child accomplish an important goal.

### Concrete Operational Thinking

The concrete operational thinker is guided by logic rather than by perception, can reverse operations mentally, and can decenter, that is, consider two aspects of a relationship, such as length and density of a row, simultaneously. Because of these skills, the concrete operational child can conserve number and can understand operations on number such as addition and subtraction.

The concrete operational child still needs to learn mathematical ideas through manipulation of objects. However, unlike the preoperational child, the concrete operational child understands relationships among the various actions and operations performed. Information derived from combining four cubes with two cubes no longer remains isolated from information derived from combining five cubes with one cube. In fact, a concrete operational child understands that the number 6 can be formed in yet another way, by combining two sets of three objects each. It is the ability to understand relationships, itself based on the ability to conserve number, that sets the concrete operational child apart from the preoperational child and makes the learning of math skills such as addition and subtraction both possible and appropriate.

## MATHEMATICAL CONCEPTS AND SKILLS FOR YOUNG CHILDREN

### Classification

The ability to classify objects—to place objects together in terms of a defining attribute or attributes—is basic to all math skills. In order to determine the number of a particular object or to decide if there is more of one thing than another, children must first differentiate among objects and organize them into classes.

Classification is also important as a basis for children's understanding of part–whole relationships. For example, blue triangles and red triangles are both subsets of the general class of triangles. Addition, subtraction, and fractions all involve part–whole relationships, which are logically similar to the triangle illustration.

### Number and Numeration

Mathematical concepts can be grouped into several categories. The concepts which receive the most attention in the early years are those dealing with number and numeration. Such concepts answer questions related to "How many?" "Which one?" or "Which group has more or less?"

Relative ideas of "How many?" are first obtained by children by matching objects from one set with objects from another set. This is called *matching one to one*. An absolute numerical answer to the question "How many?" is not obtained, but we can get answers to the question of which group has more and which less. Concepts of equivalence and nonequivalence enter in here. Such questions are very basic and do not require that children know names for numbers or that they be able to count. Matching one to one, however, does require the beginnings of the understanding that quantity and spatial arrangement are not related. For example, notice in Box 9-1 that initially, a preoperational child confronted with the conservation of number task cannot even match objects one to one. Rows beginning and ending at different points in space are assumed to be unequal in quantity, while those beginning and ending at the same points are assumed to be equal in quantity, regardless of the rows' actual equality.

The next skills involve *recognition and naming of number properties*. A child learns to recognize a group of one, a group of two, and so on. Pointing to each object in a group one at a time while saying the number words in order is called *counting*. Small groups, usually those of up to three objects, can be recognized quickly by preschool children without counting. Larger groups usually must be counted to determine their number properties.

The question of how far preoperational children may profitably be taught to count is an important one. The question arises out of concern that children understand the relationships among numbers, for example, how 10 and 15 or 10 and 20 are related, and not merely learn to count by ones to numbers over 10 as if there were no relationship among numbers.

At issue here is the concept of grouping in *base ten,* which is how our number system is organized. This means that ones are grouped into groups of ten objects each; groups of ten objects each are, in turn, placed into groups of ten; these groups, now containing one-hundred objects each, are themselves grouped into groups of ten, and so on. The number 15, for example, is one group of ten and five ones; the number 20 is two groups of ten and no ones; the number 246 in composed of two groups of one hundred, four groups of ten, and six ones. Although the preoperational child may not grasp these relationships, it may be useful to stress the composition of numbers in terms of such groupings by naming the numbers over 10 with names that explicitly call attention to them. For example, the numbers between 10 and 20 could be named "10 and 1," "10 and 2," "10 and 3," and so on. The more common counting names, eleven, twelve, thirteen, and so on, could also be used, but not exclusively, because they reveal nothing about the base-ten groupings of each number.

There is some evidence that young children spontaneously create names based on groupings for numbers over 10. Drummond (1922) reported that a child used words such as forty-ten, forty-eleven, forty-twelve, instead of saying 50, 51, and 52. Ginsburg (1977) also discusses reports of unschooled children in some African tribes who have been observed, for example, to call 20 "ten-ten," and 30 "twenty-ten." What we do not know, of course, is whether children reported to have noticed such relationships are still preoperational. In any event, in counting with young children, there may be some value in using words which explicitly indicate the base-ten structure of numbers; certainly with concrete operational children, such groupings need to be pointed out and described: "15 is made of one group of ten and five ones." In addition, when children spontaneously create names for numbers which indicate that they have noticed relationships ("twenty-ten" for 30, for example), we should praise rather than correct their "error."

A child who understands groups with different number properties and who can count can begin to *combine and separate groups.* These skills build a concrete basis for the operations on number which we know as addition and multiplication (combining), and subtraction and division (separating). As we stated earlier, the results of various actions of combining and separating objects will not be related in any coherent way by the preoperational child, although the result of each separate action may be correctly determined. For example, the preoperational child may determine that combining two cubes with four cubes results in a group of six cubes, or that separating two cubes from a group of four cubes leaves two cubes.

However, these bits of information will not be related to other discoveries and organized into a coherent group of relationships. The concrete operational child, however, will be able to coordinate relationships and can derive and organize addition and subtraction facts.

The skills discussed so far have not involved *reading* or *writing numerals*. They have involved manipulation of objects and the use of verbal labels only. Children must, of course, learn to *read and write numerals*. The question is, When? The best answer to this question seems to be, "When the symbols have some meaning for the child; when he or she can count to the quantity represented by the numeral." There is evidence which suggests that children have difficulty learning to read numerals (remember their names) if they have not yet learned to count to the quantity represented by the numeral (Wang et al., 1971). While children can learn to read numerals under these conditions, considerable drill and practice are required. We believe it is useless to ask children to read symbols that hold no meaning for them; it is also an inept strategy, if children learn them more easily after they understand what the numerals mean.

Preoperational children may become confused at times when confronted with written symbols for two-digit numbers, even if they can count to the amount represented. For example, a child who can count to 15 might read the numeral 15 as "1 and 5" or "5 and 1" (reading from right to left). Or, a child might read the numeral 32 as "3 and 2." What is not understood is the concept of *place value*, or the notion that the position of a numeral indicates its value and the specific name it is given. Since our number system is based on groups of ten, the value of any numeral is either itself (ones), ten times itself (tens), or multiples of ten times itself (hundreds, thousands, and so on). But an understanding of place value rests on an understanding of groupings in base ten, which we discussed earlier. While preoperational children can learn to read numerals such as 15, 17, and 20 and to count out by ones the number of objects these numerals represent, the significance of the placement of the numerals—that the 1 in 15 indicates one group of ten and that the 5 indicates five ones—is not adequately appreciated. As a result, children may have difficulty reading all but the most frequently encountered two-digit numerals, which they learned by memory.

Concrete operational children can comprehend place value. They will need to be told which is the ones' place, the tens' place, and so on. They will have a good background for understanding the relationship of one place to another when dealing with numbers greater than 10 if grouping in tens and ones has been stressed from the beginning. For example, if a child knows that 11 can also be called "10 and 1," it is an easy transition to understand that when it is written, a 1 is placed in the tens' place and another 1 is placed in the ones' place.

Children will also need to learn to read and write symbols other than numerals. These symbols do not represent number properties, but actions that are to be performed on numbers. At first, these will include the addition sign ( + ), subtraction sign ( – ), and the equals sign ( = ). None of these should be introduced until the child has had extensive practice with the manipulations which these signs represent. Practice with objects, for example, would utilize verbal descriptions such as "4 and 5 *make* 9 altogether."

Children must also learn to read and write what we know as *facts*. There are facts of addition, subtraction, multiplication, and division. These are all the possible combinations of each of the numbers from 0 to 9 for each of the four operations on number. Addition facts include 1 and 1, 1 and 2, 1 and 3, and so on. Subtraction facts include 3 take away 1, 2 take away 1, 1 take away 1, and so on. Multiplication facts include one group of 1, two groups of 1, three groups of 1, and so on, while division facts include the number of groups of 1 there are in 3, the number of groups of 1 there are in 2, the number of groups of 1 there are in 1, and so on. All the facts result from and have their basis in the manipulation of objects (combining and separating them). What we usually think of as facts, however, are these manipulations in written form, such as $5 + 2 = 7$ or $4 - 2 = 2$.

One goal of a mathematics program in the early years is to help children gain facility with the facts in symbolized, or written, form. But children must understand *in action* what the different operations are before the written symbols will have any meaning. They must know, for example, that addition involves combining sets, that subtraction involves separating sets, that multiplication involves combining *equal* subsets, and that division involves separating a set into *equal* subsets. Without such understandings, facts will not have much meaning for children and a great deal of rote drill will be required to learn them. When children understand the basis for the facts, they have a framework from which to remember them; although practice is still required, less practice will be needed.

A final skill which children must master as they begin to manipulate symbols on paper is the use of algorithms, or rules specific to each of the four operations on number (addition, subtraction, multiplication, and division). Algorithms are based on the facts for each operation and on the concept of place value. For example, when we add two-digit numbers such as 28 and 15, there are rules about starting with the column on the right and about carrying the ten ones that result from the addition of 8 and 5. Children who have received adequate experience in practicing facts and working with place value should adopt algorithms with relative ease. Teachers may wish to refer to any good text on elementary mathematics to review algorithms.

### Measurement

A second concept area which is stressed in the mathematics instruction of young children is measurement. Measurement, like number and numeration, deals with questions of how many and how much. In measurement, however, the quantity to be assessed is continuous rather than discrete. In number and numeration, one deals with separate (discrete) objects which are combined or separated in order to ascertain how many; in measurement, one deals with a whole something (continuous), which is then described in terms of smaller units.

DIRECT MEASUREMENT. There are four general areas of direct measurement with which young children should gain familiarity: (1) length, (2) weight, (3) volume, and (4) area. Through measurement activities, children will gain a concept of length distinct from that of weight, a concept of weight distinct from that of volume, and a concept of area distinct from that of volume.

Children must also understand units if they are to understand measurement. *The purpose of measurement is to describe something in terms of smaller parts of itself.* In order to do this, smaller pieces, or units, must be used to talk about the larger pieces. Although the adult world uses standard units such as inches, feet, yards, or meters, anything can be used as a unit as long as it possesses the distinctive characteristic of the object being measured. For example, a piece of string, a pencil, or a popsicle stick could be used as a unit of measure for length. Marbles, golf tees, or washers could be used as units of measure of weight. Squares of paper, mosaic tiles, or index cards could be used as units for measuring area

*Children need experience with nonstandard units before they use standard units.* Children need to see the separate pieces that make up a measurement tool. This is often a vague concept when standard units are used at the beginning. For example, children have difficulty understanding what an inch is when their only exposure to inches is a twelve-inch ruler. The use of nonstandard units also permits children to gain appreciation for the practicality of standard units. Children can see for themselves that it is difficult to talk about how long something is when measured with toothpicks by one person and with popsicle sticks by someone else. It is the use of standard units that enables us to communicate clearly with someone about the quantity of an object. After children have experiences with nonstandard units, they can be introduced to standard units.

Another measurement concept involves the selection of appropriate units for the object being measured. This concept requires understanding the relationship between the size of the unit and the accuracy of the measurement as well as between the size of the unit and the effort required to obtain the measurement. For example, it is more tedious to measure the length of a room with a toothpick than with a foot-long dowel rod, although the toothpick might result in the more accurate measurement. This conflict between effort and accuracy could be resolved by measuring with the dowel rod until a complete length no longer fits and then finishing up with toothpicks. That is how a system of measurement is designed. We can describe the length of a room by stating that it is two meters and three centimeters long. Typically, the measurement is done with a yard or meter stick and reported in feet and inches or meters and centimeters. When children use unit blocks to build a road across the room and you see that it is seven long blocks and two short blocks long, you know that the children are getting the basis of this idea.

The characteristics of preoperational thinking explain some common confusions noted when preschool children engage in measurement experiences. For example, if one child measures a table's width with toothpicks while another measures it with popsicle sticks, the children discover that it takes fewer popsicle sticks than toothpicks to span the table. The children are likely to conclude that the width of the table is not constant, but is greater when measured by toothpicks than by popsicle sticks; after all, it took more toothpicks than popsicle sticks to go across the table. The difficulty is that they cannot decenter and reason: It takes more toothpicks because they are shorter than the popsicle sticks—the width of the table, however, does not change.

INDIRECT MEASUREMENT.    The four areas of measurement discussed above deal with direct measurement of the quantity of one thing in relation to another. There are other areas of measurement which involve indirect assessments because the quantity to be measured is not concrete. Time and temperature are nonconcrete quantities whose measurement is introduced to young children.

Most children learn to "tell" time and read a thermometer during the first few years of elementary school. These competencies do not, however, indicate that children understand the mathematics of measuring time and temperature. They indicate only that children have learned to read clocks and thermometers.

In order to understand the difference between reading and understanding the measurement of time and temperature, it might be helpful to discuss the development of children's concepts of time. This development has been illustrated in research conducted by Piaget (1969).

Piaget's research indicates that preprimary children think tools for measuring time are controlled by their own actions. They think that if they swing their arm fast, sand will fall through a sand timer faster than if they swing their arm slowly. They have no concept of objective time separate from their own subjective time.

It is not surprising that the young child should view time subjectively. Time seems to vary depending on what we are doing. Even adults experience days when time seems either to drag or to fly. Time is perceived psychologically, and these perceptions often do not match the objective measurements of clocks. Therefore, preschool children who have had little experience with tools for objectifying time view it as purely subjective.

Primary-age children realize that the time it takes for clock hands to move a certain distance or for the sand to run out of a sand timer is the same regardless of the speed of any actions they might perform. Their concept of time is still not entirely accurate, however. For example, if one were to place two race tracks (one short, one long) on a table and race two cars down them making sure that they started and stopped at the same time, most primary children would probably declare that the car on the longer track took more time than the other car to move down the track. They would not understand that cars can move different distances in the same time. They lack a *concept of speed,* which would resolve the conflict.

With regard to clocks, young children think it takes longer for the hands of a clock with a large face to go from one numeral to another than it takes the hands of a clock with a smaller face. This indicates that even for the primary child, time is still not completely objective. Although it is no longer connected to the child's actions, it is thought to reside in the timepieces themselves, as if each were keeping its own time. Until children reach the age of nine or ten they do not fully understand that time is objective and that timepieces all keep the same time; that clocks are synchronized. It is again the concept of speed that leads to this understanding.

Understanding how to tell time requires understanding measurement, number, and numeration. For example, seconds, minutes, and hours are simply different-sized units for measuring a continuous quantity, in this case the abstract quantity, time. To understand the relationship of one of these units to the others, children must realize that it takes more smaller units (seconds, for example) than larger units (minutes, for example) to measure the same quantity.

We already mentioned the difficulty preoperational children have realizing that the number of units required to measure a given quantity does not influence the quantity; that more seconds than minutes result because of the smaller size of the second unit, not due to variations in the amount of time measured. For this reason, preschool children are not capable of understanding segments of time such as seconds, minutes, or hours. Nor do they have the number and numeration skills to deal with clock time. Many preschoolers, for example, cannot count to 60 or understand that "quarter past five" is the same as "fifteen minutes past five" because "quarter" indicates a fourth of something and fifteen minutes is the same as one-fourth of sixty minutes.

It is little wonder in view of the complex skills involved that the teaching of time is reserved for the primary grades. Preschool children indicate and understand time in terms of the order of events in their day: "When do we have snack?" "After we have cleanup," or "Before we go outside to play." Preschoolers can also learn to associate the position of the clock hands with events of their day. "When it is snack time, the big hand points to the 6 and the little hand points to the 10." However, this is not the same as actually learning in detail the units for measuring time, how these relate to each other, and the number and numeration skills required to designate various relationships. These skills are beyond the ability of most preschool children to comprehend.

Calendar time is also difficult for preschool children to understand, for the same reasons that clock time is difficult. However, children can begin to learn the order and names of days of the week, the events that occur on certain days of the week and not others, and the physical structure of a calendar. For example, they begin to see that the days of the week repeat themselves in a specific order for each week. Children must have access to a calendar to acquire such learning, however, and they must use it in meaningful ways. For example, children can cross off one day at a time on the classroom calendar as they attend school each day. They can see that they do not attend school on certain days, usually on the weekend. They also see that days of the week repeat themselves in a certain order and that days of the week and weeks in a month are "used up," requiring that a new month be posted. Children enjoy hanging pictures on certain days of the month to indicate special events, such as a birthday or school trip, and counting the number of days until the event arrives. Even with reference to a calendar, however, a child might inquire about how long it will be before some event. The teacher might again try to explain duration in terms of events the child understands: "You will go home and sleep once and then come to school and go home and sleep again, and then come back to school again. That will be the day we will go to the park. See, here is today on the calendar. This is Monday. Tomorrow will be Tuesday. It is on Wednesday—this day here—that we will go to the park."

### Geometry

Concepts related to geometry are also recognized as appropriate learnings for young children. It should quickly be pointed out that the formal geometry known to most adults is not what is being suggested. The unique cognitive abilities of young children do not equip them for dealing with logical proofs. However, young children can learn about geometric concepts on a concrete level.

Understandings related to geometry include the *ability to identify geometric figures and solids.* Many children can recognize and sort into like shapes, circles, squares, and triangles as early as three years of age, and they will learn the names readily. By five, children will typically be able to describe these basic shapes—circles are round, squares have four sides, and triangles have three. Squares and rectangles may be confused, however, and while children may see that an equilateral triangle does not look like a scalene triangle, they will typically not understand exactly what the difference is.

Geometric solids are distinguishable on the basis of the characteristics of their surfaces. Surfaces of solids are either flat or curved. Some solids have only flat surfaces (cubes, pyramids, rectangular prisms), others have both flat and curved surfaces (cones, cylinders), whereas a sphere has only one curved surface.

Geometry competencies for young children also include the *ability to construct geometric figures and solids,* for example, with a geoboard or with paper and pencil. It takes time for children to learn to draw difficult shapes such as diamonds or rhombuses, for example. It is even difficult at first, for them to learn to draw closed figures such as circles, squares, and triangles differently from each other. Young preschoolers, for example, may draw a circle, square, and triangle in the following way when shown a model of each and asked to draw them (Piaget, 1967):

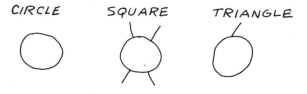

Gradually, children are able to understand the precise ways in which these figures differ—curved versus straight lines, number of sides and angles, and so on. Experience feeling the various shapes (for example, with attribute blocks) and trying to make the various figures on paper or on a geoboard is necessary for children to discover *the relationships that make each figure different from the others.*

## Money

Young children can also begin to develop an understanding of money. First, children must *recognize and name common coins and bills:* which coins are called "penny," "dime," and "quarter." Second, they must understand the *value of each piece of money.* Third, children must understand the *exchange rate of one coin for another* or of *coins for a bill,* or of *one bill for others.*

To understand the value of coins and bills and the exchange rate of one coin for another, children must have counting skills, an understanding of various sized units and of conservation of number, and knowledge of addition and subtraction. For example, a preoperational child will usually prefer to be given twenty-five pennies, rather than two dimes and a nickel, in exchange for a quarter: More coins equal more money, the child reasons. The child does not understand that although more pennies (small units) than dimes and nickels (larger units) are required in exchange for a quarter, they represent the same amount of money.

Preschool children can learn to recognize and name common coins and bills and learn the value of the smaller coins in terms of pennies: A nickel is worth five pennies; a dime is worth ten pennies. Few preschool children will truly understand that fifteen pennies is less money than a quarter, and wise teachers do not waste their time trying to convince them. We should point out, however, that some preschool children have observed that one quarter will buy more candy or other valued objects than will ten pennies, and they will request the quarter if given an opportunity. Whether they understand exactly why the quarter buys more is another matter, although the observation suggests that one way children learn the value of coins and their relationship to each other is by using them to purchase real items.

# GENERAL METHODS
# OF TEACHING MATHEMATICS
# TO YOUNG CHILDREN

## Integrating Mathematics Learning
## and Other Content Areas

Preschool children learn mathematics skills best in the context of meaningful experiences. They want to know if they have a fair share of the blocks, how many colors they have used on their painting, how many days must pass before their birthday or Halloween will arrive, and how many more laps a friend may make around the paved tricycle path before his or her turn is up. Preschool teachers can help children learn mathematical skills by interacting with children in these situations to help them compare groups of objects numerically (for example, to see that they have as many or more blocks than a friend), count days on a calendar, or determine how many more laps can be made if ten is the limit and a child has already made six.

Concrete operational children do not depend on meaningful contexts for learning math skills to the same extent as preoperational children. In other words, the learning of mathematics skills by the concrete operational child need not be tied as closely to real experiences because hopefully, by this time the child understands that such skills are useful in real life. However, even for the concrete operational child, mathematics skills still must be meaningful in that they must make sense; this requires that children continue to be given access to manipulative materials.

### Providing Materials that Serve as Good Models of Mathematical Ideas

Although much math skill learning can take place as children participate in meaningful experiences, it is useful as well to provide specific materials designed to teach math concepts. These materials would be included in a math center in classrooms organized as we suggested in Chapter 3. In primary classrooms not organized in centers, the materials might be stored in a cabinet or closet and children would use them at their desk or group table. A list of materials to be included in a math center is provided in Box 9–2.

BOX 9–2   *MATERIALS FOR A MATH CENTER*

---

#### Commercial Materials

| | |
|---|---|
| one-inch cubes | attribute blocks |
| pegs and pegboards | play money |
| Unifix Cubes | felt shapes |
| felt numerals | sand timer |
| pan balance | plastic straws |
| Cuisenaire rods | ruler |
| abacus | meter stick |
| wooden tabletop unit blocks | yardstick |
| nesting cubes | scissors |
| dominoes | magic markers |
| number/shape puzzles | pencils |
| number/shape lotto games | glue |

#### Teacher-Gathered Materials

| | |
|---|---|
| string, yarn, ribbon | IBM cards |
| bottle caps | index cards |
| old deck of playing cards | old clocks |
| plastic containers of various sizes | Formica squares |
| buttons | fabric swatches |
| styrofoam pieces | dried beans |
| pebbles | small carpet squares |
| egg cartons | washers |
| paper clips and paper fasteners | |

---

---

### Teacher-Made Materials

| | |
|---|---|
| sandpaper numerals | tagboard numeral cards |
| felt board | felt shapes |
| geoboards | one-inch graph paper |
| clock face | |

---

## Tying the Language of Mathematics to Concrete Experiences

As we discussed earlier, symbolic knowledge is used to represent other forms of knowledge: Terms and labels are understood when children understand the concepts they represent. The language of mathematics must be learned by children as they interact with concrete objects. The vocabulary children need to become familiar with includes number names and shape words and terms such as heavy–light, long–short, wide–narrow, large–small, more–less, high–low, first–last, whole–part, and many–few.

An alert teacher provides labels in many situations throughout a school day: "You have five red buttons on your shirt—one, two, three, four, five." "That's a long line you painted on your paper." "Jessica can go first today; you went first yesterday." "You have one group of ten pegs here, and four pegs left over. What number is that?"

## ACTIVITIES FOR MATHEMATICS INSTRUCTION

The remainder of this chapter deals with ideas for classroom mathematics instruction. The organization of the practical ideas follows the order in which the mathematical concepts and skills have been presented. The activities included are of two types: (1) those planned and designed for the specific purpose of providing children with opportunities to learn or practice a particular skill and (2) those planned to meet goals which may not be concerned primarily with mathematics, but from which mathematical learnings can be abstracted if the teacher is aware of this potential.

### Classification

1. **Activity:**   Button bin (PP)

   *Materials:*   A large container such as a plastic ice-cream carton; a large variety of buttons which vary in as many attributes as possible, such as size, shape, color, and material; a flat container with separated spaces. (Egg cartons or trays used to separate layers of apple or orange crates work well.)

*Procedure:*    Make container of buttons and trays available for children to work with. Verbal guidance, such as "Put the ones you think are alike together," should be ample for most children. Sometimes, more guidance is necessary to help a child start. In that case, ask the child to choose a button and place it in a space. Then select a button which is similar and place it in the same space, stating how they are alike.

2. **Activity:**    Making necklaces (PP)

*Materials:*    Wooden beads in various colors and shapes; shoestrings for stringing the beads.
*Procedure:*    Have a container with a variety of beads available for children to work with. Ask questions such as "Can you make a necklace with just three kinds of beads?" or "Can you make a necklace of beads that are all alike in one way, two ways, three ways?"

3. **Activity:**    Junk box (PP)

*Materials:*    Odds and ends of materials which might include a clothespin, several bottle caps, a pencil, an empty pharmacy bottle, a paper clip, a safety pin, a golf tee, several corks, several pebbles, a hickory nut, a toothpick, and so on; several small containers to sort objects into.
*Procedure:*    Ask the children to "put together those objects which they think belong together." It is important that the children be allowed to select their own criteria for the classes, although the guiding adult should inquire from time to time what the criteria are by asking, "Why did you put those together?"

4. **Activity:**    Paper shapes (PP-P)

*Materials:*    Red, yellow, and blue construction paper to make the following:

> two large triangles of each color
> two middle-sized triangles of each color
> two small triangles of each color
> (same as above for circles)
> (same as above for squares)

*Procedure:*    Ask children to put together the shapes they think are alike. After a child has classified the shapes one way, you might suggest that the child think of another way it could be done.

Number and Numeration

## MATCHING ONE TO ONE

1. Activity:   Felt board (PP)

   *Materials:*   Multiple copies of several different felt cutouts; felt board.
   *Procedure:*   Have felt boards and felt cutouts available for children's use.
   Ask questions such as "Are there as many ＿＿ as ＿＿?"

2. Activity:   Getting dressed (PP)

   *Materials:*   Boots, mittens, hats, coats, or whatever clothing is appropriate
   for weather and climatic conditions.
   *Procedure:*   While helping children dress for outdoor play or for going
   home, comment about the fact that there is one mitten for each hand, one
   boot for each foot, one hat for one head, one armhole for each arm, and so on.

3. Activity:   Outdoor play (PP)

   *Materials:*   Usual outdoor equipment such as swings, tricycles, old tires,
   sand toys, and so on.
   *Procedure:*   There is always a certain number of each piece of
   equipment—perhaps six swings, four tires, four tricycles, and three sand
   pails and shovels. The number of children who wish to use the equipment
   usually varies from day to day and from one time of day to another.
   Sometimes there are more children who want to play with a particular item
   than there are items available. At other times, there are more of the item than
   there are children demanding to use it. At still other times, the number of
   items and number of children are the same. Teachers can use these situations
   by verbalizing about them: "There are just enough sand pails to go around."
   " Do you suppose someone else would like a tricycle? I see we have an extra
   one right now." " Well, let's see if we can't find something else to do for
   awhile. All the swings are taken. We have more children than we have
   swings, so we'll have to take turns."

4. Activity:   Fill the cups (PP)

   *Materials:*   Egg cartons cut into pieces of one section, two sections, three
   sections, and so on; rocks, marbles, plastic discs, or other small objects to
   place in the sections; container to hold objects chosen.
   *Procedure:*   Have materials available in math center. Instruct children to
   "give each cup an object." Because of the structure of the materials, the child

will be matching a set of one cup with a set of one rock, a set of two cups with a set of two rocks, and so on.

5. **Activity:**   Peg-boards (PP)

*Materials:*   Any of the commercial peg and peg-board sets.
*Procedure:*   Interact with a child who is using these materials by asking questions such as "Can you make another line of pegs that has as many as this one?" or "Which of your lines has more? Which has less?"

6. **Activity:**   Snack time (PP)

*Materials:*   Cups and napkins; napkins and straws with cartons, if milk rather than juice is served.
*Procedure:*   Select children to pass out napkins and cups or napkins, milk, and straws. Allow children to obtain these supplies from their storage places rather than giving items to children precounted. Young children typically will obtain a "bunch" and pass these out to children, and then go back to obtain more and pass these out, until each child has all the needed items. By using this procedure, children match children with straws, milk, or napkins and come face to face with concepts of "less than," "more than," and " the same as."

7. **Activity:**   Cleanup time (PP)

*Materials:*   Any materials or objects in the room which have specific slots, holes, or spots for storage. For example, there is one pair of scissors for each section of the egg carton, a cap for each magic marker, a jar of paste for each contact-paper circle stuck on the shelf, and one pencil for each hole in the pencil holder. These organization schemes provide children with experiences in matching one to one.

## RECOGNIZING AND NAMING SETS AND COUNTING

Any of the activities and experiences already discussed can also be used to develop the above-named competencies. Guidance, however, would need to include different questions. For example, a matching-one-to-one question might be "Can you make a row here that has as many as that row over there?" A question related to helping children recognize and name sets might be "How many are there here?" A similar question would encourage counting. The materials can be the same in each case, but the questions vary.

1. **Activity:** Set cards (PP–P)

**Materials:** One-inch cubes; twenty-four tagboard cards, each 7-by-6-inches, one-inch graph paper run on ditto, cut into 6-by-5-inch rectangles. (Glue graph paper on one side of tagboard cards.) Prepare three cards for each number from 2 to 10 by coloring different arrangements of squares (See Figure 9–1.)

**Procedure:** Child finds the cards with the same number. Ask the child to find cards with the same number. Help the child name the number. Encourage the child to make sure the cards are the same by placing cubes over the squares, first on one card and then on the other two. It is important that the child use the same cubes on all cards to stress the idea that the cards all represent the same number.

**Suggestions and Variations:** It is not wise to include all the cards at once with preprimary children. Cards for numbers 3 through 6 might be enough to start. Remember that preoperational children typically deny that different arrangements are the same number.

**FIGURE 9-1** Set cards.

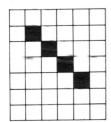 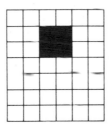 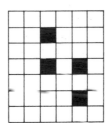

2. **Activity:** Snack time (PP–P)

**Materials:** Cups, cookies, straws, napkins; any of the items used at snack time.

**Procedure:** Children can be selected to help pass items to the rest of the children. Earlier, in the section on matching one to one, we suggested that children determine the correct amount of any item simply by matching items with children. Later, helpers can count the children and then count out the required number of items.

**Suggestions and Variations:** Encourage young children to use the matching-one-to-one method before the counting method. It is a good idea for one child at each table to be responsible for the children at the table. In this way, the numbers do not get very large. Four-year-olds may have difficulty counting out items for a group of twenty-five children.

3. **Activity:**   Outdoor play (PP)

*Materials:*   All outdoor equipment.
*Procedure:*   Use opportunities to help children recognize the number properties of sets of outdoor equipment. For example, perhaps there are five old tires, six swings, and three tricycles. Children can also be encouraged to count the number of "cupcakes" they make out of sand in the sandbox, the number of rungs they climb on a ladder, the number of times they catch a ball, and so on.

4. **Activity:**   Beanbag toss (PP–P)

*Materials:*   Several beanbags or small balls; a basket or box to toss beanbags into.
*Procedure:*   Help children set up an area for the beanbag toss game. Nothing should be in the path of the thrown object. Limit the game to two or three children at a time. Use a chalkboard or piece of paper to keep score. Every time a child is able to toss the beanbag into the container, place a tally beside the child's name. At the end of the game, count the tallies.

## READING NUMERALS AND ASSOCIATING THEM WITH THE NUMBERS THEY REPRESENT

1. **Activity:**   Numeral concentration game (PP)

*Materials:*   Twenty 3-by-5-inch tagboard cards. Write one numeral on each card making two cards each for every numeral from 0 to 9. Store the cards in a small box or clasp envelope.
*Procedure:*   Two or three children play. Place cards face down. Children take turns turning over two cards at a time. If the cards are identical, the child keeps them. If they are not, the child returns them face down to the center of the table. The game continues until all pairs have been picked up.
*Suggestions and Variations:*   An individual child can use the materials. The child searches through the cards and matches up the pairs. Regular playing cards may be used.

2. **Activity:**   Felt numerals and felt cutouts (PP–P)

*Materials:*   Felt board, felt numerals, and felt cutouts. (Select felt cutouts so that different quantities of each type are available. For example, six ducks, three stars, one rabbit, eight circles, seven apples, four squares, and five rectangles might be provided.)

*Procedure:* Children can be encouraged to place the numerals and cutouts on the felt board. Provide the numeral name and help match the numerals with the proper sets.

*Suggestions and Variations:* A "felt" board can be made by attaching a piece of cotton flannel to a section of cardboard with rubber cement. Flannel can also be attached with staples, thumb tacks, or tape to a low bulletin board, the back of a bookshelf, or the side of a metal cabinet.

3. Activity: Junk and numeral cards (PP–P)

*Materials:* Ten 3-by-5-inch tagboard cards with the numerals 1 through 10 written on them with a felt-tipped marker; a box of objects such as bottle caps, acorns, golf tees, paper clips, corks, and so on. (Provide different quantities of some of the objects, for example, one clothespin and one small pencil, two acorns, two golf tees, three corks, four paper clips, five dried beans, five paper fasteners, and so on.)

*Procedure:* Child classifies objects and puts identical ones together. Child matches numeral cards with sets having that number property. Ask questions such as "Which ones are alike?" "How many are in this group?" and "Which card would you place with this group?"

4. Activity: Rook deck pickup (PP–P)

*Materials:* Rook deck cards.

*Procedure:* Two children play. Cards are placed face down on the table. Children take turns turning over one card at a time. First child to call out numeral name gets to keep the card. Child who has the most at the end wins.

*Suggestions and Variations:* Do not include cards with numerals over 10 until children can identify the first ten with ease and can count to 20.

## COMBINING AND SEPARATING OBJECTS

1. Activity: Peg-boards (PP–P)

*Materials:* Pegs and peg-boards.

*Procedure:* Ask questions such as "How many pegs would you have if you put the two red ones and the four blue ones together?" "How many would there be altogether if we put two pegs in each row?" "How many would you have left if you took the three blue ones out of the board?"

2. Activity:    Cubes (PP–P)

**Materials:**    Commercial one-inch colored cubes.
**Procedure:**    Encourage children to combine and separate the blocks in different ways. The same questions used with the peg-board activity are appropriate here also.

3. Activity:    Jar lids and beans (K–P)

**Materials:**    Twelve baby-food jar lids with ten cardboard discs cut to fit loosely inside ten of the lids (label each with a numeral so there is one each for the numerals 1 through 10); any type of dried beans; small container with a lid for the beans; larger box to hold both lids and the container of beans.
**Procedure:**    The child starts with the lid labeled "1" and works up through the lid labeled "10." The child places as many beans in the lid as the label says. The child must then separate these beans into the two nonlabeled lids in as many different ways as he or she can. Children can make drawings of their discoveries.
**Suggestions and Variations:**    The teacher can prepare paper with circles to represent the lids already drawn so that the child's task of recording is simplified. Children then need only to draw pictures of the beans. Young children will often form twice the number of combinations for a number because they will consider 4 + 1 and 1 + 4 to be different ways to make 5. This introduces children to the concept of commutativity.

**FIGURE 9-2**    Record form for jar lids with numerical labels.

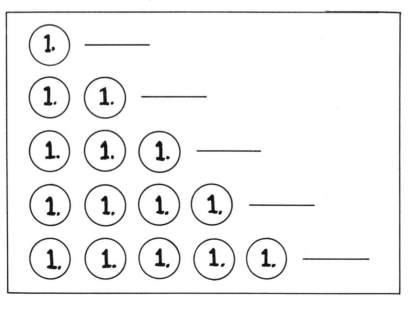

The use of three lids rather than two can introduce children to the idea of associativity. The materials can also be altered in order to stress addition of equal sets (multiplication). Provide thirty lids and thirty cardboard inserts. Label the inserts to make five each for numerals 1 through 6. Prepare dittoed record forms as shown in Figure 9-2.

Children fill the lids with beans according to the numeral in the lid. The child counts the number of beans in lids in each row to determine what one group of one equals, two groups of one equal, three groups of one equal, and so on.

## WORKING WITH BASE TEN

### 1. Activity:   Peg-boards (PP-P)

*Materials:*   Any of the commercial peg and peg-board materials.

*Procedure:*   The structure of the materials encourages children to group pegs in tens. As rows are filled with pegs, the teacher can ask children to count all the pegs. Perhaps they have filled one row and have placed three pegs in the next. When children count all the pegs, they begin to get the idea that 13 is made of one group of tens, and three ones. Verbalize this by saying, "Oh, 13 has one group of tens, and three ones." Later, ask children to make different numbers on the peg-board, such as 15, 21, 25, and so on. In this way, children will gain an idea of the composition of these numbers in terms of groups of tens and ones.

*Suggestions and Variations:*   Remember that for a long time, young children (three-year-olds in particular) enjoy merely placing the pegs in the peg-board. They often make groups of different colors. During this first exploratory stage, do not force children to conceptualize the mathematical concepts that may be apparent in what they are doing. When it appears that children have had sufficient time to explore, and at the point where they are filling each row before placing pegs in the next row, you can ask the children how many pegs there are in each row.

### 2. Activity:   Base-ten cards (K-P)

*Materials:*   A set of tagboard cards with the same dimensions as the peg-boards or smaller ones made to scale. Make dots on each card to correspond to numbers from 11 to 99.

*Procedure:*   Children name the number represented by the dots on the cards by stating the number of tens and ones that are drawn in. For example, the sample card shown in Figure 9-3 would be called "two tens and one one."

Children can also be asked to give the counting name for the number, which in this case is 21.

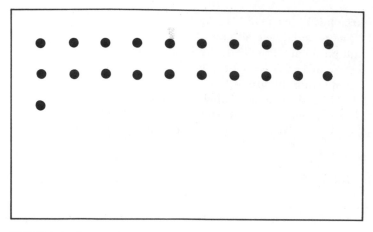

**FIGURE 9-3**  Base ten cards.

*Suggestions and Variations:*  Children can work with cards individually or with each other. A game can be played by turning all cards face down. Children take turns turning a card over and naming it. They may keep those they name correctly. The winner is the child who has the most cards at the end of the game.

3. **Activity:**  Popsicle-stick numbers (P)

*Materials:*  At least one-hundred sticks, rubber bands.
*Procedure:*  Ask children to pick a number and then count out that many popsicle sticks. Children group these in tens by placing a rubber band around each bunch. They can see what their number looks like in base ten. Provide verbal labels such as "you have two groups of tens and three ones. That is number 23."

## ADDITION, SUBTRACTION, MULTIPLICATION, AND DIVISION FACTS

1. **Activity:**  Dominoes (P)

*Materials:*  Commercial dominoes or teacher-made domino cards.
*Procedure:*  Two children divide the dominoes between them. Each child selects a number between 1 and 10. They alternate turns and may place one domino at either end of the line of dominoes to make their number. They may use any fact they can to make their number. For example, if a child's number is 6 and one of the end dominoes is 2, a child could make 6 by match-

ing the 2 with a 4, saying, "4 and 2 make 6." The first child to run out of dominoes wins.

2. **Activity:** Mixed-up odometer (P)

**Materials:** A die; a sturdy box lid at least two inches deep and with one side at least ten inches long; fifty tagboard cards 2 by 1½ inches with a numeral from 0 to 9 written on each so there are five cards for each numeral; five small metal notebook rings. (Use a paper punch to make one hole in the top of each numeral card and five holes at equal intervals on one side of the box lid. Mix up the numeral cards and then attach ten to each of the five metal notebook rings. Attach rings and numeral cards to holes punched in lid so numerals face out.)

**Procedure:** Two children may play. Children take turns tossing the die into the box lid. The child must make the number shown on the die in any way possible with the numeral cards by using any addition, subtraction, multiplication, or division fact, using one or more cards. When a card has been used, it is flipped over the box lid. A child who can keep making the number on the die may keep flipping the cards. When a child can no longer make the number, all the cards are flipped back and it is the other child's turn to throw the die. A tally is kept for each child to indicate the number of ways the number was made on each turn. The child with the most tallies at the end of five or ten rounds wins.

3. **Activity:** Multiplication race (P)

**Materials:** Pair of dice labeled with numerals; small plastic discs in various colors or other small objects suitable for markers; game board made of heavy cardboard. (Draw "road" or "track" to wind around board. Mark road into small segments so that the road contains at least 150 segments. Label the end segments "start" and "finish.")

**Procedure:** Two or four children may play. Children take turns throwing the dice, determining the product of the two numbers thrown, and moving their marker that many spaces. The first child to reach the finish line wins.

**Suggestions and Variations:** The same game can be used to practice addition, subtraction, or division facts. It is interesting to play using division facts because a player can make a move only after rolling two numbers, one of which can be *evenly* divided by the other.

4. **Activity:** Card train (P)

**Materials:** Thirty 3-by-5-inch tagboard cards numbered from 1 to 9.
**Procedure:** Two or three children may play. All cards are placed in a deck. One card is turned over to start. Then children take turns drawing a

card and putting it down next to the last card played. The child must state the answer to the fact represented by the two cards. Addition, subtraction, and multiplication facts may be practiced with this game. Players who cannot state the needed facts accurately must keep the cards they draw. The object is to end the game holding as few cards as possible.

## USING PLACE VALUE

1. **Activity:**   Finding the tens and ones (P)

   **Materials:**   Popsicle sticks; rubber bands; numeral cards (11 through 50); tens and ones chart made by drawing a line down the center of an 8½-by-11-inch piece of white construction paper and labeling the left side "TENS" and the right side "ONES."
   **Procedure:**   Two children can work together, or children can work individually. A child draws a numeral card and counts out that many sticks. The child then groups the sticks in bundles of ten and places them in the tens' space on the chart. Ones are placed in the ones' place on the chart.

2. **Activity:**   Odometer race (P)

   **Materials:**   Popsicle sticks; rubber bands; sturdy box lid at least two inches deep and with one side at least 5 inches long; thirty tagboard cards 2-by-1½ inches with numerals 0 through 9 written on them (three cards for each numeral); three small metal notebook rings. (Use a paper punch to make holes in tagboard cards and in the box lid. Order the numerals facing out so that 9 is in the back, and 0 is in the front.)
   **Procedure:**   Two children may work at once. A child throws the dice, picks up that many popsicle sticks, and groups them into ones and tens using the rubber bands to hold the tens in bunches. The child then flips the numeral cards so they represent that number. Player then passes the popsicle bundles to the other child who throws the dice, organizes the additional sticks into ones and tens, and flips the odometer to represent the new number. This continues until the odometer reaches 100. The child holding the sticks when 100 is reached wins.

3. **Activity:**   Peg-board (P)

   **Materials:**   Pegs and peg-board; pencil and paper.
   **Procedure:**   Two children work together. One child places pegs in the peg-board to make a number. The second child must write on a paper the numeral which represents that number. The children then exchange tasks. Children gain practice in writing two-digit numerals and thus use the concept of place value.

Measurement

## INVESTIGATING LENGTH

1. Activity:    Measuring ourselves (PP–K)

   *Materials:*    White paper, 36 inches wide or wider (cut a length as long as tallest teacher in class and mount lengthwise on the wall); colored construction paper cut into 1-by-3-inch rectangles and 1-by-12-inch rectangles (use one color for each size strip).
   *Procedure:*    Children stand with their backs against the paper. Make a mark just over their heads and then make a 1-inch-wide line from this mark to the floor (a yardstick or meter stick is handy for this). The child fills in the height-mark with pieces of colored construction paper. Some children will paste all 1-by-3-inch strips on the paper. Others will use all 1-by-12-inch strips, while others will use a variety of sizes. Children will notice how many strips it takes to make their height and the heights of other children. Help them notice that more strips are needed when mostly smaller strips are used.

2. Activity:    Dressing up (PP–K)

   *Materials:*    A variety of dress-up clothes, including items that vary in length such as jackets, shirts, skirts, and dresses.
   *Procedure:*    Place items in dress-up area for children to play with. Comment on the lengths of the items on the children who are wearing them.

3. Activity:    Block play (PP–K)

   *Materials:*    Unit blocks.
   *Procedure:*    Encourage children to play with the blocks. Provide firsthand experiences such as walks and field trips to see roads, bridges, and buildings. Since the blocks are designed on a units basis, children who use them will discover the concept of units. Children find out that the same length can be built with many different combinations of blocks. Children also gain an idea of linear measurement from block experiences because they are measuring the room in blocks when they build roads or rivers or any other structure which has length.

4. Activity:    Outdoor play (PP–P)

   *Materials:*    Lengths of rope knotted at one-meter intervals; small and large plastic balls.
   *Procedure:*    Two children should play together. One child throws the ball as far as possible. The other child spots the landing. The distance is then measured with the rope.

A plank measures the distance between two blocks.

*Suggestions and Variations:*   With young children, the distance should be discussed in global terms such as "very long way," "longer than the last time," "three knots this time." With older children, the distances can be described in terms of meters (the distance between each knot). Older children can keep records of their ball throwing and determine how many throws it took them to reach a total of five meters, ten meters, half a kilometer, and so on.

## 5. Activity:   Sticks (K–P)

*Materials:*   Toothpicks, popsicle sticks, long Tinker-toy sticks, a dowel rod.

*Procedure:*   Ask children to find out how many toothpicks must be used to make a line as long as the popsicle stick, the Tinker-toy stick, and the dowel rod. Ask how many popsicle sticks are required to make a line as long as the Tinker-toy stick and the dowel rod, and so on. Children solve the problems by placing the sticks down end to end.

*Suggestions and Variations:*   Children can be asked to predict what they think the answers will be. Older children can be asked to measure themselves with the dowel rod and then figure out how many toothpicks, popsicle sticks, or Tinker-toy sticks would equal their height.

6. Activity:    Measure the parts (K–P)

*Materials:*    Yarn or string, scissors, construction paper; picture assignment cards with the following body sections drawn on them: (1) heel to knee, (2) heel to toe, (3) knee to waist, (4) waist to shoulder, (5) shoulder to elbow, (6) elbow to wrist, (7) wrist to fingertips. (Indicate the exact area to be measured by marking pictures with red lines. Place a caption at the top of each card naming the section to be measured.)

*Procedure:*    Children could work in pairs to measure each other. Measurements should be taken in yarn or string, and a piece should be cut to represent the length of each body segment. These can then be mounted on paper, perhaps from the smallest to the largest, and labeled.

## INVESTIGATING WEIGHT

1. Activity:    Pan balance (PP–P)

*Materials:*    A sensitive pan balance can be made from scrap lumber, salad-dressing-jar lids, string, and a strip of peg-board or a yardstick with holes drilled at two-inch intervals. Build a stand with the scrap lumber. The peg-board or yardstick makes the arm of the balance. The lids, suspended with the string or wire, serve as the pans. Also provide an egg carton with the following materials stored separately in the sections: soda-bottle caps, dried beans, washers, paper clips, golf tees, glass marbles, small corks, a ping-pong ball, nuts, bolts, paper fasteners, identical buttons.

*Procedure:*    Encourage children to experiment to find things that weigh the same or to discover how many of one item are required to balance another.

*Suggestions and Variations:*    Children's explorations with a pan balance can be quite extensive. A series of directions and questions are listed below. They are clustered to indicate those that might be placed on one assignment card.

1. Put one bottle cap on one side of the pan balance. Find something heavier than the bottle cap. Find something lighter than the bottle cap.
2. Put a clothespin on one side of the pan balance. Find as many objects or combinations of objects as you can that weigh the same as the clothespin. Keep a record of what you find.
3. Two bottle caps  =    ?   beans
   Two bottle caps  =    ?   golf tees
   Two bottle caps  =    ?   washers
   Two bottle caps  =    ?   paper clips
   (These may be pictures instead of words.)

4. Put the following objects in order beginning with the lightest:

   bottle cap
   washer
   cork
   golf tee
   bean

5. Find something which is one-half as heavy as a paper clip.
   Find something that is twice as heavy as a golf tee.
   Find something that is five times heavier than a paper clip.

6. Can you find a way to balance two washers with four washers?

7. How many bottle caps does it take to balance one cube? How many bottle caps would it take to balance two cubes? three cubes? four cubes? Check to see if your guesses were correct.

8. Find as many pairs of objects as you can which are different in size and shape but that weigh the same. Make a record of what you find.

9. Drop a washer into the pan of water. Does it sink or float?
   Find five objects which weigh more than the washer. Predict whether they will sink or float.
   Check to see if you were right.

10. Find two objects that are different in size and shape but that weigh the same. Place them both in water. Do they both do the same thing?
    Find other pairs and check them the same way.

11. Fill identical pill bottles with sand, salt, and flour. Do they weigh the same? Explain.

12. Fill four different pill bottles with water, corn syrup, mineral oil, and rubbing alcohol. Which liquid weighs the most? The least? Guess, and then check your guess with the balance.

## 2. Activity:   Store play (PP–K)

*Materials:*   A pan balance or kitchen scale; grocery store set-up, including empty boxes and containers and plastic fruit and vegetables which are typically weighed in the produce department.

*Procedure:*   Take children on a trip to a grocery store before or soon after the grocery store is set up so they can see that some items are weighed for customers. Children will incorporate this knowledge into their store play if appropriate props are made available. Make suggestions about how much items might weigh, such as half a pound, one pound, and so on.

*Suggestions and Variations:*   Young children tend to exaggerate prices and weights of store items. They typically say something weighs "thirty-six-eight pounds." Teachers should not be too vigilant in correcting these unrealistic notions, although suggestions during play that you want half a pound of apples or one pound of grapes are very appropriate. Children then model these more realistic behaviors.

### 3. Activity:    Cooking (PP–P)

*Materials:*    Kitchen scales; cooking utensils and equipment; recipe for some food which requires fruit in an amount designated by weight (for example, applesauce recipes often call for so many pounds of apples).
*Procedure:*    Permit children to assemble the ingredients and measure out the correct amount of the weighed item.
*Suggestions and Variations:*    Take a small group of children to the store to shop for fresh fruits or vegetables to be prepared for snack. The adult who accompanies the children should point out to them that the produce must be weighed and should make sure the store worker relays to the children the weights of the items purchased.

### 4. Activity:    Objects in ounces (P)

*Materials:*    Various objects which range in weight from one ounce to sixteen ounces; a pan balance.
*Procedure:*    Make materials available for children. Encourage children to find objects which increase in weight by one ounce and to put the objects in order as they test them. Use terms such as half a pound and one pound when children use the eight-ounce and sixteen-ounce weights and explain that these are other names for these weights.

### 5. Activity:    Match a pound (P)

*Materials:*    Objects such as washers, nuts, screws, marbles, and so on, in large enough quantities to make more than a pound of each; pan balance; set of weights.
*Procedure:*    Two children work together. One child selects an object and fills the pan balance until it contains one pound of the item. The second child must then guess how many of another item would equal a pound and thus balance the first item. The child then places that many objects on the balance to see if the guess was right. If it is not, the child should determine with the weights how many ounces over or under a pound the guess was.

## MEASURING AREA

### 1. Activity:    Crazy shapes (KP)

*Materials:*    Irregular shapes cut from colored construction paper; graph paper (made with ditto).

*Procedure:*    Encourage children to guess which shape they think covers up the most area. Then have them trace the shapes on graph paper and count the number of squares covered by each.

2. **Activity:**    Blocks and rugs (PP–K)

*Materials:*    Unit blocks; carpet samples of different sizes and shapes.
*Procedure:*    Include carpet samples stored near the block area so that children can use them in their block play. Children will use them as rugs on the floors of their houses and will find out that it takes more smaller pieces than larger pieces to cover an area.

3. **Activity:**    Setting the table (PP)

*Materials:*    Equipment for dramatic play, including table, chairs, and dishes. (Include place mats of different sizes and shapes in the house play props.)
*Procedure:*    Have equipment available for children. Encourage children to put place mats on the table when they set it for "meals." Children will notice that different place mats cover the table differently or take up more area.

4. **Activity:**    Increasing squares (P)

*Materials:*    Geoboards and rubber bands.
*Procedure:*    Make materials available for children. As children work, suggest that they enclose an inch square with a rubber band. Then ask them to extend the lengths of each side of the rubber band an inch at a time, each time noting how many squares are enclosed by the rubber band. Children will notice that as the sides of the square are increased by one inch, the area of the enclosed square increases much more. They will see how the area of a rectangular figure is related to the length of its sides and will also gain an intuitive grasp of what squaring a number means.
*Suggestions and Variations:*    Be sure to use the correct vocabulary in describing the area enclosed by the rubber band (that is, one *square* inch, four *square* inches, and so on).

5. **Activity:**    Center squares (P)

*Materials:*    Graph paper run from ditto master; make graph paper so that squares are one-inch square.
*Procedure:*    Ask the child to pencil around a square in the center of the paper and then find the next biggest square and pencil around it. Encourge the child to keep finding the next biggest square until no more squares can be

enclosed. Encourage the child to count the number of square inches enclosed in each square and to label them.

## MEASURING VOLUME

1. **Activity:**   Boxes and blocks (PP–K)

   *Materials:*   Set of one-inch cubes; boxes of different shapes, some of equal sizes and others varying in size.
   *Procedure:*   Make cubes and boxes available on the classroom shelf in a suitable container. When a child selects this item to work with, the teacher should ask questions which encourage the child to notice that some boxes hold more cubes than others. If boxes are appropriately selected, children can also notice that although some boxes are different in shape, they hold the same number of cubes.

2. **Activity:**   Blocks cleanup (PP–K)

   *Materials:*   Set of unit blocks; shelves for storing blocks.
   *Procedure:*   As children clean up blocks after playing, they will notice that fewer large blocks can fit into the same space that smaller blocks fit into. Point this out occasionally, as when helping children clean up.

3. **Activity:**   Water play (PP–P)

   *Materials:*   Suitable tub for holding water; containers selected so that a variety of sizes and shapes are provided. (Make sure some containers vary in shape but are identical in size.)
   *Procedure:*   Provide water play as an activity. Ask children questions such as (1) Which one holds more, this one or that one? (2) How many of these little ones does it take to fill that big one? (3) Can you find two containers which are different shapes but hold the same amount of water?
   *Suggestions and Variations:*   As children are able to keep records of their work, they can make charts to represent their findings. They might make a chart representing the containers in the order of the amount of water they hold, or they might make charts which indicate how the containers are related to each other (how many of one it takes to fill the other).

4. **Activity:**   Cooking (PP–P)

   *Materials:*   Ingredients for recipe; cooking utensils.
   *Procedure:*   Select recipe which requires liquid measurements. Puddings, Jell-O, cakes, and ice cream are good examples. Gather a small group of children to do the cooking. Have children do all the measuring.

*Suggestions and Variations:*   Some system for selecting cooking groups is usually necessary to ensure that everyone gets a fair number of turns. You can divide the children into cooking groups and then make sure the groups take turns, or children can have turns as their names come up on a class list. It's best to keep cooking groups no larger than four members so that all children can be actively involved.

5. **Activity:**   Half-pint card game (P)

*Materials:*   Tagboard cards with sketches and written labels for cups, pints, and quarts. Make the following set of cards:

> eight cup-cards
> twelve pint-cards
> twelve quart-cards
> one half-pint card

*Procedure:*   Three or four children may play. All cards are dealt to players. Players then draw from each other as in the game Old Maid. Players may lay cards on the table in groups which equal a pint, quart, or gallon. The half-pint card may not be combined with any other. The person left holding this card at the end of the game loses.

*Suggestions and Variations:*   Children will need to know the relationship of one liquid measure to another. A chart of such relationships can be helpful, and children can refer to this during the game.

## UNDERSTANDING THAT TIME IS NOT CONTROLLED BY ONE'S ACTIONS

1. **Activity:**   Time your turn (PP–K)

*Materials:*   Sand timers and design cubes and patterns.
*Procedure:*   Encourage two children to work with the design cubes. Encourage the children to use the sand timer to designate the length of each turn. This will help children develop a concept of time as an arbitrary and objective segment separate from their own actions.

2. **Activity:**   Sand timer experiment (PP–K)

*Materials:*   Two sand timers, identical in size.
*Procedure:*   Two children are needed to do this activity. Each child has a sand timer. The children should allow the sand timers to run simultaneously to make sure they take the same amount of time to empty. The children

then decide some action to perform while the sand timer is running. One child should perform the action at a fast rate, while the other should perform it at a slower rate. They should watch the sand timers to see if they empty at the same time.

*Suggestions and Variations:*   Children should be asked to predict what they think the outcome will be.

# UNDERSTANDING THAT TIME IS INDEPENDENT OF THE MEASURING DEVICE

1. **Activity:**   Baking (PP-P)

*Materials:*   Ingredients and utensils for cookies, bread, or cake recipes; at least two clocks with different face dimensions (one large and one small); one paper or cardboard clock face with hands.
*Procedure:*   Mix recipe and place mixture in the oven. Set the paper or cardboard clock face at the time the real clocks will read when the food is finished baking. Children will notice that the small and large clocks read the same time when the food is finished; the teacher should ask them to check both clocks.

2. **Activity:**   Cleanup time (PP-P)

*Materials:*   At least two clocks, one with a large face, one with a small face; paper or cardboard clock faces.
*Procedure:*   Warn children several minutes before cleanup time that cleanup will begin at a certain time. Set the cardboard clock for the time you have said. The real clocks should be placed where children can see them easily. Refer to the clocks when announcing the final cleanup.

3. **Activity:**   Clocks (K-P)

*Materials:*   A variety of clocks—big, small, electric, and so on.
*Procedure:*   Children can work with the clocks, setting them all for the same time and then checking to see if they always read the same time regardless of their physical dimensions or characteristics.
*Suggestions and Variations:*   Add a metronome to the clock collection. Children can count how many strokes of the metronome it takes for the hands of each clock to move from one numeral to another. This helps children understand that no matter what the distance, the amount of time measured remains the same.

Geometry

## IDENTIFYING GEOMETRIC FIGURES
## AND SOLIDS

1. **Activity:**   Paper shapes (PP–K)

    *Materials:*   Geometric figures cut from colored construction paper. (Include triangles, rectangles, circles, squares, diamonds, trapezoids, octagons, and any other figures you wish.)
    *Procedure:*   Make figures available in a container on a shelf in the math center. As children work with figures, interact to help them find figures that are alike and provide their names.
    *Suggestions and Variations:*   After children have had experience identifying figures which are different, variations *within* a type of figure can be provided. For example, a box containing just triangles of different kinds could be available. Several of each kind should be provided so that children can search for those that are alike.

2. **Activity:**   A walk (PP–K)

    *Materials:*   The neighborhood.
    *Procedure:*   Take a few children for a walk to look for different geometric figures and solids. Adults provide verbal labels for what the children see.

3. **Activity:**   Shape bingo (PP–K)

    *Materials:*   Bingo cards made from tagboard; figures made with colored construction paper; call cards made with tagboard and construction paper.
    *Procedure:*   The game is played just like regular bingo. Children should do the calling so that they can practice the names of the figures.

4. **Activity:**   Containers (PP–K)

    *Materials:*   A variety of boxes and cans representing different solids.
    *Procedure:*   Set up a display using one container for each solid. Make labels to place by each type of solid. Have other containers available nearby in a box. Children can find containers which are of the same type as those on display. Help children read the labels and note the distinguishing characteristics of each type.

5. **Activity:**   Templates (PP–K)

    *Materials:*   Pencils or crayons, paper, cardboard templates. (Use a mat knife to cut figures out of the centers of pieces of cardboard.)

*Procedure:*   Make templates available in the math center. Children can use them to trace different figures on paper. Provide verbal labels for the figures children trace.

6. **Activity:**   Block solids (PP–K)

   *Materials:*   Full set of unit blocks.
   *Procedure:*   Unit blocks include cylinders, cubes, and so on. As children use the blocks, provide names for the different solids.

7. **Activity:**   Wooden block diagrams (PP–K)

   *Materials:*   One small block of each shape from unit block set; tag-board cut about 8½ by 11 inches. (Select one block and trace around each of its sides on a piece of tagboard. Repeat for all the different blocks, drawing only one block on each piece of tagboard. See Figure 9-4.)
   *Procedure:*   Place blocks and tagboard diagrams in a box available to children. Children try to match each tagboard diagram with the block it was drawn from.
   *Suggestions and Variations:*   Sometimes, blocks of unusual shapes can be obtained from scrap boxes in a wood shop or lumber yard. These make interesting diagrams.

**FIGURE 9-4**   Block surface diagrams.

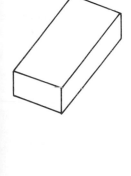
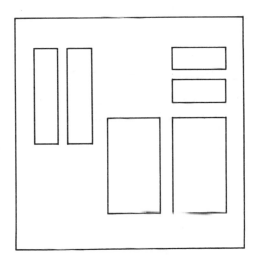

## CONSTRUCTING GEOMETRIC
## FIGURES AND SOLIDS

1. **Activity:**   Geoboard construction (K–P)

     *Materials:*   Geoboards, colored rubber bands.
     *Procedure:*   As children make figures on the geoboards, ask questions such as "Can you change that square into two triangles?" "Can you change that square into a rectangle?"
     *Suggestions and Variations:*   Assignment cards might be helpful with this activity. You can make sets in different colors to indicate those that go together. The cards for each set could then be numbered on the back so children will know in which order to follow the directions.

2. **Activity:**   Sand constructions (PP–K)

     *Materials:*   Empty plastic and metal containers of all sizes and shapes; wet sand in sand table or tub.
     *Procedure:*   Make empty containers available for children to use in the sand. Encourage children to pack the containers with wet sand and then to dump the contents out. The wet sand will take the shape of the container. Help children notice the features of the sand constructions they make.

3. **Activity:**   Peg-board constructions (K–P)

     *Materials:*   Pegs and peg-boards.
     *Procedure:*   Encourage children to use pegs to enclose different geometric figures on the peg-boards. Again, assignment cards might be useful. For example, directions might include asking children to make as many different figures as they can that have three sides, four sides, and so on.
     *Suggestions and Variations:*   This activity may be used with older preprimary children, although it may be too difficult for them.

4. **Activity:**   Tangrams (K–P)

     *Materials:*   Paper geometric figures that can be combined to make various figures; tangram assignment cards that illustrate possible figures. (See Figure 9–5.) Figures and assignment cards should be organized into sets by color coding; make figures and assignment cards of each set out of the same color paper.)
     *Procedure:*   Make materials available. Provide names for the figures children make.
     *Suggestions and Variations:*   Put out only three or four sets at one time. After children have explored these for awhile, put out several new sets.

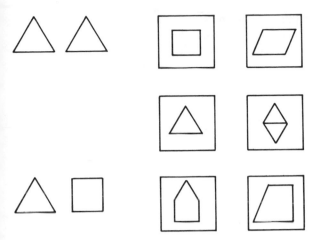

FIGURE 9-5   Tangram puzzles.

## RECOGNIZING AND NAMING COMMON COINS AND BILLS

1. **Activity:**   Store play (PP–K)

   ***Materials:***   Play money; empty food cartons of various types; shelves or some other arrangement for organizing containers as a store.
   ***Procedure:***   Encourage children to engage in store play. Join the play from time to time and provide information about the names of coins and bills. For example, you might play the role of cashier. When children offer the money to pay for their purchases, say, "That will be forty cents. Do you have four dimes, or do you have a quarter and a dime and a nickel?" You can then help search for the appropriate coins from among the child's play money.
   ***Suggestions and Variations:***   For preschool children, the stress is not on learning the value of money (for example, that forty cents is forty pennies, eight nickels, four dimes, and so on), but on recognizing certain coins as being a penny, a dime, or a nickel. The example given above is just one way to get children to attend to the characteristics and names of specific coins.

2. **Activity:**   Shopping trips (PP–K)

   ***Materials:***   Shopping list and money.
   ***Procedure:***   When going on a shopping trip, take along a variety of coins and bills. Give each child some of the money. For examle, one child might carry the dime and nickel, another might carry the quarter, and a third might carry a dollar bill. Tell children the names of the pieces of money they are

asked to carry. While on the way to the store, check once or twice to make sure each child still has the money, for example, "John, do you still have the dime and nickel?" When the actual purchase is made, ask the children to place their money in the cashier's hand: "John, give the cashier your dime and nickel. Joshua, give the cashier your dollar bill." Change can be distributed among the children to carry back to school, and the coins can be named again as they are given to each child.

*Suggestions and Variations:*    Checking the money on the way to the store is for the purpose of naming the money again. Be careful not to do this in a way which suggests to children that you do not trust them with money.

3. Activity:    Money poster (PP–K)

*Materials:*    A variety of coins and bills; poster board, clear contact paper, tape, rubber cement.

(Use tape or rubber cement to attach coins to poster board. Cover entire display with a sheet of contact paper so that a one-inch edge folds back on the underside.)

*Procedure:*    Place the poster on a bulletin board or wherever children can see it clearly and easily. Talk with children about the various coins and bills. Name coins children do not know.

*Suggestions and Variations:*    Small versions of the poster can be placed in an appropriate container on a shelf in the math center.

## UNDERSTANDING THE VALUE OF EACH PIECE OF MONEY

1. Activity:    How many pennies? (PP–K)

*Materials:*    Nickel, dime, quarter and at least twenty-five pennies; appropriate container to hold the money.

*Procedure:*    During activity time, help individual children count out the number of pennies that equals each of the other coins.

*Suggestions and Variations:*    This activity is not appropriate for the younger preschool child because a concept of number and the ability to count to 5, 10, and 25 are required. The activity is appropriate for many older four-year-olds and most five-year-olds.

2. Activity:    Money chart (PP–K)

Refer to activity #6 on page 374 of the chapter on Social Science and to Figure 10–6 on page 375 of the same chapter.

# UNDERSTANDING THE EXCHANGE
# RATES OF VARIOUS PIECES OF MONEY

1. **Activity:**   Money chart (K–P)

   **Materials:**   Nickels, dimes, quarters, and a fifty-cent piece; poster board; contact paper. (Make a money chart similar to the money chart in activity #1 in the preceding section, but instead of using pennies, use nickels. A dime would be shown to equal two nickels, a quarter would be shown to equal five nickels, and a fifty-cent piece would be shown to equal ten nickels. Other charts can be made to illustrate other exchange values. For example, the values of quarters, fifty-cent pieces, and dollar bills in a combination of dimes and nickels could be illustrated.)
   **Procedure:**   Make these charts available to children in the math area. Talk with children about the charts.

2. **Activity:**   Shopping trip (PP–K)

   **Materials:**   A variety of coins and a shopping list.
   **Procedure:**   When shopping for multiples of one item (five apples, three goldfish, and so on), find out the cost of each one. Then give each child who is making the trip money for one item, making sure each one has different coins. For example, if an apple costs twelve cents, give one child two nickels and two pennies, give a second child one dime and two pennies, and give a third child twelve pennies. They will see that each amount of money buys the same item.
   **Suggestions and Variations:**   This activity is not appropriate for younger preschool children. They do not understand that one dime and ten pennies are equal in value. They think that more pieces of money equal more money. Older four-year-olds begin to understand that more pieces do not necessarily mean more money, and they may profit from this activity.

3. **Activity:**   Extra change (P)

   Refer to activity #5 on page 374 of the chapter on Social Science for this activity.

## REFERENCES

DRUMMOND, M.   *The Psychology and Teaching of Number.* New York: World Book Company, 1922.
FURTH, H.G.   *Piaget and Knowledge.* Englewood Cliffs, N.J.: Prentice-Hall, 1969.

GINSBURG, H.    *Children's Arithmetic: The Learning Process.* New York: D. Van Nostrand, 1977.

KAMII, C.    *Number in Preschool and Kindergarten.* Washington, D.C.: National Association for the Education of Young Children, 1982.

KAMII, C., and DEVRIES, R.    *Piaget, Children, and Number.* Washington, D.C.: National Association for the Education of Young Children, 1976.

———.    Piaget for early education. In C. Day and R. Parker, eds., *The Preschool in Action.* Boston: Allyn and Bacon, 1977.

PIAGET, J.    *The Child's Conception of Number.* New York: W.W. Norton and Company, Inc., 1965

———.    *The Child's Conception of Time.* New York: Ballantine, 1969.

———.    and INHELDER, B.    *The Child's Conception of Space.* New York: W.W. Norton and Company, Inc., 1967.

WANG, M.C., RESNICK, L.B., and BOOZER, R.F.    The sequence of development of some early mathematics behaviors. *Child Development* 42(1971): 1767–1778.

## ADDITIONAL RESOURCES

### Books for Teachers

COPELAND, R. W.    *How children learn mathematics.* Third Edition. New York: Macmillan Pub. Co., Inc., 1979.

RESNICK, L., and FORD, W.    *The psychology of mathematics for instruction.* Hillsdale, New Jersey: Lawrence Erlbaum Associates, Pub., 19.

ZASLAVSKY, C.    *Preparing young children for math: A book of games.* New York: Schocken Books, 1981.

### Books for Children

ANNO, M.    *Anno's Counting Book.* New York: Thomas Y. Crowell, Co., 1977.

BROWN, M.    *One, Two, Three: An Animal Counting Book.* Boston: Little, Brown and Co., 1976.

HOBAN, T.    *Count and See.* New York: Macmillan Pub. Co., 1972.

———.    *More Than One.* New York: Greenwillow Books, 1981.

———.    *Shapes and Things.* New York: Macmillan Pub. Co., 1971.

KEATS, E.    *Over in the Meadow.* Bristol, Fla.: Four Winds Press, 1972.

SCARRY, R.    *Best Counting Book Ever.* New York: Random House, 1975.

SENDAK, M.    *Seven Little Monsters.* New York: Harper and Row, Pub., 1977.

SHARMAT, M. W.    *The 329th Friend.* Bristol Fla.: Four Winds Press, 1979.

THOMPSON, S. L.    *One More Thing, Dad.* Chicago: Albert Whitman, 1980.

WILDSMITH, B.    *1, 2, 3's.* New York: Franklin Watts, Inc., 1965.

ZASLAVSKY, C.    *Count on Your Fingers African Style.* New York: Crowell Junior Books, 1980.

# 10
# SOCIAL SCIENCE

Social sciences are important because no other area of study so directly affects children's understandings of themselves as persons and as members of groups. Through studying social science, children develop self-understanding, an awareness and respect for others, as well as skills in group interaction and social problem-solving.

Social science is concerned not only with the study of people and their interactions with others but also with the total environment. It transmits a way of life, while building knowledge, skills, attitudes, and values that enable children to function responsibly and effectively in a mobile and highly technological society.

A socially competent child is more willing to explore new things—toys, relationships, space, and tasks—than a child who is socially incompetent. The child's social competency provides a strong sense of confidence and security which facilitates exploration of the environment. Unfortunately, the possibility that social competencies are just as important, or perhaps more critical, than intellectual skills is often not considered.

One reason for the limitation of social science instruction is the current "back to basics" movement. The social sciences have taken a back seat to other areas of the curriculum such as reading, handwriting, and mathematics. The fact that social science education can include meaningful reading, handwriting, and computation is often ignored. And what could be more "basic" than learning how to get along with other human beings, learning about one's cultural heritage, and developing skills, knowledge, and values that characterize a responsible citizen in society?

A second reason for the limitation of social science instruction is the myth that the content of social science is too remote for young children, that their lives are not affected by events that are typically included in social science content. However, young children are constantly exposed to the harsh realities of life. Information about people and places in their community as well as in the far corners of the world is heard on the radio and seen on television every day. Those children who are not actually involved in aspects of life such as poverty, discrimination, riots, crime, violence, and wars hear and see documentaries about them regularly. Due to the complexity of society, young children need help in interpreting and understanding these events. In addition, it is never too early for young children to receive assistance in learning better ways to communicate and live harmoniously with others. Learning about self, others, and the world is a lifelong process which begins during infancy and expands as the child grows older.

This chapter will help teachers understand (1) the nature of the social sciences, (2) how children think and acquire knowledge about social science, (3) the goals and concepts appropriate for young children, and (4) instructional strategies and activities which will help children develop competencies in the social sciences.

# THE NATURE OF SOCIAL SCIENCE

Suppose you were asked to identify the nature and purpose of the social sciences. What would you say this area of study is to accomplish in early education? Your answer might be: Social science is really learning about people—how and where they live; how they form and structure societies; how they govern themselves; how they provide for their material and psychological needs; how they use and misuse the resources of the earth; and how and why they love and hate each other (Jarolimek, 1977).

Social science refers to an organized body of knowledge which facilitates the development of skills and attitudes related to social competence. For example, when children study phenomena from sociology, they gain knowledge about how people live in communities as well as about how services are provided in those communities. As children engage in experiences, they develop skills related to gathering, organizing, and presenting information. Young children also learn to share and work with others. Through the social learning process, they formulate values and attitudes about people.

Social science is an interdisciplinary science that tries to understand physical, human, and psychological interactions. It includes disciplines such as geography, ecology, psychology, sociology, economics, political science, anthropology, and history. These areas will be described below.

## Psychology: Individual Aspects of Human Behavior

Every individual has basic needs. They may be classified as primary and secondary. Primary needs such as food, rest, and maintenance of body temperature are primarily physical. Secondary needs are primarily psychological. These include the need to be recognized, accepted, and successful in life. Many of these needs are inherited by the individual, while others are transmitted through a particular culture. Individuals constantly attempt to satisfy both physical and psychological needs. Apparently, the need for self fulfillment is a pervasive and lifelong desire.

## Anthropology and History: Need to Understand Culture and the Past

Anthropology is the study of human beings, their culture and growth toward civilization. This discipline is primarily concerned with the development of social institutions, religion, arts and crafts, language, and physical and mental traits of the individual. People feel the need to understand the past, to see how it affects the present and to consider its implications for the future. A great sense of pride derives from tracing family "roots."

Cross-cultural studies in anthropology have documented the wide range of capabilities of human beings. Different groups of people living in different parts of the world have developed varied lifestyles. Anthropological studies reflecting affluence and poverty or urban and rural life demonstrate these vast differences. There are many cultural groups in a given society that need to be explored in the preschool and primary grades.

Events of the past were often recorded by individuals. Studying these historical events has taught adults the concepts of change and continuity as regards human life. Learning how and why people live a particular way has become an informative and interesting experience. Where events were not recorded, traces left by past groups allow those who are interested to make inferences about predecessors. Most adults and children enjoy knowing about the past and want to know much more, especially if it reflects their own past.

### Geography and Ecology:
### The Physical Environment

Geographiers study and describe the earth. As people began to move from one place to another, they noticed that places differed from one another. Geographical knowledge became extremely useful for travelers, military leaders, explorers, and those engaged in trade and commerce.

Not only is geographical knowledge useful to people, but the physical features of the environment directly affect people's lives. People who live in an environment where there are natural resources are likely to earn their living from these resources. Conversely, the environment has been affected by people. Land masses have been connected with bridges and tunnels. Streams have been dammed and land has been irrigated and changed from barren to productive. Minerals have been dug out from the earth. Ecologists warn that the face of the earth is fragile and that the complex effect of changes must be understood if life on earth is to survive.

Modern life has influenced the environment. Environmental education evolved due to the exploitation and waste of natural resources. For example, due to pollution, fresh water and fish are not plentiful in some areas. Forests, trees, and wildlife are no longer in abundance due to forest fires and the actions of people. In addition, combustion engines and manufacturing plants create large quantities of harmful hydrocarbons, which pollute the air. If the present rate of contamination persists, the possibility exists that the earth could experience a disaster, reducing the quality of life.

In the early childhood classroom, young children can be provided geographical knowledge and many experiences related to ecological problems. Teachers can help children develop ecological concepts as they teach them to conserve materials in the classroom.

## Sociology and Political Science:
## Need to Understand Society and
## Governance

The way in which people organize themselves into groups, social classes, and institutions is referred to as sociology. The family is the basic social unit and source of the most fundamental learnings in most cultures. When family members affiliate with others outside the family structure, they become members of larger groups, which require rules and institutions in order that people live together peacefully and meet their needs.

Societies have developed ways of establishing and maintaining social order. The system consists of laws governing how groups of people should live together and receive fair treatment. The laws reflect the values, beliefs, and attitudes consistent with the political system of the society. When people violate laws, they are usually punished and removed from other people in the community. Eventually, children learn that laws not only limit what people can do, but also have a protective function. Social science education helps children develop the concepts of rules and laws needed for orderly living.

## Economics: The Production,
## Consumption, Distribution, and
## Exchange of Goods and Services

Economics is the study of the production, distribution, exchange, and consumption of goods and services that people need or want. These processes involve an interrelated web of relationships. Goods and services produced and consumed by individuals are related to the economic system. However, there are critical differences between people's needs and desires, and the things they can have. The concept of scarcity—the difference between the unlimited wants of people and the limited goods, services, and materials available is a major consideration in the social sciences.

Monetary systems serve as a vehicle of exchange for goods and services. Without such systems people would need to trade goods and services directly for essential commodities. The interdependence of people in the world makes exchange and trade a necessity in the modern world. Money makes such trading easier.

## CHILDREN AND THE SOCIAL
## SCIENCES

In order for teachers to plan and implement social science programs, they need to be cognizant of the relationships between children's development and their social learnings. In particular, they must consider (1) children's social development, (2) children's cognitive development, and (3) children's moral development.

### Children's Social Development

THE FAMILY.    The first and perhaps most important and continuing agent of the child's socialization is the family. Whether in a nuclear or extended family, with a single parent, or in some type of communal arrangement, the child learns social patterns and skills within the context of the family (Seefeldt, 1977). During infancy, the parents are usually the primary agents of socialization. When the parent is continuously in contact with the infant, love, security, and care are provided, resulting in an attachment between the infant and parent.

Socialization is greatly influenced by type of family. *Authoritative* family styles reflect respect for the child, establish limits, and provide reasons for rules. For example, the authoritative parent might say to the child, "You can't play with the ball now, your brother has it," Or "I can't allow you to hurt anyone else." Children who are reared in families of this nature are more likely to become socially active, open-minded, and outgoing. On the other hand, children who are reared in *authoritarian* families usually become obedient, conforming and dependent; they are subject to arbitrary rules that are not accompanied by reasons. For example, at the birthday party a parent might say, "Stop pushing other children in line who are waiting for ice cream," yet never give an explanation as to why the behavior should be discontinued (Baumrind, 1972)

Some parents are overprotective. Children reared under these conditions can become dependent on adults and unable to explore the world for themselves. When parents limit children's social contacts and discourage friendships with other children, social development can be delayed.

SEX-ROLE DEVELOPMENT.    A fundamental characteristic of personality is sex role orientation, which refers to the masculine or feminine pattern of behavior affecting all social relations. Some sex differences in behavior are evident very early in life. Male infants cry more, sleep less, and demand more attention than females. Female infants are more sensitive to cold, touch, and sounds.

Sex differences in toy preferences also appear early in life. Parents purchase different toys for boys and girls. Parents give boys more trucks or wheel toys to play with while girls are given more dolls. Thus, parental selection of toys may affect sex differences in toy preferences among children.

According to Maccoby and Jacklin (1974), children learn both male and female roles through observation, but they perform whichever is reinforced or called for in a particular situation. Children know how to be both boyish and girlish. Once a child understands the basic concept of gender constancy, there is an awareness that the gender is not going to change. The behavior actually demonstrated depends on models and what parents, teachers, and peers reinforce. Media also affects young children's behavioral performance.

In our culture, stereotyped male qualities, such as independence, logic, and order, are highly valued. Consequently, girls may imitate men more than boys imitate women. Behaving as a tomboy is acceptable for a young girl, while feminine behavior in a boy is not. It appears that girls' sex roles are more flexible than boys'. (Bee, 1981).

SOCIOECONOMIC CLASS.    Social class greatly influences social development in young children. Each socioeconomic class has different models of socialization. Socioeconomic class influences the way parents rear their children and dictates what children will wear and to whom and in what manner they will relate. For example, middle class parents often insist that their children relate only to other middle class children with similar experiences and values. Teachers should be aware of the influence of socioeconomic status on children and attempt to understand and accept the differences children bring with them to the school setting.

SCHOOL.    Children initially become socialized through the context of the family, but once in a school setting, new ways of behaving, relating, and socializing are required. Children find that they must share space, materials, toys, and adults with other children. They must also learn to cooperate, see another viewpoint, and work together for group cohesion. Children who feel good about themselves are most likely to make the difficult adjustments necessary for group living in the school (Seefeldt, 1977). In the classroom, the teacher becomes the agent of socialization, setting the rules, limits, and standards for behavior. A teacher provides the children with a model to imitate and reinforces those behaviors considered desirable in the classroom.

## Children's Cognitive Development

PREOPERATIONAL THINKING.    Children between the ages of two and seven or eight possess preoperational thought patterns. The preoperational child thinks from a limited perspective due to perceptual orientation. Thus, judgments about the world are based on how it looks to the child. Several characteristics of preoperational thinking are described below.

EGOCENTRICITY.    Young children's thinking is egocentric (Piaget, 1969). This characteristic influences their ability to understand the affective objectives and knowledge of social science instruction. Children are egocentric in that they see things through their own perspective and do not realize that there are other ways of viewing things. Consequently, children are not concerned with logical justification of their points of view. Egocentric thinking presents a barrier to the intrusion of the opinions of others. This means that young children have difficulty imagining, for instance, what another person's lifestyle is like, particularly if it is quite different from their own.

Egocentricity also makes it difficult for children to understand the concept of interdependence. Socially, this concept involves the mutual dependence of two children. A young child may still be unaware that one's own action of hitting another child is what makes that child cry. As a result, the child may repeat the behavior until an adult intervenes. Though most preprimary children understand relationships better than that, their understanding is still quite limited.

Social relations are influenced by egocentricity as well as by the tendency of young children's thinking to be dominated by perception rather than by logic. Children often appear selfish because they literally see the world only from their own point of view. Therefore, it is not unusual to see two three-year-olds engaged in a tug of war about the same toy, each yelling, "I want it, I want it." Despite the very strong feelings of each child about wanting the toy, neither seems to understand that the other has strong feelings, too.

ANIMISM.    False assumptions and conclusions are common in children's thinking because children draw inferences from observations and experiences which are salient to them. Very young children believe that everything is alive and has feelings and reactions. Some children do not develop this viewpoint, but perceive that everything that moves is alive, such as cars and blowing leaves. Children may develop the idea that anything that moves is being moved by somebody on purpose. For instance, many children think that the sun and moon, and other inanimate objects that move are alive or have someone moving them (Brophy, 1977).

The fearfulness of young children in strange places may reflect this animism. It is not unusual for a child to go on a field trip and express fear and anxiety in the unfamiliar setting. Animistic ideas gradually disappear as children learn to identify the essential and invariant properties of living things. Six- seven- and eight-year-old children learn some of the ways in which inanimate objects can move without human intervention.

PHYSICAL AND SOCIAL CAUSALITY.    Young children's sense of causality is very different from that of older children and adults. Often, young children believe that when two events occur in succession, the first one causes the second. If, for example, a young child raises the window shade in the morning and sees the sun coming up over the horizon, he or she may believe that raising the window shade caused the sun to rise. Piaget's daughter announced one afternoon when she had not taken her nap, "I haven't had my nap so it isn't afternoon." She thought that the nap "caused" the afternoon (Piaget, 1969). Primary age children begin to understand that two things occurring together may not be causally related.

TIME AND SPACE.    Young children's thinking is still egocentric in relation to time concepts. Children have difficulty understanding both a sequence of events and duration of time. A three-year-old is aware of the sequence of events when it is "time for dinner" or "time for bed," but often only *after* behaviors of family members indicate the beginning of the particular event. Sequences involving days or weeks are even more difficult for preschool children to comprehend. For example, it is not unusual for children to ask the teacher daily when the class will be leaving for the field trip planned for next week. Sequences within a day are generally understood before longer sequences, such as yesterday, today, tomorrow, last week, and this week.

Specific durations of time take even more time to understand than daily sequences. "Five minutes," "twenty minutes," "half an hour" mean little to a preschooler.

Limited time understandings during the early years confuse children about age concepts. Young children tend to confuse age with height. The person who is bigger is older, regardless of birth order, the young child reasons. They do not know who was born first, their mothers or their grandmothers, because both are the same size (Piaget, 1970). By the end of the preoperational years, when children begin to coordinate concepts of succession and duration, they separate the idea of age from size.

In addition to limitations in understanding time, young children have limited ability to understand spatial representations. When a teacher shows that New York and California are but eight inches apart on a map, it is difficult to imagine that if one were to ride in an automobile, it would take five or six days and nights to go from one state to the other. Children also have limited ability to orient themselves on a map and perceive the relationships between one area and another.

The study of social science can probably help children develop their thinking. Experiences which allow children to see, hear, and think about other people, times, and places gradually increase children's ability to look at things from several points of view. For young children, real-life, firsthand experiences and the chance to reproduce these experiences in their play are the most valuable strategies for teaching the social sciences. Books, pictures, films, and filmstrips are also valuable resources.

Technical aspects of social science, such as map and compass reading, require understandings of symbols, scale, spatial relationships, and directionality. These concepts are difficult for preprimary children. Therefore, it would be wise for teachers not to attempt to deal with these concepts abstractly until children reach kindergarten age. The younger child can, however, deal with basic, concrete concepts. For example, it would be reasonable to ask a child whose house is near a church to describe where the church is in relation to the house. Perhaps the child would answer that it is between his or her house and that of a friend.

CHILDREN'S MORAL DEVELOPMENT.    Social science is concerned with moral development and understanding social rules. Since morality refers to conscious intentions and awareness of the implications of behavior, young children are described as "premoral" until they overcome egocentrism. They tend to respond to socialization pressures by repeating behavior that brings acceptance and rewards, and they usually avoid behavior that brings rejection and punishment. Young children will control their behavior in response to socialization demands, but this control is based solely on desires to obtain rewards rather than on any general concepts of right or wrong.

According to Piaget (1965), children's moral sense arises from the interaction between their developing thought structures and their gradually widening social experience. The first stage of this moral sense is referred to as *moral realism*. At this stage, a young child thinks that all rules should be obeyed because they are real objects, or things, rather than psychological constructs. When children reach the stage of *moral relativism,* they are aware that rules are created and agreed upon by individuals cooperating together.

Since perception is so dominant in young children's thinking, they judge the "goodness" or "badness" of an act, not by the intentions of the person who performs the act, but by the amount of damage that results (Piaget, 1965). A child who accidently bumps into someone's block building and knocks the whole structure down is likely to upset another child a great deal more than one who intentionally knocks down just a few. The visible damage, rather than the motivation, is used to judge the act. Adults would judge the intentions and not the actual damage. As adults help children interpret the difference between one situation and the other, children gradually begin to behave differently in the two situations; as they do, social relations improve. Young children must have opportunities to interact with one another if they are to learn how to deal with these interactions, and they must have support and guidance from adults.

As in all curriculum areas, concepts in social science will not appear fully developed. For example, a young child asks, "Are you my friend?" Adults may answer "yes," give the child a smile and a hug, and go about their business without another thought. But the concept of "friend" is an abstract concept which the child is still struggling to understand. What is a friend? What do friends do? Do friends sometimes do things you do not like? Can they still be your friends? Time, experience, and guidance from an understanding teacher will bring answers to these questions. It is important to remember that children have difficulty dealing with abstractions and need as much concrete information as they can obtain.

## SOCIAL SCIENCE GOALS AND CONCEPTS FOR YOUNG CHILDREN

Social science has a principal goal of developing individuals who can contribute to a society. This requires both instructional content and experiences enabling children to understand their immediate environment and eventually, the larger world. As children acquire knowledge in the social sciences, they also develop the skills of relating to others. Concomitantly, values and attitudes form which help children develop respect for themselves and others. The four major goals in teaching social science are (1) understanding about self and the family, (2) the development of knowledge and understandings related to people and society, (3) the development of skills that promote learning about society and how to function in society, and (4) the formation of values and attitudes.

Due to the limited experience and egocentricity of young children, a major portion of the social science curriculum centers on the children themselves—their own life histories, homes, families, feelings, and needs. A second portion of content extends to children's peers and the school environment and a third to people and society.

## Understanding Self and the Family

UNDERSTANDING SELF.    One often hears, "Sheila is just like her mother," and "Ralph is the exact image of his father." In the formation of self-concept, a child is highly influenced by adult responses and behaviors and particularly by what the child believes adults think of him or her. Although parents are very important in promoting the child's self image, the teacher is also an influential agent. A teacher's expectations of the child's behaviors can serve as a self-fulfilling prophecy.

A child comes to recognize himself or herself as a unique entity. While a child is a human being who shares certain physical characteristics in common with other human beings, there are particular qualities that set one apart from others. As the child becomes aware of physical differences, an appreciation can be developed for all people, regardless of religious, ethnic, or cultural considerations.

EACH INDIVIDUAL HAS WORTH AND DIGNITY.    Our democratic heritage has a core which consists of human dignity and self-worth. The goals for social science instruction include promoting these qualities in children. As children develop feelings of self-worth, they translate these feelings to others. When children find that people listen to them, respond with interest and pleasure, and show appreciation for their accomplishments, they feel good about themselves. As a result of their good feelings, they are able to respond to others in a positive manner, expressing respect for others.

PERSONAL HISTORY.    Every human being has an ancestry. Exposing children to genealogy is an important goal of social science. Children can be helped to understand their own heritage and ancestry. Becoming aware of the roots of one's heritage can help develop a sense of pride and respect for ancestors. Grandparents and great grandparents can take on greater meaning for the child.

But what about the ancestry of an adopted child? Although an adopted child does not share the genetic heritage of the parents, he or she shares the heritage of tradition and will feel a sense of belonging to the family when learning about parents' ancestors.

FEELINGS CAN BE EXPRESSED IN ACCEPTABLE WAYS.    Joy, anger, sadness, frustration, and inadequacy are feelings experienced by all human beings and need to be accepted as part of the human organism. Children must be allowed to express their feelings in an acceptable manner. For example, children need to express anger, joy, and sadness. However, neither angry children nor joyous children can be allowed to harm themselves or others. Rather, they can be given outlets to release the emotion in a more constructive manner.

DEATH AS A FACT OF LIFE.    If death is a fact of life, something from which no person will escape, why are people reluctant to consider it? Adults often attempt to protect young children from knowing about death. The dead goldfish is hastily removed from the tank and a similar fish put in to replace it. Such acts on the part of the teacher or parent may have undesirable side effects. The child could conclude, mistakenly, that the loss of a loved one is of little importance, because attention is readily transferred to something or someone else. Young children cannot be protected from death any more than adults can protect themselves. Trying to insulate children from the reality of death keeps them from fulfilling the need to know and to feel. It is important for children to understand death in the context of life—birth, living, and dying are all parts of the same process.

Basic understandings regarding death should be introduced to children. However, these concepts should be determined by the questions children ask as well as by their developmental stages. It is imperative that feelings accompany cognitive teaching. Wise teachers will encourage children to share their feelings about death and dying as the need arises or as planned in the curriculum.

DIVORCE AND THE YOUNG CHILD.    How do children react to divorce? Each child will react differently based upon emotional maturity and level of sensitivity. Younger children will most likely have more difficulty in restructuring their lives than older children. From three to six years of age is a critical period for children of divorced families because it embraces the time when boys' and girls' limited understanding may lead them to think they are to blame for their parents' difficulties. All children are affected by the crisis, particularly immediately following the divorce and, usually, for a period of one to two years after (Hetherington, et al, 1979).

The sensitive teacher can give the child assurance and moral support during the crisis period. It becomes important for the teacher to be a good listener. It is therapeutic for a child to talk things over with someone who understands and is remote from the situation at home.

THE FAMILY UNIT IS BASIC IN A SOCIETY.    The family unit is basic in a society because the family is the first socialization agent and stable factor in a person's life. Family stability helps one to adjust to the cultural context of society. All children are members of families, although there are not always biological ties. Children can learn about the roles and interdependence of family members in an economic, social, and psychological posture.

ALTERNATIVE FAMILY STRUCTURES.    Although all children are members of families, the basic composition is not necessarily the traditional model reflecting mother, father, and children. Children live with two parents, one parent, in foster homes, or in homes where they have been adopted. Children are part of the various structures and need to become aware of the things all groups functioning as families have in common as well as the uniqueness of each family.

## Understanding People and Society

PEOPLE HAVE RIGHTS.    People have rights which must be respected. These include the right to work, the right to privacy, the right to one's own opinion, and the right to personal property. Many of these rights are significant to the dominant culture in the United States. For example, not all people living within the borders of the country hold personal property rights as a value; instead, the properties they own belong to the group as a whole. Nevertheless, since personal and public property rights are basic to the legal and economic structure in the United States, it would probably be helpful for all children to gain some understanding of these rights.

The classroom climate is very important where there are children with handicaps. These children often need to be given special consideration. Nonhandicapped children should be taught how to relate to and respect the rights of children with special needs. When children understand the nature of the handicap, they are most likely to offer assistance and support; when children see a warm caring model, they are most likely to imitate the behavior and relate in a respectful manner.

PEOPLE HAVE RESPONSIBILITIES.    When people live together, they must assume responsibility for their own behavior and for the welfare of the group. Learning to take such responsibility is a goal closely tied to that of dignity and self-worth. When self-discipline becomes internalized, the child is aware of his or her role and responsibilities in the classroom whether the teacher is absent or present.

PEOPLE HAVE NEEDS AND DESIRES.    Basic needs such as food, clothing, and shelter must be fulfilled before psychological and other needs are attended to. Needs may be defined as things that are essential to life. People also want goods and services which they believe will make life more pleasant and enjoyable; we may call these *desires*. It is wise for children to begin to learn to distinguish between primary and secondary needs and desires.

WHEN PEOPLE LIVE IN GROUPS, RULES ARE NEEDED.    In order for people to live comfortably together, rules must be established. These rules serve as guidelines for behavior and protectors of security and safety. Young children should begin to make and apply rules in order to live together as a cohesive group. When children formulate the rules, they are more likely to understand and apply them consistently. The climate of the environment will be more appealing when rules are applied by all members of the class.

PEOPLE LIVE IN COMMUNITIES.    As people establish their dwellings in a particular area, it becomes a community. Each community serves the purpose of protection, convenience, and often assistance. Children should become acquainted with the features of their community. They can then represent their community in the form of picture maps and begin to develop map-reading skills. These skills may be transferred when exploring communities other than their own. The goal here is to help children notice differences among communities and determine reasons for these differences.

PEOPLE PRODUCE AND CONSUME GOODS AND SERVICES.    American society is such a complex macrocosm that needs and desires cannot be satisfied independently or even by bartering. In order to satisfy needs and desires, people produce goods or offer services in exchange for money. In turn, they use the money for purchasing the goods and services they want from others. Children can begin to learn the basics of our economic system.

PEOPLE DO DIFFERENT TYPES OF WORK.    Children can be introduced to persons who represent a wide spectrum of occupations, such as dentists, attorneys, firemen, janitors, law-enforcement workers, mechanics, and architects. They can also become acquainted with the occupations of their parents and learn to respect their careers. As children become aware of the wide range of work roles, they may begin to look forward to growing up and assuming one of these roles. The teacher can support the young child's natural respect for the work of nonprofessional workers such as garbage collectors and ice-cream vendors.

PEOPLE TRAVEL IN VARIOUS WAYS AND SEND MESSAGES.    For several decades, transportation and communication have been used as means of bringing people together. People travel great distances in short periods of time in order to be together. Another means of coming together is by written and verbal communication. Children can begin to understand the many ways in which people travel and communicate as well as to develop skills in using the vehicles of communication. Writing letters and telephoning are familiar means used in the child's home for communication.

PEOPLE COME FROM MANY CULTURES.    Most children today come into contact with people from many different cultural backgrounds, either in their own communities, in the city, when traveling, or from the mass media. It is imperative that children know, understand, and have respect for other people, regardless of the color of their skin or of differences in speech or behavioral patterns. Basic to gaining this appreciation and respect for cultural differences are positive experiences with representatives of different cultures. Knowledge of the history and customs of all people is extremely valuable.

IMPORTANT PEOPLE, PAST AND PRESENT.    Through the efforts and contributions of past generations, many accomplishments have been made in government, business, institutions, and public services. People of all races and countries had great ideas and performed good deeds. Although young children cannot relate to this historical perspective by dates, they can nevertheless learn about contributions and deeds of famous people. Current events can often be the starting point for teaching about historical events.

UNDERSTANDING CULTURAL DIVERSITY.    In order for children to understand the diversity of various cultures, they need to work through racial awareness. Mary Ellen Goodman (1964) demonstrated that racial awareness begins as early as three years of age. By age five, the beginning of racial attitudes can be expected. At around seven years of age, full-blown racial attitudes are established.

Throughout the time when racial awareness is developing, many stereotypes are formed. Stereotypes are described as beliefs or opinions about a particular culture, ethnic group, or nation. Stereotypes serve as a barrier to understanding and appreciating cultural and ethnic diversity. These developing stereotypes can form the basis for racist and sexist thinking. Children need information and contact with all people so that they will not overgeneralize based on limited information and contact.

Teachers should emphasize the truth when teaching about the nature and impact of sexism, racism, and prejudicial thinking. The favorable as well as unfavorable aspects of a culture need to be introduced. The commonalities of people should be emphasized, but the teacher should not preclude consideration of important cultural and ethnic differences.

### Values, Customs, and Traditions

FORMATION OF VALUES.    Young children establish values at an early age. Values are the basis for inner guidance and direction. They are acquired from socializing experiences provided by adult models and demands. Of all the goals in the social sciences, the formation of values is the most important and most difficult. It is impossible for teachers, who are significant persons in young children's lives, not to impart their values to them. However, very often these values may be in conflict with values children bring from home. Teachers can respect the values of the home to the extent that they are not in conflict with their own carefully considered goals. For example, if the value of the home is one of complete adult respect where the child must listen when adults are talking, then the teacher has to respect this value of the family. However the teacher may encourage children to interact with adults rather than merely listen to them.

CUSTOMS AND TRADITIONS.    Every nation has holidays which derived from historical and religious events. The customs and traditions which have grown up around these holidays are part of the rich heritage of a people. Often in a pluralistic society, the richness of this heritage is lost as persons from different backgrounds become interspersed throughout society. For example, in the spring, most people have a festival which celebrates new life. For Jews, it is the Passover which celebrates a life free from bondage. For Christians, it is the Resurrection, in which it is believed that Jesus brought people hope for a new life. Easter eggs and Easter bunnies are symbols of new life, but nothing more. Yet for many children, all Easter means is that the Easter bunny comes and brings eggs and other goodies and that often they get new clothing for the occasion.

It is wise for teachers to develop a significant goal for teaching young children about customs and traditions. Teachers should help children appreciate the meaning of holidays as well as helping children enjoy the traditions and customs which surround them. Traditions and customs of people are expressed in their art, music, drama, dress, food, and food service. Children need many experiences which give them exposure to many customs and traditions.

## METHODS FOR TEACHING
## SOCIAL SCIENCE

Social science teaching can occur throughout the entire day. The way in which a teacher organizes the classroom, the amount of freedom and flexibility permitted, the reward versus punishment system, the rules established and enforced, the sharing of materials, and independent versus group activities—all are factors contributing to developing children's social science concepts and understandings.

Various kinds of learning activities are used to introduce the young child to the social world: working in small groups; participating in discussions, process activities, or construction; hearing and reading stories; or drawing and working at learning centers.

Young children need to be actively involved in the learning process. Learning encounters need to be more than sessions in which children merely sit and listen. Teachers must plan a program of varied learning activities for children. It is helpful to make children actively responsible for learning by asking often for ''feedback'' in response to instruction. For example, before a trip to the museum, remind children to observe particular artifacts while at the museum so that the artifacts can be discussed upon return to the classroom or at a later date. When children are given focus and direction before an activity, learning becomes an interactive process.

The following methods provide a variety of suggestions for teaching the social sciences.

### Teacher Modeling
### and Classroom Management

The teacher serves as a model for young children, who tend to behave according to the role that the significant adult models. Therefore, it is necessary for teachers to display the behaviors which they verbalize. In other words, it is not ''Do as I say,'' but ''Do as I do.''

Creating an organized environment is most important for the teacher and children. Classroom management is simplified when children are aware of the rules and when the rules are applied consistently by the teacher. When there are inconsistencies, children often become confused and resort to disruptive and destructive behavior.

### Conducting Group Discussions

As children interact together in a group, there will be concerns and issues to be resolved. The teacher can present the situation that has aroused concern and elicit from the children their reactions, feelings, explanations, and suggestions for solution. The teacher can summarize the suggestions and decisions. The main role of the teacher is that of facilitator and moderator.

Group discussions can help children to understand and verbalize their feelings and to realize that others have similar feelings. Because young children have difficulty understanding another's point of view due to their egocentric thought, the source of group discussions should be concrete situations, whether problems or pleasures, which the children have encountered.

## Using Books

Many social science concepts and understandings can be developed through children's literature. Good books can be read to children in order for them to receive information and derive enjoyment. Children who can read, can be encouraged to engage in independent reading concerning social science concepts.

As children browse through books, their interest and curiosity can be awakened. Discussion can also be stimulated. However, discussions can be relatively spontaneous, with the teacher following the children's cues in guiding the conversation.

In many classrooms, books are stacked on the shelves in a disorderly fashion. They are not frequently rotated from cupboard to shelves, nor are they displayed in an appealing manner. The disarray does not encourage children to browse and read books. Since a desire to read and reading itself are the keys to successful learning, attractive displays of good children's literature are crucial.

## Dealing with Controversial Issues

Since young children are exposed to various value systems, it becomes difficult for them to understand and deal with particular issues. Busing of children and incorporating religion in the school program are current controversial issues. A teacher who values busing in order to promote integration may plan activities to promote understandings of this concept. However, the teacher must (1) avoid taking sides on a controversial issue and (2) present information on which children can base their own decisions.

Teachers should not raise ideas with negative connotations unless they are brought up by the children. If a child says that his or her parents believe that minorities are stupid, then the teacher might explore with children the meanings of such words as *stupid* and *lazy*. Following this experience, the teacher might ask a child if a minority child with whom he or she has played is stupid or lazy. No further comment is needed after the question. The child's response is accepted. If pressed for an opinion on an issue, teachers should, after having presented appropriate information, explain what they think and why. They can then suggest that children talk the issue over with their parents.

## Teaching for Cultural Awareness

One way teachers can promote understandings regarding cultural awareness is to use a comparative structure. When studying traditional American harvest celebrations such as Thanksgiving, children can make a cross-cultural exploration into the ways harvest time is celebrated elsewhere in the world. For example, Jewish festivals or the English harvest may be discussed. As children learn about the problems of life in the city, they can make a comparative study of problems faced by the people of suburban and rural areas. In addition, learning about family lifestyles represented by children in a class that includes blacks can be extended to include a cross-cultural study of families in Africa.

FIELD TRIPS.    Field trips can be most worthwhile experiences for children since they provide direct, hands-on learning experiences. In many instances, field trips provide children with opportunities for observation, data collection, inference, and drawing conclusions. Children should be helped to focus their attention on the purpose of the trip before they go and guidance should be provided throughout. Often, the time following the trip is more important than the trip itself because of the follow-up activities that can occur. For example, children might utilize art media, dance, movement, literature, audio-visual materials, dramatic play, or discussions related to the trip. Having an experience and then acting on it can be a springboard to concepts and values basic to social learnings.

USING MOTION PICTURES.    Through films and filmstrips, teachers can convey important ideas about the world. Seeing a film on different kinds of houses after hearing the teacher read a story about particular kinds of houses helps the children develop the concept. What children learn from the teacher is reinforced by what they learn from the film or filmstrip.

USING KITS.    Publishers have developed many commercial kits which often contain useful materials. Teachers can best use these materials when they are so familiar with the kits that they are able to extrapolate materials which match the needs and interests of the children and adapt the ideas to individual styles of teaching.

STUDY PRINTS.    Photographs provide appealing windows of the world for children. Therefore, a fundamental resource in learning about the social world is what is commonly called the "study print package." It consists of a coordinated series of photographs on a particular topic. A set of study prints of life in the city might show a congested downtown intersection, a business district, a community redevelopment project, shoppers in a downtown department store, and so on. Teachers can help children become proficient in reading pictures.

Children can use study prints to create photo stories associated with concepts being studied. Working in groups of two or three persons, children select individual pictures and arrange them on the floor so that they tell a story. It is also valuable for the teacher to use transparency slides. Learning becomes personalized when a teacher is able to share materials such as these with the children.

TEACHER-PLANNED UNITS.    For many years, the traditional way to construct a unit has been to select a topic for study, determine what the objectives are, and then plan activities to meet the objectives. Often, a culminating activity would be planned to evaluate the children's progress toward attaining the objectives. However, this pattern often results in children simply giving back to the teacher the learning planned for them without expanding their thinking beyond the simple content presented.

We suggest that a far richer experience involves a web structure—a central axis or concept with interrelated concepts—in which an experience is planned that all the children will share. In planning, the teacher considers all the different directions the children's interests might take and tries to provide resources which will help them as they follow these interests. Individual explorations are encouraged. For example, a trip to a bakery is planned. Some children might become interested in where wheat comes from and how it is grown. Other children might be fascinated with the process involved in mixing and baking the bread. What causes it to rise? A few might be interested only in tasting the bread but will have other related interests, such as the buying or selling of bread. The skillful teacher thinks of other avenues for study and is alert for cues from the children which indicate the direction their interest has taken. Research in books or oral, written, or picture reports may follow from such an experience shared by primary age children.

INDIVIDUALIZED INSTRUCTION.    Individualized instruction is a technique that teachers use to create an activity-oriented classroom. Within a classroom, the goals are different for each child, as are the means used to attain the goals. Individualization helps to maintain interest as each child makes meaningful discoveries. As young children seek a variety of sources, they can help each other understand that more than one point of view is possible. Tolerance of different opinions can be encouraged. By allowing children to read materials at different levels or to look at various picture books and refer to different types of resources, the teacher helps to avoid frustration. Individualization simply implies an acceptance of individual differences.

USING RESOURCE PERSONS.    Whenever possible, young children should have concrete experiences; this promotes enthusiasm, interest, and concept development. Sometimes, such experiences can be arranged by having visitors come to the classroom. A parent of a Vietnamese child could be invited to share something significant about that culture. Whether the parent engages in storytelling, shows a collection of artifacts, or engages in a cooking experience, the children's interest about the culture could be expanded through the experience.

### Understanding Oneself and the Family

## UNDERSTANDING ONESELF AND OTHERS

1. **Activity:**    This is I (PP–K)

**Materials:**    Butcher paper, crayons, scissors.
**Procedure:**    Make paper and crayons available to children in art area or other area where there is floor space. Encourage children to trace around a

friend and then have the friend trace around them. Children can then color in their body drawings. Display body drawings in the classroom or the corridor.

2. Activity:   Mirroring (PP–K)

*Materials:*   Mirror.
*Procedure:*   Install a full-length mirror in a corner or place a mirror on a stand. Encourage children to get to know themselves by seeing who they are. Promote discussions about facial features, hair texture and length, body parts, and how specific parts function. Also discuss clothing worn by the children.
*Suggestions and Variations:*   Have the children find partners and stand opposite each other. One child is the mirror and duplicates the actions of the partner for a period of time. Later, roles are exchanged. Body movements can be mirrored at first; later, children can perform more complex facial mirroring.

3. Activity:   The "ME" collage (K–P)

*Materials:*   Magazines.
*Procedure:*   Have children clip magazine pictures as they prepare a collage that reveals things about themselves. Discuss the things they might include:

> Birthplace—picture from home or picture of similar area from magazine
> Baby pictures—picture from home
> Family—people, pets
> Things they like—foods, sports, recreation
> Where they have lived or traveled—cities, towns, farm, parks

4. Activity:   My photograph (PP–K)

*Materials:*   Polaroid camera, film.
*Procedure:*   In order to develop a sense of identity in children, use a Polaroid camera and take the children's pictures. Discuss physical characteristics. Use the pictures to label the children's storage area. Also, the pictures can be used as an attendance check. Children can take pictures from a large pocket chart and place them on the bulletin board to indicate their presence.

5. Activity:   Movie time (K–P)

*Materials:*   8 mm movie camera, film.
*Procedure:*   Take 8 mm movies of the children in the classroom while they are engaged in a variety of activities. Show the movies at a particular time of the day to the children. The movies permit the children to observe themselves in motion and in relation to other children and adults in the room.

## 6. Activity:   My voice (K-P)

*Materials:*   Toy telephones, tape recorder.
*Procedure:*   When a child hears a recording of his or her voice, it helps to develop a sense of identity. Invite children to use the toy telephones in the classroom for a conversation and record their voices on tape. Play the tape so that children can hear their own telephone conversations. If children have problems coming up with situations, structure the situation by suggesting who they call and the general content to be discussed.
*Suggestions and Variations:*   Borrow a set of telephones provided by the local telephone company. Encourage the children to engage in telephone conversations as often as they desire.


## HELPING CHILDREN LEARN THAT
## THEY AND OTHERS ARE OF WORTH

## 1. Activity:   All of us (PP-P)

*Materials:*   Construction paper, film, Polaroid camera.
*Procedure:*   Take snapshots of the children, or have them take pictures of each other. Place pictures in an album or book made by mounting pictures on construction paper. Place the book in the library with other books so that children can look at it.
*Suggestions and Variations:*   Children can label their own pictures and write a sentence about themselves. Teachers can take dictation for younger children.
Encourage children to bring a baby picture of themselves. Place it in photo album with their other picture, or make a complete "baby book."
Take slides of the children engaged in activities at school. Show these to the children some day during story or group time.

## 2. Activity:   My pictures (PP-P)

*Materials:*   Easels, poster paints, brushes, paper, crayons.
*Procedure:*   Make materials available in the art center. When children draw figures, pause to ask who the persons are, what they are doing in this particular scene, and so on.

## 3. Activity:   Sing our names (PP-K)

*Materials:*   Autoharp, piano, or teacher's voice alone.
*Procedure:*   During song time, sing "I See a Boy [Girl] with a Yellow Shirt [dress, pants, shoes] or, "Who Are You?" Any simple tune will do.

One's very own place suggests
respect for each child.

Look at the child who has been selected. The child sings back, "I am Steve."
This is a particularly good song during the first few weeks of school since it
helps children learn each other's names.

4. **Activity:**   Everyone has a place (PP-P)

*Materials:*   Some set-up—cubbies, bins, shelves—to serve as individual
storage spaces for children's personal possessions.
*Procedure:*   Designate individual places by labeling spaces with children's
names. Encourage children to store personal belongings in these spaces, and
encourage them to respect each other's places.

## UNDERSTANDING ONE'S OWN
## PERSONAL HISTORY

1. **Activity:**   My special day (PP-K)

*Materials:*   Cake, ice cream, other birthday celebration items.
*Procedure:*   Celebrate each child's birthday in some appropriate way,
such as serving the special treats at snack and singing "Happy Birthday." Inquire how old the child is with this birthday.

2. **Activity:**   My Past and present (K–P)

*Materials:*   Photographs.
*Procedure:*   Ask the children to bring to school photographs of themselves taken earlier in their lives. When photographs are received, build a time line which shows how each individual looked at various stages in life. Place the display on a bulletin board. The time line should stimulate conversation regarding previous and present experiences encountered by the children.
*Suggestions and Variations:*   Invite one child each week to bring photographs which were taken when younger. Fill a bulletin board with pictures, using the theme "Child of the Week." Use another child's photographs the following week. Continue until all children have had a turn.

3. **Activity:**   Family historians (K–P)

*Materials:*   None.
*Procedure:*   Invite relatives of the children to come and share their recollections of childhood. Parents can describe what they did as children—their favorite games, things they liked to do, eat, or see. Also, parents might be able to give the children information about the history of the school building, such as what stood on the site before the building, how the area has changed, and so on.

4. **Activity:**   Where did it come from? (PP–P)

*Materials:*   Common items in the classroom, children's personal possessions.
*Procedure:*   Talk with children about the items. Help them think about where the materials for making each item came from, where the item was before it came to the classroom or the child's house, and where it might end up some day.

5. **Activity:**   Family roots (P)

*Materials:*   Charts.
*Procedure:*   This project involves parents and teaches children about their ancestry. Children take small charts home and ask their families about the history of the family. (See sample chart in Figure 10–1.)

6. **Activity:**   Family tree (P)

*Materials:*   Construction paper, pens, scissors.
*Procedure:*   The children can construct a family tree using the information they collect. Children may cut out a representation of a tree and put the names of family members on slips of construction paper. Attach the name

| MY FAMILY | | | |
|---|---|---|---|
| MOTHER<br>FATHER<br>BROTHER(S)<br>SISTER(S) | NAME | BIRTHPLACE | DATE |
| MOTHER<br>FATHER<br>BROTHER(S)<br>SISTER(S) | MOTHER'S FAMILY<br>NAME | BIRTHPLACE | DATE |
| MOTHER<br>FATHER<br>BROTHER(S)<br>SISTER(S) | FATHER'S FAMILY<br>NAME | BIRTHPLACE | DATE |

**FIGURE 10-1**  My Family.

cards to the tree; put on the immediate family first and then the extended-family members.

## HANDLING FEELINGS IN DESIRABLE WAYS

1. **Activity:**   Accepting feelings (PP–P)

*Materials:*   None.

*Procedure:*   With young children, emotions are often on the surface. Children become angry, sad, and happy very easily. When children express any of these feelings, teachers should accept them and not make statements like "Oh come on now, big brave boys don't cry." While teachers should not always accept the behavior which accompanies anger (hitting, hurting, damaging things), they should demonstrate acceptance of the feeling. This can be done by helping the child find a different way of expressing it. For example, if in anger one child begins hitting another, the teacher should stop the hitting and say to the child, "Tell her you are angry that she took your truck away and that you want it back."

*Suggestions and Variations:*   Primary age children can discuss conflict situations in stories or dramatic presentations and relate any solutions to problems they may have encountered. In dramatic play, children will act out feelings they have had or that they think others have had. They will spank or kiss the doll, kick at the pretend dog, act exasperated at pretend spouses or children. Teachers should observe children during dramatic play and ask appropriate questions, perhaps at group time. "John, you sure seemed angry at the baby today. What did the baby do?"

It is appropriate at times for teachers to model the expression of feelings in dramatic play. The teacher can do this by becoming a participant. The teacher should not dominate the play (give orders, determine roles, and so on) but could ask permission to play and ask to be given a role to assume. Through such role playing, it is possible to introduce new ways to express feelings. For example, anger over something the baby did can be expressed in a discussion with a spouse or friend, or verbally to the baby, rather than through physical attacks on the baby.

2. **Activity:**   Story time (PP–P)

   *Materials:*   Children's literature.
   *Procedure:*   Select books with focus on feelings *(Snowy Day, A Letter to Amy, Curious George, Where the Wild Things Are, Ping)*. After reading the story, ask children what feelings the story characters expressed. Ask children to relate situations in which they felt the same way as the characters.

3. **Activity:**   Tell it like it is (K–P)

   *Materials:*   Game board, pictures expressing six to eight different emotions.
   *Procedure:*   The children and teacher sit in a circle around the game board. Each child in turn spins the spinner. When it stops, the child examines the face it is pointing to and enacts the emotion that face seems to portray. The child may explain the emotion he or she is enacting.
   *Suggestions and Variations:*   As children enact the emotions, they can examine their faces in a mirror or tape record what they say. The game board may be illustrated as shown in Figure 10-2.

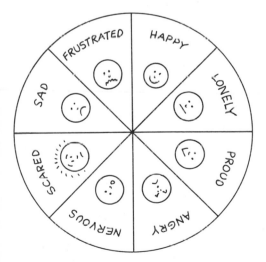

FIGURE 10-2

4. Activity:    Expressing feelings (P)

*Materials:*    None.
*Procedure:*    Begin a discussion with children and use open-ended sentences for them to complete orally. These sentences help children probe their feelings and express them with little fear. For example:

> I feel really happy when . . . .
> When I get big, I am going to . . . .
> Once I really got scared because . . . .
> When I'm all alone, I pretend . . . .
> I get really mad when . . . .

## COPING WITH DEATH AND DIVORCE

1. Activity:    My friend (P)

*Materials:*    Children's literature.
*Procedure:*    Read *A Taste of Blackberries* by Doris B. Smith. It is the story of a boy who goes from denial, anger, and guilt to ultimately accepting the death of his close friend. This book may be helpful to a child who has experienced the death of a family member or close friend.
*Suggestions and Variations:*    Use the filmstrip and tape interpretation of the story.

2. Activity:    My parents (K–P)

*Materials:*    Doll house with figures.
*Procedure:*    Often, children need to release their feelings about their divorced parents. It is often easier to project feelings through another character than through oneself. Encourage children of divorced parents to act out their feelings using doll house figures. Various roles of mother and father may be presented. Use their expressions as a springboard for later discussions.

3. Activity:    Learning about divorce (K–P)

*Materials:*    Children's literature.
*Procedure:*    Have access to books pertaining to divorce. Read these books to children and allow them to discuss the content of the books. Films and filmstrips may also be shown. These forms of media often enable children to better understand the concept of divorce and to identify with others who have had similar experiences.

# LEARNING ABOUT FAMILIES

1. **Activity:**    Dramatic play—house (PP–K)

   *Materials:*    Toy refrigerator, stove, cabinets, table, chairs, bed, chest of drawers, trays, measuring cup, spoons, bowls, pans, dishes and other items common to a house. (See page 172 for dramatic play.)

   *Procedure:*    Encourage children to play in the house area. As children play, take cues from what you hear and observe, and build toward a recognition of interdependent family roles based on such cues. For example, one child says, "You be the mother; you stay home and keep house while I go to work." The second child shows some reluctance to take this kind of "mother" role. You might then suggest that both "mother" and "father" go to work, and ask what kind of work each parent does.

   *Suggestions and Variations:*    As children show interest, house-cleaning implements, tools, clocks, old radios, and other items might be added, and the children might assume roles of house cleaner, appliance fixer, cook, and so on.

2. **Activity:**    The family (PP–P)

   *Materials:*    None.
   *Procedure:*    In a group meeting, ask children to talk about their families. Who lives in each child's house? Children may include goldfish, dogs, cats, and other pets as family members. Later, show pictures of different types of families, ranging from those with one parent and one child to families with parents, grandparents, several children, and a menagerie of pets. Discussion may cover such questions as: What makes a family? Can one person be a family? Why do we live in families? Such a discussion could occur at story time after the children have listened to a story related to families.

3. **Activity:**    Family jobs (PP–K)

   *Materials:*    Felt board; cut-out pictures of family members and of work tools and objects—garden hose, dishes, washing machine, hammer, and so on—pictures of kitchen, yard, laundry, and other areas of the home. (Pictures should have strips of sandpaper or felt pasted on the back for use on felt board.)

   *Procedure:*    Make materials available for children during activity time. As children match people and objects they work with, help them discuss how this work is accomplished in their own families. Usually, two or three children will gather around to talk and compare how their families divide up work.

4. **Activity:**   Different kinds of families (PP–K)

**Materials:**   Felt board; figures for all possible family members (children, mother, father, aunt, uncle, grandmother, grandfather, and so on) backed for use on a felt board.
**Procedure:**   Make materials available for children. Stop by occasionally and talk with individual children about the members of their own families.
**Suggestions and Variations:**   Be sure to include figures from a variety of ethnic backgrounds, particularly if children in the class are from different ethnic groups.

5. **Activity:**   Family survey (P)

**Materials:**   Paper, pencils, crayons, graph paper.
**Procedure:**   Ask children to collect data about their families. Data might include:

1. Family members
2. Family occupations
3. Family size

Have chidren report back to class what they have found out. Help a small group of children make graphs which summarize the data. For example, a graph illustrating family size might look like the one shown in Figure 10–3.

**FIGURE  10-3**   Graph of family size.

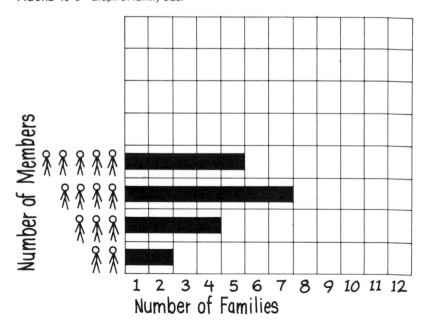

Help children see how to indicate on the graph that fewer families had two and three members than had four and five members.

6. **Activity:** Are there any more at home like you? (PP–K)

   **Materials:** Poster paper or construction paper, felt pens or crayons, rulers.
   **Procedure:** Have children talk about how many people there are in their families. Set up a large bar graph. The vertical axis consists of the number of family members, and the horizontal axis includes the name of each child in the class. Each child fills in a bar (with teacher help) using a felt pen or crayon in order to show how many people are in the family. (See Figure 10–4.)

| FAMILY GRAPH | | | | | | |
|---|---|---|---|---|---|---|
| 7 | | | | | | |
| 6 | | | | | | |
| 5 | | | | | | |
| 4 | | | | | | |
| 3 | | | | | | |
| 2 | | | | | | |
| 1 | | | | | | |
| NAME | TIM | AMY | JOEY | KIM | MARIA | DEWITT |

**FIGURE 10-4** Family graph.

Understanding People and Society

## UNDERSTANDING THAT PEOPLE HAVE RIGHTS

1. **Activity:** Everyone has a place (PP–P)

   **Materials:** Same as in activity on page 359.
   **Procedure:** Same as in activity on 359.

2. **Activity:** Classroom spaces (PP–P)

   **Materials:** Whole classroom.
   **Procedure:** Arrange the classroom so that children can find a private

space to be alone if they want to be. This will not be one child's personal space, but will be used by any child when the need arises and the space is not in use.

3. Activity:    Honoring a child's work (PP-P)

   *Materials:*   The child's work.
   *Procedure:*   Permission to keep, display, file, send home, or destroy work should be obtained from each child. On rare occasions, it may be necessary to go against the child's wishes on this issue. If this is the case, discuss this decision with the child. Children's work should also be protected from destruction by others in the classroom. This will require procedures for helping children store their work in safe places.

4. Activity:    Group time (PP-K)

   *Materials:*   None.
   *Procedure:*   Having children engage in small group work is often helpful in developing social awareness and a sense of the rights of others. Children practice good listening skills by giving another child the right to speak; in turn, the other child responds accordingly.

## UNDERSTANDING THAT PEOPLE HAVE RESPONSIBILITIES

1. Activity:    Cleanup time (PP-P)

   *Materials:*   Everything in the classroom.
   *Procedure:*   Children can be encouraged to put away and clean up materials and equipment. Encouragement can be provided first by organizing the room so that everything has a place. Labeling can help ensure that children remember where things go. In addition to these structural encouragements, teachers also need to remind children to put things away. During the first weeks of school, talk with children about putting things away and why it is important. When a child forgets, a gentle verbal reminder such as "Oh, Sue, you will need to put the puzzle back before you start painting. I'll wait here at the easel while you go do that" will help. During general cleanup after activity time, pitch in and help. Comments such as "I'll get these things here; can you get the blocks over there?" or "What can I do to help?" or "Can you help me here?" are appropriate.

2. **Activity:** Snack (PP–P)

*Materials:* Items for snack.
*Procedure:* Children can be involved in the preparation and serving of snack. Snack is usually an enjoyable activity for children, and children can become responsible for preparation, serving, and cleanup associated with it.

3. **Activity:** Classroom jobs (PP–P)

*Materials:* Materials in the classroom.
*Procedure:* All classrooms have routine tasks which must be performed; plants need to be watered, animals need to be fed, materials need to be straightened, lunch money needs to be collected. Children can assume responsibility for these tasks. Refer to page 52 of Chapter III for suggestions for scheduling this work.

4. **Activity:** Completing tasks agreed upon (PP–P)

*Materials:* Classroom materials and equipment.
*Procedure:* Teachers and children will make agreements about work to be completed. Maybe a young child has agreed to finish a boat made of wood. Perhaps an older child has decided to read a certain number of pages in a book. Children should be expected to finish the work they have agreed to do. There will be some work about which no such agreements are made, and decisions about whether to complete this work may be left to the child.
*Suggestions and Variations:* Teachers can offer good guidance at the time the agreement is made to avoid setting unreasonable expectations. In addition, teachers should keep in mind that children's ability to think and plan ahead and then carry out such plans is related to their developmental level. A three-year-old can be expected to follow through with cleaning up one last play area before going on to a new one if the child and the teacher have just talked it over. But a three-year-old cannot be expected to decide on Monday what to do during activity time on Tuesday, Wednesday, Thursday, and Friday. On the other hand, it would not be unreasonable to expect a second grader to plan out activities for a week at a time, although some plans would no doubt be tentative. Of course, the second grader has the advantage of being able to write down such plans.

5. **Activity:** Clean scene (K–P)

*Materials:* Large litter bags; crayons, markers and other materials for decorating bags; poster paper.

*Procedure:*    Each child is given a litter bag to decorate. In small groups, the children collaborate on making posters and leaflets. (Example: We're cleaning up; how about you?) These leaflets may be reproduced. Later, the children will take a field trip through the area on which they decide to concentrate, picking up litter, putting up their posters, and distributing their leaflets. Areas may include the school, the playground, streets surrounding the school, or around the neighborhood. (The leaflets may also be sent home.)

6. **Activity:**   Taking roles (K–P)

*Materials:*    Puppets and puppet stage.
*Procedure:*    Invite children to use the puppets and stage. Let children improvise their own stories or give children a story to provide a context for the puppet actions. (See p. 134 for details of puppet making.) The following story provides a context:

> This story is about Maurice. One morning, it was time to go to school and Maurice could not find a book that he borrowed from the school library. His mother began to help him look for the book. Although Maurice had a book-shelf in his room, he never put things where they belong. After searching for some time, Maurice had to go to school without the book which was due. Of course, by now Maurice was late for school. His mother talked to him about putting things where they belong and suggested that after school he should begin the search again. What should Maurice do? If the book is found, where should it be placed? Have you ever lost anything by putting things in the wrong place?

## UNDERSTANDING THAT PEOPLE HAVE NEEDS AND DESIRES

1. **Activity:**   Your house and mine (PP–K)

*Materials:*    Pictures.
*Procedure:*    Mount pictures of homes where children can see them. These might include a house, apartment, trailer, houseboat, igloo, hut, and so on. Discuss differences and similarities among the homes with children who stop by to look.
*Suggestions and Variations:*    Have a flannel board with cut-out items of different kinds of houses. Allow children to show the kind of houses in which they live. Take a walk in the community to look at different types of homes. Make the children aware of the materials that are used in construction of various types of homes. Include materials such as long grass, bamboo, sticks, leather, stone, wood, and brick. Discuss parts of a house, such as roof,

eaves, windows, doors, rooms, chimneys. The land area around houses can also be mentioned. Encourage children to construct houses from materials such as blocks.

2. **Activity:**   Where we live (K–P)

**Materials:**   Paper, pencils, butcher paper.
**Procedure:**   Ask children to find out what type of home (apartment, duplex, single-family home, mobile home) they live in. Help children make a graph to illustrate their data.

3. **Activity:**   What families buy (K–P)

**Materials:**   Paper, pencils, crayons.
**Procedure:**   Encourage children to ask their parents what things their families buy. Have them report back to the class. Help children make a list of all the items families must buy, such as food, clothing, household items, and so on.
**Suggestions and Variations:**   Invite to the class people who produce some of the items children have determined that families buy. Preferably, the visitors should be parents of the children. In this way, children can begin to understand that families must produce in order to consume.

4. **Aotivity:**   Fixing things (P–PP)

**Materials:**   Glue, wood putty, tape, contact paper, oilcan, screw-driver.
**Procedure:**   Involve children in the care and repair of classroom equipment. If books are torn or worn, or if puzzle pieces are lost, fix or replace them and have children help. Children love to tighten screws and oil squeaky tricycles or doors. Children should be helped to understand that more needs and desires can be met if equipment is cared for properly.

5. **Activity:**   Needs or desires (K–P)

**Materials:**   Magazines, butcher paper, scissors, paste, marking pens.
**Procedure:**   Have a discussion with children noting the difference between things we need and things we would like to have. Cite some examples. You can prepare a bulletin board for the children. Label one section "Needs" and the other, "Desires." Tell the children to cut out pictures of various products from magazines and paste them in the appropriate section of the bulletin board. The board may look like the one shown in Figure 10-5.

FIGURE 10-5

## UNDERSTANDING HOW INDIVIDUALS
## LIVE TOGETHER IN GROUPS

1. **Activity:** Classroom ground rules (PP-P)

   *Materials:* None.
   *Procedure:* As problems arise, discuss with children how they can be solved. Help children develop rules for the class. Rules might include what a child is to do when finished with a piece of equipment. Another rule might specify when certain activities can occur (maybe hammering can only occur during a specific half-hour). Teachers will need to initiate some rule making at the beginning of the year, but other rules can be developed with the children.

2. **Activity:** Reasonable rules (K-P)

   *Materials:* Poster paper, marking pens, magazine pictures, construction paper.
   *Procedure:* Teacher and children sit in a circle and discuss why rules are important. Have children suggest what rules the class needs to help it run smoothly and safely. As each rule is decided on, write it on a chalkboard or poster board. When all rules have been agreed upon, teacher and children cooperate to make an illustrated poster for each rule, using drawings or pictures from magazines in addition to the written rules.

3. **Activity:** Learn the law (K-P)

   *Materials:* Poster paper, tagboard, pencils, crayons, marking pens.
   *Procedure:* Help children identify some specific community laws that affect children's lives—traffic, safety, littering, petty theft, and so on.

Have each child make a poster stating and illustrating the law he or she thinks is most important. Display the posters around the room and in the corridors of the school.

4. Activity:   Traffic signs (PP–K)

*Materials:*   Red, yellow, and green construction paper; egg cartons; glue.
*Procedure:*   Place circles (2½ inches in diameter) of red, yellow, and green construction paper, the tops of egg cartons, and glue on a table. In the morning planning circle, tell children that materials for making traffic signs are on the table. Ask them to recall which color is at the top, which is in the middle, and which is at the bottom. Also discuss what each color means. Discuss why we need traffic signals. Encourage children to use their signals with roads made of blocks or while playing outdoors with wheel toys.
*Suggestions and Variations:*   Before introducing above materials, take children for a walk to observe the nearest traffic signal. Help children discuss the signals and their contribution to safety.

5. Activity:   School safety procedures (P)

*Materials:*   Traffic pattern schedules for the school in case of fire; outdoor playground schedules for school; lunchroom facility schedules for the school.
*Procedure:*   Arrange to have children obtain the above schedules from the school office. Help them discuss the relationship of these schedules and procedures to the comfort and safety of all classes who use the school.

## UNDERSTANDING THAT PEOPLE LIVE IN COMMUNITIES

1. Activity:   Our neighborhood (K–P)

*Materials:*   Blocks, boxes, wrapping paper, felt marker, construction paper.
*Procedure:*   Encourage children to make their own maps, beginning with their home and their neighbor's house. Give children large sheets of manila paper and crayons. A discussion of their street should precede this experience.
*Suggestions and Variations:*   Have a small group of children who live in close proximity lay out a representation of their street. Give the children strips of masking tape to place on the floor in the block area. After completion of their street, allow the children to trace the path from each other's homes following the map layout.
Encourage children to make a drawing of the school and nearby places on a

large strip of wrapping paper placed on the floor. Begin with the school, trace the route, and put in key places. The teacher should help children label certain streets.

Encourage children to discover directions from school to home, to neighborhood market, to library, and so on. Have the children also note distance in blocks from school to home, to the store, or to a friend's house.

Children might be asked to bring in pictures of their homes. Have children pin the pictures of their homes in the appropriate space on the map.

Take the children to the top of a tall building or tower so they can look down on the entire community. This enables children to see in one glance the whole area that is mapped.

2. Activity:   Model in blocks (PP–P)

   *Materials:*   Unit blocks.
   *Procedure:*   Encourage kindergarten and primary age children to make a model of the room out of unit blocks. Once they have made the three-dimensional model, primary children may like to draw it as a two-dimensional model.

3. Activity:   Sand map (PP–P)

   *Materials:*   Sand table and sand; tin cans, blocks, small vehicles.
   *Procedure:*   Encourage older children to build cities or a model of their classroom in the sand.

4. Activity:   Hidden treasures (PP–P)

   *Materials:*   Paper, pencils, toy trucks, balls, jump ropes, and so on.
   *Procedure:*   Hide small play items on the playground. Draw maps to indicate their location. Give maps to the children so that they may try to find the items.

5. Activity:   Trip map (K–P)

   *Materials:*   Paper and pencil.
   *Procedure:*   Plan a short trip near the school to see something, gather pebbles, and so on. Draw maps for the children to use to find their destination. The adult accompanying the children should help them use their maps.

6. Activity:   Felt town (K–P)

   *Materials:*   Large flannel board; various colors of felt pieces; cardboard outlines of buildings, vehicles, trees, shrubs, and so on; marking pen; poster paper.

*Procedure:*    Discuss the children's community in reference to buildings, parks, and streets. A felt community which represents the community in which the children reside can be planned. Children can use cardboard outlines as patterns for cutting out pieces of felt to form buildings. Children arrange the felt pieces on the flannel board to represent the community. Each building can be discussed in terms of its function in the community.

*Suggestions and Variations:*    A three-dimensional community can be made from blocks and other building toys.

7. **Activity:**   Map-a-thon (K–P)

*Materials:*    Butcher paper, pencils, crayons, pens, construction paper, and other materials such as yarn, tinfoil, glue; map of the area.

*Procedure:*    Examine with children a map of the community or neighborhood. Afterwards, take a walk through the community and note points of interest. Use a large piece of butcher paper and a map of the area to help children draw an illustrated map of the community. Hang the map in the classroom upon completion.

## UNDERSTANDING PRODUCTION AND CONSUMPTION AND THE USE OF MONEY

1. **Activity:**   Cashier and customer (PP–K)

*Materials:*    Dramatic play area set up as a store; cash register or money box; play money.

*Procedure:*    As children play, encourage them to take the roles of cashier and customer. Explain what each does (young children often think the cashier gives money to the customer, since they see the change). Information about what the cashier and customer do can be illustrated well if you enter the play in one of these roles.

*Suggestions and Variations:*    Trips to a store to purchase items needed for the class will help children better understand the cashier-customer relationship. Books about stores can help, too.

2. **Activity:**   Supermarket visit (PP–K)

*Materials:*    None.

*Procedure:*    Take a small group of children to the supermarket to see produce and other items being delivered. Then permit children to observe at the check-out counter. They will notice people buying items they saw being delivered.

*Suggestions and Variations:*    If you live where it is feasible, children might visit a vegetable farm in order to understand where the food comes from that they see being unloaded from the delivery trucks at the store.

Allow children to purchase produce they have seen being delivered to the store. These items can be prepared for snack.

3. **Activity:**    Orchard and applesauce (PP-P)

   *Materials:*    Usual preparation for a trip. Saucepan, paring knife, hot plate, bowl, spoon.
   *Procedure:*    Take a group of children to an apple orchard to see apples being picked (and perhaps pick their own). Purchase some apples to make applesauce.
   *Suggestions and Variations:*    Similar trips can be taken to a maple-sugar farm, an orange grove, a dairy farm, or a vegetable farm.

4. **Activity:**    Coin names (PP-K)

   *Materials:*    Real money coins.
   *Procedure:*    Have materials available for children to work with during activity time. As children examine the coins, help them name them—penny, nickel, dime, quarter.
   *Suggestions and Variations:*    If possible, permit children to use the coins in dramatic play as they engage in buying and selling commodities.

5. **Activity:**    Extra change (P)

   *Materials:*    Sixteen nickels, nine dimes, three quarters.
   *Procedure:*    Two children may play. The coins are mixed up in a box and blindly divided between the two children. The children must arrange their coins in pairs or groups that are equal. For example, they can pair a dime with two nickels because each is the same amount of money. They might also pair a group of three nickels and one dime with a quarter. The child who has the most extra change loses the round. Play five rounds to a game. The child who wins more rounds wins the game.

6. **Activity:**    Money chart (PP-K)

   *Materials:*    Forty pennies, one nickel, one dime, one quarter.
   *Procedure:*    Make a chart to illustrate the exchange of each coin in terms of pennies. Cover the chart with contact paper. Display it where children can refer to it easily. Figure 10-6 shows a sketch of such a chart.

7. **Activity:**    Foreign currency (P)

   *Materials:*    Foreign currency
   *Procedure:*    Invite a money collector to share a small foreign currency display with children; or ask children to check at home to see if they can bring

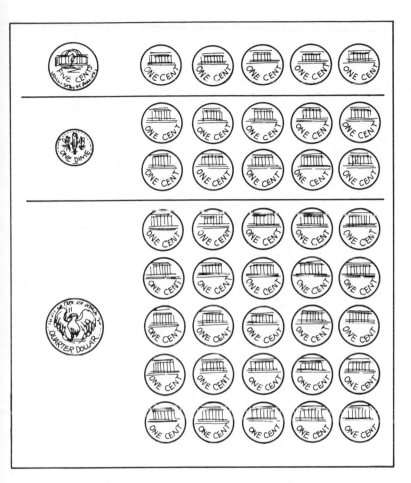

**FIGURE 10-6**  Money chart.

a piece of foreign currency. Explain the value of the foreign currency by relating it to U.S. currency.

## UNDERSTANDING THAT PEOPLE DO DIFFERENT KINDS OF WORK

1. **Activity:**   Visiting nurse (PP–P)

*Materials:*   Tape measure, tongue depressors, cotton swabs, mask, scales, nurse's cap, thermometer.
*Procedure:*   Invite a nurse to visit the classroom to discuss the nurse's role and the kinds of tools it requires. The nurse should demonstrate the use of each tool. Set up props in the housekeeping corner. Encourage dramatic play.

*Suggestions and Variations:*   Give each child bits of gauze, Band-Aids, cotton, and adhesive tape to make a collage. They will talk about the medical uses for these items as they use them. Interact verbally and add information as needed.

Invite other people in to talk about their work. Encourage such visitors to bring tools and equipment associated with their work, because this helps young children understand better what it is that the person does.

2. **Activity:**   Visiting people at work (PP-P)

*Materials:*   None.
*Procedure:*   Make the usual trip preparations, including notes from home and briefing of the people to be visited. Any type of worker may be visited. Those that are popular with young children include police officers, firefighters, medical workers, road equipment operators, glass blowers, delivery workers, and farmers.

3. **Activity:**   What parents do (PP-K)

*Materials:*   Paper, pencils, magazines, scissors, glue, construction paper.
*Procedure:*   Ask children to find out what kind of work their parents do. They can then cut out a picture of someone engaged in that type of work and paste it in a construction-paper book. This can become a class book.
*Suggestions and Variations:*   Because in any community there may be parents who for periods of time do not work, it might be wise to suggest this activity as something children may want to pursue, or may not. In this way, those children whose parents do not presently have jobs will not be forced into an uncomfortable situation. Parents may be invited to the classroom to demonstrate and discuss the type of work they do.


## UNDERSTANDING TRANSPORTATION AND COMMUNICATION

1. **Activity:**   Getting to school (PP-K)

*Materials:*   Large sheet of butcher paper, glue, pencil; cutouts of buses, cars, trains, bicycles, and figures walking.
*Procedure:*   Attach butcher paper to a space on the wall at a low height. Place cutouts in a container near the butcher paper. Place pencils and glue there also. Encourage children to select the cutout that indicates the way they travel to school. They can write their names on the cutouts and glue them in the appropriate column on the paper. In this way, children will make a picture graph depicting the number of children arriving at school each way.

*Suggestions and Variations:*    Children can be provided with magazines to find a picture of their mode of travel. They can cut it out and then place it on the graph. The graph might appear like the one in Figure 10-7.

2. **Activity:**    Transportation models (K–P)

*Materials:*    Model cars, trains, airplanes, boats, and so on.
*Procedure:*    Set up an area which can be used for displaying models. Ask children to bring in any models they have at home. Books can be selected to accompany the display. While talking with children who view the display, help them notice details of the models and understand how each is used.

3. **Activity:**    Wheels (PP–P)

*Materials:*    Blocks, box, wagon.
*Procedure:*    Encourage children to compare the effort required to move a box of blocks with and without the aid of a wagon. Relate this experience to the construction of most modes of travel. All vehicles carry heavy loads. All (with few exceptions) have wheels.

**FIGURE 10-7**    Graphs of modes of travel to school.

4. **Activity:**   Airplanes (PP–P)

   *Materials:*   None.
   *Procedure:*   Make field trip arrangements as usual. Take the children (all or a small group) to an airport. They should see airplanes; people arriving and departing; planes being loaded, unloaded, and cleaned. Go inside a plane. The children can compare the baggage cart with their own experience in moving blocks at school.
   *Suggestions and Variations:*   Trips to visit trains, boats, and trucks might also be planned. Primary age children may like to obtain schedules for the different modes of travel so that they can compare the time each takes to reach the same destination.

5. **Activity:**   Truck traffic (K–P)

   *Materials:*   Books, pictures; pencil and paper.
   *Procedure:*   Read books to children which are about different kinds of trucks. Display pictures of different types of trucks. Then, allow a small group of children to go sit by the street (accompanied by a high-school student or other adult) and observe the number of each kind of truck that passes by. Help the children make a graph which illustrates their findings. Through questioning, try to help children think of reasons why they saw certain types of trucks and not others. Questions would include: "Where do you think the refrigerated dairy trucks are going?" "Where might the cement truck be going?"

6. **Activity:**   Writing letters (PP–P)

   *Materials:*   Paper, crayons, pencils, envelopes, and stamps.
   *Procedure:*   Make materials available to children in the writing center. Encourage children to write a letter to someone in their family. You may need to take dictation from young children. Somewhat older children will need to know how to spell some words. These can be written on scraps of paper and then copied by the child. When the letters are finished, take the children to a nearby mailbox and mail the letters.
   *Suggestions and Variations:*   Draw a picture to be mailed home. If a holiday or special day is approaching, make cards for the occasion. When picture or card is completed, have children deposit in a mailbox.
   Take the children to visit a post office. They can see what happens to a letter in preparation for delivery. Encourage children to make a cardboard mailbox for the classroom to use in dramatic play. Letters can be "mailed" to friends in the class. Try to arrange for the children in your class to write letters to children in a class at a different school or to children in another class at the same school.

Young children learn about communication systems by pretending to use them.

7. **Activity:**   Using the telephone (PP–P)

**Materials:**   Toy telephones, real telephones (in school office).
**Procedure:**   Toy telephones can be placed in the dramatic play area. Children can also be asked to do telephoning for the class on real phones when this seems appropriate. For example, primary age children can call stores in order to locate a particular item needed by the class or may call a museum to check its visiting hours.

8. **Activity:**   Talking machines (PP–P)

**Materials:**   Two-way radios, intercom system, walkie-talkie, and so on.
**Procedure:**   Try to use any of the above to help children understand how people can talk with each other across distance. A visit to the school office to see the intercom system would be interesting. A police officer who visits the class can show children a two-way radio.

9. **Activity:**   Audio codes (K–P)

**Materials:**   Any devices for tapping out messages (pencil tapping on the table, musical triangle, and so on.).
**Procedure:**   Let children experiment with making up codes and sending messages to each other.

10. Activity:   Radio and TV stations (K–P)

*Materials:*   None.
*Procedure:*   Arrange for field trips to the stations for small groups of children. Be sure children have some notion of what happens at a radio or TV station.

## UNDERSTANDING THAT PEOPLE COME FROM MANY CULTURES

1. Activity:   Pictures of people (PP–P)

*Materials:*   Portfolio of pictures.
*Procedure:*   In the picture file and on bulletin-board displays, include pictures of Afro, Asian, Native, and Mexican Americans as well as others who have distinctive appearance, dress, and hair styles. The pictures should represent people from a variety of ethnic groups in ordinary dress and hair styles as well as in dress and hair styles reflecting their cultural heritage.

A Native American tells school children about tribes.

It is wise to plan for visitors to stay to talk with individual children.

## 2. Activity:   Native Americans (PP–P)

**Materials:**   Artifacts such as beaded or concho belts, jewelry, woven rugs, pottery, and baskets made by Native Americans who live in your area.

**Procedure:**   Invite a Native American professional person or leader to visit your class. Ask the guest to tell the class about his or her place of birth, schooling, occupation, and family. (It is important to demonstrate to children that Indians are people whose lives are similar to those of their own families. Few live by choice in teepees, hogans, or adobe huts with no modern conveniences.) An Native American visitor who was reared on a reservation may talk about a life quite different from that of the children in the class. The man in the photo on page 380 is a member of the Mohawk Indian tribe who discussed Indian tribes and their locations with the children.

**Suggestions and Variations:**   Follow the visit by making a display of Native American artifacts. If the museum in your community has a display depicting Indians living as they did years ago, arrange for a field trip. Study other ethnic groups in similar ways.

## 3. Activity:   Oh, you beautiful doll (K–P)

**Materials:**   Pictures of traditional costumes—huraches, kimonos, sombreros, obi sashes, zori sandals—scissors, paste, pens, construction paper, scraps of fabric, feathers, leather scraps, doll pattern.

*Procedure:*   Encourage the children to examine and discuss the pictures of costumes. Each child gets scissors, paste, and a pattern for cutting out paper dolls. Materials for making costumes are put out where all the children can choose from among them. Upon completion of the project, display the dolls with a brief description written or dictated by the children.

## UNDERSTANDING IMPORTANT PEOPLE, PAST AND PRESENT

1. **Activity:**   Black Americans (P)

   *Materials and Procedure:*   Use the *Boning Profile of Black Americans* and the *Gallery of Great Afro-Americans* to stimulate discussion regarding black Americans. Show the pictures and relate the historical evidence to the children. At a later date, ask children to relate some of the contributions that certain blacks have made.
   *Suggestions and Variations:*   Children may be interested in using the overhead projector and the transparencies to make silhouettes of the black Americans discussed, and then to use the silhouettes to make a book.

2. **Activity:**   Getting to know Americans of the past (PP–P)

   *Materials:*   Pictures and books.
   *Procedure:*   Introduce some famous Americans to the children by displaying their pictures. Persons such as George Washington, Frederick Douglass, Abraham Lincoln, Crispus Attucks, Susan B. Anthony, Amelia Earhart, and George Washington Carver would be appropriate. Read stories about these persons and talk about why they were important.

3. **Activity:**   Current important people (PP–P)

   *Materials:*   Magazines, newspapers, other sources of pictures and reading materials about current events.
   *Procedure:*   Display pictures and place reading materials where children have access to them. Discuss with children the deeds the people in the pictures are performing and why their actions are important. Encourage older children to collect newspaper and magazine articles and pictures and bring them to class.

4. **Activity:**   What things are unique? (K)

   *Materials:*   Paper, scissors.
   *Procedure:*   Discuss diversity in nature. The snowflake is a good example, because no two snowflakes are alike. Show children how to cut paper

snowflakes to demonstrate the variety produced. Display the snowflakes on the bulletin board with the caption: No Snowflakes Are Alike. Mount pictures of the children on the snowflakes.

5. Activity:    Contributions of others (P)

*Materials:*    None.
*Procedure:*    Focus on broad topics that make it possible to observe the contributions of people from many different ethnic groups. Consider topics such as the following: Music around the World; Art through the Ages; Living in the City; Foods for the World; and Folklore and Mythology. Within such studies, children learn that cultures have distinctive qualities and contributions. They also discover human needs such as eating and the problems of living together.

6. Activity:    World book of heroes and heroines (P)

*Materials:*    Pictures of heroes and heroines of different cultures (for example, Martin Luther King); writing paper, pencils, construction paper.
*Procedure:*    Divide a bulletin board into sections, one for each of several cultures. Mount pictures of heroes and heroines under the appropriate culture and label. Allow each child to choose one hero or heroine to study. The children will work independently while doing research in simple encyclopedias, articles, and dictionaries. Each child will prepare a short report on a chosen subject and share it with the class. All the reports will be "bound" to form the *World Book of Heroes and Heroines.*

## FORMING VALUES

1. Activity:    Classroom purchases (PP-P)

*Materials:*    None.
*Procedure:*    Involve children if possible in decisions about classroom purchases. If children are involved, there are bound to be differences of opinion among them regarding what should be purchased for the classroom. These discussions provide excellent opportunities for children to think about and discuss what they think is important and why, as well as for them to begin to appreciate that people have different values.

2. Activity:    Open-ended story (K-P)

*Materials:*    Stories involving choice and decisions.
*Procedure:*    Select a story children have not previously heard in which the principal character must make a decision whether or not to do something. For

example, in *Pet Show* by Ezra Jack Keats, Archie must make two decisions: (1) whether or not to say something when the little old lady shows up with *his* cat and (2) what to do when the judges award her a prize for the cat. You might stop and ask the children what they think Archie did when the little old lady showed up at the pet show. After accepting the children's answers without giving any indication of right or wrong, complete the story. Discussion following the story may center on the children's speculation of why Archie acted as he did. Teachers should avoid moralizing, however.

## UNDERSTANDING CUSTOMS AND TRADITIONS

1. **Activity:**   Foods (PP–P)

   *Materials:*   Magazines, scissors, paste, construction paper, food.
   *Procedure:*   Have students bring old magazines to school or collect some yourself. Allow children to look for food pictures in the magazines that are part of black, Native American, Asian American, Mexican, and other cultures. Recipes or picture books may be made by cutting out and pasting pictures of these foods on construction paper. Staple or sew sheets of paper together for a booklet to add to the reading center.
   *Suggestions and Variations:*   Ask international children or children from minorities to bring to class food representative of their culture. Have a tasting party. On another day, take children on a trip to a local supermarket. Help children to identify foods at the market that are typical of certain cultures. If possible, purchase a few of the foods to prepare at school.
   Try to include interesting and representative foods for snack from time to time and discuss their significance to different groups. At holiday time, help children prepare foods which are traditional for the holiday (pumpkin pie, cranberry sauce, plum pudding).

2. **Activity:**   Christmas and Hanukkah (PP–P)

   *Materials:*   Pictures, books, food items.
   *Procedure:*   Read the book *A Day of Winter* by Betty Miles. Relate to the children that Christmas and Hanukkah come during the winter season. Discuss with the children how their families spend these holidays.
   *Suggestions and Variations:*   Make and decorate Christmas cookies or cupcakes. String cranberries or popcorn for a tree, perhaps a natural one growing in the school yard. The cranberries and popcorn can be eaten by the birds. Light a Menorah and sing some Chanukah songs. Allow children to play with a dreidel.

3. **Activity:**   Costumes (PP–P)

*Materials:*   Pictures or real items which illustrate dress for special occasions in different cultures.

4. **Activity:**   Cultural Literature (PP–P)

*Materials:*   Literature pertaining to countries such as China, Japan, Thailand, Canada, Mexico, Austria, Denmark, Russia, Scotland, and Sweden. Select books which are stories about customs and traditions in these countries.
*Procedure:*   Read stories to the children. Discuss the story with the children. Questions might include:

1. What did these people do that we do not do? Or that we do?
2. What do they have in their homes that we do not have? Or that we have?
3. What was the special occasion in the story?
4. How would we celebrate the special occasion?

*Suggestions and Variations:*   Help older children locate the countries on a globe or map. Relate differences in customs and traditions to differences in climate and terrain where appropriate. For example, traditional festival foods depend on their availability in the area. Introduce songs, dances, and games of children of other lands. Invite a parent or other resource person from another country to visit the classroom and tell about the customs and traditions there.

5. **Activity:**   Films and filmstrips (PP–P)

*Materials:*   Appropriate films and filmstrips depicting people of other countries celebrating special occasions; equipment and space to show films or filmstrips.
*Procedure:*   Films or filmstrips may either be shown to the whole group at story time or they may be viewed by small groups during activity time. Discussion of the films and filmstrips should follow viewing.
*Suggestions and Variations:*   In perhaps no other area of study are films and filmstrips more useful than in helping children understand customs and traditions of other people. They should be used as frequently as possible. Also, watch local television listings to find similar presentations on TV. A note sent home with the children indicating the time and channel of the program will help ensure that the child will be able to watch it.

## REFERENCES

BAUMRIND, D.   Socialization and instrumental competence in young children. In W.W. Hartup, ed., *The Young Child: Reviews of Research,* Vol. 2. Washington, D.C.: National Association for the Education of Young Children, 1972.

BEE, H.   *The Developing Child.* 3rd ed. New York: Harper and Row, Pub., 1981.

BROPHY, J. E.   *Child Development and Socialization.* Chicago: Science Research Associates, Inc., 1977.

DAMON, W.   *The Social World of the Child.* San Francisco, Calif.: Jossey-Bass, 1977.

GOODMAN, M. E.   *The Culture of Childhood.* New York: Teacher's College Press, 1970

HERSH, R., PAOLITTO, D., and REIMER, J.   *Promoting Moral Growth.* New York: Longman, 1979.

HETHERINGTON, E. M., COX, M., and COX, R.   Play and social interaction in children following divorce. *Journal of Social Issues,* 35, no. 4 (1979).

HILLIARD, A. G.   How should we assess children's social competence? *Young Children* 33, no. 5 (1979).

JAROLIMEK, J.   *Social Studies in Elementary Education.* 5th ed. New York: Macmillan, 1977.

———.   and WALSH, H.   *Readings for Social Studies in Elementary Education.* 3rd ed. New York: Macmillan, 1974.

KLUG, J.   What the world needs now: Environmental education for young children. *Young Children* 26, no. 5 (1971).

MACCOBY, E. E., and JACKLIN, C. N.   *The Psychology of Sex Differences.* Stanford, Calif.: Stanford University Press, 1974.

PIAGET, J.   *The Moral Judgment of the Child.* New York: Free Press, 1965.

———.   *The Child's Conception of Time.* New York: Basic Books, 1970.

———.   and INHELDER, B.   *The Psychology of the Child.* New York: Basic Books, 1969.

PHILLIPS, J. L.   *The Origins of Intellect: Piaget's Theory.* 2nd ed. San Francisco, Calif.: W. H. Freeman & Company Publishers, 1975.

PLOGHOFT, M., and SHUSTER, A.   *Social Science Education in the Elementary School.* 2nd ed. Columbus, Ohio: Chas E. Merrill, 1976.

ROSEN, H.   *The Development of Sociomoral Knowledge: A Cognitive-Structural Approach.* New York: Columbia University Press, 1980.

RUBIN, Z.   *Children's Friendship.* Cambridge, Mass.: Harvard University Press, 1980

SEEFELDT, C.   *Social Studies for the Preschool-Primary Child.* Columbus, Ohio: Chas E. Merrill, 1977.

———.   Is today tomorrow? History for young children. *Young Children* 30, no. 2 (1975).

TABA, H., ET AL.   *A Teacher's Handbook to Elementary Social Studies: An Inductive Approach.* Reading, Mass.: Addison-Wesley, 1971.

WALSH, H. M.   *Introducing the Young Child to the Social World.* New York: Macmillan, 1980.

WINDMILLER, M., LAMBERT, N., and TURIEL, E.   *Moral Development and Socialization.* Boston: Allyn and Bacon, 1980.

YOUNISS, J.   *Parents and Peers in Social Development.* Chicago: University of Chicago Press, 1980.

## REFERENCES FOR TEACHERS

BONING, R.   *Profiles of Black Americans.* Rockville Center: Dexter and Westbrook, LTU, 1969.

EMMONS, F., and COBIA. J.   Introducing Anthropological concepts in the primary grades. *Social Education* 32 (1968): 248–250.

GOODMAN, M. E.   *The Culture of Childhood.* New York: Teachers College Press, 1970.

JAROLIMEK, J.   Skills teaching in the primary grades. *Social Education* 31 (1967): 222–223;234.

KRANZ, P.L., and OSTLER, R.   Adult expectations of children—Do as I say, not as I do. *Young Children* 29 (1974): 277–279.

MITCHELL, L. S.   *Young Geographers.* New York: Bank Street College of Education, 1971.

MOYER, J.E.   *Bases for World Understanding and Cooperation.* Association for Supervision and Curriculum Development, 1970.

MUGGE, D.J.   Are young children ready to study the social sciences? *Elementary School Journal* 68 (February 1968).

SEEFELDT, C.   Is today tomorrow? History for young children. *Young Children* 30 (1975): 99–106.

SPODEK, B.   Social studies for young children: Identifying intellectual goals. *Social Education* 38 (1974): 40–53.

*American Indians.*   Inglewood, Calif.: Educational Insights, Inc., 1973.

*Black Studies.*   Inglewood, Calf.: Educational Insights, Inc., 1973.

*Career Card File.*   Niles, Ill.: Developmental Learning Materials, 1976.

*Drama of Social Studies.*   Chicago, Ill.: Creative Teaching Press, 1971.

*Social Studies Strategies.*   Inglewood, Calif.: Educational Insights, Inc., 1974.

*Where I Am.*   Niles, Ill.: Developmental Learning Materials, 1977.

*The Weewish Tree.*   A magazine of Indian America for young people. American Indian Historical Society, 1451 Masonic Avenue, San Francisco, California 94117.

## ADDITIONAL RESOURCES

### Children's Books

AARDEMA, V.   *The Riddle of the Drum.* New York: Four Winds Press, 1979. A handsome prince must solve a riddle in order to win the hand of the princess in marriage. This Mexican cumulative tale relates how the prince finds people to help him win his prize.

BAKER, B. F.   *What is Black?* New York: Franklin Watts, 1969. The author poses questions about the things in the world that may be black. A positive concept of blackness is provided for the child.

BALIAN, L.   *I Love You, Mary Jane.* New York: Abingdon, 1967. Mary Jane is a big lovable shaggy dog who has a birthday party for the neighborhood children. The party is a wonderful success with balloons, games, ice cream and, best of all, Mary Jane's special gift to each guest.

BARTLETT, R. M.   *Thanksgiving Day.* New York: Thomas Y. Crowell, 1965. This book provides a brief history of giving thanks at harvest time. It begins in ancient Greece and proceeds to the present with emphasis on the Pilgrims and their Thanksgiving celebration.

BEIM, J.   *Swimming Hole.* New York: Morrow, 1951. This story depicts prejudices in children. Steve, a caucasian boy, does not want to play at the swimming hole because there are two black boys with the group. The other boys leave Steve alone until he gets a sunburn which turns him bright red. Then Steve realizes that color is only skin deep. The story is warmly told with nice illustrations.

BEIM, J., and BEIM, L.   *Two is a Team.* New York: Knopf, 1945. The author relates the teamwork of two young boys. They get into trouble as they race their new wagons. As a result, both boys get a job and work as a team in order to pay for the damage.

BERGER, T.   *How Does It Feel When Your Parents Get a Divorce?* New York: Messner, 1977. Anger, fright, and sadness about divorce are explored in this book of photographs.

BROMBALL, W.  *Peter's Three Friends.* New York: Knopf, 1964. This story tells how friendships might develop. Peter and his three friends share some interesting experiences.

BROWNER, R.  *Every One Has a Name.* New York: Henry Z. Walck, 1961. A delightful book which has illustrations of animals and a text that rhymes. Human relations are stressed, and the message is that although people may look different, everyone is of worth and has a name.

BUCHHEIMER, N.  *Let's Go to the Post Office.* New York: Putnam's 1964. The author provides an overview of how mail is sorted, canceled, tied into bundles, put into pouches, and loaded onto mail trucks.

BUCKLEY, H.  *The Little Boy and the Birthdays.* New York: Lothrop, Lee and Shepard Co., 1965. A little boy discovers that it is important for him to remember the birthdays of others, just as he hopes they will remember his. This book helps build an understanding of mutual exchange and respect for one another.

————.  *Grandmother and I.* New York: Lothrop, Lee and Shepard Co., 1961. A young girl experiences times when grandmother's lap is better than anyone else's.

CAINES, J.  *Daddy.* New York: Harper and Row, Pub., 1977. The little girl of a divorced family has a very special relatioinship with her father.

CHANDLER, E. W.  *Five Cent, Five Cent.* Chicago: Albert Whitman & Co., 1967. A Liberian child, Kolu, learns how to earn money; Jack learns that money comes through working and cannot just be taken. Concepts of work and honesty are expressed.

CLARK, A. N.  *In My Mother's House.* New York: Viking, 1941. Authentic illustrations and account of life among the Tewa Indians of New Mexico. Ms. Clark has written a number of books on various Indian tribes and Mexican families in the Southwest.

CLIFTON, L.  *Everett Anderson's 1-2-3.* New York: Holt, Rinehart and Winston, 1977. Everett tries to understand when Mom says that sometimes two can be lonely.

COHEN, M.  *Will I Have a Friend?* New York: Macmillan, 1967. Jim is very apprehensive about his first day in school and asks his father, "Will I have a friend?" All seem to be friends and pay no attention to Jim. At rest time, Paul notices Jim. Afterwards, they play together.

CROSBY, B.  *It's Time.* New York: Harper & Row, Pub., 1964. Mabel Ann and Patrick are very good friends until the subject of sharing comes up. Then both want to have what the other one has. Each child wants all the toys. They finally learn the benefits of sharing.

DePAOLA, T.  *Nana Upstairs and Nana Downstairs.* New York: Putnam's 1973. A young boy's love for his great-grandmother and his grandmother helps ease his adjustment to their deaths.

————.  *Watch Out for the Chicken Feet in Your Soup.* Englewood-Cliffs, N.J.: Prentice-Hall, 1974. An embarrassed grandson sees his grandmother through the eye of a friend— and likes what he sees.

ETS, M. H.  *Just Me.* New York: Viking, 1965. The author relates the experiences and the love shared between father and son. A little boy imitates all the inhabitants of the farmyard and woods. But he runs as only he alone can do to meet his father.

————.  *Gilberto and the Wind.* New York: Viking, 1963. Gilberto has many experiences with the wind. Sometimes it does what he wants it to; sometimes it does not. The wind and Gilberto grow tired and fall asleep.

EVANS, E. K.  *People are Important.* New York: Capital Publishing Company, 1957. The author shows that people are more important than their customs. The differences among people in language, dress, food, types of dwellings, and ways of doing things are explained. To understand that our ways may seem strange to others is the first step in getting along with the people of the world.

FOSTER, D. V.  *A Pocketful of Seasons.* New York: Lothrop, and Shepard Co., 1971. This book relates seasonal changes. A boy picks up something from each season for his pocket.

FREEMAN, D.   *Corduroy*. New York: Viking, 1968. The author tells the story of a toy bear named Corduroy and a little black girl, Lisa, who wishes to buy him. Feelings are stressed in the book.

GREENE, C.   *Doctors and Nurses*. New York: Harper & Row, Pub., 1963. The author relates the things that people must study to learn an area of medicine. She also focuses on how doctors and nurses help people who are sick.

——.   *Railroad Engineers and Airplane Pilots*. New York: Harper & Row, Pub. 1964. This book contains information about railroad engineers and airplane pilots. Their roles are carefully explained.

HAWKINSON, J., and HAWKINSON, L.   *Little Boy Who Lives up High*. Chicago: Albert Whitman and Co., 1967. This story is about Ricky, who lives in an apartment building. Ricky notices the differences in the view when he is in his high-rise apartment and when he is walking on the street. The environment of the city is vividly portrayed.

HILL, E.   *Evans' Corner*. Chicago: Holt, Rinehart and Winston, 1967. The author depicts the need in a child to share and help others. Evans is a little boy who longs for a place to call his own. He discovers a corner in his apartment and begins to collect items for his corner. His mother helps him realize that this alone cannot make him happy, but that he must help others, too.

HOBAN, R.   *Bedtime for Francis*. New York: Harper & Row, Pub. 1968. A badger acts like a child as she tries to put off going to bed.

——.   *A Birthday for Francis*. New York: Harper & Row, 1968. Jealous Francis, feeling left out, turns her back on the preparation for her sister's birthday. But she becomes generous at the party and exchanges words with her sister.

HOETHE, L., and HOETHE, R.   *Houses around the World*. New York: Scribner's, 1973. The authors discuss and illustrate all kinds of houses from various parts of the world. They emphasize how houses differ depending upon the climate, building materials, and nature of people.

HOLSCLAW, C.   *Just One Me*. Chicago: Follett Corporation, 1967. The author illustrates the imagination of a black boy. Jimmy's father always told him he could be anything he wanted to be. So Jimmy wonders what it would be like to be a tree, the wind, or an airplane. But Jimmy decides, "If there's just one me, that's what I really want to be."

HUGHES, S   *David and Dog*. Englewood Cliffs, N.J.: Prentice-Hall, 1978. When David loses his prized stuffed dog, his older sister unselfishly saves the day.

KEATS, E. J.   *Peter's Chair*. New York: Harper & Row, Pub., 1967. The author conveys to the reader how a little boy grows up. Peter seemed to resent the idea that his little sister was going to use his cradle and then his crib. In his moment of frustration, he decided to move. He moved outside and took his chair. Peter soon discovered that he did not fit into the chair. He was too big.

——.   *Whistle for Willie*. New York: Viking, 1964. This is the story of a little boy who wanted to be able to whistle for his dog the way big boys do. Peter eventually learns how to whistle after much practice.

——.   *A Letter to Amy*. New York: Harper & Row, Pub., 1968. This delightful story for preschoolers is about a black boy who is having a birthday party and sends Amy an invitation. He has quite a time trying to mail the letter, but finally succeeds. When the party begins, Amy is not present, and Peter is sad. But finally Amy appears.

——.   *Pet Show*. New York: Collier Books, 1972. There is to be a pet show and Archie cannot find his cat. A little old lady shows up with Archie's cat and wins a ribbon for the cat with the longest whiskers. Archie's substitute pet is a germ in a jar. He wins a prize for the quietest pet. He also wins a friend in the little old lady.

KESSLER, E., and KESSLER, L.   *The Big Red Bus*. Garden City, N.Y.: Doubleday, 1964. The author illustrates a bus ride. The scenes and flow of traffic are clearly explained. The author also brings out the way it feels to be riding in a big bus.

KINDRED, W.   *Lucky Wilma.* New York: Dial Press, 1978. The book demonstrates that children need not be miserable because their parents divorce.

KIRN, A.   *Two Pesos for Catalina.* Skokie, Ill.: Rand McNally, 1961. When Catalina finds a tourist's bracelet and returns it, she is given two pesos as a reward. Much of the story revolves around her trying to decide what to buy at the market in Taxco. Aspects of Mexican rural life are shown. A glossary of Spanish terms is included.

KRAVETZ, N.   *Two for a Walk.* New York: Oxford University Press, 1954. The author shares the experiences of John and Tony as they visit a grocery store, a barber shop, a pet shop, a construction site, and a fire station.

KUSKIN, K.   *Just Like Everyone Else.* New York: Harper & Row, 1959. The adventures of a boy named Jonathon are shared. He gets up, gets dressed, eats breakfast, and goes to school. He follows the same routine as most children of his age.

LENSKI, L.   *Davy Goes Places.* New York: Henry Z. Walck, 1961. This story is about a boy who goes to visit his grandpa. This visit, which is very delightful for him, involves rides on many different vehicles.

LEXAU, J.   *Emily and the Klunky Baby and the Nextdoor Dog.* New York: Dial Press, 1972. Emily feels neglected. She takes her klunky baby brother when she runs away from home to find her divorced father.

LIANG, Y.   *Tommy and Dee Dee.* New York: Henry Z. Walck, 1953. The eighth day of the twelfth Chinese month is exciting for Dee Dee and his sister, Bao, for this is the beginning of the Chinese New Year Festival. The children have a delightful day eating, decorating the house, and shopping for food and presents. They also see a parade and fireworks at night. Tommy does the same kind of thing, but in another country.

MAYER, M.   *Beauty and the Beast.* New York: Four Winds Press, 1978. In this well-known tale, a beautiful princess breaks the spell which has kept a handsome prince trapped inside an ugly beast.

MCCLOSKEY, R.   *Blueberries for Sal.* New York: Viking, 1966. This book tells the story of a little girl and her mother as they go blueberry hunting in Maine. During their hunt, they meet a mother bear and a cub.

MCDERMOTT, G.   *Arrow to the Sun.* New York: Viking, 1974. This Caldecott-award-winning Pueblo Indian tale is beautifully illustrated and tells the story of how the spirit of the Lord of the Sun was brought to Earth.

MCGOVERN, A.   *Why It's a Holiday.* Eau Claire, Wisc.: E. M. Hale and Co., 1960. The author explains why certain days are legal holidays. She tells the story of many religious holidays and other special days.

PAPAS, W.   *No Mules.* New York: Coward, McCann and Geoghegan, 1967. This book relates the experiences of an African boy, Faan, who has difficulty going shopping with his mule, Solo.

PATTERSON, L.   *Christmas in Britain and Scandinavia.* Champaign, Ill.: Garrard Publishing Company, 1970. The author discusses Christmas traditions in all the Scandinavian and British countries. She explains and shows pictures of decorations, songs, and food.

REICH, H.   *Children and Their Mothers.* New York: Hill and Wang, 1964. This is a book of excellent photographs of children with their mothers in countries in Europe, Asia, Africa, and North and South America.

ROSS, G.   *When Lucy Went Away.* New York: Dutton, 1976. Lucy is a special but too independent cat. When she disappears, her young owners are left to struggle with her loss.

ROTH, E.   *Children and Their Fathers.* New York: Hill and Wang, 1962. The book shows pictures of children and their fathers from different countries.

ROWE, J.   *City Workers.* New York: Franklin Watts, 1969. Various kinds of work are illustrated in this book. The book provides children with some understanding of the different types of work that need to be done in a city.

SANDBERG, I., and SANDBERG, L.  *The Boy with Many Houses.* New York: Delacorte Press, 1968. A boy who has lived in a number of different houses tries to build one for himself. He gets into trouble with the cleaning lady, his mother, father, sister, and brother. Finally, his brother helps him build a house in the yard.

SCHWEITZER, B. B.  *Amigo.* New York: Macmillan, 1963. Francisco wants a dog whom he plans to call Amigo. His parents tell him they cannot afford to feed a dog. Finally, his mother suggests a prairie dog. The story switches to a prairie dog who wants a human boy. Amigo and Francisco meet and each thinks he has tamed the other.

SCOTT, A. H.  *Sam.* New York: McGraw-Hill, 1967. This is a sensitive story which dramatizes a childhood experience. Sam is a little boy who wants to play, but his family does not want to play with him. He finally sits and cries. His mother knows what is wrong with him, and she solves the problem when she takes him into the kitchen with her and gives him a job.

SHOWERS, P.  *Your Skin and Mine.* New York: Thomas Y. Crowell, 1965. This book explains to the young child that everyone is covered from head to toe with a protective covering that keeps out germs, helps you feel, and keeps you warm or cold. The text tells clearly and simply how melanin gives color to the skin, that skin comes in two layers, and what happens when the skin is cut or damaged.

SIMON, N.  *Hanukkah.* New York: Thomas Y. Crowell, 1966. A description of this holiday is given with rituals and customs as observed all over the world.

——.  *What Do I Say?* Chicago: Albert Whitman and Co., 1967. Manuel's home life and school days are depicted in attractive illustrations and in easy-to-read answers to the question "What do I say?"

STEIN, S.  *A Hospital Story.* Suffern, N.Y.: Danbury Press, 1974. Photographs of experiences in a hospital.

UDRY, J.  *What Mary Jo Shared.* Chicago: Albert Whitman and Co., 1967. It is sharing time at school. Mary Jo does not know what to share, because everything she wants to share is always shared by someone else. One day, Mary Jo shares her father with the children.

——.  *Let's Be Enemies.* New York: Harper & Row, Pub., 1961. John is unhappy because his friend is too bossy, and when John tells him this, the two boys say they will stop being friends. Instead, they agree it would be more fun to go skating together.

——.  *Mary Jo's Grandmother.* New York: Whitman, 1970. Mary Jo's grandmother has an accident and it is up to Mary Jo to go for help.

VIGNA J.  *Couldn't We Have a Turtle Instead?* Chicago: Albert Whitman, 1975. Anticipation is not exactly running high for the new baby in the family.

VIORST, J.  *Alexander, Who Used to Be Rich Last Sunday.* New York: Atheneum, 1978. Alexander all too quickly discovers the elusiveness of money, just when he thinks he's rich.

——.  *Rosie and Michael.* New York: Atheneum, 1974. Friendship can overcome all problems—according to Rosie and Michael.

WABER, B.  *Just Like Abraham Lincoln.* Boston: Houghton Mifflin Co., 1964. A small boy has a neighbor who looks just like Abraham Lincoln and who tells him stories about Abraham Lincoln.

WHITE, A.  *Walter in Love.* New York: Lothrop, Lee & Shepard Co., 1973. An amusing tale of love between Walter and Tita. Love overcomes Walter's problem of dyslexia.

YASHIMO, T.  *Seashore Story.* New York: Viking, 1967. Japanese children vacationing at the seashore ask to hear a story of Urashima, an ancient fisherman. This story is told to the children several times at their request.

——.  *Umbrella.* New York: Viking, 1958. Momo is a Japanese girl living in New York.

On her third birthday she is given an umbrella. There is a long wait for a rainy day when Momo can enjoy the sound of the rain on her umbrella.

YOUNG, M.    *Martin Luther King, Jr.* New York: Franklin Watts, 1968. The story of Martin Luther King and his fight for freedom and equality for black Americans.

ZOLOTOW, C.    *The Quarreling Book.* New York: Harper & Row, Pub. 1963. Gruffness and anger are passed along from person to person until a little dog starts a chain of happiness that reverses the trend. This is a pleasant picture book that hints about emotional maturity.

———.    *My Grandson Lew.* New York: Harper & Row, Pub., 1974. A mother and son remember Grandpa—together.

# INDEX

## W

9513

1